APPLIED CRYPTANALYSIS

BICENTENNIAL
1807
⊕WILEY
2007
BICENTENNIAL

THE WILEY BICENTENNIAL—KNOWLEDGE FOR GENERATIONS

$\mathcal{E}$ach generation has its unique needs and aspirations. When Charles Wiley first opened his small printing shop in lower Manhattan in 1807, it was a generation of boundless potential searching for an identity. And we were there, helping to define a new American literary tradition. Over half a century later, in the midst of the Second Industrial Revolution, it was a generation focused on building the future. Once again, we were there, supplying the critical scientific, technical, and engineering knowledge that helped frame the world. Throughout the 20th Century, and into the new millennium, nations began to reach out beyond their own borders and a new international community was born. Wiley was there, expanding its operations around the world to enable a global exchange of ideas, opinions, and know-how.

For 200 years, Wiley has been an integral part of each generation's journey, enabling the flow of information and understanding necessary to meet their needs and fulfill their aspirations. Today, bold new technologies are changing the way we live and learn. Wiley will be there, providing you the must-have knowledge you need to imagine new worlds, new possibilities, and new opportunities.

Generations come and go, but you can always count on Wiley to provide you the knowledge you need, when and where you need it!

WILLIAM J. PESCE
PRESIDENT AND CHIEF EXECUTIVE OFFICER

PETER BOOTH WILEY
CHAIRMAN OF THE BOARD

APPLIED CRYPTANALYSIS

Breaking Ciphers in the Real World

Mark Stamp
Richard M. Low

San Jose State University
San Jose, CA

BICENTENNIAL
BICENTENNIAL
1807
WILEY
2007
BICENTENNIAL
BICENTENNIAL

WILEY-INTERSCIENCE
A JOHN WILEY & SONS, INC., PUBLICATION

Library of Congress Cataloging-in-Publication Data:

Stamp, Mark.
  Applied cryptanalysis : breaking ciphers in the real world / Mark Stamp,
Richard M. Low.
      p. cm.
  Includes bibliographical references and index.
  ISBN 978-0-470-11486-5 (pbk.)
  1. Computer security. 2. Data encryption (Computer science) 3.
Cryptography. I. Low, Richard M., 1967– II. Title.
  QA76.9.A25S687 2007
  005.8'2—dc22   2007001277

Printed in the United States of America.

10 9 8 7 6 5 4 3 2 1

To Melody, Austin, and Miles — MSS

To Amy — RML

Contents

Preface

To paraphrase Barbie, "cryptanalysis is hard" [6]. Unfortunately, many cryptanalysis papers seem to be written in their own impenetrable secret code, making the subject appear to be even more difficult than it really is.

In this book, we strive to present applied cryptanalytic attacks in an accessible form. Here, we are focused on practical attacks that actually break real-world systems, not attacks that merely indicate some theoretical weakness in a cipher. Consequently, we consider real ciphers and, primarily, modern ciphers. Many attacks that satisfy our criteria are scattered throughout the literature.[1] With a few notable exceptions, these papers require a Herculean effort to digest and understand. One of our goals is to lift this unintentional veil on the exciting and fascinating field of cryptanalysis.

Most of the topics presented in this book require only a modest mathematical background. Some of the public key topics are inherently more mathematical, but in every case we have strived to minimize the advanced mathematics. We also believe that we have provided enough background information so that the book is essentially self-contained. Some of the more advanced mathematical topics are treated briefly in the Appendix. Any motivated upper-division undergraduate student—in any technical field of study— should be able to tackle this book. Some of the material is not easy, but those who persist will be rewarded with a solid understanding of cryptanalysis, as well as the knowledge, tools, and experience to confidently explore cutting-edge cryptanalytic topics.

We have provided an extensive set of problems for each chapter. A few of these problems are relatively easy, but most range from moderate to somewhat challenging. Generally, we have tried to avoid obvious problems of the "implement such-and-such attack" variety. Of course, it is useful and instructive to implement an attack, but the problems are intended to reinforce and expand on material presented in the text, without placing an overwhelming burden on the reader. A fairly complete solutions manual is available to instructors directly from your Wiley representative.

---

[1]A large percentage of the cryptanalysis literature is informal in the sense that many papers never receive any formal peer review. Although the academic peer-review process suffers from a multitude of sins, no peer review is no better.

To really understand the material in this book, it is necessary to work a significant number of the problems. Cryptanalysis is definitely not a spectator sport. We believe that the computer is an essential cryptanalytic tool. It is not coincidental that many of the homework problems require some computer programming.

For the terminally cryptanalytically insane, we have created a collection of challenge problems. These problems, which are posted on the textbook website at

> http://cs.sjsu.edu/faculty/stamp/crypto/

consist primarily of cryptanalytic challenges based on the ciphers and attacks presented in the text. A few research-oriented problems are also included. Each problem carries a difficulty rating so that you will have some idea of what you might be getting into. For each challenge problem, a small prize[2] is offered to the first solver. We promise to update the website as the challenge problems are solved. The website includes source code and test vectors for many of the ciphers discussed here. In addition, a complete set of quality PowerPoint slides is available.

The text is organized around four major themes, namely, classic ciphers (Chapters 1 and 2), symmetric ciphers (Chapters 3 and 4), hash functions (Chapter 5), and public key crypto (Chapters 6 and 7). The specific topics covered in each chapter are summarized below:

Chapter	Topics
1. Classic Ciphers	Pen-and-paper systems
2. World War II Ciphers	Enigma, Purple, Sigaba
3. Stream Ciphers	Shift registers, correlation attacks, ORYX, RC4, PKZIP
4. Block Ciphers	Block cipher modes, MAC, Hellman's TMTO, CMEA, Akelarre, FEAL
5. Hash Functions	HMAC, birthday attacks, Nostradamus attack, MD4, MD5
6. Public Key Systems	Knapsack, Diffie-Hellman, Arithmetica, RSA Rabin, NTRU, ElGamal
7. Public Key Attacks	Factoring, discrete log, RSA timing attacks, RSA glitching attack

---

[2]The emphasis here is on "small."

The first author wrote Chapters 2 through 5 and 7, while the second author wrote the majority of Chapters 1 and 6. The first author extensively edited all chapters to give the book a more consistent "look and feel." The first author did his best to resist including too many bad jokes, but some proved irresistible. Most of these have, mercifully, been relegated to footnotes.

The majority of the book consists of a series of cryptanalytic vignettes, organized by topic. Chapters 3, 4, and 5 each begin with a relatively generic method of attack (correlation attacks, Hellman's TMTO and birthday attacks, respectively). These attacks are interesting in their own right, but each also serves as an introduction to the type of cipher under consideration. Each of these chapters then segues into the cryptanalysis of specific ciphers.

For public key crypto, the introductory material has been expanded to an entire chapter. In Chapter 6, several public key systems are introduced and discussed from the perspective of relatively straightforward attacks or implementation issues that can lead to weaknesses. Then selected public key attacks are covered in depth in Chapter 7.

The chapters are highly independent of each other, as are many of the sections within chapters. The most dependent chapters are 6 and 7, which cover public key crypto. In addition, some familiarity with hashing (Chapter 5) would be useful before diving into the public key material. The terminology and background covered in Chapter 1 is used throughout the text. Regardless of your background in cryptography, we recommend that you read Chapter 1 first, since terminology is not consistent throughout the crypto world. Not only is crypto terminology inconsistent, but notation is even worse. Notation-wise, we have tried to be as internally consistent as possible. Consequently, our notation often differs from the original source.

The first author's information security textbook [142] covers four major topics, one of which is cryptography. The only significant overlap between [142] and this book is Hellman's time-memory trade-off attack, discussed here in Section 4.4. A brief section on the knapsack attack is also included in both books; here, in Section 6.2.

Finally, we apologize in advance for the inevitable "bugs" in this book. Any computer program of sufficient size has bugs and it is more difficult to debug a textbook than a program, since there is at least some hope of getting a program to misbehave during testing. There is no method to "exercise" a textbook other than to proofread it and to teach from it —the more times the better. The first author has taught virtually all of the material in this text, and several careful proofreadings have been done. Nevertheless, it is a sure bet that errors remain. Please tell us of any bugs you find. We would also appreciate any other comments you have regarding this book.

Mark Stamp
Richard M. Low
San Jose State University

About the Authors

Mark Stamp has an extensive background in information security in general and cryptography in particular, having spent more than seven years as a Cryptologic Mathematician at the National Security Agency. His other relevant experience includes two years as Chief Cryptologic Scientist at a small Silicon Valley startup company. Since the demise of his startup company in 2002, he has been a faculty member in the department of computer science at San Jose State University, where he primarily teaches courses in information security. In 2005, Dr. Stamp published his first textbook, *Information Security: Principles and Practice* (Wiley Interscience).

Richard M. Low has a PhD in mathematics and is a faculty member in the department of mathematics at San Jose State University. His research interests include cryptography, combinatorics and group theory. In addition to teaching mathematics, he has conducted a popular cryptography seminar at SJSU.

Acknowledgments

I want to thank the following San Jose State University students who contributed significantly to the indicated sections: Heather Kwong (Enigma); Thang Dao (Purple); Wing On Chan and Ethan Le (Sigaba); Thuy Nguyen-phuc (ORYX); Bevan Jones and Daniel Tu (Akelarre); Tom Austin, Ying Zhang, and Narayana Kashyap (MD5); Ramya Venkataramu (RSA timing attack); Natalia Khuri (RSA); Edward Yin (Chapter 2 solutions).

As always, thanks to my PhD advisor, Clyde F. Martin. Clyde is the one who introduced me to cryptography.

Richard Low deserves credit for enthusiastically signing on to this project and for convincing me to persevere at a couple of points where I was ready to throw in the towel. He also tolerated my occasional rants very well.

A very special thanks to Wan-Teh Chang for his careful reading of most sections of this book. Wan-Teh has an excellent eye for detail and he provided numerous corrections and useful suggestions.

Thanks are due to all of the people at Wiley who were involved with this book. In particular, I want to thank Paul Petralia, Whitney A. Lesch, and Kellsee Chu who were extremely helpful throughout.

Last but certainly not least, thanks to my lovely wife, Melody, and my two boys, Austin and Miles, for their patience during the seemingly endless hours I spent working on this project.

— MSS

My love of mathematics was cultivated by many of my former math teachers (from junior high school to graduate school). Those that come particularly to mind include: Joseph Buckley, Gary Chartrand, Daniel Goldston, Doug Harik, Philip Hsieh, Sin-Min Lee, John Martino, John Mitchem, Thomas Richardson, Gerhard Ringel, Jerome Schroeder, Michael Slack, Arthur Stoddart, Sandra Swanson, Arthur White, Gregg Whitnah, and Kung-Wei Yang. Thank you for showing me the way.

— RML

Chapter 1

Classic Ciphers

You are in a maze of twisty little passages, all alike.
— Adventure

1.1 Introduction

Most of this chapter is devoted to introducing terminology and discussing a select few classic "pen and paper" ciphers. Our goal here is not to cover classical cryptography in detail, since there are already many excellent sources of information on such ciphers. For example, Kahn's history [74] has a general discussion of virtually every cipher developed prior to its original publication date of 1967, Barr [7] presents a readable introduction to cryptography, Spillman [139] nicely covers the cryptanalysis of several classic cipher systems and Bauer [8] provides rigorous coverage of a large number of classical crypto topics. The ciphers we discuss in this chapter have been selected to illustrate a few important points that arise in upcoming chapters.

Even if you are familiar with classical cryptosystems, you should read the next two sections where terminology is discussed, since the terminology in cryptography is not always consistent. In addition, the material in Sections 1.4.3 and 1.4.4 is directly referenced in upcoming chapters.

1.2 Good Guys and Bad Guys

In cryptography, it is traditional that Alice and Bob are the good guys who are trying to communicate securely over an insecure channel. We employ Trudy (the "intruder") as our generic bad guy. Some books have a whole cast of bad guys with the name indicating the particular evil activity (Eve, the eavesdropper, for example), but we use Trudy as our all-purpose bad "guy".

1

Since this is a cryptanalysis book, we often play the role of Trudy. Trudy is an inherently more interesting character than boring old Alice and Bob, and this is part of what makes cryptanalysis so much more fun than cryptography. Trudy does not have to play by any preconceived set of rules. However, it is important to remember that attacks on real systems are almost certainly illegal, so do not attempt to play Trudy in the real world.

1.3   Terminology

Cryptology is the art and science of making and breaking "secret codes." Cryptology can be subdivided into *cryptography* (the art and science of making secret codes) and *cryptanalysis* (the breaking of secret codes). The secret codes themselves are known as *ciphers* or *cryptosystems*. In this book, we are focused on cryptanalysis, but many topics in cryptography naturally arise.

It is common practice to use the term cryptography as a synonym for cryptology, and we generally follow this practice. In fact, we often use *crypto* as shorthand for cryptology, cryptography, cryptanalysis, or any variety of other crypto-related topics. The precise meaning should be clear from the context.

The original readable message is the *plaintext*, while the *ciphertext* is the unreadable text that results from *encrypting* the plaintext. *Decryption* is the inverse process, where the ciphertext is converted into plaintext.

A *key* is used to configure a cryptosystem. All classic systems are *symmetric ciphers*, meaning that the same key is used to encrypt as to decrypt. In so-called *public key cryptography* the encryption and decryption keys are different, which means that the encryption key can be made public, but the decryption key must remain private. We cover public key cryptosystems in Chapters 6 and 7, while all of the remaining chapters—including the remaining sections of this chapter—deal with symmetric ciphers.

Note that decryption is distinct from cryptanalysis, since cryptanalysis implies an attack of some sort has been used to read the messages, while decryption implies that the plaintext has been retrieved using the key by the expected process. Of course, if Trudy recovers the key via cryptanalysis, then she can simply decrypt a particular ciphertext.

The typical encryption and decryption process is illustrated in Figure 1.1, where P_i is the ith unit of plaintext (which may be a bit, a letter, a word, or a larger block, depending on the particular cipher), C_i is the corresponding unit of ciphertext, and the squiggly line represents the transmission of the ciphertext over an insecure channel.

There are several generic types of attacks on ciphers. In a *ciphertext only* attack, the attacker attempts to recover the key or plaintext from the ciphertext. In particular, in a ciphertext-only attack, the cryptanalyst does

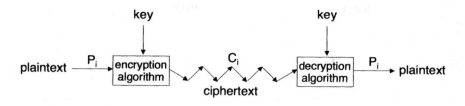

Figure 1.1: Encryption and decryption.

not know any of the underlying plaintext. A basic assumption is that the ciphertext is always available to an attacker. After all, if the ciphertext is not available to the attacker, why bother to encrypt?

In a *known plaintext* attack, Trudy has the ciphertext as well as some of the corresponding plaintext. This might give the attacker some advantage over the ciphertext only scenario—certainly the attacker is no worse off with known plaintext. If Trudy knows all of the plaintext, there is probably not much point in bothering to attack the system, so the implicit assumption is that the amount of known plaintext is relatively limited.

As the name implies, in a *chosen plaintext* attack, an adversary can choose the plaintext and then obtain the corresponding ciphertext. This can only help the attacker, as compared to a known plaintext scenario. Similarly, in a *chosen ciphertext* attack, the cryptanalyst chooses ciphertext and gets to see the corresponding plaintext. There are also *related key* attacks, where the attacker can break the system if two keys are used that happen to be related in some very special way. While this may seem somewhat esoteric, we will see an example of a real-world related key attack in Chapter 3.

In most cases, recovering the key is Trudy's ultimate goal, but there are attacks that recover the plaintext without revealing the key. A cipher is generally not considered secure unless it is secure against all plausible attacks. Cryptographers are, by nature, a paranoid bunch, so "plausible" is usually defined very broadly.

Kerckhoffs' Principle is one of the fundamental concepts underlying cryptography. This principle states that the strength of a cryptosystem depends only on the key and, in particular, the security does not depend on keeping the encryption algorithm secret. This principle is generally construed even more broadly to imply that the attacker knows the protocols and overall system in which a cryptosystem is used. Adherence to Kerckhoffs' Principle should ensure that the security of a cryptosystem does not depend on the much-dreaded "security by obscurity", since the security does not depend on a secret algorithm. Unfortunately, there are many real-world pressures that can lead to violations of Kerckhoffs' Principle, usually with disastrous consequences.

Why do we insist on Kerckhoffs' Principle? After all, the attacker's job certainly must be more difficult if the crypto algorithm is unknown. In part, the answer is that Kerckhoffs' Principle is just a codification of reality—algorithms never remain secret for long so it is far better to find flaws beforehand, rather than after an algorithm is embedded in millions of applications dispersed across the globe. It also happens to be true that designing a secure cipher is not easy, and it is made all the more difficult when efficiency is an issue, which is usually the case. An extensive peer review process is essential before any algorithm can be considered sufficiently secure for use. We will see several real-world examples that illustrate the wisdom of Kerckhoffs in upcoming chapters.

Suppose that Alice encrypts a message and sends the ciphertext to Bob. Figure 1.2 illustrates what information is available to Alice, Bob and the attacker, Trudy. At a minimum we assume that Trudy has access to the ciphertext and, by Kerckhoffs' Principle, she also knows how the crypto algorithm works. In some cases, Trudy may have additional information, such as known plaintext, chosen plaintext, etc.

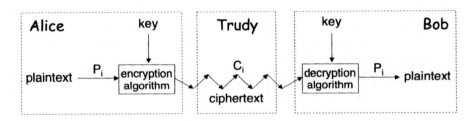

Figure 1.2: Who knows what.

In the next section we highlight a few selected classic crypto topics. We also discuss some important cryptanalytic principles and we provide details on a few specific ciphers that are relevant to later chapters.

1.4 Selected Classic Crypto Topics

If you have done much traveling, you know that it is almost impossible to see everything, and if you try, you are bound to regret it. It is usually far more productive to avoid the "tourist death march" and instead focus on a few specific interesting locations. We will take a similar approach here as we peruse selected classic crypto topics, stopping at a few points of interest, but making no attempt to cover every possible topic along the way. Since our focus in the remainder of the book is cryptanalysis, we emphasize attacks on the classic ciphers that we cover.

Since ancient times, cryptography has been used for military and diplomatic purposes. In the remainder of this chapter we consider a few specific examples of classic ciphers. These ciphers have been carefully selected to illustrate important topics that arise in the study of modern ciphers presented in subsequent chapters.

The history of crypto is itself a fascinating topic, but it is not our focus here. For more crypto history, a good crypto timeline can be found at [104] and there is always Kahn's book [74]. For a more in-depth technical look at classic ciphers, see Bauer's fine book [8].

1.4.1   Transposition Ciphers

Transposition ciphers jumble the letters of the message in a way that is designed to confuse the attacker, but can be unjumbled by the intended recipient. The concept of transposition is an important one and is widely used in the design of modern ciphers, as will be seen in subsequent chapters. Note that the key must provide sufficient information to unscramble the ciphertext.

Scytale

One of the earliest recorded uses of cryptography was the Spartan *scytale* (circa 500 B.C.). A thin strip of parchment was wrapped helically around a cylindrical rod and the message was written across the rod, with each letter on a successive turn of the parchment. The strip was unwound and delivered to the receiver. The message could then be decrypted with the use of an identical cylindrical rod. To anyone who intercepted the message, and did not understand the encryption technique, the message would appear to be a jumble of letters. A clever cryptanalyst with access to a number of rods of various diameters will soon recover the plaintext.

For the scytale cipher, which is an example of a transposition cipher, the key is the rod (or its diameter). This is a very weak cipher since the system could be easily broken by anyone who understands the encryption method.

Columnar Transposition

Suppose we have plaintext SEETHELIGHT and we want to encrypt this using a *columnar transposition cipher*. We first put the plaintext into the rows of an array of some given dimension. Then we read the ciphertext out of the columns. The key consists of the the number of columns in the array. For example, suppose we choose the key to be four, which means that we write the plaintext in four columns as

$$
\begin{bmatrix}
S & E & E & T \\
H & E & L & I \\
G & H & T & X
\end{bmatrix},
$$

where the final X is used as to fill out the array. The ciphertext is then read from the columns, which in this case yields SHGEEHELTTIX. The intended recipient, who knows the number of columns, can put the ciphertext into an appropriate-sized array and read the plaintext out from the rows.

Not surprisingly, a columnar transposition is not particularly strong. To perform a ciphertext only attack on this cipher, we simply need to test all possible decrypts using c columns, where c is a divisor of the number of characters in the ciphertext.

Keyword Columnar Transposition

The columnar transposition cipher can be strengthened by using a keyword, where the keyword determines the order in which the columns of ciphertext are transcribed. We refer to this as a *keyword columnar transposition cipher*. For example, consider encrypting the plaintext CRYPTOISFUN using a keyword columnar transposition cipher with keyword MATH, again using four columns. In this case, we get the array

$$
\begin{array}{cccc}
M & A & T & H \\
\left[\begin{array}{cccc}
C & R & Y & P \\
T & O & I & S \\
F & U & N & X
\end{array}\right]
\end{array}.
$$

The ciphertext is read from the columns in alphabetical order (as determined by the keyword), so that, in this example, the ciphertext is ROUPSXCTFYIN.

Is it possible to conduct a ciphertext-only attack on a keyword columnar transposition cipher? It is certainly not as straightforward as attacking a non-keyword columnar cipher. Suppose we obtain the ciphertext

VOESA IVENE MRTNL EANGE WTNIM HTMEE ADLTR NISHO DWOEH

which we believe was encrypted using a keyword columnar transposition. Our goal is to recover the key and the plaintext. First, note that there are 45 letters in the ciphertext. Assuming the array is not a single column or row, the array could have any of the following dimensions: 9×5, 5×9, 15×3 or 3×15. Suppose that we first try a 9×5 array. Then we have the ciphertext array in Table 1.1.

We focus our attention on the top row of the array in Table 1.1. If we permute the columns as shown in Table 1.2, we see the word GIVE in the first row and we see words or partial words in the other rows. Therefore, we have almost certainly recovered the key.

This method is somewhat ad hoc, but the process could be automated, provided we can automatically recognize likely plaintexts. In this example, we have recovered the encryption key 24013 and the plaintext is

GIVE ME SOMEWHERE TO STAND AND I WILL MOVE THE EARTH.

Table 1.1: Ciphertext Array

0	1	2	3	4
V	E	G	M	I
O	M	E	E	S
E	R	W	E	H
S	T	T	A	O
A	N	N	D	D
I	L	I	L	W
V	E	M	T	O
E	A	H	R	E
N	N	T	N	H

Table 1.2: Permuted Ciphertext Array

2	4	0	1	3
G	I	V	E	M
E	S	O	M	E
W	H	E	R	E
T	O	S	T	A
N	D	A	N	D
I	W	I	L	L
M	O	V	E	T
H	E	E	A	R
T	H	N	N	N

There are many ways to systematically mix the letters of the plaintext. For example, we can strengthen the columnar transposition cipher by allowing the permutation of columns and rows. Since two transpositions are involved, this is known as a *double transposition cipher*, which we briefly describe next.

Double Transposition Cipher

To encrypt with a double transposition cipher, we first write the plaintext into an array of a given size and then permute the rows and columns according to specified permutations. For example, suppose we write the plaintext ATTACKATDAWN into a 3×4 array:

$$\begin{bmatrix} A & T & T & A \\ C & K & A & T \\ D & A & W & N \end{bmatrix}.$$

Now if we transpose the rows according to $(0, 1, 2) \rightarrow (2, 1, 0)$ and then transpose the columns according to $(0, 1, 2, 3) \rightarrow (3, 1, 0, 2)$, we obtain

$$\begin{bmatrix} A & T & T & A \\ C & K & A & T \\ D & A & W & N \end{bmatrix} \longrightarrow \begin{bmatrix} D & A & W & N \\ C & K & A & T \\ A & T & T & A \end{bmatrix} \longrightarrow \begin{bmatrix} N & A & D & W \\ T & K & C & A \\ A & T & A & T \end{bmatrix}.$$

The ciphertext is read directly from the final array:

NADWTKCAATAT.

For the double transposition, the key consists of the size of the matrix and the row and column permutations. The recipient who knows the key can simply put the ciphertext into the appropriate sized matrix and undo the permutations to recover the plaintext.

If Trudy happens to know the size of the matrix used in a double transposition, she can insert the ciphertext into a matrix of the appropriate size. She can then try to unscramble the columns to reveal words (or partial words). Once the column transposition has been undone, she can easily unscramble the rows; see Problem 12 for an example. This attack illustrates the fundamental principle of *divide and conquer.* That is, Trudy can recover the double transposition key in parts, instead of attacking the entire key all at once. There are many examples of divide and conquer attacks throughout the remainder of this book.

In spite of the inherent divide and conquer attack, the double transposition cipher is relatively strong—at least in comparison to many other classic cipher. The interested reader is directed to [88] for a thorough cryptanalysis of the double transposition.

1.4.2 Substitution Ciphers

Like transposition, substitution is a crucial concept in the design of modern ciphers. In fact, Shannon's [133] two fundamental principles for the design of symmetric ciphers are *confusion* and *diffusion*, which, roughly, correspond to the classic concepts of substitution and transposition, respectively. These are still the guiding principles in the design of symmetric ciphers.

In this section we discuss several classic substitution ciphers. We highlight some of the clever techniques that can be brought to bear to attack such ciphers.

Caesar's Cipher

In 50 B.C., Gaius Julius Caesar described the use of a specific cipher that goes by the name of *Caesar's cipher.*[1] In Caesar's cipher, encryption is ac-

---

[1]Historians generally agree that the Caesar's cipher was named after the Roman dictator, not the salad.

complished by replacing each plaintext letter with its corresponding "shift-by-three" letter, that is, A is replaced by D, B is replaced by E, C is replaced by F, and so on. At the end of the alphabet, a wrap around occurs, with X replaced by A, Y replaced by B and Z replaced by C. Decryption is accomplished by replacing each ciphertext letter with its corresponding left-shift-by-three letter, again, taking the wrap around into account.

Suppose we assign numerical values $0, 1, \ldots, 25$ to the letters A, B, ..., Z, respectively, Let p_i be the ith plaintext letter of a given message, and c_i the corresponding ith ciphertext letter. Then Caesar's cipher can be mathematically stated as $c_i = p_i + 3 \pmod{26}$ and, therefore, $p_i = c_i - 3 \pmod{26}$. In Caesar's cipher, the key is "3", which is not very secure, since there is only one key—anyone who knows that the Caesar's cipher is being used can immediately decrypt the message.

Simple Substitution

A *simple substitution* (or *mono-alphabetic substitution*) cipher is a generalization of the Caesar's cipher where the key can be any permutation of the alphabet. For the simple substitution, there are $26! \approx 2^{88}$ keys available. This is too many keys for any attacker to simply try them all, but even with this huge number of keys, the simple substitution cipher is insecure. Before we discuss the attack on the simple substitution, we consider a few special types of related ciphers that have been used in the past.

Nomenclator

Circa 1400, a type of cipher known as a *nomenclator* was invented and came into widespread use by trading states in Europe and by the Catholic Church. A nomenclator is a book that describes how letters, syllables, and words are converted into ciphertext and vice versa. In effect, this is a hybrid between a simple substitution and a codebook cipher (described below), and it has a larger number of possible keys than a simple substitution cipher. All else being equal (which it never is), this should make the cryptanalyst's job more difficult.

Poly-alphabetic Substitution

During the Renaissance, the first *poly-alphabetic substitution* cipher was invented by one Leon Battista Alberti (1404–1472). Such a cipher is essentially a variable simple substitution cipher, that is, a different substitution alphabet is used for different parts of the message. In Alberti's cipher, this was accomplished by use of a device that included an inner and outer cipher wheel with the alphabet written in particular ways on each wheel. The inner wheel freely rotated allowing the two alphabets to be aligned in any fashion, with each alignment generating a different (simple) substitution. As the message was encrypted, differing substitution alphabets could be used, as determined by both parties in advance, or as specified within the message itself.

In his book *Traicté des Chiffres*, Blaise de Vigenère (1585) discusses a poly-alphabetic substitution that uses a 26×26 rectangular array of letters. The first row of the array is $\mathsf{A}, \mathsf{B}, \mathsf{C}, \ldots, \mathsf{Z}$, and each succeeding row is a cyclic left shift of the preceding one. A keyword can then be used to determine which of the cipher alphabets to use at each position in the text. In this way, all "shift-by-n" simple substitutions are readily available for use. The Vigenère cipher, and its cryptanalysis, is discussed below.

Affine Cipher

An *affine* cipher is a simple substitution where $c_i = ap_i + b$ (mod 26). Here, the constants a and b are integers in the range 0 to 25 (as are p_i and c_i). To decrypt uniquely—always a nice feature for a cipher system—we must have $\gcd(a, 26) = 1$. Consequently, there are $26 \cdot \phi(26) = 312$ affine ciphers for the English language, where ϕ is the Euler-phi function (see the Appendix for a definition of the ϕ function). The decryption function for the affine cipher is $p_i = a^{-1}(c_i - b)$ (mod 26), where $aa^{-1} = 1$ (mod 26), that is, a^{-1} is the multiplicative inverse of a, modulo 26.

Affine ciphers are weak for several reasons, but the most obvious problem is that they have a small *keyspace*. A ciphertext only attack can be performed by conducting a brute force search of all 312 possible key pairs (a, b). This attack is trivial, provided we can recognize the plaintext when we see it (or, better yet, automatically test for it).

Simple Substitution Cryptanalysis

Trying all possible keys is known as an *exhaustive key search*, and this attack is always an option for Trudy. If there are N possible keys, then Trudy will, on average, need to try about half of these, that is, $N/2$ of the keys, before she can expect to find the correct key. Therefore, the first rule of cryptography is that any cipher must have a large enough keyspace so that an exhaustive search is impractical. However, a large keyspace does not ensure that a cipher is secure. To see that this is the case, we next consider an attack that will work against any simple substitution cipher and, in the general case, requires far less work than an exhaustive key search. This attack relies on the fact that statistical information that is present in the plaintext language "leaks" through a simple substitution.

Suppose we have a reasonably large ciphertext message generated by a simple substitution, and we know that the underlying plaintext is English. Consider the English letter frequency information in Table 1.3, which was compiled from a 7834-letter sample of written English. By simply computing letter frequency counts on our ciphertext, we can make educated guesses as to which plaintext letters correspond to some of the ciphertext letters. For example, the most common ciphertext letter probably corresponds to plaintext E. We can obtain additional statistical information by making use of digraphs (pairs of letters) and common trigraphs (triples). This type of statistical attack on a simple substitution, is very effective. After a few letters have been guessed correctly, partial words will start to appear and the cipher should then quickly unravel.

Table 1.3: English Letter Frequencies as Percentages

Letter	Relative Frequency	Letter	Relative Frequency
A	8.399	N	6.778
B	1.442	O	7.493
C	2.527	P	1.991
D	4.800	Q	0.077
E	12.15	R	6.063
F	2.132	S	6.319
G	2.323	T	8.999
H	6.025	U	2.783
I	6.485	V	0.996
J	0.102	W	2.464
K	0.689	X	0.204
L	4.008	Y	2.157
M	2.566	Z	0.025

Vigenère Cipher

Recall that a poly-alphabetic substitution cipher uses multiple simple substitutions to encrypt a message. The Vigenère cipher is a classic poly-alphabetic substitution cipher. The World War II cipher machines discussed in Chapter 2 are more recent examples of poly-alphabetic substitutions.

In the Vigenère cipher, a key of the form $K = (k_0, k_1, \ldots, k_{n-1})$, where each $k_i \in \{0, 1, \ldots, 25\}$, is used to encipher the plaintext. Here, each k_i represents a particular shift of the alphabet. To encrypt a message,

$$c_i = p_i + k_{i \, (\text{mod } n)} (\text{mod } 26)$$

and to decrypt

$$p_i = c_i - k_{i \, (\text{mod } n)} (\text{mod } 26).$$

For example, suppose $K = (12, 0, 19, 7)$, which corresponds to the keyword MATH (since M corresponds to a shift of 12, A corresponds to a shift of 0, and so on). Using this keyword, the the plaintext SECRETMESSAGE is encrypted as EEVYQTFLESTNQ.

Next, we cryptanalyze the Vigenère cipher. But first, note that a poly-alphabetic substitution (such as the Vigenère cipher) does not preserve plain-text letter frequencies to the same degree as a mono-alphabetic substitution. Furthermore, if the number of alphabets is large relative to the message size, the plaintext letter frequencies will not be preserved at all. Therefore, the generic simple substitution attack discussed above will not work on a poly-alphabetic substitution.

However, the Vigenère cipher is vulnerable to a slightly more sophisticated statistical attack. To see how this works, first consider a Vigenère cipher with a small keyword. Suppose that the following ciphertext was created using a Vigenère cipher with a three-lettered keyword:

$$
\begin{array}{llllllll}
\text{RLWRV} & \text{MRLAQ} & \text{EDUEQ} & \text{QWGKI} & \text{LFMFE} & \text{XZYXA} & \text{QXGJH} & \text{FMXKM} & \text{QWRLA} \\
\text{LKLFE} & \text{LGWCL} & \text{SOLMX} & \text{RLWPI} & \text{OCVWL} & \text{SKNIS} & \text{IMFES} & \text{JUVAR} & \text{MFEXZ} \\
\text{CVWUS} & \text{MJHTC} & \text{RGRVM} & \text{RLSZS} & \text{MREFW} & \text{XZGRY} & \text{RLWPI} & \text{OMYDB} & \text{SFJCT} \\
\text{CAZYX} & \text{AQ.}
\end{array} \tag{1.1}
$$

To recover the key and decrypt the message, we can make use of the fact that the ciphertext is composed of three simple substitutions. To accomplish this, we tabulate the letter frequencies for the sets

$$ S_0 = \{c_0, c_3, c_6, \dots\}, \quad S_1 = \{c_1, c_4, c_7, \dots\}, \quad \text{and} \quad S_2 = \{c_2, c_5, c_8, \dots\}, $$

where c_i is the ith ciphertext letter. Doing so, we obtain the results in Tables 1.4, 1.5, and 1.6, respectively.

Table 1.4: Letter Frequencies in S_0

Letter	R	Q	U	K	F	E	Y	J	M	L	G	P	C	N	I	Z	W	B
Frequency	10	4	3	1	2	3	2	3	3	4	2	2	2	4	1	1	1	1

Table 1.5: Letter Frequencies in S_1

Letter	L	V	E	W	I	M	X	Q	K	S	H	R	Y	C	A
Frequency	6	5	4	2	4	4	7	1	1	6	1	2	1	1	1

From the S_0 ciphertext in Table 1.4, we might reasonably guess that ciphertext R corresponds to plaintext E, T, N, O, R, I, A or S, which gives us

Table 1.6: Letter Frequencies in S_2

Letter	W	M	A	D	Q	G	L	F	Z	K	C	O	X	S	J	T	Y
Frequency	6	4	5	2	1	3	3	5	4	2	1	3	1	2	1	2	1

candidate values for k_0, namely $k_0 \in \{13, 24, 4, 3, 0, 9, 17, 25\}$. Similarly, for set S_1, ciphertext X might correspond to plaintext E, T, N, O, R, I, A or S, from which we obtain likely values for k_1, and from set S_2, ciphertext W likely correspond to plaintext E, T, N, O, R, I, A or S. The corresponding likely keyword letters are tabulated in Table 1.7.

Table 1.7: Likely Keyword Letters

k_0	k_1	k_2
N	T	S
Y	E	D
E	K	J
D	J	I
A	G	F
J	P	O
R	X	W
Z	F	E

The combinations of likely keyword letters in Table 1.7 yield $8^3 = 2^9$ putative keywords. By testing each of these putative keyword on the first few letters of the ciphertext, we can easily determine which, if any, is the actual keyword. For this example, we find that $(k_0, k_1, k_2) = (24, 4, 18)$, which corresponds to YES, and the original plaintext is

```
THE TRUTH IS ALWAYS SOMETHING THAT IS TOLD, NOT
SOMETHING THAT IS KNOWN. IF THERE WERE NO SPEAKING
OR WRITING, THERE WOULD BE NO TRUTH ABOUT ANYTHING.
THERE WOULD ONLY BE WHAT IS.
```

This attack provides a significant shortcut as compared to trying all possible $26^3 \approx 2^{14}$ keywords.

Knowing the length of the keyword used in a Vigenère cipher helps greatly in the cryptanalysis. If the keyword is known, and the message is long enough, we can simply perform letter frequency counts on the associated sets of ciphertext to begin solving for the plaintext. However, it is not so obvious how to determine the length of an unknown keyword. Next, we consider two methods for approximating the length of the keyword in a Vigenère cipher.

Friederich W. Kasiski (1805–1881) was a major in the East Prussian infantry regiment and the author of the cryptologic text *Die Geheimschriften und die Dechiffer-kunst*. Kasiski developed a test (amazingly, known as the Kasiski Test), that can sometimes be used to find the length of a keyword used in a cipher such as the Vigenère. It relies on the occasional coincidental alignment of letter groups in plaintext with the keyword. To attack a periodic cipher using the Kasiski Test, we find repeated letter groups in the ciphertext and tabulate the separations between them. The greatest common divisor of these separations (or a divisor of it) gives a possible length for the keyword.

For example, suppose we encrypt the plaintext

THECHILDISFATHEROFTHEMAN

with a Vigenère cipher using the keyword **POETRY**. The resulting ciphertext is

IVIVYGARMLMYIVIKFDIVIFRL.

Notice that the second occurrence of the ciphertext letters **IVI** begins exactly 12 letters after the first, and the third occurrence of **IVI** occurs exactly six letters after the second. Therefore, it is likely that the length of the keyword is a divisor of six. In this case, the keyword length is exactly six.

Index of Coincidence

While working at the Riverbank Laboratory, William F. Friedman (1891–1969) developed the *index of coincidence*. For a given ciphertext, the index of coincidence I is defined to be the probability that two randomly selected letters in the ciphertext represent the same plaintext symbol.

For a given ciphertext, let $n_0, n_1, \ldots, n_{25}$ be the respective letter counts of $A, B, C, \ldots, Z$ in the ciphertext, and set $n = n_0 + n_1 + \cdots + n_{25}$. Then, the index of coincidence can be computed as

$$I = \frac{\binom{n_0}{2} + \binom{n_1}{2} + \cdots + \binom{n_{25}}{2}}{\binom{n}{2}} = \frac{1}{n(n-1)} \sum_{i=0}^{25} n_i(n_i - 1). \qquad (1.2)$$

To see why the index of coincidence gives us useful information, first note that the empirical probability of randomly selecting two identical letters from a large English plaintext is

$$\sum_{i=0}^{25} p_i^2 \approx 0.065,$$

where p_0 is the probability of selecting an **A**, p_1 is the probability of selecting a **B**, and so on, and the values of p_i are given in Table 1.3. This implies that an (English) ciphertext having an index of coincidence $I \approx 0.065$ is probably associated with a mono-alphabetic substitution cipher, since this statistic will not change if the letters are simply relabeled (which is the effect of encrypting with a simple substitution).

The longer and more random a Vigenère cipher keyword is, the more evenly the letters are distributed throughout the ciphertext. With a very long and very random keyword, we would expect to find

$$I \approx 26 \left(\frac{1}{26} \right)^2 = \frac{1}{26} \approx 0.03846.$$

Therefore, a ciphertext having $I \approx 0.03846$ could be associated with a poly-alphabetic cipher using a large keyword. Note that for any English ciphertext, the index of coincidence I must satisfy $0.03846 \leq I \leq 0.065$.

The question remains as to how to determine the length of the keyword of a Vigenère cipher using the index of coincidence. The main weakness of the Vigenère (or any similar periodic cipher) is that two identical characters occurring a distance apart that is a multiple of the key length will be encrypted identically. In such cryptosystems, the key length k can be approximated by a function involving the index of coincidence I and the length of the ciphertext n. The following example illustrates this technique.

Suppose an English plaintext containing n letters is encrypted using a Vigenère cipher, with a keyword of length k, where, for simplicity, we assume n is a multiple of k. Now suppose that we arrange the ciphertext letters into a rectangular array of n/k rows and k columns, from left to right, top to bottom. If we select two letters from different columns in the array, this would be similar to choosing from a collection of letters that is uniformly distributed, since the keyword is more-or-less "random". In this case, the portion of pairs of identical letters is, approximately,

$$0.03846 \binom{k}{2} \left(\frac{n}{k} \right)^2 = 0.03846 \frac{n^2(k-1)}{2k}.$$

On the other hand, if the two selected letters are from the same column, this would correspond to choosing from ciphertext having a symbol distribution similar to printed English plaintext, since, in effect, a simple substitution is applied to each column. In this case, the portion of pairs of identical letters is approximately

$$0.065 \binom{\frac{n}{k}}{2} k = 0.065 \frac{1}{2} \left(\frac{n}{k} \right) \left(\frac{n}{k} - 1 \right) k = 0.065 \left(\frac{n(n-k)}{2k} \right).$$

Therefore, the index of coincidence satisfies

$$I \approx \frac{0.03846 \frac{n^2(k-1)}{2k} + 0.065 \left(\frac{n(n-k)}{2k} \right)}{\binom{n}{2}}$$

$$= \frac{0.03846n(k-1) + (0.065)(n-k)}{k(n-1)}. \tag{1.3}$$

The attacker, Trudy, does not know k, but she can solve for k in (1.3) to obtain

$$k \approx \frac{0.02654n}{(0.065 - I) + n(I - 0.03846)}. \tag{1.4}$$

Then given n and I, which are easily computed from the ciphertext, Trudy can approximate k, the number of letters in the keyword of the underlying Vigenère cipher.

The index of coincidence was a cryptologic breakthrough, since it can be used to gain information about poly-alphabetic substitution ciphers. Friedman's work on the index of coincidence was one of his most important contributions to cryptology, and it provided invaluable information to cryptanalysts during WWII, where poly-alphabetic ciphers played a major role.

Hill Cipher

As a final example of a substitution cipher, we consider the Hill cipher, which was introduced by mathematician Lester Hill in 1929 [67]. The Hill cipher is interesting since it is a pre-modern block cipher. The idea behind the Hill cipher is to create a substitution cipher with an extremely large "alphabet". Such a system is more resilient to cryptanalysis that relies on letter frequency counts and statistical analysis of the plaintext language. However, the cipher is linear which makes it vulnerable to a relatively straightforward known plaintext attack. The description of the Hill cipher requires some elementary linear algebra; see the Appendix for the necessary background information.

Suppose that Alice wants to send a message to Bob and they have decided to use the Hill cipher. First, the plaintext is divided into blocks $p_0, p_1, p_2, \ldots$, each consisting of n letters. Alice then chooses an $n \times n$ invertible matrix A, with the entries reduced modulo 26, which acts as the key. Encryption is accomplished by computing the ciphertext as $c_i = Ap_i \pmod{26}$ for each plaintext block p_i. Bob decrypts the message by computing $A^{-1}c_i \pmod{26}$, for each ciphertext block c_i, where A^{-1} is the inverse of A, modulo 26.

For example, suppose Alice wants to send the plaintext MEETMEHERE, using the encryption matrix

$$A = \begin{bmatrix} 22 & 13 \\ 11 & 5 \end{bmatrix}. \tag{1.5}$$

Converting letters to numbers, Alice finds

$$\mathtt{MEETMEHERE} = (12, 4, 4, 19, 12, 4, 7, 4, 17, 4).$$

Next, she divides the plaintext into blocks of length two and then represents each block as a column vector, which yields

$$p_0 = \begin{bmatrix} 12 \\ 4 \end{bmatrix}, \ p_1 = \begin{bmatrix} 4 \\ 19 \end{bmatrix}, \ p_2 = \begin{bmatrix} 12 \\ 4 \end{bmatrix}, \ p_3 = \begin{bmatrix} 7 \\ 4 \end{bmatrix}, \ p_4 = \begin{bmatrix} 17 \\ 4 \end{bmatrix}.$$

To encrypt, Alice computes $c_i = Ap_i \pmod{26}$ for each column vector p_i. In this example, the resulting ciphertext is

$$c_0 = \begin{bmatrix} 4 \\ 22 \end{bmatrix}, \ c_1 = \begin{bmatrix} 23 \\ 9 \end{bmatrix}, \ c_2 = \begin{bmatrix} 4 \\ 22 \end{bmatrix}, \ c_3 = \begin{bmatrix} 24 \\ 19 \end{bmatrix}, \ c_4 = \begin{bmatrix} 10 \\ 25 \end{bmatrix}.$$

Converting into letters, we have

$$(4, 22, 23, 9, 4, 22, 24, 19, 10, 25) = \mathtt{EWXJEWYTKZ},$$

which Alice sends to Bob. When Bob receives the ciphertext, he breaks it into blocks c_i of length two and treats these as column vectors. He then decrypts the message by computing $p_i = A^{-1}c_i \pmod{26}$ for each ciphertext block c_i.

The Hill cipher, with an invertible matrix $A \pmod{26}$ and block length n, can be viewed as a substitution cipher utilizing an alphabet of 26^n possible "letters" and the expected letter frequency distribution in the ciphertext is far more uniform than that of the plaintext. This makes a ciphertext only attack generally impractical. However, the Hill cipher is highly vulnerable to a known plaintext attack.

Suppose that Trudy suspects Alice of using a Hill cipher with an $n \times n$ encryption matrix A. Further, suppose that Trudy can obtain ciphertext blocks c_i, for $i = 0, 1, \ldots, n-1$, where each block is of length n, as well as the corresponding plaintext blocks, that is, p_i, for $i = 0, 1, \ldots, n-1$. Then Trudy may be able to recover the key A as follows: Let P and C be the $n \times n$ matrices whose columns are formed by the plaintext p_i and ciphertext c_i, respectively. Then $AP = C$ and if it is the case that $\gcd(\det(P), 26) = 1$, the matrix $P^{-1} \pmod{26}$ exists. If the inverse matrix exists, Trudy can compute P^{-1} and from P^{-1} she can determine A via $A = CP^{-1}$. Once Trudy finds A, the decryption matrix A^{-1} is easily calculated.

The Hill cipher is an example of a *linear cipher*. The linearity of the Hill cipher effectively creates a large number of substitutions, which is desirable. However, the linear structure can be exploited, since linear equations are easy to solve. The lesson here is that a cipher must have some nonlinear component. However, linear components are useful and, in fact, modern ciphers combine both linearity and nonlinearity. In Shannon's terminology [133], linearity provides an effective method to increase diffusion while nonlinearity is essential for confusion.

1.4.3   One-Time Pad

In 1917, Gilbert Vernam and Joseph Mauborgne invented a cipher system
which would eventually become known as the *one-time pad*. When correctly
used, this system is invulnerable to a ciphertext only attack. This is the only
real-world cipher that is provably secure.

Suppose Alice wants to send a message to Bob and she wants to encrypt
her message using a one-time pad. Alice first converts her plaintext message P
into binary. She then generates a random binary key K of the same length
as P. Encryption is accomplished by adding K to P, bit by bit, modulo 2,
to obtain the ciphertext C. That is, $C = P \oplus K$, where "$\oplus$" is XOR.

To recover the plaintext P from the ciphertext C, Bob, knowing the key K,
computes $C \oplus K = (P \oplus K) \oplus K = P$. For example, suppose $P = 01001100$
and $K = 11010110$. Then

$$C = P \oplus K = 01001100 \oplus 11010110 = 10011010$$

and P can be recovered from C via

$$P = C \oplus K = 10011010 \oplus 11010110 = 01001100.$$

The one-time pad is immune to a ciphertext only attack, since the ciphertext yields no information about the plaintext, other than its length. To
see why this is true, consider the eight-letter alphabet in Table 1.8, with the
given binary encodings.

Table 1.8: Abbreviated Alphabet

Letter	C	A	T	D	O	G	E	N
Binary	000	001	010	100	011	101	110	111

The plaintext message CAT is encoded as 000 001 010. Suppose the
key $K = 110\ 100\ 001$ is used for encryption. Then the ciphertext is given
by $C = 110\ 101\ 111$ which corresponds to EGN. Now, suppose Trudy intercepts C and she guesses the putative key $K' = 010\ 110\ 010$. Using K', Trudy
computes the putative plaintext

$$P' = C \oplus K' = 110\ 101\ 111 \oplus 010\ 110\ 010 = 100\ 011\ 101$$

which corresponds to the message DOG. Based on the ciphertext and the putative plaintext, Trudy has no way to judge whether the message DOG is any
more likely than the message CAT, or any other three letter message that can
be spelled from the eight letters in Table 1.8. That is, "decrypting" C with
any one of the possible $8^3 = 512$ keys gives one of the 512 possible plaintext
messages and the ciphertext itself gives no hint as to which of these is correct.

The "one-time" in the one-time pad is crucial. If a key K is used more than once, then the one-time pad (which is, technically, no longer a one-time pad) is subject to an attack. Different messages encrypted with the same key are said to be in *depth*.

Suppose that plaintext messages P_0 and P_1 are in depth, that is, both are encrypted with a one-time pad using the same key K, yielding ciphertexts C_0 and C_1, respectively. Then if Trudy obtains both ciphertexts, she can compute

$$C_0 \oplus C_1 = (P_0 \oplus K) \oplus (P_1 \oplus K) = P_0 \oplus P_1,$$

that is, Trudy can obtain the XOR of the two plaintexts. It might then be possible for Trudy to "peel apart" these two messages, depending on the properties of the plaintext. The fundamental issue here is that the attacker can, in effect, use one of the messages as a check on any guess for the other message (or the key). Consequently, the ciphertext now provides information about the underlying plaintext and the security can no longer be assured. The problem only gets worse (or, from Trudy's perspective, better) the more the one-time pad is reused.

An obvious practical problem with the one-time pad is that a key having the same length as the plaintext must be securely transmitted to the recipient, and this key can only be used once. If the key can be securely distributed, why not send the message by the same means, in which case there is no need to encrypt?

However, it is important to note that there are some cases where a one-time pad is practical. In some situations it may be easy to send the key at a particular time, and then use it at a later time when it would be difficult or impossible to communicate securely. For example, in the 1930s and 1940s, the Soviet Union used a one-time pad cipher to transmit intelligence gathered from spies in the United States. Soviet agents would simply bring their one-time pads with them when entering the United States, then use these to encrypt sensitive messages as necessary. In fact, these one-time pads were often used more than once and, as a result, many of the messages were eventually broken by United States cryptanalysts. The famous Project VENONA [151] details this impressive cryptanalytic success. The VENONA decrypts provide tremendous insight into Soviet spying in general, and nuclear espionage in particular.

Modern *stream ciphers* are a generalization of the one-time pad, where provable security is traded for practicality. In a stream cipher a short secret key is "stretched" into a long pseudo-random string of bits, which is then used just like a one-time pad. The provable security is lost since the number of possible keys is much smaller than the number of possible messages. Stream ciphers are discussed in Chapter 3.

1.4.4   Codebook Ciphers

Finally, we discuss codebook ciphers, which are, literally, books filled with "codes". In a classic codebook cipher, there are two books, one of which has the plaintext words (or phrases) listed in alphabetical order, each of which is adjacent to its corresponding codeword. A particular word or phrase is encrypted by looking it up in the codebook and replacing it with the appropriate codeword. A corresponding codebook indexed by codewords is used to decrypt. For example, Table 1.9 contains an excerpt from a famous (encryption) codebook of World War I. In fact, this excerpt is from the codebook that was used to encrypt the infamous Zimmermann Telegram [149]. In this particular codebook, the plaintext consists of German words and the ciphertext consists of 5-digit numbers. The inverse codebook, where the words are indexed by the corresponding 5-digit codewords, would be used to decrypt.

Table 1.9: Excerpt from World War I German Codebook

plaintext	ciphertext
Februar	13605
fest	13732
finanzielle	13850
folgender	13918
Frieden	17142
Friedenschluss	17149
⋮	⋮

The security of a classic codebook cipher depends heavily on the physical security of the book itself. That is, the book must be protected from capture by the enemy. In addition, statistical attacks such as those described above for the simple substitution cipher apply equally to codebooks, although the amount of data required to attack a codebook would be much larger. This is due to the fact that the size of the "alphabet" is larger for a codebook, and consequently much more data must be collected before the statistical information can rise above the noise.

As late as World War II, codebooks were in widespread use. Cryptographers realized that these ciphers were subject to statistical attack, so codebooks were regularly replaced with new codebooks. Since this was an expensive and risky process, it was necessary to extend the life of a codebook as much as possible. To this end, an *additive* book was generally used.

Suppose that for a particular codebook cipher, the codewords are all 5-digit numbers. Then the additive book would consist of a long list of randomly generated 5-digit numbers. After a plaintext message had been converted to a series of 5-digit codewords, a random starting point in the additive book would be selected, and the subsequent 5-digit additives would be added to the codewords to create the ciphertext. For a codebook with 5-digit codewords, the addition would be taken modulo 100,000. In this case, the ith ciphertext word would be

$$C_i = F(P_i) + A_j \;(\mathrm{mod}\; 100{,}000),$$

where $F(X)$ is the result of looking up plaintext word X in the codebook, A_j is the additive and P_i is the plaintext. To decrypt,

$$P_i = F^{-1}(C_i - A_j \;(\mathrm{mod}\; 100{,}000)),$$

where $F^{-1}(Y)$ is the plaintext word that corresponds to codeword Y. Note that the additive book is required to encrypt or decrypt a message.

Often, the starting point in the additive book was selected at random by the sender and sent in the clear (or in a slightly obfuscated form) at the start of the transmission. The additive information was part of the *message indicator* (MI). In general, an MI includes any information (other than the key) needed by the recipient to decrypt the message correctly. More examples of MIs appear in the next chapter, where we discuss World War II cipher machines.

Note that if the additive material were only used once, the resulting cipher would be a one-time pad and therefore, provably secure. However, in practice, the additive was reused multiple times and, therefore, any messages sent with overlapping additives would have their codewords "encrypted" with the same additives. Therefore, any messages with overlapping additive sequences could be used to gather the statistical information needed to attack the underlying codebook. In effect, the additive book simply increased the amount of ciphertext required to mount a statistical attack on the codebook, which is precisely the effect the cryptographers hoped to achieve.

Modern *block ciphers* are, in a sense, the descendants of classic codebook ciphers. In addition, the concept of an additive also lives on, in the form of a so-called *initialization vector* (IV), which is often used with block ciphers (and sometimes with stream ciphers as well). The use of IVs in block ciphers is discussed in detail in Chapter 4.

1.5 Summary

In this chapter, we introduced the basic terminology used in the remaining chapters, and we gave an overview of a few selected classical cryptosystems. These classic systems illustrate many of the important concepts seen in later chapters where we analyze modern ciphers.

We also considered various aspects of elementary cryptanalysis. Specifically, we mentioned attacks based on each of the following:

- Exhaustive key search.

- Divide and conquer.

- Statistical weaknesses.

- Linearity of the underlying cipher.

These same cryptanalytic principles appear in various forms throughout the subsequent chapters of this book.

The remaining chapters are primarily focused on case studies illustrating the cryptanlysis of specific real-world ciphers. In the next chapter we discuss the cryptanalysis of the three most famous cipher machines from World War II. Then we turn our attention to modern ciphers, including examples of stream ciphers, block ciphers, hash functions and public key systems. All of these attacks are "applied" in the sense that they are realistic attacks that can be used to break the security of real ciphers.

1.6   Problems

1. Many companies use proprietary cryptosystems. Google to find a specific example of a company that has violated Kerckhoffs' Principle.

2. Edgar Allan Poe's 1843 short story, "The Gold Bug," features a cryptanalytic attack. What type of cipher is broken and how?

3. Solve the following congruence: $19x = 3 \pmod{26}$.

4. Fill in the missing steps in the derivation of the formula for the index of coincidence in (1.2).

5. Consider the ciphertext QJKES REOGH GXXRE OXEO, which was generated using an affine cipher. Recover the decryption function and decipher the message. Hint: Plaintext T encrypts to ciphertext H and plaintext O encrypts to ciphertext E.

6. Decrypt the ciphertext

   TNFOS FOZSW PZLOC GQAOZ WAGQR PJZPN ABCZP QDOGR AMTHA
   RAXTB AGZJO GMTHA RAVAP ZW.

   Hint: This is from a simple substitution cipher and the word "liberty" appears in the plaintext.

7. Cryptanalyze the following message, which is from a Vigenère cipher with a 3-letter English keyword:

   CTMYR DOIBS RESRR RIJYR EBYLD IYMLC CYQXS RRMLQ FSDXF
   OWFKT CYJRR IQZSM X.

8. Write a computer program to calculate the index of coincidence for an English ciphertext. Compute the index of coincidence for the ciphertext in (1.1).

9. Using the result of Problem 8, compute k in (1.4) for the ciphertext in (1.1).

10. Write a computer program to approximate the key length for a Vigenère ciphertext. Verify your program on the ciphertext in (1.1).

11. The following ciphertext is from a columnar transposition cipher:

    TSEHVAIESSRYIYQ.

    Find the corresponding plaintext.

12. The following ciphertext is from a double transposition cipher, where the encryption matrix is 10×11:

    TNOSSKAIMAGAEITMHETHTSRHXXIHEUXDX
    NUEIDSATDTDDSARAHHENTTTDSOUIOEART
    FHDAOMWYWFERTNEONFDYAHSEIMEDGRWTA
    TISURUARTHJ.

    Find the corresponding plaintext.

13. Verify the derivation of (1.4), which can be used to find the number of letters in the keyword of a Vigenère cipher.

14. Consider the Hill cipher with matrix A as given in (1.5).

    a. Find $A^{-1} \pmod{26}$.

    b. Using the result of part a, decrypt the ciphertext EWXJEWYTKZ and verify that the corresponding plaintext is MEETMEHERE.

    c. Using the same A matrix as in part a, decrypt the ciphertext

    QCNDVUHLKGANIYVUWEGMWTNHHXXD.

15. Consider a one-time pad using the letter encodings in Table 1.8. Suppose that Trudy intercepts $C = 110\ 101\ 111$.

    a. Find a putative key K' such that the corresponding putative plaintext P' yields the word GET.

    b. Find another putative key K'' such that the corresponding putative plaintext is TAG.

16. Using the codebook excerpt in Table 1.9 and the additive sequence

$$A_0 = 88,900, \quad A_1 = 92,331, \quad A_2 = 23,546$$

encrypt and decrypt the plaintext message

folgender Frieden Februar.

Assume that the additive arithmetic is taken modulo 100,000. Show all intermediate steps.

17. Consider two ciphers, Cipher A and Cipher B, and suppose that Cipher A has a 64-bit key, while Cipher B has a 128-bit key. Alice prefers Cipher A, while Bob wants the additional security provided by a 128-bit key, so he insists on Cipher B. As a compromise, Alice proposes that they use Cipher A, but they encrypt each message twice, using two independent 64-bit keys. Assuming that no shortcut attack is available for either cipher, is Alice's approach sound?

Chapter 2

World War II Ciphers

...obstacles do not exist to be surrendered to, but only to be broken.
— Adolf Hitler, *Mein Kampf*

2.1 Introduction

In the previous chapter, we covered a few classic "pen and paper" cipher
systems. In this chapter we discuss the three most famous World War II
era cipher machines. We first consider the German Enigma and we present
enough cryptanalysis to illustrate a serious weakness in the cipher. Then
comes the Japanese Purple cipher and its cryptanalysis. Finally, we consider the American Sigaba machine which was never broken during its service
lifetime. We present an attack on Sigaba that would have been impractical
using WWII technology, but nicely illustrates the strong points of the cipher
as compared to the Enigma and Purple.

It is important to remember that World War II was the first significant
use of cryptographic machines. This was necessitated by the vast increase
in the volume of communication required for modern, highly mobile military
operations. Prior to WWII, most military cipher systems were codebooks,
with additives used to increase the amount of data required to successfully
recover the codebook. Obviously, the security of a codebook depends on the
physical security of the book itself. With the advent of machine cryptosystems, much more ciphertext was available to the cryptanalyst, which changed
the nature of the threat considerably. With a cipher machine, physical security of the machine was almost irrelevant in comparison to the statistical
properties of the cipher itself. However, the developers and users of these
early machine systems failed to fully grasp the changed nature of the threat,
since their thinking was grounded in the earlier codebook era. Consequently,
they tended to overemphasize the importance of the physical security of the

25

machine, as opposed to the statistical security of the ciphertext, as discussed in some detail in [23]. We return to this theme at the end of the chapter after we have analyzed the most famous cipher machines of the war.

While there are many sources of information on WWII ciphers, much of the information is unreliable. Among the best sources are [23, 29].

2.2   Enigma

> *It may well be doubted whether human ingenuity can construct an enigma...*
> *which human ingenuity may not, by proper application, resolve.*
> — Edgar Allen Poe, *The Gold Bug*

The Enigma cipher was used by Germany prior to and throughout World War II. The forerunner of the military Enigma machine was originally developed by Arthur Scherbius as a commercial device. The Enigma was patented in the 1920s but it continued to evolve over time. However, all versions of the Enigma are "rotor" machines, and they share certain additional common features.

The German military eventually become interested in the Enigma and, after further modifications, it became the primary cipher system for all branches of the German military. The German government also used the Enigma for diplomatic communications. It is estimated that approximately 100,000 Enigma machines were constructed, about 40,000 of those during World War II. The version of Enigma that we describe here was used by the German military throughout World War II [47].

The Enigma was broken by the Allies, and the intelligence it provided was invaluable—as evidence by its cover name, ULTRA. The Germans had an unwavering belief in the security of the Enigma, and they continued to use it for vital communications long after there were clear indications that it had been compromised. Although it is impossible to precisely quantify the effect of Enigma decrypts on the outcome of the war, it is not farfetched to suggest that the intelligence provided by Enigma decrypts may have shortened the war in Europe by a year, saving hundreds of thousands of lives.

2.2.1   Enigma Cipher Machine

An Enigma cipher machine appears in Figure 2.1, where the keyboard—essentially, a mechanical typewriter—and "lightboard" are visible. The front panel consists of cables plugged into what appears to be an old-fashioned telephone switchboard. This switchboard (or plugboard) is known by its German name, *stecker*. There are also three *rotors* visible near the top of the machine.

Figure 2.1: Enigma cipher [46].

Before encrypting a message, the operator had to initialize the device. The initial settings include various rotor settings and the stecker cable pluggings. These initial settings constitute the key.

Once the machine had been initialized, the message was typed on the keyboard, and the as each plaintext letter was typed, the corresponding ciphertext letter was illuminated on the lightboard. The ciphertext letters were written down as they appeared on the lightboard, to be subsequently transmitted, typically by radio.

To decrypt, the recipient's Enigma had to be initialize in exactly the same way as the sender's. Then when the ciphertext was typed into the keyboard, the corresponding plaintext letters would appear on the lightboard.

The cryptographically significant components of the Enigma are illustrated in Figure 2.2. These components and the way that they interact are described below.

To encrypt, a plaintext letter is entered on the keyboard. This letter first passes through the stecker, then, in turn, through each of the three rotors, through the reflector, back through each of the three rotors, back through the stecker, and, finally, the resulting ciphertext letter is illuminated on the lightboard. Each rotor—as well as the reflector—consists of a hard-wired permutation of the 26 letters. Rotors as cryptographic elements are discussed in detail in Section 2.2.3.

In the example illustrated in Figure 2.2, the plaintext letter C is typed on the keyboard, which is mapped to S due to the stecker cable connecting C to S. The letter S then passes through the rotors, the reflector, and back through the rotors. The net effect of all the rotors and the reflector is a permutation of the alphabet. In the example in Figure 2.2, S has been permuted to Z, which then becomes L due to the stecker cable between L and Z. Finally, the

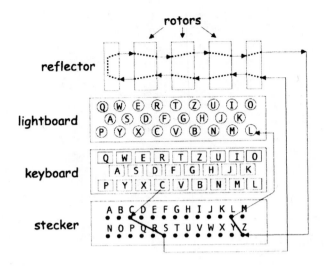

Figure 2.2: Enigma diagram [142].

letter L is illuminated on the lightboard.

We use the following notation for the various permutations in the Enigma:

$$R_r = \text{rightmost rotor}$$
$$R_m = \text{middle rotor}$$
$$R_\ell = \text{leftmost rotor}$$
$$T = \text{reflector}$$
$$S = \text{stecker.}$$

If plaintext letter x encrypts to ciphertext letter y, from Figure 2.2, we have

$$y = S^{-1}R_r^{-1}R_m^{-1}R_\ell^{-1}TR_\ell R_m R_r S(x)$$
$$= (R_\ell R_m R_r S)^{-1}T(R_\ell R_m R_r)S(x). \tag{2.1}$$

If that is all there were to the Enigma, it would be nothing more than a glorified simple substitution (or mono-alphabetic substitution) cipher, with the initial settings determining the permutation. However, each time a keyboard letter is typed, the rightmost rotor steps one position, and the other rotors step in an odometer-like fashion—almost [26, 63].[1] That is, the middle

---

[1] The "almost" is due to the mechanical system used to step the rotors, which causes the middle rotor to occasionally step twice in succession. Whenever a rotor steps, it causes the rotor to its right to also step. Suppose that the middle rotor just stepped to the position that engages the ratchet mechanism that will cause the leftmost rotor to step when the next letter is typed. Then when the next letter is typed, the left rotor will step, and this will also

rotor steps once for each 26 steps of the right rotor and the left rotor steps once for each 26 steps of the middle rotor. The reflector can be viewed as a fixed rotor since it permutes the letters, but it does not rotate. The net effect is that the overall permutation changes with each letter typed. Due to the odometer effect, the permutations R_r, R_m, and R_ℓ vary with time, but T and S do not.

Figure 2.3 illustrates the stepping of a single Engima rotor. This example shows the direction that the rotors step. Note that to the operator, the letters appear in alphabetical order.

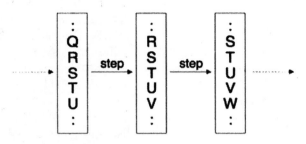

Figure 2.3: Enigma rotor.

The Enigma is a substitution cipher where each letter is encrypted based on a permutation of the alphabet. But the Enigma is far from simple since whenever a letter is encrypted (or decrypted), the permutation changes. That is, the Enigma is a poly-alphabetic substitution cipher, with an enormous number of possible alphabets.

2.2.2   Enigma Keyspace

The cryptographically significant components of the Enigma cipher are the stecker, the three rotors, and the reflector. The Enigma key consists of the configuration of the cipher used to encrypt and decrypt a particular message. The variable settings that comprise the key are the following:

1. The choice of rotors.

2. The position of a movable ring on each of the two rightmost rotors. This ring allows the outer part of the rotor (labeled with the 26 letters) to rotate with respect to the inner part of the ring (where the actual permutation is wired).[2] Rotating this ring shifts the permutation and

---

cause the middle rotor to step again. The middle rotor thereby steps twice in succession, violating the odometer effect. Note that this same ratcheting mechanism causes the right rotor to step whenever the middle rotor steps, but since the right rotor already steps for each letter typed, there is no noticeable effect on the right rotor.

[2]This is analogous to rotating the position of a car tire relative to the rim.

the point at which the odometer effect occurs relative to the letters on the rotors.

3. The initial position of each rotor.

4. The number and plugging of the wires in the stecker.

5. The choice of reflector.

As mentioned above, each rotor implements a permutation of the 26 letters of the alphabet. The movable rings can be set to any of the 26 positions corresponding to the letters.

Each rotor is initially set to one of the 26 positions on the rotor, which are labeled with **A** through **Z**. The stecker is similar to an old-fashioned telephone switchboard, with 26 holes, each labeled with a letter of the alphabet. The stecker can have from 0 to 13 cables, where each cable connects a pair of letters. The reflector implements a permutation of the 26 letters, with the restriction that no letter can be permuted to itself, since this would cause a short circuit. Consequently, the reflector is equivalent to a stecker with 13 cables.

Since there are three rotors, each containing a permutation of the 26 letters, there are

$$26! \cdot 26! \cdot 26! \approx 2^{265}$$

ways to select and place rotors in the machine. In addition, the number of ways to set the two movable rings—which determine when the odometer-like effects occurs—is $26 \cdot 26 \approx 2^{9.4}$.

The initial position of each of these rotors can be set to any one of 26 positions, so there are $26 \cdot 26 \cdot 26 = 2^{14.1}$ ways to initialize the rotors. However, this number should not be included in our count, since the different initial positions are all equivalent to some other rotor in some standard position. That is, if we assume that each rotor is initially set to, say, **A** then setting a particular rotor to, say, **B** is equivalent to some other rotor initially set to **A**. Consequently, the factor of 2^{265} obtained in the previous paragraph includes all rotors in all possible initial positions.

Finally, we must consider the stecker. Let $F(p)$ be the number of ways to plug p cables in the stecker. From Problem 2, we have

$$F(p) = \binom{26}{2p}(2p-1)(2p-3)\cdots 1.$$

The values of $F(p)$ are tabulated in Table 2.1.

Summing the entries in Table 2.1, we find that there are more than $2^{48.9}$ possible stecker configurations. Note that maximum occurs with 11 cables and that $F(10) \approx 2^{47.1}$. As mentioned above, the Enigma reflector is equivalent

Table 2.1: Stecker Combinations

$F(0) = 2^0$	$F(1) \approx 2^{8.3}$
$F(2) \approx 2^{15.5}$	$F(3) \approx 2^{21.7}$
$F(4) \approx 2^{27.3}$	$F(5) \approx 2^{32.2}$
$F(6) \approx 2^{36.5}$	$F(7) \approx 2^{40.2}$
$F(8) \approx 2^{43.3}$	$F(9) \approx 2^{45.6}$
$F(10) \approx 2^{47.1}$	$F(11) \approx 2^{47.5}$
$F(12) \approx 2^{46.5}$	$F(13) \approx 2^{42.8}$

to a stecker with 13 cables. Consequently, there are $F(13) \approx 2^{42.8}$ different reflectors.

Combining all of these results, we find that, in principle, the size of the Enigma keyspace is about

$$2^{265} \cdot 2^{9.4} \cdot 2^{48.9} \cdot 2^{42.8} \approx 2^{366}.$$

That is, the theoretical keyspace of the Enigma is equivalent to a 366 bit key. Since modern ciphers seldom employ more than a 256 bit key, this gives some indication as to why the Germans had such great—but ultimately misplaced—confidence in the Enigma.

However, this astronomical number of keys is misleading. From Problem 3, we see that under the practical limitations of actual use by the German military, only about 2^{77} Enigma keys were available. This is still an enormous number and an exhaustive key search would have been out of the question using 1940s technology. Fortunately for the civilized world, shortcut attacks exist. But before we discuss an attack, we first take a brief detour to consider rotors as cryptographic elements.

2.2.3   Rotors

Rotors were commonly employed in cipher machines during the first half of the 20th century. The Enigma may be the most famous rotor machine, but we will see another when we discuss the Sigaba cipher. From a crypto-engineering standpoint, the appeal of a rotor is that it is possible to generate a large number of distinct permutations in a robust manner from a relatively simple electro-mechanical device. Such considerations were particularly important in the pre-computer era. In fact, the Enigma was an extremely durable piece of hardware, which was usable for tactical military communications.

The Japanese Purple cipher—discussed in Section 2.3—is a non-rotor polyalphabetic cipher that was a contemporary of the Enigma. In contrast to the Enigma, Purple was a bulky and fragile device that could never have survived under battlefield conditions.

Hardware rotors are easy to understand, but it is slightly awkward to mathematically specify the permutations that correspond to the various positions of the rotor. A good analysis of these issues can be found in [90]; here we briefly discuss some of the main points.

For simplicity, consider a rotor with four letter, A through D. Assuming the signal travels from left to right, the rotor illustrated in Figure 2.4 permutes ABCD to CDBA, that is, A is permuted to C, B is permuted to D, C is permuted to B and D is permuted to A. The inverse permutation, DCAB in our notation, can be obtained by simply passing a signal through the rotors from right-to-left instead of left-to-right. This is a useful feature, since we can decrypt with the same hardware used to encrypt. The Enigma takes this one step further—it is its own inverse, so that the same machine with exactly the same settings can be used to encrypt and decrypt (see Problem 6).

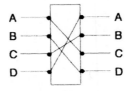

Figure 2.4: Rotor.

Now suppose that the rotor in Figure 2.4 steps once. Note that only the rotor itself—represented by the rectangle—rotates, not the electrical contacts at the edge of the rotor. We assume that the rotor steps "up," that is, the contact that was at B is now at A and so on, with the contact that was at A wrapping around to D. The shift of the rotor in Figure 2.4 is illustrated in Figure 2.5. The resulting shifted permutation is CADB, which is, perhaps, not an obvious shift of the original permutation, CDBA.

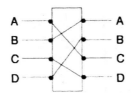

Figure 2.5: Stepped rotor.

In general, it is not difficult to determine the rotor shift of a permutation. The crucial point is that it is the offsets, or displacements, that shift. For example, in the permutation CDBA, the letter A is permuted to C, which is an offset of 2 positions, the letter B is permuted to D, which is an offset of 2, the letter C is permuted to B which is an offset of 3 (around the rotor) and D is permuted to A which is an offset of 1, so the sequence of offsets for the permutation CDBA is $(2, 2, 3, 1)$. Cyclically shifting this sequence yields $(2, 3, 1, 2)$ which corresponds to the permutation CADB, which is the rotor shift that appears in Figure 2.5. Problem 1 provides more details on rotor shifting.

As mentioned above, one of the primary advantages of rotors is that they provide a simple electro-mechanical means to generate a large number of different permutations. Combining multiple rotors in series increases the number of permutations exponentially. For example, in Figure 2.6, C is permuted to A, while a shift of rotor L, denoted by $\sigma(L)$ and illustrated in Figure 2.7, causes C to be permuted to B. That is, stepping any single rotor changes the overall permutation.

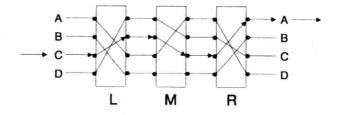

Figure 2.6: Three rotors.

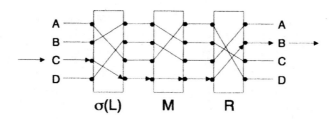

Figure 2.7: Rotor L steps.

With this simple three rotor scheme, we can generate a cycle of 64 permutations of ABCD by stepping through the 64 settings for the three rotors. Of course, not all of these permutations will be unique, since there are only 24 distinct permutations of the four letters ABCD. But the sequence of permutations is at least as significant as the actual generated permutations. Also, selecting different initial settings for the rotors, we can generate a dfferent sequence of permutations, and by selecting a different set of rotors, we can generate different sequences of permutations. As with a single rotor, it is easy to obtain the inverse permutations from a series of rotors by simply passing the signal through the rotors in the opposite direction. Of course, the inverse permutations are needed for decryption.

2.2.4 Enigma Attack

Polish cryptanalysts led by Marian Rejewski, Henryk Zygalski, and Jerzy Różycki were the first to successfully attack the Engima; see [148] for a good discussion of the details of their attack. Their challenge was greatly complicated by the fact that they did not know the rotors in use. Through some clever mathematics, and a small, but crucial, piece of espionage [2], they were able to recover the rotor permutation from ciphertext. This certainly ranks as one of the greatest cryptanalytic successes of the entire war.

When Poland fell to the Nazis in 1939, Rejewski, Zygalski and Różycki fled to France. After France fell under the Nazi onslaught the Poles audaciously continued their cryptanalytic work from unoccupied Vichy France. The brilliant cryptanalytic work of Rejewski's team eventually made its way to Britain, where the British were rightly amazed. A group of British cryptanalysts that included Gordon Welchman and computing pioneer Alan Turing took up the Enigma challenge.

The Enigma attack that we describe here is similar to one developed by Turing, but much simplified. Our attack—which relies on known plaintext—is easily implemented on a modern computer, but would have been impractical using WWII technology. The essential idea is that, initially, we can ignore the stecker and make a guess for the remainder of the key. From Problem 3, there are less than 2^{30} such guesses. For each of these, we use information derived from known plaintext (a "crib" in WWII terminology) to eliminate incorrect guesses. In the process, the stecker is only a minor nuisance and, in fact, when we complete the attack, we will have recovered most—if not all—of the stecker settings as well.

Suppose that for a given ciphertext, we know the plaintext and corresponding ciphertext in Table 2.2. We make use of this data in the attack described below.

Table 2.2: Enigma Known Plaintext Example

i	0	1	2	3	4	5	6	7	8	9	10	11	12	13	14	15	16	17	18	19	20	21	22	23
Plaintext	O	B	E	R	K	O	M	M	A	N	D	O	D	E	R	W	E	H	R	M	A	C	H	T
Ciphertext	Z	M	G	E	R	F	E	W	M	L	K	M	T	A	W	X	T	S	W	V	U	I	N	Z

Let $S(x)$ be the effect of the stecker when a letter x passes through the stecker from the keyboard. Then $S^{-1}(x)$ is the effect of the stecker when x passes through the stecker in the other direction. For a given initial setting, let P_i be the permutation at step i, that is, P_i is the permutation determined by the composition of the three rotors, followed by the reflector, followed by the three rotors—in the opposite direction—at step i. Using the notation in (2.1), we obtain

$$P_i = S^{-1} R_r^{-1} R_m^{-1} R_\ell^{-1} T R_\ell R_m R_r S,$$

where, to simplify the notation, we ignore the dependence of R_ℓ, R_m, and R_r on i.

Since P_i is a permutation, its inverse, P_i^{-1} exists. Due to the rotation of the rotors, the permutation varies with each letter typed. Consequently, P_i does indeed depend on i.

The Enigma attack we present here exploits "cycles" that occur in the known plaintext and corresponding ciphertext. Consider, for example, the column labeled "8" in Table 2.2. The plaintext letter A passes through the stecker, then through P_8 and, finally, through S^{-1} to yield the ciphertext M, that is, $S^{-1} P_8 S(\mathtt{A}) = \mathtt{M}$ which we can rewrite as $P_8 S(\mathtt{A}) = S(\mathtt{M})$. Then from the known plaintext in Table 2.2, we have

$$P_8 S(\mathtt{A}) = S(\mathtt{M})$$
$$P_6 S(\mathtt{M}) = S(\mathtt{E})$$
$$P_{13} S(\mathtt{E}) = S(\mathtt{A})$$

which can be combined to yield the cycle

$$S(\mathtt{E}) = P_6 P_8 P_{13} S(\mathtt{E}). \qquad (2.2)$$

Suppose that we select one of the possible initial settings for the machine, neglecting the stecker. Then all P_i and P_i^{-1} that correspond to this setting are known. Now suppose that we guess, say, $S(\mathtt{E}) = \mathtt{G}$, that is, we guess that E and G are connected by a cable in the stecker plugboard. If it is actually the case that the stecker has a wire connecting E and G, and if our guess for the initial settings of the machine is correct, then from (2.2) we must have

$$\mathtt{G} = P_6 P_8 P_{13}(\mathtt{G}). \qquad (2.3)$$

If we try all 26 choices for $S(\mathtt{E})$ and (2.2) is never satisfied, then we know that our guess for the rotor settings is incorrect and we can eliminate this choice. We would like to use this observation to reduce the number or rotor settings, ideally, to just one. However, if we find any guess for $S(\mathtt{E})$ for which (2.2) holds, then we cannot rule out the current rotor settings. Unfortunately, there are 26 possible guesses for $S(\mathtt{E})$ and for each, there is a $1/26$ chance that (2.2) holds at random. Consequently, we obtain no reduction in the number of possible keys from this one cycle.

Fortunately, all is not lost. We can easily find an additional cycle involving $S(\texttt{E})$, which can then be used in combination with (2.2) to reduce the number of possible rotor settings. For example, we can combine the four equations

$$S(\texttt{E}) = P_3 S(\texttt{R})$$
$$S(\texttt{W}) = P_{14} S(\texttt{R})$$
$$S(\texttt{W}) = P_7 S(\texttt{M})$$
$$S(\texttt{E}) = P_6 S(\texttt{M})$$

to obtain

$$S(\texttt{E}) = P_3 P_{14}^{-1} P_7 P_6^{-1} S(\texttt{E}).$$

Now if we guess, say, $S(\texttt{E}) = \texttt{G}$, we have two equations that must hold if this guess is correct. There are still 26 choices for $S(\texttt{E})$, but with two cycles, there is only a $(1/26)^2$ chance that they both hold at random. Therefore, with two cycles in $S(\texttt{E})$, we can reduce the number of viable machine settings (that is, keys) by a factor of 26. We can easily develop an attack based on this observation. Using only two cycles, the attack is outlined in Table 2.3. However, several additional cycles would be required to uniquely determine the key.

Table 2.3: Enigma Attack

```
// Given: Cycles C_0 and C_1 for S(E)
// (L_0, L_1, ..., L_25) = (A, B, ..., Z)
for each rotor setting
      Compute required permutations to test C_0 and C_1
      for j = 0 to 25
            S(E) = L_j
            if C_0 and C_1 hold then
                  save putative rotor settings and S(E) value L_j
            end if
      next j
next rotor setting
```

To reiterate, the crucial observation here is that once we specify the rotor settings, all permutations $P_0, P_1, P_2, \ldots$ and $P_0^{-1}, P_1^{-1}, P_2^{-1}, \ldots$ are known. Then if we substitute a putative value for $S(\texttt{E})$, we can immediately check the validity of both cycle equations. For an incorrect guess of $S(\texttt{E})$ (or incorrect rotor settings) there is a $1/26$ chance any given cycle will hold true. But with two cycles, there is only a $(1/26)^2$ chance that both cycle equations will hold true. Consequently, with two cycles involving $S(\texttt{E})$, we can reduce the number of possible initial rotor settings by a factor of 26. Since there are about 2^{30} rotor settings, after completing the "attack" in Table 2.3, we expect to have about $2^{30}/26 \approx 2^{25.3}$ putative rotor settings remaining.

The attack in Table 2.3 can be extended to more than two cycles, in which case we obtain a proportionally greater reduction in the number of surviving keys. With a sufficient number of cycles, we can uniquely identify the initial rotor settings. In fact, with n pairs of cycles we expect to reduce the number of possible keys by a factor of 26^n. Therefore, with a sufficient number of cycles, we can recover the key.

Amazingly, by recovering the initial rotor settings in this manner, stecker values are also recovered—essentially for free. However, any stecker values that do not contribute to a cycle will remain unknown, but once the rotor settings have been determined, the remaining unknown stecker settings are easy to determine; see Problem 9. It is interesting to note that in spite of an enormous number of possible settings, the stecker contributes little to the security of the Enigma.

2.2.5   More Secure Enigma?

Several of the design features of the Enigma conspired to create weaknesses that were exploited by the Allies. For example, the fact that the right rotor is the "fast" rotor (i.e., the right rotor steps with each letter typed) was said to be crucial in one particular attack. If instead, the left rotor had stepped with each letter—and the designers of the Enigma could just as easily have chosen any of the rotors as the fast rotor—this particular attack would not have succeeded [23].

The attack described in this section would still work, regardless of which rotors are fast, medium, and slow. However, in spite of it being extremely efficient by modern standards, the attack presented here would have been impractical using 1940s technology. The practical attacks of World War II required that the cryptanalyst reduce the number of cases to be tested to a small number. Many clever techniques were developed to squeeze as much information as possible from the messages before attempting an attack. In addition, much effort was expended finding suitable *cribs* (known plaintext) since all of the practical attacks required known plaintext.

Is there any relatively simple modification to the Enigma that would prevent the attack discussed in this section? We leave this as an exercise (Problem 13). It is important to note that our attack exploits the fact that the rotors can, in a sense, be isolated from the stecker. Any modifications designed to prevent this attack must take this fact into account.

2.3   Purple

> *The Japanese Government regrets to have to*
> *notify hereby the American Government that in view of the attitude*
> *of the American Government it cannot but consider that it is impossible*
> *to reach an agreement through further negotiations.*
> — From the "14-part message" [72]

The World War II era Japanese cipher machine *Angooki Taipu B* was known to Allied cryptanalysts as Purple—due to the color of the binders used to hold information on the cipher. The Japanese used Purple to encrypt diplomatic traffic and it was in use from the late 1930s until the end of the war. Contrary to some reports, Purple was not used to encrypt tactical Naval communications—that was the role of the JN-25 cipher [23]. In particular, it was JN-25 decrypts (not Purple decrypts, as is sometimes claimed [75]) that provided the information enabling American pilots to shoot down Admiral Yamamoto's airplane in 1943.

2.3.1   Purple Cipher Machine

No intact Purple cipher machine was ever captured by the Allies. Figure 2.8 shows a fragment of a Purple machine that was discovered in Berlin at the end of WWII.

Figure 2.8: Fragment of a Purple cipher machine [117].

The most famous Purple ciphetext was the so-called 14-part message, sent from Tokyo to Washington on December 6, 1941, in which Japan broke off negotiations with the United States. The Japanese ambassador was instructed to present the message to U.S. officials at 1:00pm (Washington time) on December 7, 1941, but due to difficulties with the decryption and translation to English, the message was not delivered to Secretary of State Cordell Hull until 2:30 pm. By the time Hull was handed the message, he knew of the attack on Pearl Harbor, which had begun an hour earlier. Hull's blistering response to the Japanese ambassador included the following [71]:

> In all my 50 years of public service I have never seen a document that was more crowded with infamous falsehoods and distortions ... on a scale so huge that I never imagined until today that any Government on this planet was capable of uttering them.

American cryptanalysts led by Frank Rowlett had previously broken Purple[3] and the Americans actually decrypted the 14-part message before the Japanese diplomats in Washington had done so. Although the message contained no specific threat, it clearly represented a serious change in the status quo. The codebreakers' report reached General George Marshall who sent a warning to Hawaii on the morning of December 7. However, due to various delays, the warning did not reach the commanders in Hawaii until after the Japanese attack was over. These events have fueled endless conspiracy theories to the effect that political leaders in Washington knowingly let the attack occur as a way to obtain public backing for war. What these conspiracy theorists lack in fact, they more than compensate for in paranoia.

Purple is inherently weaker than Enigma. Nevertheless, the successful cryptanalysis of Purple is sometimes regarded as the greatest cryptanalytic triumph of World War II. The reason for this apparent contradiction is that while the Enigma machine was known to the Allies, the Purple machine was not—in fact, no intact Purple cipher machine was ever recovered, before, during, or after the war. In comparison, even the Polish cryptanalysts who recovered the Enigma rotors by analyzing ciphertext knew the inner workings of the device. Before Purple could be attacked, its operation first had to be diagnosed based primarily on observed ciphertext. This remarkable diagnostic effort is what people are referring to (implicitly, in many cases) when they discuss the great cryptanalytic success in breaking Purple.

Here, we provide a complete description of the cryptographic functions of the Purple cipher, but we do not attempt to give precise details on the mechanical operation of the actual cipher machine that was used by the Japanese. From the fragments of Purple machines that were found after the war, most of the details of the machine are known. It was a complex and intricate piece of engineering, with a "rat's nest" of nearly 2000 wires used to implement its various permutations. For details on the mechanical operation of the Purple machine, see the article [52].

The Purple cipher (in encryption mode) is illustrated in Figure 2.9. When a plaintext letter is typed on the input keyboard, it passes through a plug-

---

[3]The intelligence garnered from Purple decrypts was given the cover name MAGIC, which is an indicator of its perceived value.

board which permutes the letters. The permuted letters are then split into a group of six letters—the "sixes"—and a group of 20 letters—the "twenties." Internally, the sixes consist of the vowels

$$\text{AEIOUY,} \tag{2.4}$$

while the twenties are the consonants

$$\text{BCDFGHJKLMNPQRSTVWXZ.} \tag{2.5}$$

We refer to this unusual feature of Purple as the "6-20 split."

The input plugboard permutation enables any six letters to be connected to the internal sixes in (2.4). If, after passing through the input plugboard, the resulting letter is permuted to one of the sixes, it then passes through a permutation, denoted by S in Figure 2.9, before being permuted by the output plugboard. The resulting letter is then sent to the output device. If, on the other hand, the plugboard permutation yields a twenties letter, the letter passes through three permutations, denoted L, M, and R in Figure 2.9, before being permuted by the output plugboard. Again, the resulting letter is then sent to the output device.

As used by the Japanese, the output plugboard and input plugboard permutations were always the same. In fact, the Purple simulators built by the Allies used only a single physical plugboard, which could not have accurately modeled Purple if the input and output permutations were different.

As can be seen in Figure 2.9, internally the sixes are permuted to sixes and the twenties are permuted to twenties. This was a major flaw that was carried over from a predecessor of Purple, a cipher known as Red. Why it was carried over is not clear, since there was no inherent limitation of Purple that necessitated such a split. In fact, two variants of Purple were used by the Japanese (Coral and Jade) that did not employ the 6-20 split. As discussed below, the 6-20 split was a crucial weakness that was exploited by the cryptanalysts who broke Purple.

Each of S, L, M, and R cycle thorough a series of 25 fixed permutations, with S stepping once for each letter typed, and exactly one of L, M, or R stepping for each letter—which of these steps is determined by S as will be described shortly. Each of the S permutations is a permutation of the six vowels in (2.4), while each of the L, M, and R permutations is a permutation of the twenty consonants in (2.5).

Like Enigma, Purple is a poly-alphabetic substitution cipher. However, the mechanisms employed by the two ciphers are completely different. Recall that Enigma is a rotor machine, where each rotor has a single hardwired permutation, and as a result of the rotor motion, the overall Enigma permutation changes with each letter. In contrast, Purple uses switches, where each step of a switch changes to a different permutation. That is, instead

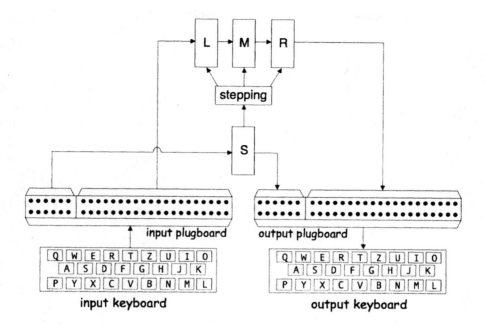

Figure 2.9: Purple encryption.

of using permutations wired to rotors—which only requires one permutation per rotor—each step of Purple's S, L, M, and R "switches" to a different, unrelated, hardwired permutation. Consequently, we refer to S, L, M, and R as switches and Purple as a *stepping switch* machine.

While the distinction between rotors and switches might seem relatively minor, it is actually a major difference. For one thing, a stepping switch machine like Purple is inherently more complex and difficult to engineer than a rotor machine. From a cryptanlytic point of view, a rotor machine provides an elegant way to generate a large number of permutations, while a comparable stepping switch machine must be far more complex. There are also significant differences between the types of permutations that can be generated by Purple and Enigma, as discussed below and in Problem 16.

The Purple encryption formula depending on whether the letter being encrypted corresponds to a "six" or "twenty". Let x be the given input letter and let y be the corresponding output letter. Then we can denote the encryption by

$$y = \begin{cases} P_O^{-1} P_R P_M P_L P_I(x) & \text{if } P_I(x) \text{ is one of the twenties} \\ P_O^{-1} P_S P_I(x) & \text{if } P_I(x) \text{ is one of the sixes} \end{cases} \tag{2.6}$$

where P_I is the input plugboard permutation (when going from the input keyboard to the switches), P_O is the output plugboard permutation (from the output keyboard to the plugboard). Note that P_I and P_O^{-1} follow the direction of the arrows in Figure 2.9. Also, P_L, P_M, and P_R are the left, middle, and right twenties permutations, respectively, and P_S is the sixes permutation. As mentioned above, the Japanese always selected $P_I = P_O$.

A major practical difference between Purple and Enigma is that Purple is not its own inverse (Problem 6 asks you to show that Enigma is its own inverse). This means that decryption with Purple is more complicated than with Enigma. Since decryption requires the inverse permutations, Purple can be decrypted by reversing the flow through the diagram in Figure 2.9, as illustrated in Figure 2.10. This implies that the output plugboard is used for input and the input plugboard for output. Of course, if the plugboards have identical permutations (as, apparently, was always the case with Purple), then it does not matter which plugboard is used for input and which is used for output.

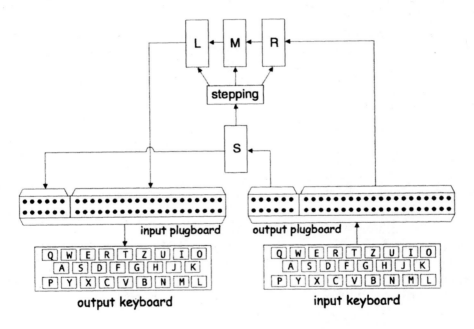

Figure 2.10: Purple decryption.

The decryption formula corresponding to (2.6) is

$$x = \begin{cases} P_I^{-1} P_L^{-1} P_M^{-1} P_R^{-1} P_O(y) & \text{if } P_O(y) \text{ is one of the twenties} \\ P_I^{-1} P_S^{-1} P_O(y) & \text{if } P_O(y) \text{ is one of the sixes.} \end{cases}$$

Since the decryption formula works for any choice of P_I and P_O, why did the Japanese always select $P_I = P_O$? If $P_I = P_O$, then a single plugboard can be used. Assuming there were two physical plugboards present in Purple, perhaps it was the case that it was easy to swap the input and output keyboards, but not the plugboards. If so, then it would still be possible to decrypt when $P_I \neq P_O$, but the plugboards would have to be wired with the inverse permutations to do so. This would have necessitated different encryption and decryption settings and, in particular, would have made it difficult to do trial encryptions and decryptions, which could be used to verify the key settings.

In contrast to the Enigma, Purple plugboards are not necessarily their own inverse, since the plugboards do not connect pairs of letters, as is the case with Enigma. Instead, the Purple plugboards connect 26 letters to 26 letters so they can implement any permutation.

Since there are 25 steps on each of the switches S, L, M, and R, each switch has a cycle length of 25. Since exactly one of the switches L, M, or R steps with each letter, overall, the twenties have a cycle length of $25 \cdot 25 \cdot 25 = 15,625$, while the sixes have a cycle length of 25. As mentioned above, the S switch determines which of L, M, or R steps. When setting the Purple cipher, it is necessary to specify which of L, M and R are "fast," "medium," and "slow" switches. The fact that only one of the twenties switches steps with each letter leads to a somewhat complicated stepping process, which we now describe.

The specification of fast, medium, and slow switches is part of the keying process and does not change during the encryption of a message. The sixes switch, S, simply steps once for each letter encrypted, cycling through its 25 permutations. Exactly one of L, M, and R steps with each encryption, with the stepping determined as follows. Number the permutations on each of the switches 0 through 24. The fast twenties switch steps each time, except for the following two cases:

- If the sixes switch S is in position 24, then the medium switch steps.

- If the S switch is in position 23 and the medium switch is in position 24, then the slow switch steps.

The result is that the S switch and exactly one of the twenties switches step for each letter typed, and both the S switch and the selected twenties switch step simultaneously.

Two examples of switch stepping appear in Table 2.4, where L is the fast twenties switch, M is the medium twenties switch, and R is the slow twenties switch. The left-hand example in Table 2.4 illustrates the case where the medium switch steps, while the right-hand example illustrates the stepping of the slow switch.

Purple stepping is more complicated than the simple odometer effect employed by the Engima rotors. But the ever-so-slight advantage of the Pur-

Table 2.4: Medium Switch Steps and Slow Switch Steps

S	L	M	R
20	0	10	7
21	1	10	7
22	2	10	7
23	3	10	7
24	4	10	7
0	4	11	7
1	5	11	7
2	6	11	7
3	7	11	7

S	L	M	R
20	0	24	4
21	1	24	4
22	2	24	4
23	3	24	4
24	3	24	5
0	3	0	5
1	4	0	5
2	5	0	5
3	6	0	5

ple stepping method is that the period length of the twenties is maximized, whereas in Enigma, the period length is reduced slightly, since more than one rotor steps at the rollover points. However, the additional complexity of the Purple stepping more than offsets any possible advantage due to the greater period length.

2.3.2 Purple Keyspace

Now we consider the size of the Purple keyspace. Suppose for a moment that the permutations on the switches were selectable. Then the Purple keyspace would be enormous—just the selection of the S, L, M, and R permutations would give

$$(6!)^{25} \cdot (20!)^{75} \approx 2^{237} \cdot 2^{4581} = 2^{4818}$$

possible keys.

However, given the design of Purple, it was not possible to change the hardwired permutations, so we compute the keyspace assuming that the permutations are fixed. Under this restriction, the Purple key consists of the following:

1. Initial settings of the switches S, L, M, and R: There are $25^4 \approx 2^{18.6}$ ways to initialize these switches.

2. Choose fast, medium, and slow switches from L, M, and R: Since these can be selected in any order, there are $6 \approx 2^{2.6}$ combinations.

3. Select input and output plugboard permutations: If the input and output plugboards can be chosen independently, there are $(26!)^2 \approx 2^{176.8}$ combinations.

Therefore, the theoretical keyspace for Purple is approximately of size 2^{198}, equivalent to a 198-bit key. However, all but a factor of $2^{21.2}$ of this comes from the plugboard settings. In fact, the Japanese always used the same plugboard for both input and output, which immediately reduces the keyspace to $2^{109.6}$.

The Purple plugboard is a very weak cryptographic element and, consequently, the effective keyspace is little more than 2^{21}. However, this presupposes that the switch permutations are known to the cryptanalyst, which was not the case when Rowlett and his team began their analysis of Purple. Consequently, the real cryptanalytic challenge for the Allies was to understand the inner workings of Purple and to recover the internal permutations—all without ever having seen the machine. Once this was accomplished, the actual decryption would not be difficult.

In fact, the Japanese only used a very small fraction of the (already small) effective keyspace. Once the machine had been diagnosed, and a relatively simple message indicator (MI) system had been broken, the Allies could decrypt messages as quickly as—and sometimes faster than—the Japanese. In effect, maintaining the secret design of Purple was essential to maintain its security. It is hard to imagine a more striking violation of Kerckhoffs' Principle. The fact that the Allies were able to break Purple without ever laying hands on an actual machine argues strongly for the wisdom of Kerckhoffs.

In the next section we consider the diagnosis of Purple. This was the crucial cryptanalytic challenge in breaking Purple.

2.3.3   Purple Diagnosis

No Purple cipher machine was available to Frank Rowlett, the American cryptanalyst most closely associated with the cryptanalysis of Purple. This meant that he first had to *diagnose* the machine before he could hope to break it. That is, he had to reconstruct the inner workings of the machine using the only available information, namely, intercepted ciphertext and knowledge of prior Japanese cryptosystems. In some cases, known plaintext was also available, and this would prove crucial to the diagnostic effort.

Recall that ciphertext messages are said to be in *depth* if they are encrypted using the same key. If n messages are all encrypted with the same key, then we refer to this as a depth of n legs. It is also possible to have an offset depth, where the messages do not begin on the same key, but from some point onward the messages go into depth.

Suppose that the matched plaintext and ciphertext message snippets in Table 2.5 were generated by a cipher that uses a time-varying permutation of the alphabet. The Enigma cipher, for example, works in this manner. Purple is slightly more complicated due to the 6-20 split, but we ignore this issue for now.

Table 2.5: Matched Plaintext and Ciphertext

i	0	1	2	3	4	5	6	7	8	9	10	11
Plaintext	P	E	A	R	L	H	A	R	B	O	R	X
Ciphertext	J	K	F	H	N	V	P	G	P	G	P	Y
Plaintext	T	O	R	A	T	O	R	A	T	O	R	A
Ciphertext	K	P	L	T	H	D	W	V	J	L	O	P
Plaintext	M	I	D	W	A	Y	I	S	L	A	N	D
Ciphertext	X	H	T	E	S	A	G	N	K	O	L	I

Furthermore, suppose the messages in Table 2.5 form a 3-legged depth. Then the permutation at each position of the three messages is the same. Let P_i be the ith permutation generated by this cipher for this particular key. Then we have some information on the first several permutations. For example, we know that P_0 maps plaintext P to ciphertext J, plaintext T to ciphertext K and plaintext M to ciphertext X. Also, P_1 maps E to K and O to P, and I to H, and so on. In this way, we can partially reconstruct the permutations, and the more legs of depth that are available, the more information on each permutation we obtain.

While it was clear to Rowlett and his team that Purple was a substitution cipher, it was unclear how the permutations were generated. The cryptanalysts had knowledge of previous Japanese cipher machines, as well as knowledge of other cryptographic devices of the time, including rotor machines. The knowledge of an earlier Japanese cipher known as Red proved most valuable.

The Red cipher employed an unusual split of the alphabet into sixes and twenties, which was carried over into Purple. Initially, the Red cipher split the alphabet into the six vowels, AEIOUY, and the remaining twenty consonant. Substituting vowels for vowels and consonants for consonants was also used in some other ciphers of the time. This split reduced the cost of cabling the ciphertext messages, since the resulting messages were considered "pronounceable"—even though the ciphertext was gibberish—and therefore were charged a lower rate than messages consisting of random letters [52]. But encrypting vowels to vowels is a serious weakness, since some messages can be inferred simply based on the placement of vowels within the ciphertext. The Japanese apparently realized this was a weakness and usage of the Red cipher was modified so that any six letters could act as the sixes. This is precisely the same situation as with Purple.

The ciphertext sixes would be expected to each occur with the average probability of the corresponding plaintext sixes, and similarly, each ciphertext twenties letter would occur with the average probability of the plaintext twenties. For most random selections of six letters from the alphabet, the selected letters will occur at either a higher or lower average frequency than the remaining letters (see Problems 14 and 15). For example, if the plaintext letter E is among the sixes, and the other sixes are all letters of average frequency, then the expected frequency of each of the ciphertext sixes will be higher than the expected frequency of each of the ciphertext twenties. Therefore, the ciphertext sixes can usually be determined simply from a frequency count of individual ciphertext letters. That is, the six highest-frequency or six lowest-frequency letters are most likely the sixes. Once the sixes have been isolated, it is relatively easy to determine the sixes permutations from a small amount of known plaintext, since in Purple there are only 25 sixes permutations.

Using their knowledge of the Red cipher, Rowlett's team was quick to realize that Purple also employed a 6-20 split. They were then able to reconstruct the sixes permutations. But the twenties proved far more difficult to crack.

The output permutations generated by a switch-based cipher, such as Purple, have certain identifiable characteristics. For example, consider the permutations in Table 2.6, which were generated by a process analogous to that used by Purple to generate its twenties permutation. In this example, there are three banks of permutations, as with the twenties permutations in Purple, but here each of the switches contains just three permutations (as opposed to 25 for Purple), giving a cycle length of $3^3 = 27$.

Table 2.6: Successive Permutations

	0	1	2	3	4	5	6
P_0	5	6	1	0	2	3	4
P_1	5	0	6	1	3	2	4
P_2	5	6	0	3	1	4	2
P_3	6	1	0	4	5	2	3
P_4	4	2	1	6	5	0	3
P_5	6	0	4	1	2	5	3
P_6	6	1	5	2	3	0	4
P_7	6	2	1	5	0	3	4
P_8	5	3	2	6	0	1	4
P_9	3	4	6	5	1	0	2
P_{10}	5	0	3	6	4	1	2
P_{11}	2	1	3	4	6	0	5

Consider permutations P_4 and P_5 in Table 2.6. The element in position 0 of P_4 is 4, while the 4 is in position 2 of P_5. That is, the first element of P_4 is offset by 2 in P_5. The element in position 1 of P_4 is a 2 and the 2 appears in position 4 of P_5, so these have an offset of 3. Continuing in this manner, we see that the offsets, or differences, between the elements of P_4 and the corresponding elements of P_5 are $(2, 3, 1, 4, 1, 3, 0)$. As explained in Section 2.2.3, consecutive permutations from a rotor all share the same difference sequence. The difference sequence for P_5 and P_6 is different than between P_4 and P_5, so we can be sure that these three permutations were not generated by consecutive shifts of a single rotor.

Now if we compute the difference sequence for permutations P_8 and P_9, we see that it is the same as for P_4 and P_5. This is not coincidental. In fact, it is consistent with these two pairs being compositions of (non-rotor) permutations; see Problem 17. It was precisely this sort of observation that was the crucial breakthrough in the diagnosis of Purple.

Once we realize that the permutations in Table 2.6 are compositions of permutations, we can solve for the individual permutations (or an equivalent set) as follows. Most likely, P_4 and P_5 are consecutive "fast" permutations with the same settings for the medium and slow permutations. Suppose the L switch is the fast switch and let L_0 be the fast permutation in P_4 and L_1 be the fast permutation in P_5. Then $R_i M_j L_0(0) = R_i M_j L_1(2)$, for some i and j, which implies that $L_0(0) = L_1(2)$. Continuing, we can determine the permutation L_1 in terms of L_0. Using the appropriate rows from Table 2.6, we can also determine L_2 in terms of L_0. Then we are free to arbitrarily select L_0, thereby fixing L_1 and L_2. With the L permutations determined, we can similarly determine the M permutations. Finally, when determining the R permutations, there will be no freedom to specify one of the permutations; see Problem 18 at the end of this chapter for more details on this particular example.

Is it feasible to obtain data analogous to that in Table 2.6 for the Purple cipher? If there happens to be a large number of messages in depth with known plaintext, then the encryption permutations are at least partially exposed by the various legs of depth, and the more legs of depth available, the more information there is on the underlying permutation at each position. In fact, this is essentially what occurred and this is what enabled Rowlett and his team to diagnose Purple. The American cryptanalysts had deduced the general structure of Purple, but it took a large volume of messages in depth, with known plaintext, before they could recover the actual permutations [23]. The American cryptanalysts were then able to construct machines that were functionally equivalent to Purple—one such Purple "analog" is pictured in Figure 2.11.

Recall that Polish cryptanalysts were able to recover the Enigma rotor wirings from ciphertext analysis. But the Poles knew how the Enigma worked, whereas in the case of Purple, the cryptanalysts did not know the inner workings of the machine. However, Purple is, from a cryptanalytic point

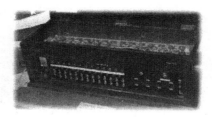

Figure 2.11: Purple analog [105].

of view, a simpler device than Enigma. We have more to say about the comparison between Purple and Enigma in Section 2.3.5, below.

2.3.4 Decrypting Purple

Once Purple had been diagnosed, reading messages was relatively easy. The Japanese restricted the number of initial switch settings to a very small number (originally, 120 and later 240), presumably, to avoid offset depths. In addition, only about 1000 plugboard settings were ever used. Consequently, analysts could build a dictionary of possible settings from a relatively small number of broken messages. However, not even this much work was required, since the switch settings were transmitted in a message indicator (MI) that was sent with the ciphertext. The indicators were obfuscated, but this system was relatively easy to break. Given the extremely limited keyspace used in practice, after a small number of successful decryptions, the Allies were able to decrypt received messages as quickly as the Japanese. In fact, the 14-part message was decrypted by American cryptanalysts before the Japanese had done so.

Even if the full keyspace had been used, the Purple machine would have been extremely weak once it had been diagnosed. There are only $6 \cdot 25^4 \approx 2^{21.2}$ initial switch settings. The number of plugboards, at $26! \approx 2^{88.4}$, appears to be daunting, but, as with the Enigma stecker, this is highly misleading. As a cryptographic element, the Purple plugboard is fundamentally flawed. Assuming that the switch settings are correct, putative plugboard settings that are close to the actual plugboard setting yield putative plaintext that is close to the actual plaintext. For a well-designed modern cipher, we require that any change to the key—no matter how minor—yields a putative decryption that is statistically indistinguishable from that generated by a randomly selected key.

In [52] a straightforward "hill climbing" attack is given that exploits the weakness of the Purple plugboard. This attack recovers the plugboard settings with a relatively small amount of work.

2.3.5   Purple versus Enigma

It is interesting to compare Enigma and Purple. Although Enigma had a large theoretical keyspace of some 380 bits, practical issues cut this number drastically. In particular, due to the fact that only a small number of rotors were available in practice, and the fact that the stecker adds little to the security, the number of keys that a World War II cryptanalyst had to be concerned with was about 2^{29}. However, if we implement a modern version of the Enigma in software, then any rotor is readily available and the number of effective keys rises to somewhere near 2^{290}.

In contrast, the Purple design is fundamentally flawed due to the 6-20 split. Given a fair amount of known plaintext, the sixes are easily recovered, and some messages can be read simply from knowledge of the sixes. As we observed above, with sufficient messages in depth, it is possible to diagnose Purple. If the switch settings were selected at random, without varying the plugboard settings, the limited number of such settings would result in many messages in offset depth.

It is also interesting that both the Enigma and Purple plugboards are of virtually no cryptographic value. In spite of the huge numbers of possible plugboard settings for each, they effectively add little to the keyspace.

The Purple permutations were not designed to be changed, and if we maintain that restriction, this is another major weakness of the design. But in a software version of Purple, we could easily allow the permutations to change based on the key. This would increase the keyspace by some 265 bits, which would put Purple roughly on par with the Enigma. However, the sixes could still be easily recovered, which is a serious weakness.

Consider a new cipher, Maroon,[4] which eliminates the obvious weaknesses of Purple but retains the basic design. Like Purple, Maroon is a stepping switch cipher, with four switches, which we denote S, L, M, and R. But unlike Purple, Maroon does not use the 6-20 alphabet split. Instead, each of the permutations in the switches L, M, and R is a permutation on 26 letters. We have also increased the number of permutations per switch from 25 to 26.

As with Purple, the S switch of Maroon steps once for each input letter, but, since there are no sixes, the S switch is only used to determine the stepping of the other switches. The switch stepping follows the same pattern as in Purple. The Maroon cipher is illustrated in Figure 2.12.

Maroon was designed to be comparable to Enigma, with the essential difference being that Maroon employs switched permutations instead of rotors to determine the permutation. Some comparisons of Enigma and Maroon are explored in the homework problems.

The bottom line is that, in spite of its flaws, Enigma was a much superior

---

[4]Our Maroon cipher appears to be similar to the Japanese World War II ciphers known as Jade and Coral, but precise details on these machines are somewhat sketchy.

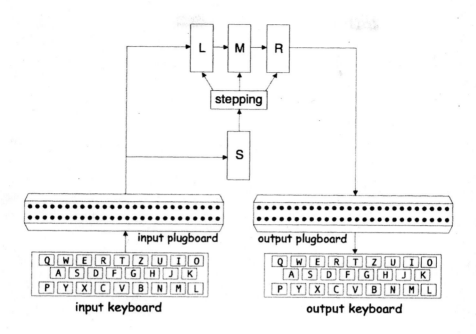

Figure 2.12: Maroon encryption.

design in comparison to Purple. The inherent flaw of the 6-20 alphabet split is a major shortcoming of Purple. Also worth noting is that Enigma machines are virtually indestructible, whereas the complexity and fragility of Purple greatly limited its potential uses.

The diagnosis problem makes the story of Purple cryptanalytically interesting. Since the cryptanlysts did not have access to a Purple machine, they were forced to reconstruct the inner workings of the device based on intercepted ciphertext. Certainly this ranks as a phenomenal cryptanalytic success. Of course, the successful attacks on Enigma—first by the Poles and then the British—also rank as amazing cryptanalytic success stories.

Comparing the diagnosis of Purple and the cryptanalysis of Enigma is somewhat ridiculous—since they are entirely different problems—but that will not prevent us from doing so. Purple was clearly the weaker machine. However, the internals of the machine were unknown to the American cryptanalysts, making it extremely challenging to diagnose, even taking into account the prior knowledge of Japanese ciphers such as Red.[5] On the other

---

[5]The 6-20 alphabet split, which was carried over from Red, was the most significant hint that was gained from previous Japanese ciphers. However, the 6-20 split would have been relatively easy to diagnose from Purple ciphertext, even without knowledge of previous Japanese ciphers. The fact that Purple uses a stepped switch design was the crucial observation needed to break the cipher.

hand, the inner workings of Enigma were completely known (at least to the British), but Enigma was inherently stronger than Purple, making any successful attack a challenging and delicate affair. So which was the greater challenge? Take your pick—you will have solid arguments in your favor no matter which you choose.

2.4 Sigaba

> *Remove the Cipher Unit from the machine,*
> *withdraw the Index Maze Spindle and remove the Index Wheels.*
> *Destroy the Index Wheels by smashing them with a heavy hammer.*
> — Sigaba operating instructions [111]

Sigaba was developed by American cryptographers—including Friedman and Rowlett—prior to World War II.[6] As far as is known, no successful attack on Sigaba was ever conducted during its service lifetime. During WWII, the Germans are said to have quit collecting Sigaba intercepts since they deemed the problem hopeless [23].

In this section we first give a detailed description of the cipher. Sigaba is a rotor machine, but its inner workings are far more complex than the Enigma. Then we consider the size of the Sigaba keyspace in some detail, followed by an outline of an attack on the machine. As we describe it, the attack is impractical—and it would have been even more so using WWII technology. Some of the problems at the end of this chapter point to improvements in the attack, which make it far more practical, but still beyond the realm of a realistic WWII-era attack. This attack highlights the crucial features of the Sigaba that make it so much more secure than Enigma or Purple.

2.4.1 Sigaba Cipher Machine

There were several variants of the basic Sigaba design, and to further muddy the water, different branches of the military used different names for the same machine. The Sigaba machine in Figure 2.13 is thought to be equivalent to the CSP-889 (used by the Navy) and the Converter M-134C or Sigaba (different names, but the same device, used by the Army). In addition, the name ECM Mark II was used during the development of the machine that would become Sigaba. Here, we stick with the name Sigaba.

The Sigaba cipher includes a typewriter keyboard for entering the plaintext (or ciphertext), and an output device for printing the corresponding

---

[6]Rowlett cited the design of Sigaba as his proudest accomplishment, not the breaking of Purple as might have been expected [23].

Figure 2.13: A Sigaba machine [105].

ciphertext (or plaintext). Like the Enigma, Sigaba is a rotor machine, but there are several important differences between the two. Cryptographically, the most significant differences are that whereas Enigma uses three rotors, Sigaba employs five rotors to permute the letters, and whereas Enigma rotors step like an odometer, the Sigaba cipher rotor motion is controlled by a set of ten additional rotors, for a total of 15 rotors. In effect, it is as if the motion of the Sigaba encryption rotors is controlled by another rotor cipher machine. This causes the Sigaba rotors to step irregularly, which is a major improvement over the Enigma and other regularly stepping rotor machines. Sigaba also lacks the Enigma's reflector and stecker. The use of irregularly stepping rotors and the lack of a reflector and Enigma-like stecker make Sigaba a stronger cipher than Enigma (the attack in Section 2.2 points to some of the weaknesses of the Enigma design). The Sigaba rotors are illustrated in Figure 2.14.

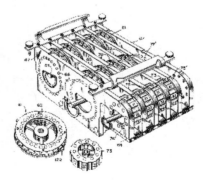

Figure 2.14: Sigaba rotors [126].

The fifteen Sigaba rotors consist of five *cipher rotors*, five *control rotors*, and five *index rotors*, where the cipher rotors permute the input letters and the other two banks of rotors drive the cipher rotors. The cipher and control rotors are interchangeable, and these rotors are also designed so they can be inserted backwards. The cipher and control rotors each permute the 26 letters. The five index rotors each permute the numbers 0 through 9 and, of course, the index rotors are not interchangeable with the other rotors. Unlike the cipher and control rotors, the index rotors cannot operate in the reverse orientation. Figure 2.15 illustrates the cryptographic components of Sigaba in encryption mode.

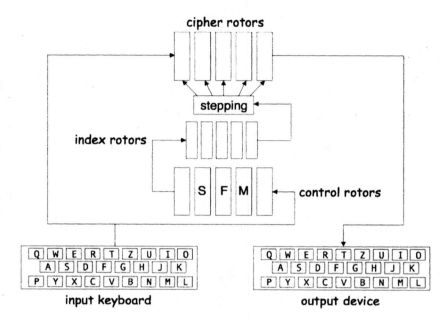

Figure 2.15: Sigaba encryption.

After a letter is encrypted or decrypted, from one to four of the cipher rotors step. The number and selection of the stepping cipher rotors is controlled by the other two banks of rotors, that is, the control and index rotors.

For each letter typed, the rightmost control rotor receives four simultaneous inputs, which we assume to be F, G, H, and I. These four letters are permuted according to the five control rotors and the resulting four permutation-dependent output letters are combined before being input to the index rotor bank. Let I_j denote the input to element j of the leftmost index rotor and A through Z the outputs of the control rotors. Then

$$
\begin{array}{lll}
I_1 = \text{B} & I_4 = \text{F} \vee \text{G} \vee \text{H} & I_7 = \text{P} \vee \text{Q} \vee \text{R} \vee \text{S} \vee \text{T} \\
I_2 = \text{C} & I_5 = \text{I} \vee \text{J} \vee \text{K} & I_8 = \text{U} \vee \text{V} \vee \text{W} \vee \text{X} \vee \text{Y} \vee \text{Z} \\
I_3 = \text{D} \vee \text{E} & I_6 = \text{L} \vee \text{M} \vee \text{N} \vee \text{O} & I_9 = \text{A}
\end{array}
\tag{2.7}
$$

where (2.7) is interpreted to mean that, for example, input 3 of the leftmost index rotor is active if output D or E (or both) results from the control rotors;

otherwise input 3 is inactive. Note that I_0 is missing, which implies that input 0 is always inactive. Since four values are input to the control rotors, due to the "OR" of the outputs, anywhere from one to four of the inputs to the index rotors are active at each step.

The middle three control rotors step in an odometer-like fashion—almost. The fast, medium, and slow control rotors are indicated by F, M, and S, respectively, in Figure 2.15, where the fast rotor steps with each letter, the medium rotor steps once for each 26 steps of the fast rotor, and the slow rotor steps once for each 26 steps of the medium rotor. The stepping of these three rotors differs from an odometer only in the order of the fast, medium and slow rotors. The initial setting of all five control rotors is adjustable, but the leftmost and rightmost control rotors do not step during encryption or decryption.

The output of the control rotor bank enters the index rotor bank. The index rotors do not step, but their order and initial positions are adjustable. For a particular message, the index rotors effectively implement a simple substitution on 0 through 9 (i.e., a fixed permutation of 0 through 9). From one to four (inclusive) of the inputs to the index rotor bank are active, and the number of active outputs is equal to the number of active inputs.

As mentioned above, the cipher and control rotors are interchangeable. In addition, each of these rotors can be inserted in either of two orientations— forward or reverse. In the reverse orientation, the letters on the cipher wheel will appear upside down to the operator.

When a rotor is in its forward orientation, the shifting is, for example, from O to N to M and so on. Figure 2.16 illustrates successive shifts of a single Sigaba cipher (or control) rotor in its forward orientation. Note that the direction of rotation of the Sigaba rotors is the same as that of the Enigma rotors. However, the labeling on the Sigaba rotors goes in the opposite direction as the Enigma; compare Figure 2.16 to Figure 2.3.

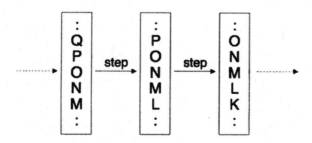

Figure 2.16: Sigaba rotor in forward orientation.

In the reverse orientation the cipher (or control) rotor shifting is from O to P to Q, with the letters appearing upside down on the rotors. The stepping

of a rotor in reverse orientation is illustrated in Figure 2.17. As discussed
in Section 2.2.3, implementing rotors in software requires some care, and re-
versed rotors create an additional complication (see Problem 21). Also, from
Figure 2.15 we see that the signal passes through the control rotors from
right-to-left, while, in encrypt mode, it passes through the cipher rotors from
left-to-right, which creates yet another slight complication when implementing Sigaba in software.

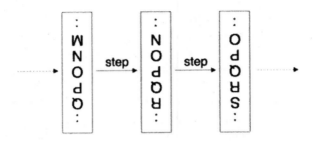

Figure 2.17: Sigaba rotor in reverse orientation.

Curiously, the Sigaba index rotors are labeled in the opposite direction of
the cipher and control rotors. That is, the numbers increase in the downward
direction as illustrated in Figure 2.18. Since the index rotors do not step
during operation of the cipher, this is not a significant issue.

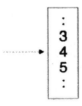

Figure 2.18: Index rotor.

An interesting quirk of Sigaba is that the letter Z is changed to X before
encrypting, and a space is changed to a Z before encrypting. If the result of
decryption is a Z, a space is output. In this way, messages can be encrypted
and decrypted with word spaces included, which makes parsing the decrypted
message easier. The only drawback is that both plaintext X and Z will be
decrypted as X. For example, for some setting of Sigaba, the plaintext message

ZERO␣ONE␣TWO␣THREE␣FOUR␣FIVE␣SIX

encrypts as

IEQDEMOKGJEYGOKWBXAIPKRHWARZODWG

and this ciphertext decrypts as

$$\text{XERO}_\sqcup\text{ONE}_\sqcup\text{TWO}_\sqcup\text{THREE}_\sqcup\text{FOUR}_\sqcup\text{FIVE}_\sqcup\text{SIX},$$

where "$\sqcup$" is a word space.

We assume that the odometer effect of the middle three control rotors occurs when a rotor steps from O to the next letter, regardless of the orientation of the rotor. For example, if the fast rotor is at O, then the fast and medium rotors will both step when the next letter is typed on the keyboard.[7]

The output value (or values) of the index rotors determines which of the cipher rotors step. Let

$$C_0 = O_0 \vee O_9$$
$$C_1 = O_7 \vee O_8$$
$$C_2 = O_5 \vee O_6$$
$$C_3 = O_3 \vee O_4$$
$$C_4 = O_1 \vee O_2$$

where O_i is the output from contact i of the index rotor bank. Then the leftmost cipher rotor steps if C_0 is active, the second (from left) cipher rotor steps if C_1 is active and so on. Since there are from one to four active outputs of the index rotors, anywhere from one to four of the cipher rotors will step with each letter typed.

To decrypt with Sigaba, all of the rotors are initialized and stepped precisely as in encryption mode, as described above. However, the inverse cipher rotor permutation must be used. This can be accomplished by feeding the ciphertext letters through the cipher rotors in the opposite direction, as illustrated in Figure 2.19.

2.4.2   Sigaba Keyspace

The Sigaba key is specified by the choice of rotors and their initial positions. If we assume that all possible rotors are available, then a different initial position simply corresponds to a different rotor. Consequently, for the calculation of the theoretical size of the Sigaba keyspace, we can assume that the rotors are all set to some standard position. Then the number of keys depends only on

1. The choice of the five cipher rotors.

2. The choice of the five control rotors.

3. The choice of the five index rotors.

---

[7]Some of the details mentioned in this section were derived from studying Sigaba software simulators, so it is possible that there are minor discrepancies with the way that an actual Sigaba machine operates. However, none of these details appear to have any significant effect on the analysis or attack discussed here.

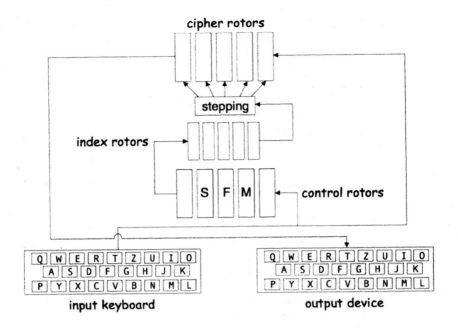

Figure 2.19: Sigaba decryption.

As with the Enigma rotors, there are 26! choices for each of the cipher and control rotors. Similarly, there are 10! choices for each of the index rotors. This gives a total keyspace of about

$$(26!)^{10} \cdot (10!)^5 \approx 2^{884} \cdot 2^{109} \approx 2^{993}.$$

However, as is the case with the Enigma and Purple ciphers, the size of the practical Sigaba keyspace is far less than this astronomical number would indicate. In practice, only ten rotors were available for the ten cipher and control rotor slots. Each of these rotors can be inserted forwards or backwards. The order of these ten rotors and their orientations (forward or reverse) must be included in the practical keyspace calculation. In addition, each of the five index rotors can be set to any of 10 positions, and each of the control rotors can be set to any of 26 positions.

In principle, each of the five cipher rotors could also be set to any of 26 positions. However, the usual Sigaba keying procedure set these rotors to a default value, then stepped the rotors in a nonstandard manner—simultaneously stepping the control rotors to their actual starting positions. In addition, the index rotors generally were inserted in one fixed order, in which case only their initial settings were variable. Taking these restrictions into account, it would appear that for Sigaba, as used in WWII, the keyspace was of size

$$10! \cdot 2^{10} \cdot 26^5 \cdot 10^5 \approx 2^{71.9},$$

as claimed in [90].

However, a careful reading of the Sigaba manual [113] reveals that the setting of the control rotors was sent in the clear as a message indicator or MI. Therefore, assuming the MI was intercepted and its meaning was known to the attacker, the actual keyspace for Sigaba—as it was generally used in WWII—was of size

$$10! \cdot 2^{10} \cdot 10^5 \approx 2^{48.4}, \tag{2.8}$$

as (correctly) stated in the article [128]. But, on the POTUS-PRIME[8] link between Roosevelt and Churchill, the control and cipher rotor settings were set independently, and neither was sent in the clear, which implies a keyspace in excess of 95 bits [128]. In the next section we provide a precise calculation of the keyspace for this particular case.

A keyspace of size $2^{48.4}$ is small enough that today it is susceptible to an exhaustive key search.[9] But a keyspace of this magnitude would have been unassailable using 1940s technology, provided no shortcut attack was available.

2.4.3   Sigaba Attack

For this attack, we assume that all three banks of rotors are set independently. We also assume that there is only one set of index rotors, and that these five rotors can be placed in any order, and that a total of ten rotors are available for use as cipher and control rotors. The control and cipher rotors can be inserted in any order and there are two orientations for each of these rotors. Under these assumptions, the keyspace is apparently of size

$$10! \cdot 2^{10} \cdot 26^{10} \cdot 5! \cdot 10^5 \approx 2^{102.3}.$$

However, due to the fact that pairs of index rotor outputs are ORed together to determine the cipher rotor stepping, effectively only

$$10!/32 = 113{,}400 \approx 2^{16.8}$$

distinct index permutations can occur. This reduces the feasible keyspace size to

$$10! \cdot 2^{10} \cdot 26^{10} \cdot 2^{16.8} \approx 2^{95.6}$$

or less.

This full keyspace of size $2^{95.6}$ was used on the POTUS-PRIME link between Roosevelt and Churchill, but not on other links. Again, this represents

---

[8]President Of The United States – PRIME Minister.

[9]The Data Encryption Standard (DES) has a 56-bit key and it has been successfully attacked by an exhaustive key search.

the largest Sigaba keyspace that was available in WWII. That is, it represents the largest practical keyspace, given the hardware that was typically available with a Sigaba machine in WWII. Increasing the number of available rotors would increase the keyspace, but we limit ourselves to the number of rotors that will fit in the device at one time, since this is typically all that was available with the cipher. Finally, we assume that all of the rotors and the inner workings of the device are known to the cryptanalyst.

Our attack requires some amount of known plaintext. This attack occurs in two phases—a primary phase and a secondary phase. In the primary phase, we try all cipher rotor settings, retaining those that are consistent with the known plaintext. Then in the secondary phase, we guess the control and index rotor settings, and again use the known plaintext, this time to whittle down the number of possible keys to a very small number of candidates.

Suppose that we have a Sigaba-encrypted ciphertext message, where the first several letters of the corresponding plaintext are known. Our goal in the primary phase is to recover the cipher rotors, their order, orientations and initial settings. Collectively, we refer to these cipher rotor initializations as the cipher rotor *settings*. In the primary phase, we strive to reduce the number of cipher rotor settings to a small number—ideally just one. We refer to an incorrect choice of cipher rotor settings as a *random* setting, while the correct setting is said to be *causal*.

For each cipher rotor setting that survives the primary phase, a secondary phase is required. This secondary phase consists of trying all possible control and index rotor settings to determine which are consistent with the known plaintext. In this way, the random primary survivors are eliminated and, in the causal case, we determine the key.

Primary Phase

We are assuming that ten different cipher rotors are available. Also, each cipher rotor has two possible orientations and 26 possible initial positions. Therefore, the number of ways to select and initialize the five cipher rotors is

$$\binom{10}{5} \cdot 5! \cdot 2^5 \cdot 26^5 \approx 2^{43.4}.$$

For each of these choices, we determine whether the setting is consistent with the known plaintext as follows.

Recall that for each letter typed, from one to four of the cipher rotor rotates. This implies that once we specify the cipher rotors, their orientations and their initial settings, the number of possible new permutations at any given step is

$$\binom{5}{1} + \binom{5}{2} + \binom{5}{3} + \binom{5}{4} = 30.$$

Now suppose that we correctly guess the cipher rotor settings at some point in time. We can then generate each of the 30 possible subsequent permutations and determine which are consistent with the next known plaintext letter. That is, we can test each of these 30 subsequent permutations to see which (if any) encrypt the next known plaintext letter to the corresponding ciphertext letter. For each surviving permutation, we can repeat this process using the next known plaintext letter and so on.

Modeling the encryption permutations as uniformly random, the matches follow a binomial distribution with $p = 1/26$ and $n = 30$, yielding an expected number of matches of $30/26 \approx 1.154$ per step. This can be viewed as a branching phenomenon, where the number of possible paths tends to increase with each known plaintext letter analyzed. That is, at each step, the number of possible paths increases, which seems to be the opposite of what we would like to see occur. Nevertheless, we can obtain useful information from this process, as outlined below, but first we consider a simple example.

Suppose we have selected five of the ten available candidate rotors as cipher rotors, and we have placed them in a specified order and selected their orientations. This, together with the initial positions of the selected cipher rotors constitutes a putative setting. Consider, for example, the case where these cipher rotors are set to AAAAA, that is, each of the five cipher rotors is initialized to A. Then we know the putative encryption permutation and if it does not encrypt the first known plaintext to the first known ciphertext, this cipher rotor setting is not causal and we can discard it. This immediately reduces the number of candidates by a factor of 26, since there is only a $1/26$ chance of a letter matching at random.

Suppose that the first letter does match. Then we must try all 30 possible steps of the five cipher rotors and save any of these that encrypt the second plaintext letter to the second ciphertext letter. Since we make 30 comparisons, The expected number of matches that occur at random is, as mentioned above, $30/26 \approx 1.154$. An example of this process is illustrated in Figure 2.20. In this example, the first letter is consistent with the initial setting AAAAA, and the first three letters are consistent with each of the given paths.

Note that at the third plaintext letter in Figure 2.20 we have two paths ending at BBBBA. Since the next step depends only on the current cipher rotor settings, and since we are only interested in the initial setting (not the entire path), we can merge these paths as illustrated in Figure 2.21. This merging is useful since it effectively reduces the number of paths under consideration, while not degrading the success of this phase of the attack.

In the random case, the analysis above holds, so that at each step we expect an increase by a factor of 1.154 (before merging). In contrast, the causal case provides a slightly higher increase on average, since we are assured one causal match, with the remaining elements matching as in the random case; see Problem 31. This gives us a method to distinguish random from

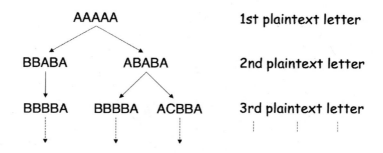

Figure 2.20: Example of consistent paths.

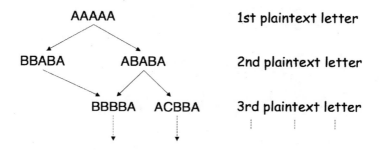

Figure 2.21: Merged paths.

causal and thereby reduce the number of random cases. Note also that only 1 in 26 of the random paths survive the first test, and many more vanish at later steps.

Suppose we are in a random case and the first plaintext letter happens to encrypt to the first ciphertext letter. Then the probability that none of the 30 possible steps yields a match for the second letter is $(25/26)^{30} \approx 0.31$, and this holds for each subsequent letter. While the total number of paths increases, the number of distinct merged paths decreases; see Problems 31 and 32.

The results in Table 2.7 illustrate typical numbers for the random case, while the results in Table 2.8 illustrate typical numbers for the causal case. For both cases, we have merged paths, as discussed above (and illustrated in Figures 2.20 and 2.21). Table 2.7 indicates that using 30 known plaintext letters, we expect only a fraction of about 0.00427 of the random cases to survive, and each of these survivors will have expanded to an average of about 16.5 paths, with a maximum for the cases tested of 84. In contrast, Table 2.8 shows that with 30 known plaintext letters, we expect the causal path to have generated about 29.6 consistent branches, with, for the 10,000 cases tested, a maximum of 151 and a minimum of one consistent path.

Table 2.7: Random Case

Steps	Average	Maximum	Tests	Nonzero
10	6.5	27	100,000	763
20	11.8	56	100,000	516
30	16.5	84	100,000	427
40	20.8	105	100,000	324
50	28.4	194	100,000	290
60	38.8	163	100,000	275
70	47.1	415	100,000	269
80	71.3	524	100,000	212
90	77.6	486	100,000	216
100	100.5	1005	100,000	203

Table 2.8: Causal Case

Steps	Average	Maximum	Minimum	Tests
10	10.2	51	1	10,000
20	19.6	94	1	10,000
30	29.6	151	1	10,000
40	40.1	237	1	10,000
50	54.1	404	1	10,000
60	69.2	566	1	10,000
70	85.0	689	1	5,000
80	105.0	829	2	5,000
90	130.4	1152	1	3,000
100	161.1	1926	1	3,000

The results in Table 2.7 show that we can eliminate the vast majority of random cases using a small amount of known plaintext. Combined with the causal results in Table 2.8, we can further reduce the number of random cases by saving only those cases that are, say, above the expected mean in the corresponding causal case. Of course, this latter refinement implies that we will sometimes discard the causal case, with the probability depending on the selected threshold. This approach provides a method for further reducing the number of primary phase survivors, at the expense of a lower probability of success. Unfortunately, Tables 2.7 and 2.8 indicate that the variance is high, so a significant number of random cases will remain for any reasonable probability of success.

The work for this part of the attack is on the order of $2^{43.4}$, since most random paths do not survive the first known plaintext test (see Problem 23 for a slightly more precise estimate). We would like to minimize the amount of known plaintext required, but we need to reduce the number of primary phase survivors as much as possible. Using the approach outlined here, it appears impractical to reduce the number of primary phase survivors by more than factor of about 2^{20}, which leaves a large number of survivors (more than 2^{20}) that must be tested in the secondary phase (see Problem 32). However, Problem 33 gives a more effective method for reducing the number of primary survivors. The paper [28] contains more information on this attack, including several further refinements.

Secondary Phase

For each of the cipher rotor settings that survived the primary phase, a secondary test is required. This secondary test will determine whether the cipher rotor setting is consistent with any setting of the control and index rotors. In the process, we eliminate random survivors from the primary phase and for the causal survivor we determine the rotor settings and thereby recover the key.

For the secondary test, we choose the order and initial positions of the index rotors and the order, orientation and initial positions of the control rotors—given the putative cipher rotor settings from the primary phase. The number of settings for the index and control rotors appears to be

$$5! \cdot 10^5 \cdot 5! \cdot 2^5 \cdot 26^5 \approx 2^{58.9}.$$

However, as noted above, there are only about $2^{16.8}$ distinct index permutations, which reduces the overall work factor to

$$2^{16.8} \cdot 5! \cdot 2^5 \cdot 26^5 \approx 2^{52.2}.$$

That is, the work factor for the secondary part of the attack appears to be on the order of $2^{52.2}$ for each putative setting that survived the primary phase. Fortunately, we can improve on this naïve implementation of the secondary phase.

Secondary Phase Refinement

To reduce the secondary work factor requires some amount of known plaintext. Here, we only outline the plan of attack, leaving the details as a challenge problem.

The interaction of the control rotors and the index rotors is illustrated in Figure 2.22, where we have collapsed the five control rotors into a single permutation (denoted as "control") and, similarly, the five index rotors are considered as a single permutation (denoted as "index"). The four inputs to the control permutation, F, G, H, and I, are activated at each step. This results in four active outputs, which are combined as indicated before being fed into the index permutation. At least one—and at most four—inputs to the index permutation will be active. The outputs from the index permutation are combined in pairs, as indicated, and these determine which of the cipher rotors, C_0 through C_4, step. At least one cipher rotor will step, and at most four will step.

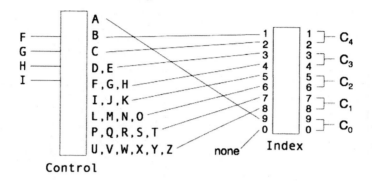

Figure 2.22: Control and index permutations.

In Figure 2.22, the control permutation changes with each letter typed, but the index permutation is fixed for the entire message. Since the control permutations are changing, we model their output as uniformly random, that is, we assume that each of the $\binom{26}{4}$ combinations of output letters is equally likely at each step. Then, due to the way that the control rotor outputs are ORed together, the inputs to the index permutation are not uniform. For example, input 8 will be active much more often than inputs 1, 2, or 9 and input 0 is never active.

The outputs of the index rotors are ORed in pairs, and the results determine the cipher rotor stepping. Therefore, if we have sufficient information on the frequency of the stepping of individual cipher rotors—which is available from known plaintext using the putative cipher rotor settings obtained in the primary phase of the attack—we can assign probabilities to the index permutations. For example, suppose that the index permutation is 5479381026, that is, input 0 is mapped to output 5, input 1 is mapped to output 4, and so on. Then by considering the pairs of outputs that determine the cipher rotor stepping, we can see that some cipher rotors will step more often than others. The data in Table 2.9 makes this more precise. For example, cipher rotor C_4 steps if either output 1 or 2 (or both) of the index permutation is active. For the index permutation in Table 2.9, inputs 6 and 8 are mapped to outputs 1 and 2, respectively. Inputs 6 and 8 of the index permutation correspond to outputs 6 and 8 of the current control permutation, and at least one of these outputs is active if one or more of the 10 letters L, M, N, O, U, V, W, X, Y, or Z, which are connected to these outputs, are active. On the other hand, C_2 steps only when output A of the control permutation is active. As a result, C_4 will step much more often than C_2.

Table 2.9: Index Permutation 5479381026

	Cipher Rotor				
	C_4	C_3	C_2	C_1	C_0
index rotor outputs	(1,2)	(3,4)	(5,6)	(7,8)	(9,0)
index rotor inputs	(6,8)	(4,1)	(0,9)	(2,5)	(3,7)
control rotor count	10	4	1	4	7

Assuming the control rotors generate random permutations, the expected number of steps for cipher rotor i depends solely on the number of control rotor output letters that feed into C_i, as illustrated in Figure 2.22. All of the 45 possible input pairs and the corresponding number of control rotor output letters are tabulated in Table 2.10.

Table 2.10: Index Permutation Input Pairs

Letters	Count	Pairs
1	3	(0,1) (0,2) (0,9)
2	4	(0,3) (1,2) (1,9) (2,9)
3	5	(0,4) (0,5) (1,3) (2,3) (3,9)
4	7	(0,6) (1,5) (2,5) (5,9) (1,4) (2,4) (4,9)
5	6	(0,7) (1,6) (2,6) (6,9) (3,4) (3,5)
6	6	(0,8) (1,7) (2,7) (7,9) (3,6) (4,5)
7	6	(1,8) (2,8) (8,9) (3,7) (4,6) (5,6)
8	3	(3,8) (4,7) (5,7)
9	3	(4,8) (5,8) (6,7)
10	1	(6,8)
11	1	(7,8)

If we have sufficient known plaintext available, we obtain information on the "count" column of Table 2.9 for each cipher rotor simply based on a count of the number of times that cipher rotor i steps. Then from the "pairs" column, we obtain putative restrictions on the index permutation. Other restrictions apply which further reduce the number of cases that must be considered; see Problem 27.

Using the available information, we can reduce the number of possible index permutations to a small fraction of the $10!/32 \approx 2^{16.8}$ permutations that we would otherwise need to consider. In fact, with sufficient known plaintext, the average number of permutations that we need to check is about 2^7 (the range is about 2^4 to 2^{10}). However, there is significant variability in the amount of known plaintext required to distinguish the control rotor counts, depending on the actual underlying index permutation.

With this refinement, the average work factor for the secondary phase of the attack is about

$$2^7 \cdot 5! \cdot 2^5 \cdot 26^5 \approx 2^{42.4},$$

which is somewhat less than the primary phase of the attack. However, this work factor applies to each survivors from the primary phase, and we expect a large number of primary survivors. Consequently, we could improve the attack by either reducing the number of primary survivors or making the secondary phase more efficient (or both).

Note that in this secondary phase, the actual index rotor settings are not—and in fact cannot be—recovered. Several details of this phase of the attack are explored more fully in Problems 27 and 28.

The typical secondary work factor for each primary survivor is on the order of 2^{43}, assuming sufficient known plaintext is available. This amount of work is clearly feasible, although the attack is not trivial to implement. The primary phase of this attack has a similar work factor and it is also feasible. However, for the attack described in this chapter, the primary phase yields a larger number of survivors, which makes the overall cost of the secondary phase high. In any case, either phase of this attack would have been far beyond the realm of 1940s technology. Nevertheless, the attack outlined above offers a dramatic shortcut as compared to an exhaustive key search, which, under the assumptions of this section, would have a work factor of about 2^{95}.

Problem 33 suggests one method for improving the attack described in this chapter. For the definitive treatment of this attack—including several improvements over the outline given in this chapter—see [28].

2.4.4 Sigaba Conclusion

Recall from (2.8), above, that Sigaba, as typically used in WWII, had a keyspace of size $2^{48.4}$, which implies that an exhaustive key search has a work factor of $2^{47.6}$. However, the Sigaba-encrypted POTUS-PRIME link between Roosevelt and Churchill used the full keyspace of more than 95 bits. It is curious that keyspaces of these sizes were chosen. From the designers' perspective, there would be no incentive to have a keyspace that is larger than a known shortcut attack, since a larger keyspace entails more secret settings and consequently more chance for errors and miscommunication.

In WWII, a work factor of $2^{47.6}$ would certainly have been untouchable, particularly for tactical communications. Nevertheless, for the strategically important communication between Allied leaders, it would be reasonable to use a larger key size, provided that the larger key actually yields additional security. Based on this logic, it would seem likely that the designers of Sigaba believed that the cipher provided a full 95 bits of security. However, in this section, we have outlined an attack that requires much less than 95 bits of work, and it is possible to improve on the attack presented here; see [28]. In any case, it would be interesting to know more about the Sigaba attacks that were considered by Rowlett and Friedman, and their reasons for choosing the key sizes as they did.

2.5 Summary

In this chapter we considered three of the most famous pre-modern cipher machines. It is striking that the vast majority of cipher machines of the World War II era (and earlier) proved to be insecure, and most were shockingly weak, at least by modern standards. As mentioned in the introduction to this chapter, this was due in part to a failure to appreciate the differences between machine systems and their predecessors, which consisted largely of codebooks. One important difference is that the amount of data that was encrypted with a machine was typically far greater than that which could be processed using a codebook. Although by modern standards, the quantity of data generated by these machines was miniscule, it was far greater than was possible using labor intensive manual systems. As a result, the cryptanalysts had a relatively large amount of data to analyze, which allowed statistical weaknesses of a cipher to be exploited. Of course, there are statistical attacks on codebook ciphers, and these were well understood. The protection of a codebook relied first and foremost on ensuring the physical security of the codebook itself. Secondarily, the use of additive sequences could extend the useful life of the codebook.

Whereas the security of a codebook depended primarily on the physical security of the book, the security of a machine system depends almost entirely on its statistical security, that is, it depends on the lack of any useful statistical information "leaking" to the attacker through the ciphertext. This was not well understood during WWII and, in fact, much effort was expended trying to maintain the physical security of cipher machines, and comparatively little was done to probe for potential statistical weaknesses. Even with the relatively secure Sigaba, it was considered absolutely essential that the machine not fall into enemy hands.

For modern cipher design, Kerckhoffs' Principle reigns supreme—at least in principle, if not always in practice. Consequently, any respectable cipher must go through an open and extensive peer-review process before it can be considered secure, with the theory being that "more eyes" will lead to "more security", particularly if those eyes belong to skilled cryptanalysts. It is also assumed that the crypto algorithm is known to the attacker. Furthermore, a cipher must be resistant to a variety of attacks, including known plaintext, chosen plaintext, adaptively chosen plaintext, and so on, even if these attacks do not seem particularly realistic in a specific application. This is all in stark contrast to the situation in WWII, where a secret design was considered essential. The bottom line is that the machine ciphers of WWII were often viewed as little more than glorified codebook ciphers, which obscured the fundamental distinctions between manual and machine cryptanalysis.

In fairness to WWII cipher designers, cryptology was not entirely scientific at the time, in part due to the lack of any solid foundation for the field. That situation began to change during WWII, and with the publication of Shannon's classic 1949 paper [133], cryptography finally emerged from the realm of "black art" into a genuine scientific discipline.

2.6   Problems

1. Consider a rotor with permutation P of $\{0, 1, 2, \ldots, n-1\}$. Suppose that P permutes i to p_i. Let d_i be the displacement of p_i, that is, $d_i = p_i - i \pmod{n}$. Find a formula for the elements of permutation P_k, the kth rotor shift of P, where the shift is in the same direction as the rotors described in Section 2.2.3. Your formula must be in terms of p_i and d_i.

2. Let $F(p)$, for $p = 0, 1, 2, \ldots, 13$, be the number of ways to plug p cables into the Enigma stecker. Show that

$$F(p) = \binom{26}{2p} \cdot (2p - 1) \cdot (2p - 3) \cdot \cdots \cdot 1.$$

3. In World War II, the German's usually used 10 cables on the stecker, only five different rotors were in general use, one reflector was in common use, and the reflector and five rotors were known to the Allies. Under these restrictions, show that there are only about 2^{77} possible Enigma keys. Also show that if we ignore the stecker, under these restrictions there are fewer than 2^{30} settings.

4. In the Enigma attack described in the text, we give the cycles

$$S(\text{E}) = P_6 P_8 P_{13} S(\text{E})$$

and

$$S(\text{E}) = P_6 P_{14}^{-1} P_7 P_6^{-1} S(\text{E}).$$

Find two more independent cycles involving $S(\text{E})$ that can be obtained from the matched plaintext and ciphertext in Table 2.2.

5. How many pairs of cycles are required in order to uniquely determine the Enigma rotor settings?

6. Prove that the Enigma is its own inverse. Hint: Suppose that the ith plaintext letter is x, and that the corresponding ith ciphertext letter is y. This implies that when the ith letter typed into the keyboard is x, the letter y is illuminated on the lightboard. Show that, for the same key settings, if the ith letter typed into the keyboard is y, then the letter x is illuminated on the lightboard.

7. What is the advantage of a cipher (such as the Enigma) that is its own inverse, as compared to a cipher that is not (such as Purple and Sigaba)?

8. For the Enigma cipher,

   a. Show that a ciphertext letter cannot be the same as the corresponding plaintext letter.

   b. Explain how this restriction gives the cryptanalyst an advantage when searching for a suitable crib.[10]

9. Consider the Enigma attack discussed in the text and suppose that only cycles of $S(\mathbf{E})$ are used to recover the correct rotor settings. Then, after the attack is completed, only the stecker value of $S(\mathbf{E})$ is known. Using only the matched plaintext and ciphertext in Table 2.2, how many additional stecker values can be recovered?

10. Write a program to simulate the Enigma cipher. Use your program to answer the following questions, where the rotor and reflector permutations are known to be

$$R_\ell = \text{EKMFLGDQVZNTOWYHXUSPAIBRCJ}$$
$$R_m = \text{BDFHJLCPRTXVZNYEIWGAKMUSQO}$$
$$R_r = \text{ESOVPZJAYQUIRHXLNFTGKDCMWB}$$
$$T = \text{YRUHQSLDPXNGOKMIEBFZCWVJAT}$$

where R_ℓ is the left rotor, R_m is the middle rotor, R_r is the right rotor, and T is the reflector. The "notch" that causes the odometer effect is at position Q for R_ℓ, V for R_m, and J for R_r. For example, the middle rotor steps when the right rotor steps from V to W.

   a. Recover the initial rotor settings given the following matched plaintext and ciphertext.

---

[10]In modern parlance, a crib is known as known plaintext.

i	0	1	2	3	4	5	6	7	8	9	10	11	12	13	14	15	16	17	18	19	20	21
Plaintext	A	D	H	O	C	A	D	L	O	C	Q	U	I	D	P	R	O	Q	U	O	S	O
Ciphertext	S	W	Z	S	O	F	C	J	M	D	C	V	U	G	E	L	H	S	M	B	G	G

i	22	23	24	25	26	27	28	29	30	31	32	33	34	35	36	37	38	39	40	41	42	43
Plaintext	L	I	T	T	L	E	T	I	M	E	S	O	M	U	C	H	T	O	K	N	O	W
Ciphertext	N	B	S	M	Q	T	Q	Z	I	Y	D	D	X	K	Y	N	E	W	J	K	Z	R

    b. Recover as much of the stecker settings as is possible from the known plaintext.

11. Suppose that the same Enigma rotors (in the same order) and reflector are used as in Problem 10, and the stecker has no cables connected. Solve for the initial rotor settings and recover the plaintext given the following ciphertext.

```
ERLORYROGGPBIMYNPRMHOUQYQETRQXTYUGGEZVBFPRIJGXRSSCJTXJBMW
JRRPKRHXYMVVYGNGYMHZURYEYYXTTHCNIRYTPVHABJLBLNUZATWXEMKRI
WWEZIZNBEOQDDDCJRZZTLRLGPIFYPHUSMBCAMNODVYSJWKTZEJCKPQYYN
ZQKKJRQQHXLFCHHFRKDHHRTYILGGXXVBLTMPGCTUWPAIXOZOPKMNRXPMO
AMSUTIFOWDFBNDNLWWLNRWMPWWGEZKJNH
```

Hint: The plaintext is English.

12. Develop a ciphertext only attack on the Enigma, assuming that all you know about the plaintext is that it is English. Analyze the work factor of your proposed attack and also estimate the minimum amount of ciphertext necessary for your attack to succeed. Assume that Enigma rotors, the rotor order, the movable ring positions, and the reflector are all known. Then you need to solve for the initial settings of the three rotors and the stecker. Hint: Since E is the most common letter in English, guess that the plaintext is EEEEE... and use this "noisy" plaintext to solve for the rotor and stecker settings.

13. Suggest modifications to the Enigma design that would make the attack discussed in Section 2.2 infeasible. Your objective is to make minor modifications to the design.

14. Suppose that the "sixes" in the Purple cipher consist of the vowels, AEIOUY. What is the expected frequency of each of the sixes and what is the expected frequency of each of the twenties? Suppose instead that the sixes consist of JKQVXZ. What is the expected frequency of each of the sixes and what is the expected frequency of each of the twenties? To answer these questions, use the English letter frequency distribution given in Table 1.3 in Chapter 1.

15. Consider the Purple cipher. For each of the $\binom{26}{6} \approx 2^{17.8}$ choices for the "sixes," let E_6 be the average frequency for each of the sixes letters and

let E_{20} be the average frequency for each of the corresponding twenties letters. For how many of these $2^{17.8}$ selections is $|E_6 - E_{20}| < 0.1\%$? To answer this question, use the English letter frequency distribution in Table 1.3 in Chapter 1, which is given as percentages.

16. Suppose that we have two ciphers, both of which encrypt elements of $\{0, 1, 2, \ldots, 7\}$ using permutations, where the permutation varies with each step. One of these, known as cipher A, is a rotor machine, analogous to the Enigma, while the other, known as cipher B, is a switch-based machine, analogous to Purple. Which of the permutations $P, Q, \ldots, W$, below, could have been generated by the A cipher and which could have been generated by the B cipher? In each case, justify your answer.

	0	1	2	3	4	5	6	7
P	5	2	1	7	6	0	4	3
Q	3	4	7	0	1	6	5	2
R	7	4	6	5	2	0	1	3
S	1	3	5	0	6	4	7	2
T	3	5	6	2	1	0	7	4
U	2	5	0	6	7	1	3	4
V	7	4	2	0	6	5	3	1
W	6	2	1	5	7	3	0	4

17. Define the permutations $P = 1203$, $Q = 2031$, $A = 0213$, and $B = 3021$.

    a. Compute PA, QA, PB, and QB, where, for example, PA denotes the permutation A followed by the permutation P. Find the difference sequence (as discussed in Section 2.3.3) for the pair PA, QA, and also for the pair PB, QB.

    b. Explain the results in part a.

    c. Why are these results relevant to the diagnosis of Purple?

18. The permutations in Table 2.6 were generated from switched permutations using a method analogous to that used in the Purple cipher. Recover the L, M, and R permutations (or an equivalent set of permutations). Hint: There are three permutations per switch. Use the permutations in lines 3, 4, and 5 to solve for the L permutations, lines 4, 8, and 9 to solve for the M permutations, and lines 0, 10, and 11 to solve for the R permutations.

19. Consider the putative matched plaintext and ciphertext pairs in Table 2.5. Explain why these could not have resulted from a 3-legged depth of either the Enigma or Purple ciphers.

20. Suppose that a permutation P is wired to a rotor. Define $\sigma(P)$ to be the resulting permutation when the rotor is shifted one step. For example, if P maps 0123456 to 6504213, then $\sigma(P)$ maps 0123456 to 4061532, $\sigma^2(P)$ maps 0123456 to 3510264, and so on (see Section 2.2.3 and Problem 1). Consider the Maroon cipher that we invented in Section 2.3. Let P_L, P_M and P_R be given permutations of the 26 letters. Suppose that the permutations on switch L are selected to be

$$P_L, \sigma(P_L), \sigma^2(P_L), \ldots, \sigma^{25}(P_L).$$

Similarly, let the rotor permutations of P_M be the permutations on the switch M and the rotor shifts of P_R be the permutations on switch R.

   a. With this choice of permutations, how is Maroon similar to—and different from—Enigma?

   b. Suppose we choose the switched permutations of Maroon to be the "rotor shifts" of a given permutation, as described above. Then Maroon generates permutations similar to those produced by a rotor machine, such as Enigma. It might, therefore, be argued that Maroon is, in some sense, more general than the Enigma, and therefore it must be at least as secure. What is wrong with this line of reasoning?

21. The Sigaba cipher rotors and control rotors can each be inserted in a forward or reverse orientation. In this problem we consider the permutation generated by a rotor inserted in a reverse orientation.

   a. Suppose that we have a rotor analogous to a Sigaba cipher rotor, except that it is labeled with 0 through 6 instead of A through Z. If the permutation on this rotor in its forward orientation is 3164205, show that the corresponding permutation when the rotor is inserted in its reverse orientation is 5263041.

   b. Given the permutation of a rotor in its forward orientation, explain how to derive the corresponding reverse rotor permutation.

22. This problem deals with the Sigaba cipher.

   a. Let $P(n)$ be the probability of exactly n active inputs to the index rotors, assuming that the control rotors generate random permutations. Find $P(n)$ for $n = 1, 2, 3, 4$.

   b. If there are n active inputs to the index rotors, then there are $\binom{10}{n}$ possible distinct active outputs. For $n = 1, 2, 3, 4$, determine the number of these $\binom{10}{n}$ outputs that result in 1, 2, 3, and 4 of the cipher rotors stepping.

    c. Let $S(n)$ be the probability that exactly n cipher rotors step. Assuming that the outputs in part b are uniformly distributed, calculate $S(n)$ for $n = 1, 2, 3, 4$.

23. In the primary phase of the Sigaba attack, using n known plaintext letters, the expected work factor is $x \cdot 2^{43.4}$ for some x. Suppose

$$x \approx 1 + p + p^2 + \cdots + p^{n-1},$$

where $p = (25/26)^{30}$, that is, p is the probability that no consistent extension of a path exists (in the random case). Under this assumption, show that the primary phase work factor is less than $2^{45.1}$ for any choice of n.

24. Write a program to generate empirical results analogous to those in Tables 2.7 and 2.8.

25. Consider a three rotor version of Sigaba, that is, assume that there are three cipher rotors, three control rotors, and three index rotors, where the rotors are the same as the actual Sigaba rotors. Assume that the stepping maze has been modified so that from one to three of the cipher rotors step with each letter encrypted or decrypted.

    a. What is the size of the theoretical keyspace for this Sigaba variant?

    b. Under assumptions analogous to those in Section 2.4.3, what is the size of the keyspace? That is, assume that only the six rotors in the machine are available for use as cipher or control rotors, the cipher and control rotors each have two orientations, only three index rotors are available, an analogous keying procedure is followed, and so on.

26. Consider a three rotor version of Sigaba, as described in Problem 25. Assume that the control rotors step in the same way as the three middle Sigaba rotors. Also, assume that the active inputs to the control rotors are F, G, and H (that is, three inputs are active, not four, as is the case for Sigaba) and the output of the control rotors are combined as in (2.7). Also, the output of the index rotor bank is combined according to

$$C_0 = O_0 \vee O_3 \vee O_9, \quad C_1 = O_2 \vee O_4 \vee O_6 \vee O_8, \quad C_2 = O_1 \vee O_5 \vee O_7.$$

With these settings, at least one of the cipher rotors will step, and at most, all three will step. Suppose that the following cipher and control rotors are available.

Rotor	Permutation
0	XQKTZMJBCWRHLGUEOIYAPDVSNF
1	FJQHVBKNMGTWLDSPZRCXYEUIOA
2	AIYOEUNPJDKSTHFZCGBLXWMRVQ
3	QJLPUOEYIAZTRMXHBCNFGDWVKS
4	KDPZWHJRQBGXNFCYEUIOALTSVM
5	EKMFLGDQVZNTOWYHXUSPAIBRCJ

Furthermore, suppose the following index rotors are available.

Rotor	Permutation
0	7591482630
1	3810592764
2	4086153297

a. Calculate the work factor for an attack on this three rotor Sigaba, using the analogous assumptions and approach as the Sigaba attack discussed in this chapter. Specify the primary work and the secondary work. Also estimate the number of known plaintext letters required.

b. Implement this three rotor Sigaba and encrypt the message below, where "␣" represents a blank space. Use the following settings: cipher rotors 234, cipher rotor orientations 101 (where 0 is the forward orientation and 1 is reverse orientation), cipher rotor initializations **ABC**, control rotors 015, control rotor orientations 110, control rotor initializations **ZYX**, index rotor ordering 201, index rotor initialization 965.

i	0	1	2	3	4	5	6	7	8	9	10	11	12	13	14	15	16	17	18	19	20
Plaintext	I	␣	A	M	␣	H	E	␣	A	S	␣	Y	O	U	␣	A	R	E	␣	H	E

i	21	22	23	24	25	26	27	28	29	30	31	32	33	34	35	36	37	38	39
Plaintext	␣	A	S	␣	Y	O	U	␣	A	R	E	␣	M	E	␣	A	N	D	␣

i	40	41	42	43	44	45	46	47	48	49	50	51	52	53	54	55	56	57	58
Plaintext	W	E	␣	A	R	E	␣	A	L	L	␣	T	O	G	E	T	H	E	R

c. Implement the attack in part a. Show that you can recover the settings used to encrypt the message given in part b.

27. This problem deals with the secondary phase of the Sigaba attack discussed in the text.

a. For any pair of inputs to the index rotors, the corresponding number of control rotor output letters ranges from 1 to 11. All pairs and their corresponding values are listed in Table 2.10. Any index permutation yields five pairs of outputs, one pair for each C_i in Figure 2.22. These five output pairs correspond to five input pairs. Since the index permutation is a permutation, the five input pairs must include each of 0 through 9 exactly once, and all 26 letters from the output control rotors must appear. Count the number of valid sets of five pairs, using Table 2.10.

    b. How many distinct groupings are there in a., where groupings are considered distinct only if the numbers are different, not just the ordering?

28. Consider the Sigaba attack discussed in the text. There are $\binom{10}{2} = 45$ choices for the pairs of index permutation inputs that get mapped to the C_i. As discussed in the text and in Problem 27, the probability that C_i is active (and, therefore, rotor i steps) is determined by the number of control rotor letters that feed into the pair of outputs that determine C_i. The number of letters that can feed into a C_i is in the range of $1, 2, 3, \ldots, 11$.

    a. For each value $k = 1, 2, 3, \ldots, 11$, determine the "stepping percentage" for C_i when it is connected to exactly k control rotor letters. These percentages will sum to much more than one, since more than one rotor generally steps. Hint: Assume all outputs of the control rotors are equally likely. Generate all $\binom{26}{4}$ of these equally likely outputs, map these to the corresponding index permutation inputs, and count the number of times that at least one element of each of the pairs in Table 2.10 occurs. Use this information to answer the question.

    b. Suppose that only one cipher rotor, say, i steps. What do you immediately know about the index permutation inputs that are combined to form C_i?

    c. Suppose that exactly two cipher rotors, say, i and j step. What do you immediately know about the index permutation inputs that are combined to form C_i and C_j?

29. For the Sigaba cipher machine, all five cipher rotors can step and three of the five control rotors can step. The two remaining control rotors and all five index rotors do not step. Since the cipher and control rotors each permute 26 letters, the maximum possible period for Sigaba is 26^8. However, in [146] it is claimed that the Sigaba cipher has a period of just 26^4, regardless of the initial settings. Write a program to determine the period of Sigaba for a given key. Use your program to verify that the Sigaba period is 26^4 for each of 100 randomly selected keys, or find a key that does not yield a period of 26^4.

30. Suppose that we create a new cipher, Sigaba Lite (SL), which is similar to Sigaba with the exception that SL uses only four cipher rotors. As with Sigaba, in SL from one to four (inclusive) of the cipher rotors steps with each letter encrypted. All other components of SL are the same as those of Sigaba. Also, SL is equipped with nine cipher and control rotors, that is, the number of rotors that will fit in the device (as is the case for Sigaba). Show that if sufficient known plaintext is available, then there is an attack on SL requiring work of about 2^{40} or less. Hint: Mimic the Sigaba attack outlined in this chapter.

31. For the primary phase of the Sigaba attack:

    a. Determine the expected number of consistent paths (without merging) in the random case and the causal case.

    b. Determine the expected number of consistent paths (with merging) in the random case and the causal case.

32. Consider the Sigaba attack discussed in this chapter.

    a. Using the results in Table 2.7, estimate the number of survivors from the primary phase, assuming that 40 know plaintext letters are available and paths are merged, but otherwise all surviving paths are saved.

    b. What is the work factor for the primary phase using the method in part a?

    c. What is the total work, including the secondary phase, for the attack as outlined in this problem?

33. This problem deals with the Sigaba attack discussed in this chapter.

    a. Compute the average probability p_i, for $i = 1, 2, 3, 4$, that precisely i cipher rotors step, where the average is taken over all possible index permutations and all possible control rotor outputs. Hint: Model the control rotor outputs as uniformly random. Then there are $\binom{26}{4}$ equally likely outputs of the control rotors and these outputs are combined as indicated in (2.7). Test each of these with each of the $10!/32$ distinct index permutations (see Section 2.4.3). Compare your results to Problem 22, part c.

    b. How can you use the result of part a of this problem to improve on the Sigaba attack described in this chapter?

Chapter 3

Stream Ciphers

If we are carried along the stream we fear nothing,
and it is only when we strive against it,
that its progress and power are discernible.
— John Owen

3.1 Introduction

Stream ciphers are a class of symmetric ciphers that operate something like a one-time pad. The crucial difference is that a stream cipher only requires a small key, whereas a one-time pad cipher requires a key that is the same length as the original message. While a one-time pad cipher is provably secure (provided it is used correctly), it is generally impractical since the key is the same length as the message. After all, if Alice and Bob can securely distribute a key that is the same length as the message, why not simply distribute the message by the same means as the key and do away with the cipher?

In a stream cipher, a relatively small key is "stretched" into a long *keystream* that can then be used just like a one-time pad. A stream cipher has far fewer keys than the number of possible keystreams, so we cannot prove that such a cipher is secure—at least not using a similar argument as is used to prove the one-time pad is secure. In effect, a stream cipher trades the provable security of a one-time pad for practicality.

A generic stream cipher is illustrated in Figure 3.1, where the key is input to the stream cipher algorithm, which then generates the keystream k_i, for $i = 0, 1, 2, \ldots$. This keystream can be generated in bits, bytes, or other sized chunks. Encryption is accomplished by XOR of the keystream k_i with the plaintext p_i to yield the ciphertext c_i. To decrypt, the same key is input to the stream cipher algorithm, so that the same keystream is generated. Then the keystream bits are XORed with the ciphertext to yield the original

plaintext. As with the one-time pad, this decryption relies on the fact that
if $c_i = p_i \oplus k_i$ then $c_i \oplus k_i = (p_i \oplus k_i) \oplus k_i = p_i$. That is, regardless of the
value of the bit k_i, we have $k_i \oplus k_i = 0$.

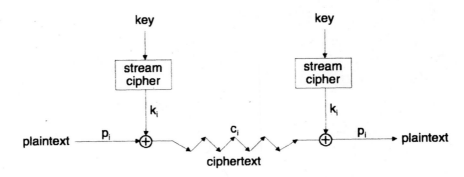

Figure 3.1: Generic stream cipher.

We must assume that Trudy, the cryptanalyst, knows (or can guess) some
of the plaintext. For a stream cipher, known plaintext and the corresponding
ciphertext immediately enables Trudy to recover part of the keystream. If
Trudy can recover more of the keystream from such a captured segment,
then the stream cipher is insecure. Therefore, the security of a stream cipher
depends on properties of the generated keystream.

But what properties should a keystream ideally satisfy? The keystream
needs to be "random," but there are many definitions of randomness, and
many of these "random" sequences would be poor keystreams. For example,
a common method for generating pseudo-random sequences is to employ a
linear congruential generator (LCG). The output from these generators satisfy
many statistical properties that make them excellent random sources for a
variety of applications (for example, simulations). The bits generated by an
LCG could be used as a keystream, with the seed value acting as the key.
However, an LCG would make a very poor stream cipher, since given a small
section of the keystream it is not difficult to determine the entire sequence [9].
This is exactly what we must avoid with a stream cipher keystream. In
other words, statistical randomness is insufficient to ensure the security of a
keystream.

The crucial property required of a keystream sequence is that it be unpredictable, or *cryptographically strong*. Intuitively, it is clear what we mean by
unpredictable, but there is no entirely satisfactory technical definition. We
discuss this problem briefly in the next section.

In this chapter we first discuss linear feedback shift registers (LFSRs),
which are often used as building blocks for stream ciphers. We also consider
correlation attacks against a particular class of LFSR-based stream cipher.

Then we discuss attacks on three specific stream ciphers, namely, ORYX, RC4 and PKZIP. Although many (if not most) stream ciphers generate their keystreams one bit at a time, coincidentally, all three of these ciphers generate their keystreams one byte at a time.

The ORYX cipher is based on shift registers. Its design is inherently weak and we present a relatively straightforward attack.

Although most stream ciphers are designed to be efficient in hardware, RC4 was specifically designed to be efficient in software implementations. The RC4 attack that we cover relies on a specific weakness in the way that the key is used. This attack is a serious concern in WEP, a wireless protocol that we briefly discuss. However, a minor modification to the way that RC4 is used in WEP renders this attack ineffective and, consequently, RC4 itself can be considered secure (when properly used) in spite of this particular attack.

PKZIP is an interesting cipher. As with RC4, the design of PKZIP is not based on shift registers, and it was designed to be highly efficient in software. The PKZIP cipher is somewhat weak, but the attack is relatively complex and involved.

3.2 Shift Registers

> *"Give your evidence," said the King;*
> *"and don't be nervous, or I'll have you executed on the spot."*
> *This did not seem to encourage the witness at all:*
> *he kept shifting from one foot to the other and in his confusion*
> *he bit a large piece out of his teacup instead of the bread-and-butter.*
> — *Alice in Wonderland*

A *shift register* consists of a series of memory elements or *stages*, each capable of containing a single bit. The register stages are initialized with an *initial fill*, then at each *step*, the contents are shifted one position to the left[1], with a new bit shifted into the rightmost position. The bit that is shifted off the left end is usually taken as the output. For the shift registers we consider, the new rightmost bit is calculated as a function of the current fill of the register. Appropriately, this function is known as the *feedback function*.

For example, consider the shift register in Figure 3.2. If the function f is given by

$$f(x_i, x_{i+1}, x_{i+2}) = 1 \oplus x_i \oplus x_{i+2} \oplus x_{i+1}x_{i+2}$$

and the initial fill is 111, then one period of the output sequence is given

---

[1] Of course, shift registers can also be viewed as shifting to the right, but for our purposes it is more convenient to consider left-shifting shift registers.

by 11100010, which happens to be a de Bruijn sequence.[2]

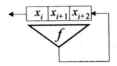

Figure 3.2: Shift register.

If a shift register has a linear feedback function, that is, if the function involves only XOR operations, not multiplication (equivalently, AND operations), then it is known as a *linear feedback shift register* (LFSR). For our purposes, LFSRs are the most important shift registers. Historically, stream ciphers employed in high data-rate systems were based on LFSRs, since shift registers are easily implemented in hardware and they can produce keystream bits at, or near, the clock speed. Today, software-based systems are capable of encrypting at extremely high data rates, which is one reason why stream ciphers in general, and LFSR-based cryptosystems in particular, are on the decline. In the realm of symmetric ciphers, software-based block ciphers are in the ascendancy, and this trend appears certain to continue. However, there remain applications where stream ciphers are preferable, such as error-prone wireless environments and some extremely resource-constrained environments.

A simple LFSR is illustrated in Figure 3.3. This type of LFSR is sometimes referred to as a *Fibonacci register*. There is another common type of linear shift register known as a *Galois register*, where the shifting and the feedback is slightly more complex. We do not discuss Galois registers further here; see [57] for more details on these two types of LFSRs.

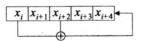

Figure 3.3: A linear feedback shift register.

The feedback function for the LFSR in Figure 3.3 is

$$x_{i+5} = x_i \oplus x_{i+2}. \tag{3.1}$$

It is standard practice to denote linear feedback functions as polynomials, where the indices become exponents. For example, x_{i+2} is represented by x^2,

---

[2]A de Bruijn sequence is a binary sequence of period 2^n in which each binary n-tuple appears exactly once, provided we consider the sequence as a cycle.

while x_{i+5} is represented by x^5 and x_i by $x^0 = 1$. Then rewriting (3.1) as $x_{i+5} \oplus x_{i+2} \oplus x_i = 0$, we have the equivalent polynomial representation

$$x^5 + x^2 + 1.$$

Such a polynomial is known as the *connection polynomial* of the LFSR, since it compactly represents the "connections" required to implement the LFSR.

There is a rich mathematical theory applicable to connection polynomials, which enables us, for example, to determine the period of the sequences generated by an LFSR. For an introduction to this mathematical theory and further pointers to the literature, see Rueppel's book [125]. There is also a corresponding theory for so-called feedback with carry shift registers (FCSRs, also known as 2-adic shift registers). An introduction to FCSRs can be found in [61].

3.2.1 Berlekamp–Massey Algorithm

Given a binary sequence, the Berlekamp–Massey Algorithm provides an efficient method to determine the smallest LFSR that can generate the sequence. Here, "size" refers to the number of stages in the LFSR. The size of the minimal LFSR is known as the *linear complexity* (or linear span) of the sequence.

Due to the threat of known plaintext attacks, a keystream must have a large period. Furthermore, due to the Berlekamp–Massey Algorithm, there must not exist any small LFSR that can generate a given keystream sequence. We expand on this point below, after we have discussed the Berlekamp–Massey Algorithm and some of its implications.

The Berlekamp–Massey Algorithm appears in Table 3.1, where

$$s = (s_0, s_1, \ldots, s_{n-1})$$

denotes the binary sequence under consideration, L is the linear complexity and $C(x)$ is the connection polynomial of the minimal LFSR. Note that the coefficients of all polynomials are to be taken modulo 2. Also, d is known as the *discrepancy*, and the connection polynomial is of the form

$$C(x) = c_0 + c_1 x + c_2 x^2 + \cdots + c_L x^L.$$

The Berlekamp–Massey Algorithm processes the sequence s sequentially and at step k, the polynomial $C(x)$ is the connection polynomial for the first $k+1$ bits of s and L is the corresponding linear complexity. At step k, if the discrepancy is $d = 0$, then the connection polynomial $C(x)$ computed at step $k-1$ is also the connection polynomial for $s_0, s_1, \ldots, s_k$ and no change to $C(x)$ or L is required. If, on the other hand, the discrepancy is $d = 1$, then $C(x)$ must be modified, and the linear complexity L increases if the current value of L lies below the $n/2$ line.

Table 3.1: Berlekamp–Massey Algorithm

// Given binary sequence $s = (s_0, s_1, s_2, \ldots, s_{n-1})$
// Find linear complexity L and connection polynomial $C(x)$
BM(s)
    $C(x) = B(x) = 1$
    $L = N = 0$
    $m = -1$
    while $N < n$ // n is length of input sequence
        $d = s_N \oplus c_1 s_{N-1} \oplus c_2 s_{N-2} \oplus \cdots \oplus c_L s_{N-L}$
        if $d == 1$ then
            $T(x) = C(x)$
            $C(x) = C(x) + B(x)x^{N-m}$
            if $L \leq N/2$ then
                $L = N + 1 - L$
                $m = N$
                $B(x) = T(x)$
            end if
        end if
        $N = N + 1$
    end while
    return(L)
end BM

Next, we illustrate the Berlekamp–Massey Algorithm. Consider the periodic sequence s, with one period given by

$$s = (s_0, s_1, \ldots, s_7) = 10011100. \tag{3.2}$$

For this sequence, the first few steps of the Berlekamp–Massey Algorithm are illustrated in Table 3.2.

For the periodic sequence (3.2), the linear complexity is $L = 6$ (Problem 1 asks for the connection polynomial). Therefore, if we let 10011 be the initial fill of the LFSR corresponding to the connection polynomial determined by the Berlekamp–Massey Algorithm, the LFSR generates the sequence s in (3.2).

Here, we do not attempt to prove the validity of the Berlekamp–Massey Algorithm, but we note in passing that the algorithm is closely related to the extended Euclidean Algorithm and continued fraction algorithms. We also note one important—but non-obvious—fact, namely, that any $2L$ consecutive bits can be used to completely determine a sequence that has linear complexity L. That is, after processing $2L$ bits through the Berlekamp–

Table 3.2: Berlekamp–Massey Example

---

sequence: $s = (s_0, s_1, \ldots, s_7) = 10011100$
initialize: $C(x) = B(x) = 1$, $L = N = 0$, $m = -1$

$\underline{N = 0}$
$d = s_0 = 1$
$T(x) = 1$, $C(x) = 1 + x$
$L = 1$, $m = 0$, $B(x) = 1$

$\underline{N = 1}$
$d = s_1 \oplus c_1 s_0 = 1$
$T(x) = 1 + x$, $C(x) = 1$

$\underline{N = 2}$
$d = s_2 \oplus c_1 s_1 \oplus c_2 s_0 = 0$

$\underline{N = 3}$
$d = s_3 \oplus c_1 s_2 \oplus c_2 s_1 \oplus c_3 s_0 = 1$
$T(x) = 1$, $C(x) = 1 + x^3$
$L = 3$, $m = 3$, $B(x) = 1$

$\underline{N = 4}$
$\vdots$

Massey Algorithm, the minimal LFSR will have been obtained. Below, we see that this property has implications for stream cipher design.

It is not too difficult to show that the Berlekamp–Massey Algorithm requires on the order of n^2 operations [62], where n is the number of bits processed and the operations are XOR. This is the most efficient known general algorithm for solving the shift register synthesis problem. However, there are more efficient algorithms for certain special cases; see Problem 4 for an example of such an algorithm.

3.2.2 Cryptographically Strong Sequences

Before illustrating the use of LFSRs in stream ciphers, we first take a slight detour to briefly consider some of the properties that keystream sequences must satisfy. Here, we relate these properties to shift registers.

Keystream sequences that are unpredictable, according to some specified set of conditions, are said to be *cryptographically strong*. However, it is important to realize that this definition is relative to the specified criteria. While we can specify necessary conditions that a keystream sequence must satisfy, there are no known sufficient conditions that ensure that a sequence is cryptographically strong. In a sense, this situation parallels cryptography in general, where the best that can be said about any practical cipher is that, as far as we know, nobody has found an efficient attack. That is, we can never prove that a cipher is absolutely secure, but we can show that it satisfies certain criteria that give us some confidence that is likely to be secure in practice.

Note that if at some point, the fill of an LFSR is all zero, then the register fill will be all zero at every subsequent step. Therefore, an upper bound on the period length of any LFSR sequence is $2^n - 1$, where n is the number of stages in the LFSR. In fact, it is possible for an LFSR to attain this upper bound, and the resulting maximal length sequences are known as *m-sequences*. For example, a 3-stage LFSR with connection polynomial $C(x) = 1 + x^2$ will generate a sequence of period length seven for any nonzero initial fill. In general, if $C(x)$ is a primitive polynomial [43], then the resulting LFSR will yield m-sequences for all nonzero initial fills.

While m-sequences have many nice statistical properties [59], they would be poor choices for keystream generators. Suppose we have a 32-bit key and we decide to use a stream cipher that consists of a 32-stage LFSR, with the connection polynomial chosen so that the resulting keystream is an m-sequence. Then if Trudy is able to obtain just 64 consecutive keystream bits, she can use the Berlekamp–Massey Algorithm to determine the entire keystream, which is of length $2^{32} - 1$. Recall that with a stream cipher, known plaintext reveals the keystream, so for this example, a very small amount of known plaintext completely breaks the cipher. Consequently, a single shift register that generates an m-sequences would be an extremely poor stream cipher, in spite of its excellent statistical properties and long period length.

In a sense, m-sequences are among the worst keystream sequences. However, it is possible to combine m-sequences to generate usable keystreams. We give examples of such keystream generators in the next section.

This discussion of m-sequences highlights the fact that, as a consequence of the Berlekamp–Massey Algorithm, a cryptographically strong keystream must have a high linear complexity. But is this sufficient? That is, if we have a sequence with a high linear complexity, can we be certain that it is a cryptographically strong keystream? In fact, it easy to see that this is not the case, since any sequence of the form

$$\underbrace{000\ldots00}_{n-1}1 \tag{3.3}$$

has linear complexity n, which can be seen from the Berlekamp–Massey Algorithm, or simply by noting that the only LFSR capable of generating (3.3) is necessarily of length n. Note that n is the maximum possible linear complexity for a sequence of period n. Nevertheless, the sequence in (3.3) obviously would not make a good keystream.

One problem with the sequence in (3.3) is that the linear complexity is, in a sense, concentrated in just a single bit. That is, the linear complexity is zero, until the last bit is processed, then the complexity jumps from the minimum to the maximum possible value. Recognizing this, Rueppel [125] proposes the *linear complexity profile* as a practical measure of the quality of a keystream. This profile is simply the graph of the linear complexity L of $s_0, s_1, \ldots, s_k$ for each $k = 0, 1, 2, \ldots$. The required L values are obtained when the linear complexity of s is computed using the Berlekamp–Massey Algorithm, so it is efficient to determine such a profile. Rueppel has shown that most sequences have a linear complexity profile that follows the $n/2$ line "closely but irregularly," and he proposes this as a criteria for judging the quality of a keystream. Figure 3.4 illustrates a linear complexity profile that satisfies Rueppel's criteria and would therefore be considered cryptographically strong by his definition.

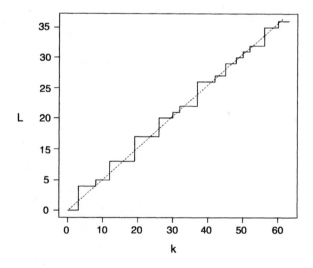

Figure 3.4: Linear complexity profile.

In [141] a different criteria for cryptographically strong sequences is considered. Although the keystream in (3.3) has the highest possible linear complexity, it differs by only one bit from the all-zero sequence, which has the minimum linear complexity. That is, the sequence in (3.3) is "too close" (in Hamming distance) to a sequence with small linear complexity. In general, if a sequence is close to a sequence with a relatively low linear complexity, then regardless of the linear complexity of the original sequence, it is an undesirable keystream. The *k-error linear complexity* is defined to be the smallest linear complexity that can be obtained when any k or fewer bits in one period of a sequence are changed from 0 to 1 or vice versa.

Given a sequence, we can plot the k-error linear complexity versus k, and for a cryptographically strong sequence, the graph should not have any large drops, particularly for relatively small k, since any such drop would indicate that a sequence with much smaller linear complexity lies close to the given keystream. We refer to the graph of the k-error linear complexity as the *k-error linear complexity profile*.

In Figure 3.5 we have illustrated an undesirable k-error linear complexity profile. This profile shows that the sequence is close to a sequence with a much smaller linear complexity, as indicated by the sharp drop below the dotted line for a relatively small value of k.

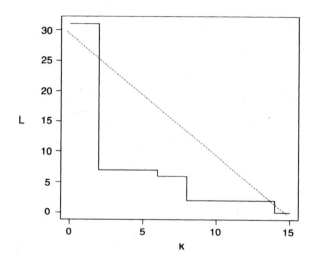

Figure 3.5: k-Error linear complexity profile.

In fact, the linear complexity profile in Figure 3.4 and the k-error linear complexity profile in Figure 3.5 were both obtained from the periodic sequence with period

$$s = 0001\ 1010\ 1001\ 1010\ 1000\ 1010\ 1001\ 1010.$$

The linear complexity profile of this particular sequence appears to satisfy Rueppel's criteria, since it follows the $n/2$ line closely and no regular pattern is evident. However, the k-error linear complexity profile indicates that this particular sequence is probably not a strong keystream, since it lies "close" to a keystream with low linear complexity. For this example, the k-error linear complexity is more informative than the linear complexity profile.

In the general case, no efficient algorithm for computing the k-error linear complexity is known. However, for the special case where s is periodic with period length 2^n, an efficient algorithm is given in [141].

3.2.3   Shift Register-Based Stream Ciphers

Due to the Berlekamp–Massey Algorithm, we cannot directly use the output of an LFSR as a stream cipher. The fundamental problem lies with the linearity of LFSRs. However, LFSRs have useful mathematical and statistical properties, so it would be desirable to construct stream ciphers based on LFSRs.

There are two generic approaches that are often used to create keystream generators based on LFSRs. One such approach is illustrated in Figure 3.6, where a nonlinear *combining function f* is applied to the contents of a shift register to yield the keystream sequence. The combining function is intended to mask the linearity of the LFSR, while taking advantage of the long period and good statistical properties of LFSR sequences.

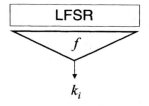

Figure 3.6: Stream cipher using one LFSR.

A second approach to constructing a keystream generator from LFSRs is illustrated in Figure 3.7. Again, the purpose of the nonlinear combining function f is to effectively hide the linearity of the underlying LFSRs. In both of these examples, the key is the initial fill of the LFSR or LFSRs.

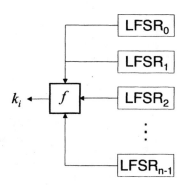

Figure 3.7: Stream cipher using n LFSRs.

The keystream generator in Figure 3.6 is actually a special case of the generator in Figure 3.7. To see that this is indeed the case, suppose that all

LFSRs in Figure 3.7, are identical to the single LFSR in Figure 3.6, except for the initial fills. Let the initial fill of $LFSR_0$ be identical to the initial fill of the LFSR in Figure 3.6, while $LFSR_1$ has as its initial fill the initial fill of $LFSR_0$ stepped once and, in general, the initial fill of $LFSR_i$ is the initial fill of $LFSR_0$ stepped i times. Then the nonlinear combining function f in Figure 3.7 has access to precisely the same bits at each step as the function f in Figure 3.6. That is, the stream cipher in Figure 3.6 is a special case of that in Figure 3.7. Consequently, in the discussion below, we restrict our attention to the more general case, as represented by Figure 3.7.

3.2.4   Correlation Attack

In this section we discuss a correlation attack on a shift register-based stream cipher. Consider the keystream generator in Figure 3.8, which consists of three small shift registers and a nonlinear combining function f. The feedback functions of the shift registers X, Y, and Z are

$$x_{i+3} = x_i \oplus x_{i+1}$$
$$y_{i+4} = y_i \oplus y_{i+3}$$
$$z_{i+5} = z_i \oplus z_{i+2}$$

respectively. Suppose that the function f, which determines the keystream bits k_i, is given by

$$k_i = f(x_i, y_i, z_i) = x_i y_i \oplus y_i z_i \oplus z_i.$$

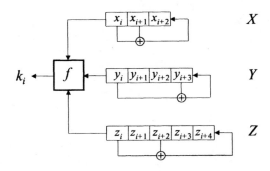

Figure 3.8: Keystream generator.

Let ℓ_X be the length of the cycle generated by the shift register X, and define ℓ_Y and ℓ_Z similarly. Then the keystream generated by stream cipher in Figure 3.8 has a cycle length of $\mathrm{lcm}(\ell_X, \ell_Y, \ell_Z)$. For the registers in Figure 3.8, the cycle length are $\ell_X = 7$, $\ell_Y = 15$, and $\ell_Z = 31$, provided that none of the initial fills are all zero and, consequently, the cycle length of this keystream generator is 3255.

To use the keystream generator in Figure 3.8 as a stream cipher, we require a 12-bit key, which is used to determine the initial fills of the registers, with the restriction that no initial fill can be all zero. If Trudy can recover the initial fills, then she has broken the stream cipher. Of course, in this example, Trudy can simply use an exhaustive search to recover the initial fills, but we use this simple example to illustrate a shortcut attack.

Suppose that the initial fill of register X is 011, register Y is 0101 and register Z is 11100. Then the key that Trudy wants to recover consists of these 12-bits of initial fill. For these initial fill bits, the first 31 output bits for registers X, Y, and Z in Figure 3.8 are given in the first three rows of Table 3.3, with the keystream given in the fourth row.

Table 3.3: Register Bits and Keystream

Bits	$i = 0, 1, 2, \ldots, 29, 30$
x_i	0111001011100101110010111001011
y_i	0101100100011110101100100011110
z_i	1110001101110101000010010110011
k_i	1111001001100101100010110101011

By Kerckhoffs' Principle, we assume that Trudy knows the LFSR feedback functions and the nonlinear boolean function f. Trudy's attack will take advantage of certain properties of the function f.

The truth table for the boolean function $f(x, y, z) = xy \oplus yz \oplus z$ is given in Table 3.4. Note that $f(x, y, z) = x$ and $f(x, y, z) = z$ both occur with probability 3/4. Trudy can take advantage of this fact to efficiently recover the initial fills (that is, the key) for the keystream generator in Figure 3.8.

Table 3.4: Truth Table for $f(x, y, z) = xy \oplus yz \oplus z$

x	y	z	xy	yz	f
0	0	0	0	0	0
0	0	1	0	0	1
0	1	0	0	0	0
0	1	1	0	1	0
1	0	0	0	0	0
1	0	1	0	0	1
1	1	0	1	0	1
1	1	1	1	1	1

The attack we consider here requires known plaintext. Since we are dealing with a stream cipher, known plaintext immediately gives Trudy the corresponding bits of the keystream.

Suppose that Trudy, via known plaintext, recovers the 31 keystream bits in the last row of Table 3.3. Trudy can then simply try all possible initial fills for the X register, and for each of these, she can generate the first 31 bits of the corresponding X sequence. For the correct initial fill of X she expects to find $k_i = x_i$ with probability 3/4, and for an incorrect initial fill she expects that the keystream will match the X register sequence with a probability of about 1/2. Therefore, Trudy can recover the X register initial fill by simply trying all 2^3 possibilities and computing the correlation with the known keystream bits for each putative fill.

For example, suppose that Trudy guesses the initial fill of X is 111. Then the first 31 bits of X would be

$$1110010111001011100101110010111.$$

If we compare these bits to the keystream bits k_i in Table 3.3, we find 15 of the 31 bits match, that is, about 1/2 of the bits match, which implies that 111 is not the correct initial fill of X. On the other hand, if Trudy tries the correct initial fill for X, namely, 011, she finds 26 matches, as can be seen in Table 3.3. Since this is close to the expected number of matches for the correct initial fill, Trudy can assume that she has found the initial fill of X. For this particular combining function f, Trudy can apply the same technique to recover the initial fill of Z, and with knowledge of the X and Z fills, she can easily recover the initial fill of Y.

In this example, the work required for the correlation attack is on the order of

$$2^2 + 2^4 + 2^3 < 2^5,$$

while a naïve exhaustive key search attack has a work factor if 2^{11}. In general, if there are n shift registers of sizes $N_0, N_1, \ldots, N_{n-1}$, respectively, then the work for an exhaustive key search attack is

$$2^{N_0 + N_1 + \cdots + N_{n-1} - 1},$$

while, in the ideal case, the work factor for a correlation attack is

$$2^{N_0 - 1} + 2^{N_1 - 1} + \cdots + 2^{N_{n-1} - 1},$$

which highlights the strength of this method of attack. This type of correlation attack is a classic divide and conquer approach.

Stream ciphers based on designs such as that in Figure 3.8 must be *correlation immune*, that is, the combining function f must not leak information about the individual shift registers. Many techniques have been proposed to combine shift registers in ways that are intended to frustrate correlation attacks. For example, in A5/1 (used in the GSM cell phone system), the shift registers step irregularly, while in E_0 (used in Bluetooth) the stepping function includes memory of previous stepping, again, creating irregular motion. For more information on correlation attacks, see [77, 99], Siegenthaler's original paper [135] or Golić's survey in [58].

Next, we turn our attention to three specific stream ciphers. The first of these, ORYX, is based on shift registers. However, the attack on ORYX that we consider does not rely on any correlation properties or similar features of the shift registers. Instead, other weaknesses in the design of ORYX are exploited. This attack is relatively straightforward, but is does require that we delve into the inner workings of the cipher.

Neither RC4 nor PKZIP—the other two stream cipher we discuss in this chapter—are based on shift registers. Instead, these ciphers are designed to be implemented in software, which makes them somewhat unusual in the world of stream ciphers. The attacks on these two ciphers are both relatively complex, with the PKZIP attack being the more intricate of the two.

3.3   ORYX

> *Oryx \O"ryx\, n. A genus of African antelopes which includes the gemsbok,*
> *the leucoryx, the bisa antelope (O. beisa),*
> *and the beatrix antelope (O. beatrix) of Arabia.*
> — dictionary.net

ORYX is a stream cipher developed by the Telecommunications Industry Association (TIA) as part of an overall cell phone security architecture.[3] The TIA system was briefly used in the late 1990s until its many security flaws were exposed. Before considering the ORYX cipher, we briefly discuss cell phone security in general.

TIA is not the only flawed cell phone security architecture. The Global System for Mobile Communications (GSM) is another cellular system that has more than its share of security issues. In GSM there are several cryptographic weaknesses, along with protocol-level flaws that open the door to many different feasible attacks [142]. The cryptographic flaws include attacks on the encryption algorithms (specifically, A5/1 and A5/2), as well as serious problems with the hash function (COMP128) that is used for authentication and key generation. These crypto problems in GSM can be traced to the fact that Kerckhoffs' Principle was violated, since the GSM crypto algorithms

---

[3]The all-uppercase rendering of ORYX is standard, but it is a mystery, since ORYX is not an acronym.

never received public scrutiny before they were installed in millions of cell phones.

In defense of GSM, it should be noted that it was designed early in the cell phone (and wireless networking) era, and it was designed with very limited security goals. In fact, contrary to what you are likely to read elsewhere, it is not unreasonable to consider GSM security a modest practical success, since none of the many potential attacks ever became a serious issue in practice [142]. However, the GSM security design goals were clearly too limited, and this is the root cause of most of the exploitable flaws. So-called "third generation" cell phones, as defined by the Third Generation Partnership Project (3GPP), have a security architecture modeled on GSM, with all of the known flaws patched [1].

The TIA cell phone security architecture was developed after most of the flaws in GSM were well-known, so you might expect that TIA would have learned from the crypto mistakes of GSM. If so, you would be mistaken.

Like GSM before it, TIA violated Kerckhoffs' Principle, with predictable results. The weak ORYX cipher discussed here is one of the consequences of the decision to use ciphers that had not been thoroughly reviewed—the weak Cellular Message Encryption Algorithm (CMEA) discussed in Chapter 4 is yet another.

The ORYX cipher was designed to encrypt data sent to and from cellular phones. Here, "data" includes voice and other messages sent over the phone. This is in contrast to "control" or signaling information, such as the number called, which was not encrypted using ORYX. Instead, the CMEA block cipher mentioned above was used to protect the confidentiality of the control information. A practical attack on CMEA is given in the next chapter.

The definitive cryptanalysis of ORYX appears in [153], where it is shown that the entire 96-bit key can be recovered with a minimal work factor, given about 25 bytes of known plaintext. The fundamental weakness in ORYX arises from the fact that, for efficiency, it generates a keystream byte at each step, when a single bit (or perhaps two) would probably be more realistic given the inherent limitations of the algorithm.

3.3.1   ORYX Cipher

The ORYX cipher employs three shift registers, which we label X, A, and B. Each register holds 32 bits. Denote the current bits of register X (that is, the fill of X) as $x_0, x_1, x_2, \ldots, x_{31}$. Similarly, let a_0 through a_{31} be the fill of register A, and b_0 through b_{31} be the fill of register B. At each step of a register, a single bit, say, y is computed as a function of the current register fill, then each bit in the register is shifted one position to the right, with the bit formerly in position 31 being discarded, and the bit y is then inserted into position 0. For more information on shift registers and their role in stream ciphers, see Section 3.2 or Rueppel's classic book [125].

When register X steps, the following sequence of operations occur

$$y = P_X(X)$$
$$x_i = x_{i-1} \text{ for } i = 31, 30, 29, \ldots, 1$$
$$x_0 = y$$

where

$$P_X(X) = x_0 \oplus x_4 \oplus x_5 \oplus x_8 \oplus x_9 \oplus x_{10} \oplus x_{13} \oplus x_{15} \oplus x_{17}$$
$$\oplus x_{18} \oplus x_{27} \oplus x_{31}.$$

Note that the feedback function P_X is linear and, consequently, X is a linear feedback shift register (LFSR). Recall that LFSRs were discussed in some detail in Section 3.2.

For register A we have

$$y = P_A(A)$$
$$a_i = a_{i-1} \text{ for } i = 31, 30, 29, \ldots, 1$$
$$a_0 = y$$

where P_A is either

$$P_{A0}(A) = a_0 \oplus a_1 \oplus a_3 \oplus a_4 \oplus a_6 \oplus a_7 \oplus a_9 \oplus a_{10} \oplus a_{11} \oplus a_{15}$$
$$\oplus a_{21} \oplus a_{22} \oplus a_{25} \oplus a_{31}$$

or

$$P_{A1}(A) = a_0 \oplus a_1 \oplus a_6 \oplus a_7 \oplus a_8 \oplus a_9 \oplus a_{10} \oplus a_{12} \oplus a_{16} \oplus a_{21}$$
$$\oplus a_{22} \oplus a_{23} \oplus a_{24} \oplus a_{25} \oplus a_{26} \oplus a_{31},$$

depending on whether bit x_{29} of register X is 0 (in which case the feedback function P_{A0} is selected) or 1 (in which case P_{A1} is selected). Note that this is somewhat analogous to the way that the Sigaba cipher uses one set of rotors to determine the stepping of another set of rotors.

For register B, a step consists of the sequence of operations

$$y = P_B(B)$$
$$b_i = b_{i-1} \text{ for } i = 31, 30, 29, \ldots, 1$$
$$b_0 = y$$

where the (linear) feedback function P_B is defined by

$$P_B(B) = b_0 \oplus b_2 \oplus b_5 \oplus b_{14} \oplus b_{15} \oplus b_{19} \oplus b_{20} \oplus b_{30} \oplus b_{31}.$$

We define one *iteration* of ORYX as follows:

1. Register X steps.

2. If $x_{29} = 0$, then register A steps using P_{A0} to generate the feedback bit. Otherwise register A steps using P_{A1}.

3. If $x_{26} = 0$, then register B steps once, otherwise register B steps twice.

4. Finally, a keystream byte is generated as

$$\text{keystreamByte} = (H(X) + L[H(A)] + L[H(B)]) \pmod{256},$$

where H selects the "high" byte of the current fill of a register (in our notation, bits 24 through 31) and L is a known permutation of the numbers $\{0, 1, 2, \ldots, 255\}$. The permutation L is variable, but it remains fixed for the duration of a given message, and L is known to the cryptanalyst. The permutation L plays a similar role to the initialization vector (IV) in RC4 or the message indicator (MI) in the WWII cipher machines discussed in Chapter 2.

Note that in ORYX, one iteration occurs before the first keystream byte is generated.

The ORYX keystream generator is illustrated in Figure 3.9, where S signifies the selection between feedback polynomials P_{A0} and P_{A1}, and C controls whether register B is "clocked" (that is, stepped) once or twice.

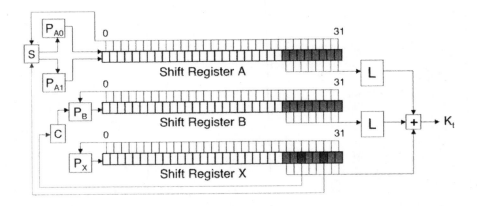

Figure 3.9: ORYX cipher.

The ORYX key consists of the initial fills of the three registers X, A, and B, while L is the (non-secret) IV. Given the initial fills, the corresponding keystream can be generated, as described above. Since each register holds 32 bits, the key is 96 bits.

Like RC4, the ORYX cipher generates its keystream one byte at a time. This improves the efficiency of the cipher, but, in the case of ORYX, it creates a serious weakness.

Denote the ORYX keystream bytes as $k_0, k_1, k_2, \ldots$. Let X, A, and B be the initial fills of the registers. Then the entire keystream is determined by these fills and the known permutation L. As mentioned above, the ORYX registers step before a keystream byte is generated. Consequently, the first keystream byte is

$$k_0 = (H(X) + L[H(A)] + L[H(B)]) \ (\text{mod } 256), \qquad (3.4)$$

where X, A, and B represent the register fills after one iteration of ORYX.

3.3.2 ORYX Attack

The ORYX attack discussed here requires that some number of keystream bytes are known. Since ORYX is a stream cipher, known plaintext together with the corresponding ciphertext would yield the necessary keystream bytes. In practice about 25 known keystream bytes suffices to recover the entire key.

The attack proceeds by trying each of the 2^{16} possible values for the pair $(H(A), H(B))$ in (3.4). Given a putative value for $(H(A), H(B))$, and assuming k_0 is known, we can solve for $H(X)$ as

$$H(X) = (k_0 - L[H(A)] - L[H(B)]) \ (\text{mod } 256).$$

Then we attempt to extend A and B by one iteration. To do so, we use the known keystream byte k_1, and solve for

$$Y = (k_1 - L[H(A)] - L[H(B)]) \ (\text{mod } 256). \qquad (3.5)$$

If the value Y can be obtained as a shift of X, then A, B, and X are consistent with the first two keystream bytes, and these partial fills are retained for the next iteration, where we attempt to further extend A and B so that they are consistent with k_2. If the value of Y in (3.5) cannot be obtained by an extension of X then the partial fills A and B are discarded.

How many ways are there to extend a given pair A and B to the next iteration?[4] Register A always shifts one position to the right so that a single new bit appears at the leftmost position in $H(A)$. Register B can shift once, in which case one new bit appears in $H(B)$, or it can shift twice, in which case two new bits appear in $H(B)$. This gives a total of 12 possible ways to extend the current fills of registers A and B. These 12 possible extensions are listed in Table 3.5. We denote the jth extension of A as $e(A, j)$ and similarly for B.

---

[4]Let me count the ways . . . .

Table 3.5: Extensions of A and B

j	Shift A	Shift B	Extend Fill A	Extend Fill B
0	1	1	0	0
1	1	1	0	1
2	1	1	1	0
3	1	1	1	1
4	1	2	1	00
5	1	2	1	01
6	1	2	1	10
7	1	2	1	11
8	1	2	0	00
9	1	2	0	01
10	1	2	0	10
11	1	2	0	11

Now we consider an example that illustrates the steps in the attack. Suppose the key—that is, the initial fills of the registers X, A, and B—is given by the register fills

$$(X, A, B) = (\text{0xdeadbeef}, \text{0x01234567}, \text{0x76543210}).$$

Since one iteration occurs before the first keystream byte is generated, we do not directly recover the initial register fills, but instead, we recover the register fills after the first iteration. Let "$\gg$" be the right shift operator. Then the attack will recover $X \gg 1$, $A \gg 1$, and either $B \gg 1$ or $B \gg 2$, depending on whether B shifts once or twice in the first iteration. In this example, these fills are

$$(X \gg 1) = \text{0xef56df77}$$
$$(A \gg 1) = \text{0x8091a2b3}$$
$$(B \gg 1) = \text{0xbb2a1908}$$
$$(B \gg 2) = \text{0xdd950c84}.$$

Once the appropriate shifted fills have been recovered, it is a simple matter to step them back to the actual initial fills and thereby recover the original 96 bit key, if desired. However, this is not necessary if the goal is simply to decrypt the message.

Trudy the cryptanalyst does not know the register fills, but we assume that she does know approximately 25 consecutive keystream bytes, and she knows the table L used for the message under consideration. Here, we only illustrate the first two steps in the attack, so we only utilize the first and second keystream bytes.

For this example, suppose

$$k_0 = \text{0xda} \quad \text{and} \quad k_1 = \text{0x31} \tag{3.6}$$

and the permutation L given in Table 3.6 was used to encrypt the message. Then, for example, $L[\text{0xa2}] = \text{0x95}$ since 0x95 appears in row 0xa and column 0x2 of Table 3.6.

Table 3.6: Example ORYX Permutation L

	0	1	2	3	4	5	6	7	8	9	a	b	c	d	e	f
0	ed	3e	0d	20	a9	c3	36	75	4c	2c	57	a3	00	ae	31	0f
1	19	4d	44	a0	11	56	18	66	09	69	6e	3d	25	9c	db	3f
2	65	58	1a	6d	ff	d7	46	b3	b1	2b	78	cf	be	26	42	2f
3	d8	d4	8e	48	05	b9	34	43	de	68	5a	aa	9d	bd	84	a2
4	3c	50	ce	8b	c5	d0	a5	77	1f	12	6b	c2	b5	e6	ab	54
5	81	22	9f	bb	5c	a8	dc	ec	2d	1e	ee	d6	6c	5f	9a	fd
6	c8	d5	94	fc	0c	1c	96	4f	f9	51	da	9b	df	e1	47	37
7	d1	eb	af	f7	a4	03	f0	c7	60	e4	f4	b4	85	f6	62	04
8	71	87	ea	17	99	1d	3a	15	52	0a	07	35	e0	70	b6	fa
9	cb	b0	86	a6	92	fb	98	55	06	4b	5d	4a	45	83	bf	16
a	7c	10	95	28	38	82	f3	6a	f8	fe	79	39	27	2a	5e	e7
b	59	b8	1b	ca	8d	d3	7b	30	33	90	d2	d9	ac	76	8f	5b
c	a7	0e	63	c4	b2	e9	97	91	53	7a	0b	41	08	c1	8c	7d
d	88	24	f5	f2	01	72	e8	80	49	13	23	9e	c6	14	73	ad
e	8a	29	ef	e5	67	61	ba	e2	7e	89	64	02	c0	21	6f	f1
f	dd	b7	c9	e3	cd	3b	93	2e	40	bc	4e	a1	cc	74	32	7f

In this attack, Trudy will try all 2^{16} guesses for the 16 bits $(H(A), H(B))$ that were used to generate k_0. Consider the case where Trudy selects

$$(H(A), H(B)) = (\text{0xb3}, \text{0x84}), \tag{3.7}$$

which is one of the 2^{16} values that she will test. In this case, Trudy computes

$$\begin{aligned} H(X) &= (k_0 - L[H(A)] - L[H(B)]) \pmod{256} \\ &= (\text{0xda} - L[\text{0xb3}] - L[\text{0x84}]) \pmod{256} \\ &= (\text{0xda} - \text{0xca} - \text{0x99}) \pmod{256} \\ &= \text{0x77}. \end{aligned}$$

Now Trudy must attempt to extend the fills X, A, and B to the next iteration by trying each of the 12 extensions listed in Table 3.5. For example, for $j = 2$ in Table 3.5, Trudy shifts each of A and B by one, and chooses 1 for the next bit of A and 0 for the next bit of B. Then the resulting "high" bytes are

$$H(A) = \text{0xd9} \quad \text{and} \quad H(B) = \text{0x42}.$$

Using these values Trudy solves for

$$H(X) = (k_1 - L[H(A)] - L[H(B)]) \ (\text{mod } 256)$$
$$= (\text{0x31} - L[\text{0xd9}] - L[\text{0x42}]) \ (\text{mod } 256)$$
$$= (\text{0x31} - \text{0x13} - \text{0xce}) \ (\text{mod } 256)$$
$$= \text{0x50}.$$

However, the previous $H(X)$ is 0x77 which can only be extended to either 0x3b or 0xbb. Therefore, this particular extension is inconsistent with the assumed $(H(A), H(B))$.

On the other hand, consider (3.7) again, and consider the case where Trudy tries to extend this fill using $j = 8$ in Table 3.5. Then she shifts A by one and B by two, choosing 0 for the next bit of A and 00 for the next two bits of B. In this case, the extensions are

$$H(A) = \text{0x59} \ \text{and} \ H(B) = \text{0x21}$$

and using these bytes Trudy solves for

$$H(X) = (k_1 - L[H(A)] - L[H(B)]) \ (\text{mod } 256)$$
$$= (\text{0x31} - L[\text{0x59}] - L[\text{0x21}]) \ (\text{mod } 256)$$
$$= (\text{0x31} - \text{0x1e} - \text{0x58}) \ (\text{mod } 256)$$
$$= \text{0xbb}.$$

This is consistent with shifting the previous value of $H(X)$ one position and filling in the new bit with 1. Therefore, Trudy retains this fill and tries to extend it further at the next iteration.

For any initial guess $(H(A), H(B))$ Trudy can solve for a consistent value of $H(X)$. Consequently, Trudy can only discover whether any guess was correct or not when she tries to extend the fills beyond the first byte. And it is possible that that some "false positives" will occur, that is, some fills will be consistent with the keystream for a few steps before failing. We carefully analyze these probabilities below. Note that, in effect, the attack we have described performs a breadth-first search. However, a depth-first search works equally well.

The attack algorithm is outlined in Table 3.7. This algorithm must be repeated for each of the 2^{16} guesses for the initial 16 bits of $(H(A), H(B))$. Recall that $e(A, j)$ is our notation from Table 3.5 for the jth extension of register A.

Once an iteration of the attack in Table 3.7 returns a solution, there is no need to continue searching, provided that a sufficient number of keystream bytes are provided to uniquely determine the key. Below, we show that with just six keystream bytes we only expect one surviving set of initial fills, and

Table 3.7: Outline of ORYX Attack

// Given: keystream bytes $k_0, k_1, k_2, \ldots, k_N$,
// table L, and a guess for initial $(H(A), H(B))$
$H(X) = (k_0 - L[H(A)] - L[H(B)]) \pmod{256}$
for $i = 1$ to N // for each keystream byte
    for each (X, A, B) // putative fill
        $T_0 = $ extend X with 0
        $T_1 = $ extend X with 1
        for $j = 0$ to 11 // for each possible extension
            $T_X = (k_i - L[H(e(A, j))] - L[H(e(B, j))]) \pmod{256}$
            if $T_X == H(T_0)$ then
                save $(T_0, e(A, j), e(B, j))$ for next iteration
            end if
            if $T_X == H(T_1)$ then
                save $(T_1, e(A, j), e(B, j))$ for next iteration
            end if
        next j
    next putative fill
next i

---

after 25 bytes we expect to have determined all of the bits of the (shifted) initial fills.

Finally, we analyze the performance of this attack. For any initial choice of $H(A)$ and $H(B)$, we can use k_0 to solve for a consistent value of $H(X)$. This implies that with just a single keystream byte available, we would obtain 65,536 consistent fills. In other words, the first keystream byte yields no reduction in the number of potential fills. However, if we have k_0 and k_1, then for each of the 65,536 fills (X, A, B) obtained in the first step, the pair (A, B) can be extended in 12 different ways, and for each of these, the implied extension of X is computed. Each valid extension must match in the seven rightmost bits of the shifted $H(X)$. Consequently, on average, only one in 128 of the extensions will survive, assuming we can model the byte comparisons as random. Since L is a permutation it is reasonable to model the computed value as a random selection from $\{0, 1, 2, \ldots, 255\}$. The bottom line is that using only k_0 and k_1, the expected number of valid fills remaining is

$$\frac{12 \cdot 65{,}536}{128} = 6144.$$

If we extend the attack to include k_2, then the expected number of surviving fills is

$$\frac{12 \cdot 6144}{128} = 576.$$

and so on. These results are tabulated in Table 3.8 along with a set of empirically obtained results. It is interesting that the empirical results match the theoretical results so closely.

Table 3.8: Number of Fills in ORYX Attack

Keystream Bytes	Expected Fills	Computed Fills
1	65,536	65,536
2	6144	6029
3	576	551
4	54	47
5	5	3
6	1	1

The results in Table 3.8 show that Trudy can expect to reduce the number of surviving fills to one single candidate using only six keystream bytes. However, to completely determine the 32 bits in each register will require at least 25 keystream bytes, since k_0 is used to determine bits 24 through 31, while each subsequent k_i determines only a single bit of registers A and X, while, on average, each keystream byte determines 1.5 bits of register B.

Since the registers step before the first keystream byte is generates, this attack does not recover the original fills (X, A, B), but instead, it recovers the fills $(X \gg 1, A \gg 1, B \gg s)$, where s is one or two, depending on whether B steps once or twice on the first iteration. In any case, given the recovered fills, it is a simple matter to determine the actual initial fills—although it is not necessary to do so to decrypt the message.

Assuming that ℓ keystream bytes are used, the expected work required for this attack is

$$12 \cdot (65{,}536 + 6144 + 576 + 54 + \ell) < 2^{20}.$$

This is an extremely efficient attack to recover a 96 bit key. The space requirement for the attack is also minimal, as explored further in Problem 13 at the end of this chapter.

3.3.3   Secure ORYX?

As mentioned above, the fundamental problem with ORYX is that it attempts to generate a byte of keystream at each iteration. While this makes for an efficient cipher, it exposes far too much of the internal state to the attacker.

Can we modify ORYX so that it is more secure? If, at each iteration, we output a single bit instead of a byte, that would probably improve the security significantly. For example, suppose we were to compute each keystream bit as

$$\text{keystreamBit} = s(X) \oplus s(L[H(A)]) \oplus s(L[H(B)]),$$

where s selects, say, the high (rightmost) bit of a word or byte. Provided that a complete iteration occurs between each keystreamBit computation, this modification would frustrate the attack discussed above—even if much more known plaintext were available—since the number of candidates to be considered would grow rapidly, instead of being reduced at each iteration. However, this modification would make the cipher eight times slower, which is almost certainly not practical for its intended application. Also, other attacks on this "secure" version of ORYX would need to be considered.

3.4 RC4

> *Suddenly she came upon a little three-legged table, all made of solid glass:*
> *there was nothing on it but a tiny golden key...*
> — *Alice in Wonderland*

RC4 was invented by Ron Rivest in 1987. The "RC" is reputedly for "Ron's Code," although officially it is "Rivest Cipher." RC4 is without doubt the most widely used stream cipher in the world today. It is used, for example, in the Secure Socket Layer (SSL), which is the de facto standard for secure transactions over the Internet, and in Wired Equivalent Privacy (WEP), a widely deployed networking protocol that purports to semi-secure a wireless local area network (LAN).

The RC4 algorithm is considered secure, if used properly. However, WEP—the Swiss cheese of security protocols—somehow managed to implement nearly all of its security functions insecurely, including RC4. As a result, there is a feasible attack on RC4 encryption as used in WEP. But before we discuss this cryptanalytic attack, we briefly mention a few of the many other security issues with WEP.

Perhaps the most egregious security problem with WEP is that it uses a cyclic redundancy check (CRC) for "integrity" protection. The primary purpose of integrity protection is to detect malicious tampering with the data—not just to detect transmission errors. While a CRC is an excellent error detection method, it is useless for cryptographic integrity, since an intelligent adversary can alter the data and, simultaneously, the CRC value so that the "integrity check" is passed. This is precisely the attack that a true cryptographic integrity check, such as a MAC or HMAC, will prevent [142]. Furthermore, since RC4 is a stream cipher, WEP encryption is linear, which allows changes to be made directly to the ciphertext—by an attacker who does not know the key or plaintext—and to the CRC value so that the receiver will not detect the tampering. The bottom line is that this supposed "integrity check" provides no cryptographic integrity whatsoever. Perhaps a CRC was used in WEP due to resource limitations, but that is no excuse for promoting the CRC calculation as an integrity check.

WEP encrypts data with the stream cipher RC4 using a long-term key that seldom (if ever) changes. To avoid repeated keystreams, an initialization vector, or IV, is sent in the clear with each message, where each packet is treated as a new message. The IV is mixed with the long-term key to produce the message key. The upshot is that the attacker, Trudy, gets to see the IVs, and any time an IV repeats, Trudy knows that the same keystream is being used to encrypt the data. Since the IV is only 24 bits, repeated IVs will occur relatively often, which implies repeated keystreams. Since a stream cipher is used, a repeated keystream is at least as bad as reuse of a one-time pad. That is, a repeated keystream provides statistical information to the attacker who could then conceivably liberate the keystream from the ciphertexts.

However, in WEP, there are several possible shortcuts that make an attacker's life easier. For example, if the attacker Trudy can send a message over the wireless link and intercept the ciphertext, then she knows the plaintext and the corresponding ciphertext, which enables her to immediately recover the keystream. This same keystream will be used to encrypt any message that bears the same IV, provided the long-term key has not changed—which it seldom does, since a key change is manual, and the key must be shared with all users of a particular wireless access point.

How realistic is it for Trudy to send a known message over the wireless link? As long as she can contact someone on the wireless LAN (for example, by sending an email message), she can potentially accomplish this trick. The primary practical difficulty for Trudy is to determine which intercepted message corresponds to her chosen plaintext.

There are many more WEP security vulnerabilities. For example, suppose that Trudy knows (or can guess) the destination IP address of a given WEP-encrypted packet. Then—without knowing the key—she can change the destination IP address to an IP address of her choosing (for example, her own IP address), and change the CRC "integrity check" so that her tampering goes undetected. WEP traffic is only encrypted from the host to the wireless access point (and vice-versa). Therefore, when the altered packet arrives at the access point, it will be decrypted and forwarded to Trudy's preferred IP address. Note that this attack is made possible by the lack of any real integrity check.

Below, we discuss a cryptanalytic attack on the RC4 stream cipher as it is used in WEP. This attack succeeds due to the specific way that WEP creates the session key from an initialization vector IV and the long-term key, not due to any inherent weakness in the RC4 algorithm itself.[5] The attack has a small work factor, and it will succeed provided that a sufficient number of IVs are observed. This clever attack, which can be considered a type of *related key* attack, is due to Fluhrer, Mantin, and Shamir [51].

3.4.1 RC4 Algorithm

RC4 is simplicity itself. At any given time, the state of the cipher consists of a lookup table S containing a permutation of all byte values, $0, 1, 2, \ldots, 255$, along with two indices i and j. When the cipher is initialized, the permutation is scrambled using a key which can be of any length from 0 to 256 bytes. In the initialization routine, the lookup table S is modified (based on the key) in such a way that S always contains a permutation of the the byte values. The RC4 initialization algorithm appears in Table 3.9.

Table 3.9: RC4 Initialization

for $i = 0$ to 255
$\quad S_i = i$
$\quad K_i = \text{key}[i \ (\text{mod} \ N)]$
next i
$j = 0$
for $i = 0$ to 255
$\quad j = (j + S_i + K_i) \ (\text{mod} \ 256)$
$\quad \text{swap}(S_i, S_j)$
next i
$i = j = 0$

The RC4 keystream is generated one byte at a time. An index is determined based on the current contents of S, and the indexed byte is selected as the keystream byte. Similar to the initialization routine, at each step the permutation S is modified so that S always contains a permutation of $\{0, 1, 2, \ldots, 255\}$. The keystream generation algorithm appears in Table 3.10.

3.4.2 RC4 Attack

In 2000, Fluhrer, Mantin, and Shamir [51] published a practical attack on RC4 encryption as it is used in the Wired Equivalent Privacy (WEP) protocol. In WEP, a non-secret 24-bit initialization vector, denoted as IV, is prepended to a long-term key and the result is used as the RC4 key. Note that the role of the IV in WEP encryption is analogous to the role that the message indicator (MI) plays in the World War II cipher machines discussed in the

---

[5]The attack does highlight a shortcoming in the RC4 initialization process—a shortcoming that can be fixed without modifying the underlying RC4 algorithm.

Table 3.10: RC4 Keystream Generator

$$i = (i + 1) \pmod{256}$$
$$j = (j + S_i) \pmod{256}$$
$$\text{swap}(S_i, S_j)$$
$$t = (S_i + S_j) \pmod{256}$$
$$\text{keystreamByte} = S_t$$

previous chapter. As with the MI in the WWII cipher machines, the WEP IV is necessary to prevent messages from being sent in *depth*. Recall that two ciphertext messages are in depth if they were encrypted using the same key. Messages in depth are a serious threat to a stream cipher.

In WEP, Trudy, the cryptanalyst, knows many ciphertext messages (packets) and their corresponding IVs, and she would like to recover the long-term key. The Fluher–Mantin–Shamir attack provides a clever, efficient, and elegant way to do just that. This attack has been successfully used to break real WEP traffic [145].

Suppose that for a particular message, the three-byte initialization vector is of the form

$$IV = (3, 255, V), \tag{3.8}$$

where V can be any byte value. Then these three IV bytes become K_0, K_1 and K_2 in the RC4 initialization algorithm of Table 3.9, while K_3 is the first byte of the unknown long-term key. That is, the message key is

$$K = (3, 255, V, K_3, K_4, \ldots), \tag{3.9}$$

where V is known to Trudy, but $K_3, K_4, K_5, \ldots$ are unknown. To understand the attack, we need to carefully consider what happens to the table S during the RC4 initialization phase when K is of the form in (3.9).

In the RC4 initialization algorithm in Table 3.9 we first set S to the identity permutation, so that we have

i	0	1	2	3	4	5	$\ldots$
S_i	0	1	2	3	4	5	$\ldots$

Suppose that K is of the form in (3.9). Then at the $i = 0$ initialization step, we compute the index $j = 0 + S_0 + K_0 = 3$ and elements i and j are swapped, resulting in the table

i	0	1	2	3	4	5	$\ldots$
S_i	3	1	2	0	4	5	$\ldots$

At the next step, $i = 1$ and $j = 3 + S_1 + K_1 = 3 + 1 + 255 = 3$, since the addition is modulo 256. Elements i and j are again swapped, giving

i	0	1	2	3	4	5	...
S_i	3	0	2	1	4	5	....

At step $i = 2$ we have $j = 3 + S_2 + K_2 = 3 + 2 + V = 5 + V$ and after the swap,

i	0	1	2	3	4	5	...	$5 + V$	...
S_i	3	0	$5 + V$	1	4	5	...	2	....

At the next step, $i = 3$ and $j = 5 + V + S_3 + K_3 = 6 + V + K_3$, where K_3 is unknown. After swapping, the lookup table is

i	0	1	2	3	4	5	...
S_i	3	0	$5 + V$	$6 + V + K_3$	4	5	...

i	...	$5 + V$	...	$6 + V + K_3$	...
S_i	...	2	...	1	...

assuming that, after reduction modulo 256, we have $6 + V + K_3 > 5 + V$. If this is not the case, then $6 + V + K_3$ will appear to the left of $5 + V$, but this has no effect on the success of the attack.

Now suppose for a moment that the RC4 initialization algorithm were to stop after the $i = 3$ step. Then if we generate the first byte of the keystream according to the algorithm in Table 3.10, we find $i = 1$ and $j = S_i = S_1 = 0$, so that $t = S_1 + S_0 = 0 + 3 = 3$. Then the first keystream byte would be

$$\text{keystreamByte} = S_3 = (6 + V + K_3) \ (\text{mod } 256). \qquad (3.10)$$

Assuming that Trudy knows (or can guess) the first byte of the plaintext, she can determine the first byte of the keystream. If this is the case, Trudy can simply solve (3.10) to obtain the first unknown key byte, since

$$K_3 = (\text{keystreamByte} - 6 - V) \ (\text{mod } 256). \qquad (3.11)$$

Unfortunately (for Trudy), the initialization phase is 256 steps instead of just four steps. But notice that as long as S_0, S_1 and S_3 are not altered in any subsequent initialization step, then (3.11) will hold. What is the chance that these three elements remain unchanged? The only way that an element can change is if it is swapped for another element. From $i = 4$ to $i = 255$ of the initialization, the i index will not affect any of these elements since it steps regularly from 4 to 255. If we treat the j index as random, then at each step, the probability that the three indices of concern are all unaffected is $253/256$. The probability that this holds for all of the final 252 initialization steps is, therefore,

$$\left(\frac{253}{256} \right)^{252} \approx 0.0513.$$

Consequently, we expect (3.11) to hold slightly more than 5% of the time. Then with a sufficient number of IVs of the form (3.8) Trudy can determine K_3 from (3.11), assuming she knows the first keystream byte in each case.

What is a sufficient number of IVs to recover K_3? If we observe n encrypted packets, each with an IV of the form (3.8), then we expect to solve for the actual K_3 using (3.11) for about $0.05n$ of these. For the remaining $0.95n$ of the cases, we expect the result of (3.11) to be a random value in $\{0, 1, 2, \ldots, 255\}$. Then the expected number of times that any particular value other than K_3 appears is about $0.95n/256$ and the correct value will have an expected count of $0.05n + 0.95n/256 \approx 0.05n$. We need to choose n large enough so that we can, with high probability, distinguish K_3 from the random "noise". If we choose $n = 60$, then we expect to see K_3 three times, while it is unlikely that we will see any random value more than twice (see also Problem 7).

This attack is easily extended to recover the remaining unknown key bytes. We illustrate the next step, that is, assuming that Trudy has recovered K_3, we show that she can recover the key byte K_4. In this case, Trudy will look for initialization vectors of the form

$$\text{IV} = (4, 255, V), \tag{3.12}$$

where V can be any value. Then at the $i = 0$ step of the initialization, $j = 0 + S_0 + K_0 = 4$ and elements i and j are swapped, resulting in

i	0	1	2	3	4	5	...
S_i	4	1	2	3	0	5	...

At the next step, $i = 1$ and $j = 4 + S_1 + K_1 = 4$ (since the addition is mod 256) and elements S_1 and S_4 are swapped, giving

i	0	1	2	3	4	5	...
S_i	4	0	2	3	1	5	...

At step $i = 2$ we have $j = 4 + S_2 + K_2 = 6 + V$ and after the swap

i	0	1	2	3	4	5	...	$6+V$	...
S_i	4	0	$6+V$	3	1	5	...	2	...

At the next step, $i = 3$ and $j = 5 + V + S_3 + K_3 = 9 + V + K_3$, and K_3 is known. After swapping

i	0	1	2	3	4	5	...
S_i	4	0	$6+V$	$9+V+K_3$	1	5	...

i	...	$6+V$	...	$9+V+K_3$	...
S_i	...	2	...	3	...

assuming that $9 + V + K_3 > 6 + V$ when the sums are taken mod 256.

Carrying this one step further, we have $i = 4$ and

$$j = 9 + V + K_3 + S_4 + K_4 = 10 + V + K_3 + K_4,$$

where only K_4 is unknown. After swapping, the table S is of the form

i	0	1	2	3	4	5	...
S_i	4	0	$6+V$	$9+V+K_3$	$10+V+K_3+K_4$	5	...

i	...	$6+V$	...	$9+V+K_3$	...	$10+V+K_3+K_4$	...
S_i	...	2	...	3	...	1	....

If the initialization were to stop at this point (after the $i = 4$ step) then for first byte of the keystream we would find $i = 1$ and $j = S_i = S_1 = 0$, so that $t = S_1 + S_0 = 4 + 0 = 4$. The resulting keystream byte would be

$$\text{keystreamByte} = S_4 = (10 + V + K_3 + K_4) \pmod{256},$$

where the only unknown is K_4. As a result

$$K_4 = (\text{keystreamByte} - 10 - V - K_3) \pmod{256}. \tag{3.13}$$

Of course, the initialization does not stop after the $i = 4$ step, but, as in the K_3 case, the chance that (3.13) holds is about 0.05. Consequently, with a sufficient number of IVs of the form (3.12), Trudy can determine K_4. Continuing in this way, any number of key bytes can be recovered, provided enough IVs of the correct form (about 60 for each key byte) are available and Trudy knows the first keystream byte of each corresponding packet.

This same technique can be extended to recover additional key bytes, $K_5, K_6, \ldots$. In fact, if a sufficient number of packets are available, a key of any length can be recovered with a trivial amount of work. This is one reason why WEP is said to be "unsafe at any key size" [154].

Consider once again the attack to recover the first unknown key byte K_3. It is worth noting that some IVs that are not of the form $(3, 255, V)$ will be useful to Trudy. For example, suppose the IV is $(2, 253, 0)$. Then after the $i = 3$ initialization step, the array S is

i	0	1	2	3	4	...	$3 + K_3$	...
S_i	0	2	1	$3+K_3$	4	...	3	....

If S_1, S_2, and S_3 are not altered in the remaining initialization steps, the first keystream byte will be $3 + K_3$, from which Trudy can recover K_3. Notice that for a given three-byte IV, Trudy can compute the initialization up through the $i = 3$ step and, by doing so, she can easily determine whether a given IV will be useful for her attack. Similar comments hold for subsequent key bytes.

By using all of the useful IVs, Trudy can reduce the number of packets she must observe before recovering the key.

Finally, we mention that it is also possible to attack RC4 if the IV is appended to the unknown key instead of being prepended (as in WEP); see [51, 96] for the details.

3.4.3 Preventing the RC4 Attack

It is easy to prevent the WEP-RC4 attack, and similar attacks that target the RC4 initialization. The standard suggestion is to add 256 steps to the initialization process, that is, after the initialization in Table 3.9 has completed, generate 256 keystream bytes according to the RC4 keystream generation algorithm in Table 3.10, and discard these bytes. Then generate the keystream in the usual way. As long as both the sender and receiver follow this procedure, no modification to the inner workings of RC4 are required. There are many other ways that the key and IV could be combined that would effectively prevent the attack described in this section; Problem 11 asks for such methods.

3.5 PKZIP

> *If you fail to abide by the terms of this license,*
> *then your conscience will haunt you for the rest of your life.*
> — ARC shareware license [66]

In the late 1980s, Phil Katz invented the ZIP file format and made it publicly available. Due to its clear superiority over the competition, the ZIP format quickly became a de facto standard—which it remains to this day. When you create, send, or receive a compressed file, you are almost certainly using Phil Katz's ZIP format.

PKZIP is an acronym for "Phil Katz's ZIP program" [114], which is a utility created by (no surprise here) Phil Katz to manage ZIP archives. PKZIP, which first appeared in 1989, was much superior to ARC, the leading compression tool of the time. ARC was developed by System Enhancement Associates, Inc., or SEA, and sold as shareware. Today we "ZIP" files, whereas for much of the 1980s people would "ARC" their files.

Prior to creating the ZIP format and his PKZIP utility, Phil Katz had developed utilities to handle ARC compressed files—tools that were, by all accounts, better then those provided by SEA. This competition did not please SEA, and they successfully sued. Shortly after these legal wranglings, Katz developed his ZIP format, and PKZIP soon far outpaced SEA's ARC utility.[6] The company Katz created, PKWare, Inc., still exists. Tragically, Phil Katz died in 2000, at age 37, as a result of alcohol abuse [106].

PKZIP is primarily a compression utility, but since ARC provided an encryption option, PKZIP needed one as well. ARC encryption was trivial—simply a repeated XOR with the password—and Katz wanted something stronger. The obvious cipher choices were DES or triple-DES, but efficiency was a major issue, as were concerns over export controls, which limited the strength of encryption that could be used on products destined for non-US markets. As a result, PKZIP used its own "homebrew" cipher, designed by Roger Schlafly [78].

Although the PKZIP cipher is weak, it is not trivial to break. Export controls in force at the time limited key sizes to 40 bits or less, and the work factor to break the PKZIP cipher is close to that limit, unless a large amount of known plaintext is available, in which case the work factor can be reduced significantly.

The PKZIP cipher employs an interesting and unorthodox design. For one thing, it may be one of the first ciphers to use "mixed-mode" arithmetic as an efficient way to achieve a degree of nonlinearity. This is a common strategy today, employed in such well-known and respected ciphers as IDEA and TEA. However, it is clear that there was little, if any, peer review of the PKZIP cipher, in violation of Kerckhoffs' Principle. Not surprisingly, PKZIP proved to be weak when exposed to the light of day.

Biham and Kocher [13] developed a known plaintext attack on the PKZIP cipher which we discuss in this section. However, the paper [13] is itself difficult to decipher—Conrad's implementation [30] is the key to understanding the Biham–Kocher attack. Attacks that require slightly less known plaintext are known [143].

3.5.1 PKZIP Cipher

We ignore the PKZIP compression process and instead focus on the encryption. Here, we are concerned with the so-called "internal representation" of the key, a 96-bit quantity derived from a user-supplied password [13]. We denote this key as three 32-bit words, X, Y, and Z. The attack will recover this key, which enables us to decrypt the message, as well as any other messages encrypted under the same password.

The PKZIP stream cipher generates one byte of keystream at each step. Being a stream cipher, the keystream is XORed with the plaintext to produce the ciphertext. The same keystream is XORed with the ciphertext to recover the plaintext.

---

[6]The success of ZIP and the rapid demise of ARC was not only due to the technical superiority of the ZIP format. Another factor was the widespread belief amongst nerds that Phil Katz had been persecuted by SEA.

Below, we follow the convention that upper case letters represent 32-bit words, while lower case represent 8-bit bytes—for the one require 16-bit quantity, we also use lower case. All arithmetic is to be taken modulo 2^{32}. As in other sections of this book, we adopt the convention that bits are numbered from left-to-right, beginning with 0. In the PKZIP attack discussed below, we often need to specify a range of bits within a byte or a 32-bit word. We use the notation $\langle A \rangle_{i \ldots j}$, where $j \geq i$, for the string of bits of length $j - i + 1$ beginning with bit i and ending with bit j of A.

The PKZIP encryption algorithm appears in Table 3.11. Here, p is the current plaintext byte, c the resulting ciphertext byte, and k is the keystream byte.

Table 3.11: PKZIP Encryption

```
// encrypt plaintext byte p
// result is ciphertext byte c
// given current X, Y, Z
k = getKeystreamByte(Z)
c = p ⊕ k
update(X, Y, Z, p)
```

The functions getKeystreamByte and update are defined in Tables 3.12 and 3.13, respectively. The decryption process is easily derived from these encryption routines.

Table 3.12: PKZIP getKeystreamByte

```
getKeystreamByte(Z)
    t = ⟨Z ∨ 3⟩₁₆...₃₁ // 16-bit quantity
    k = ⟨(t · (t ⊕ 1)) ≫ 8⟩₂₄...₃₁
    return k
end getKeystreamByte
```

$$t = \langle Z \vee 3 \rangle_{16 \ldots 31} \quad // \text{ 16-bit quantity}$$
$$k = \langle (t \cdot (t \oplus 1)) \gg 8 \rangle_{24 \ldots 31}$$

The CRC function in Table 3.13 is a cyclic redundancy check, which can be computed as shown in Table 3.14. This is the same CRC calculation used for error detection in the ZIP compression process and, undoubtedly, it is reused here for efficiency.

A more efficient way to carry out the CRC calculation in Table 3.14 is discussed in Problem 18, where it is shown that there exists a table, CRCtable[b], where for any byte b, we have

$$\mathrm{CRC}(X, b) = \langle X \rangle_{0 \ldots 23} \oplus \mathrm{CRCtable}[\langle X \rangle_{24 \ldots 31} \oplus b].$$

Table 3.13: PKZIP update

```
// update values of X, Y, Z
update(X, Y, Z, p)
    X = CRC(X,p)
    Y = (Y + ⟨X⟩₂₄...₃₁) · 134,775,813 + 1
    Z = CRC(Z,⟨Y⟩₀...₇)
end update
```

Table 3.14: PKZIP CRC Calculation

```
// X is a 32-bit integer
// b is a byte
CRC(X,b)
    X = X ⊕ b
    for i = 0 to 7
        if X is odd then
            X = (X ≫ 1) ⊕ 0xedb88320
        else // X is even
            X = X ≫ 1
        end if
    next i
    return X
end CRC
```

Problem 19 shows that there is a table, CRCinverse, that is the inverse of CRCtable in the sense that if

$$B = \langle A \rangle_{0\ldots23} \oplus \mathrm{CRCtable}[\langle A \rangle_{24\ldots31} \oplus b], \qquad (3.14)$$

then

$$A = (B \ll 8) \oplus \mathrm{CRCinverse}[\langle B \rangle_{0\ldots7}] \oplus b. \qquad (3.15)$$

Let (X_i, Y_i, Z_i) denote the 32-bit words (X, Y, Z) used to generate the ith keystream byte and let k_i be the ith keystream byte, for $i = 0, 1, 2, \ldots$. We are now in a position to discuss the Biham–Kocher attack.

3.5.2 PKZIP Attack

We first summarize the PKZIP attack, then we provide details for each of the points in the summary. We call $k_0, k_1, k_2, \ldots, k_n$ a k-list. Define p-list, X-list, Y-list, and Z-list similarly. The attack assumes known plaintext, which implies that the k-list and p-list are both known.

If we can recover any valid triple (X_i, Y_i, Z_i), then the internal state of the keystream generator is known and we can determine the keystream k_j for all $j \geq i$. This attack will enable us to find such a triple (X_i, Y_i, Z_i) with a nontrivial, but feasible, amount of work.

In outline form, the attack consists of the following steps:

1. Use the k-list to find a set of putative Z-lists.

2. For each putative Z-list, we find multiple putative Y-lists.

3. For each putative Y-list, we use the p-list to obtain a single putative X-list.

4. The true X-list must be among the putative X-lists. By using the p-list, we can determine the correct X-list, and once we find the correct X-list, we know the corresponding Y-list and Z-list, so we can determine the keystream.

A total of $n + 1$ known plaintext bytes are required.[7] We number the known plaintext bytes from 0 to n. These plaintext bytes must be consecutive, but need not be the first $n + 1$ bytes. Then each list (k-list, X-list, etc.) contains $n + 1$ elements, which are numbered from 0 to n, even though these might not represent the first $n + 1$ elements generated. Eventually, we will show that 13 consecutive known plaintexts is sufficient (that is, $n = 12$), but for now we leave n unspecified.

Next, we expand on each of the points in the attack outlined above. For this attack, we assume that we have available the p-list, that is, we have p_i, for $i = 0, 1, 2, \ldots, n$, which implies that we also know the corresponding k-list. We number the steps in the attack below to correspond with the numbers in the outline of the attack, above.

1. Problem 20 shows that given a key byte k, there are 64 choices for the value t in Table 3.12, which, in turn, gives 64 possible values for the 14 bits $\langle Z \rangle_{16\ldots29}$. Consequently, given any k_i, we have 64 putative values for $\langle Z_i \rangle_{16\ldots29}$.

   We use k_n to determine 64 putative values for $\langle Z_n \rangle_{16\ldots29}$ and we use k_{n-1} to determine 64 putative values for $\langle Z_{n-1} \rangle_{16\ldots29}$. Next, we loop over the 2^{16} possible choices for $\langle Z_n \rangle_{0\ldots15}$. For each of these, we have 64 putative $\langle Z_n \rangle_{16\ldots29}$, which implies that we have 2^{22} candidates for $\langle Z_n \rangle_{0\ldots29}$.

   From update in Table 3.13, we have

   $$Z_i = \mathrm{CRC}(Z_{i-1}, \langle Y_i \rangle_{0\ldots7})$$

---

[7]In PKZIP, the plaintext bytes are actually compressed text. This has no effect on the attack discussed here, except that we are implicitly assuming that the compressed bytes are known.

and from the inversion formula in (3.15) it follows that

$$Z_{i-1} = (Z_i \ll 8) \oplus \text{CRCinverse}[\langle Z_i \rangle_{0...7}] \oplus \langle Y_i \rangle_{0...7}. \qquad (3.16)$$

Let $i = n$ in (3.16). Then given a candidate $\langle Z_n \rangle_{0...29}$, we know bits 0 through 21 on the right-hand side of (3.16). On the left-hand side, there are 64 possible values for $\langle Z_{n-1} \rangle_{16...29}$. For the correct Z_{n-1} and Z_n, bits 16 through 21 on both sides of (3.16) must match. For any given Z_n, there is a probability of about $1/64$ that a given Z_{n-1} matches in these six known bit positions. Since we have 64 putative $\langle Z_{n-1} \rangle_{16...29}$, we expect, on average, one of these 64 to match in the corresponding bits of the given Z_n.

Once we find a $\langle Z_{n-1} \rangle_{16...29}$ that is consistent with a putative Z_n, we can then fill in bits 0 through 15 of Z_{n-1} based on the right-hand side of (3.16). At this point, we have found a (putative) pair consisting of $\langle Z_{n-1} \rangle_{0...29}$ and $\langle Z_n \rangle_{0...29}$, and we expect to find the same number of such pairs as we have putative $\langle Z_n \rangle_{0...29}$. We can repeat this process for $n-1, n-2, n-3, \ldots$, and thereby obtain complete putative Z-lists of the form $\langle Z_i \rangle_{0...29}$, for $i = 0, 1, \ldots, n$.

We can extend each putative Z_i from 30 known bits to its full 32 bits as follows. From (3.16), we have

$$(Z_i \ll 8) = Z_{i-1} \oplus \text{CRCinverse}[\langle Z_i \rangle_{0...7}] \oplus \langle Y_i \rangle_{0...7}. \qquad (3.17)$$

In this form, bits 22 and 23 are known on the right-hand side. But these correspond to bits 30 and 31 of Z_i on the left-hand side, which allows us to fill in these (previously) unknown bits on the left-hand side. In this way, for each putative Z-list, we can determine bits 30 and 31 of Z_i, for $i = 1, 2, \ldots, n$, and we can thereby complete each Z_i, except for Z_0. Note that we cannot determine bits 30 and 31 of Z_0 using (3.17), since Z_{i-1} is required on the right-hand side. Also note that the expected number of putative Z-lists is equal to the number of putative Z_n, that is, about 2^{22}.

The number of putative Z-lists can be reduced as follows. For all putative Z_i, we can determine the corresponding Z_{i-1} values, then sort the resulting lists based on Z_{i-1}, removing any duplicates. The savings provided by this refinement are explored further in Problem 29. In [13] it is suggested to carry out this reduction for 28 steps, which, it is claimed, reduces the expected number of Z-lists from 2^{22} to 2^{18}. While this reduces the work by a factor of 2^4, the price that is paid is that 28 additional known plaintext bytes must be available.

For simplicity, in the remainder of our discussion of this attack, we ignore this duplicate-reduction step. Consequently, we expect to have 2^{22} putative Z-lists.

2. At this point we have about 2^{22} putative Z-lists, each of which is of the form $Z_1, Z_2, \ldots, Z_n$. Now we rewrite (3.16) as

$$\langle Y_i \rangle_{0\ldots7} = (Z_i \ll 8) \oplus Z_{i-1} \oplus \text{CRCinverse}[\langle Z_i \rangle_{0\ldots7}], \qquad (3.18)$$

which, for each Z-list, immediately gives us $\langle Y \rangle_{0\ldots7}$ of the corresponding Y-list, that is, we obtain bits 0 through 7 of each of $Y_2, Y_3, \ldots, Y_n$. Note that Y_1 cannot be recovered using (3.18) since Z_{i-1} is required to find Y_i, and Z_0 was not recovered.

From update in Table 3.13, we have

$$Y_i = (Y_{i-1} + \langle X_i \rangle_{24\ldots31}) \cdot 134{,}775{,}813 + 1, \qquad (3.19)$$

which we rewrite as

$$(Y_i - 1) \cdot C = Y_{i-1} + \langle X_i \rangle_{24\ldots31}, \qquad (3.20)$$

where $C = 134775813^{-1} = 3645876429 \pmod{2^{32}}$. From this equation and Problem 23, it follows that with high probability we have

$$\langle (Y_i - 1) \cdot C \rangle_{0\ldots7} = \langle Y_{i-1} \rangle_{0\ldots7}. \qquad (3.21)$$

Letting $i = n$ in (3.21) we have

$$\langle (Y_n - 1) \cdot C \rangle_{0\ldots7} = \langle Y_{n-1} \rangle_{0\ldots7}.$$

Since $\langle Y_n \rangle_{0\ldots7}$ and $\langle Y_{n-1} \rangle_{0\ldots7}$ are known, we can test all 2^{24} choices for $\langle Y_n \rangle_{8\ldots31}$ against the known right-hand side. The probability of a match is $1/2^8$, so we expect to find 2^{16} putative Y_n. Note that we obtain this number of Y_n per putative Z-list, since the $\langle Y_i \rangle_{0\ldots7}$ are derived based on a particular Z-list. Since there are about 2^{22} Z-lists, at this point we have about 2^{38} partial Y-lists, each consisting of just Y_n.

Now from (3.20), we have

$$Y_{n-1} = (Y_n - 1) \cdot C - a \qquad (3.22)$$

for some unknown $a \in \{0, 1, 2, \ldots, 255\}$. Given a putative Y_n, we substitute each choice for a into (3.22) and obtain a putative Y_{n-1}. Each of these is then is tested to determine whether

$$\langle (Y_{n-1} - 1) \cdot C \rangle_{0\ldots7} = \langle Y_{n-2} \rangle_{0\ldots7}$$

holds; if so, Y_{n-1} is saved, and if not, it is discarded. Since $\langle Y_{n-2} \rangle_{0\ldots7}$ is a known 8-bit quantity, on average, we expect one of the 256 computed Y_{n-1} to pass this test. That is, the number of Y-lists does not expand at this step, where we extend each putative Y-list from Y_n to Y_{n-1}. Consequently, we expect to find about 2^{38} partial Y-lists, each consisting of Y_n and Y_{n-1}.

Now for each Y_{n-1}, there are 256 possible Y_{n-2} from

$$Y_{n-2} = (Y_{n-1} - 1) \cdot C - a$$

and, on average, only one of these will satisfy

$$\langle (Y_{n-2} - 1) \cdot C \rangle_{0\ldots 7} = \langle Y_{n-3} \rangle_{0\ldots 7}.$$

In this way we extend the putative Y-lists to include Y_{n-2}, without increasing the number of lists to more than 2^{38}. Continuing, we obtain about 2^{38} putative Y-lists, each consisting of Y_i, for $i = 3, 4, 5, \ldots, n$. Note that we cannot find Y_2 by this method, since $\langle Y_1 \rangle_{0\ldots 7}$ would be required, which is not known.

The computation of Y-lists discussed here can be made more efficient by using lookup tables. Specifically, given the byte $\langle Y_{i-1} \rangle_{0\ldots 7}$, we would simply look up the corresponding $\langle (Y_i - 1) \cdot C \rangle_{0\ldots 7}$, saving the cost of many multiplications.

3. At this point, we have about 2^{38} putative Y-list, each of the form $Y_3, Y_4, \ldots, Y_n$. For each of these we determine one corresponding X-list as follows. We rewrite (3.20) as

$$\langle X_i \rangle_{24\ldots 31} = (Y_i - 1) \cdot C - Y_{i-1}, \tag{3.23}$$

from which we immediately obtain

$$\langle X_4 \rangle_{24\ldots 31}, \langle X_5 \rangle_{24\ldots 31}, \ldots, \langle X_n \rangle_{24\ldots 31},$$

but not $\langle X_3 \rangle_{24\ldots 31}$.

Now from update in Table 3.13 together with (3.14), we have

$$X_i = \langle X_{i-1} \rangle_{0\ldots 23} \oplus \mathrm{CRCtable}[\langle X_{i-1} \rangle_{24\ldots 31} \oplus p_i]. \tag{3.24}$$

A consequence of (3.24) is that if we know one complete X_i, we can compute all bits of X_j, for $j > i$, assuming that the corresponding plaintexts p_j are known. By using the CRC inversion formula, we can also use this X_i to recover X_j for $j < i$, again, provided that the corresponding plaintexts p_j are known.

To determine one complete X_i, first note that according to (3.24) we have

$$\langle X_i \rangle_{0\ldots 23} = X_{i+1} \oplus \mathrm{CRCtable}[\langle X_i \rangle_{24\ldots 31} \oplus p_{i+1}] \tag{3.25}$$

$$\langle X_{i+1} \rangle_{0\ldots 23} = X_{i+2} \oplus \mathrm{CRCtable}[\langle X_{i+1} \rangle_{24\ldots 31} \oplus p_{i+2}] \tag{3.26}$$

$$\langle X_{i+2} \rangle_{0\ldots 23} = X_{i+3} \oplus \mathrm{CRCtable}[\langle X_{i+2} \rangle_{24\ldots 31} \oplus p_{i+3}]. \tag{3.27}$$

Since we know $\langle X_{i+3}\rangle_{24...31}$ and $\langle X_{i+2}\rangle_{24...31}$, from (3.27) we can determine $\langle X_{i+2}\rangle_{16...23}$ which gives us $\langle X_{i+2}\rangle_{16...31}$. Combining this result with (3.26), we find $\langle X_{i+1}\rangle_{8...31}$, which, together with (3.25), allows us to determine all bits of X_i. We can now use this recovered X_i and (3.24) to find putative X-lists, of the form $X_4, X_5, \ldots, X_n$, as discussed, above.[8] We obtain one putative X-list for each putative Y-list, so that the expected number of X-lists is 2^{38}.

4. Finally, to determine the correct X-list from the collection of putative X-lists, we compare the values of $\langle X_i\rangle_{24...31}$ obtained from (3.24) with the values obtained from (3.23). We expect each such comparison to reduce the number of remaining lists by a factor of 256. Since we have about 2^{38} X-lists, we need to make five such comparisons before we expect to obtain the correct X-list.

At this point we have a single X-list along with the corresponding Y-list and Z-list. Given any triple (X_i, Y_i, Z_i) we can compute the keystream k_j for all $j \geq i$ and therefore decrypt the ciphertext to recover the (compressed) plaintext.

The overall work factor for this attack is on the order of 2^{38} (the number of lists generated). The work factor can be reduced by using more known plaintext, as discussed in [13] and Problem 29.

We still need to precisely determine the minimum number of known plaintext bytes required, that is, the smallest value of n for which the attack will succeed. From (3.25), (3.26), and (3.27), we see that four consecutive $\langle X_i\rangle_{24...31}$ are needed to completely determine the X-lists. Also, five additional X_i are needed to find the correct X-list from the set of 2^{38} lists. This means nine X-list elements must be available. However, each X-list is only determined for $i = 4, 5, \ldots, n$, which implies $n = 12$ is the smallest value for which we obtain the required nine X-list elements. Since our indexing begins at 0, we need a minimum of 13 consecutive known plaintext bytes for the attack described here.

Finally, we describe a slightly different implementation of this PKZIP attack, which is easier to program. The attack discussed above requires that we store all putative Z-lists and so on. This is essential if want to do the duplicate-reduction step, where the number of of Z-lists is reduced from 2^{22} to some smaller number using additional known plaintext (see Problem 29). But if we do not employ this reduction step, we can obtain an algorithm that is easier to implement. The idea is essentially to turn the breadth-first approach described above into a depth-first attack.

---

[8]We could use (3.24) to solve for additional X_j, but only X_4 through X_n are required for this attack.

Instead of generating all of the putative Z-lists, then all of the Y-lists, followed by all of the X-lists, we generate a single Z-list, then all of the Y-lists that are consistent with this Z-list, then the X-lists that are consistent with the Y-lists. The resulting X-lists are then tested to determine whether we have found the correct list, and the entire process is repeated for each putative Z-list until the solution is found. In this way, we only need to store a relatively small set of lists at any given time—not the entire set of 2^{38} lists. This simplified attack is outlined in Table 3.15.

Table 3.15: Outline of PKZIP Attack

```
// given keystream bytes k₀, k₁, ..., k₁₂
```

$$\begin{array}{l}
\text{// given keystream bytes } k_0, k_1, \ldots, k_{12} \\
\textbf{for } i = 0, 1, \ldots, 12 \\
\quad \text{Find } \langle Z_i \rangle_{16\ldots29} \text{ consistent with } k_i \text{ // expect 64} \\
\textbf{next } i \\
\textbf{for each } \langle Z_{12} \rangle_{16\ldots29} \text{ // expect 64} \\
\quad \textbf{for each } \langle Z_{12} \rangle_{0\ldots15} \text{ // } 2^{16} \text{ choices} \\
\quad\quad \textbf{for } i = 11, 10, \ldots, 0 \\
\quad\quad\quad \text{Find } \langle Z_i \rangle_{16\ldots29} \text{ consistent with } \langle Z_{i+1} \rangle_{0\ldots29} \\
\quad\quad\quad \text{Extend } \langle Z_i \rangle_{16\ldots29} \text{ to } \langle Z_i \rangle_{0\ldots29} \\
\quad\quad \textbf{next } i \\
\quad\quad \text{Complete to } Z\text{-list: } Z_i = \langle Z_i \rangle_{0\ldots31}, \ i = 1, 2, \ldots, 12 \\
\quad\quad \text{Solve for } \langle Y_i \rangle_{0\ldots7}, \ i = 2, 3, \ldots, 12 \\
\quad\quad \text{Solve for } Y\text{-lists: } Y_i, \ i = 3, 4, \ldots, 12 \text{ // expect } 2^{16} \text{ lists} \\
\quad\quad \textbf{for each } Y\text{-list // expect } 2^{16} \\
\quad\quad\quad \text{Solve for } \langle X_i \rangle_{24\ldots31}, \ i = 4, 5, \ldots, 12 \\
\quad\quad\quad \text{Solve for } X_9 \text{ using } \langle X_9 \rangle_{24\ldots31}, \langle X_{10} \rangle_{24\ldots31}, \\
\quad\quad\quad\quad\quad\quad\quad \langle X_{11} \rangle_{24\ldots31} \text{ and } \langle X_{12} \rangle_{24\ldots31} \\
\quad\quad\quad \text{Solve for } X\text{-list: } X_i, \ i = 4, 5, \ldots, 12 \\
\quad\quad\quad \textbf{if } \langle X_i \rangle_{24\ldots31} \text{ for } i = 8, 7, 6, 5, 4 \text{ verified } \textbf{then} \\
\quad\quad\quad\quad \textbf{return } X\text{-list}, Y\text{-list}, Z\text{-list} \\
\quad\quad\quad \textbf{end if} \\
\quad\quad \textbf{next } Y\text{-list} \\
\quad \textbf{next } \langle Z_{12} \rangle_{0\ldots15} \\
\textbf{next } \langle Z_{12} \rangle_{16\ldots29}
\end{array}$$

Note that for the attack in Table 3.15, the maximum number of (X, Y, Z)-lists generated is 2^{38}, so that the expected number of lists generated before the solution is found is 2^{37}. The price we pay for this simplification is that we cannot implement the duplicate-reduction step which reduces the number of putative Z-lists, and thereby reduces the overall work factor. If more than 13 bytes of known plaintext is available, the simplified attack given here will have a higher work factor than the nonsimplified attack discussed above, provided that the duplicate-reduction step is implemented.

3.5.3   Improved PKZIP?

Unlike the ORYX cipher, for example, the Achilles' heel of the PKZIP cipher is not immediately obvious. It seems that many aspects of the design are slightly weak, and these combine to create an overall weak cipher.

However, the use of the CRC appears to be the weakest link in the chain. The problem with the CRC is that there exists a relatively simple inversion formula. Perhaps if we replace the CRC with some other operation that is harder to invert, the resulting cipher would be stronger.

Recall that the CRC calculation is of the form $Y = \text{CRC}(X,b)$, where X and Y are 32-bit integers, and b is a byte. So to replace the CRC, we need a function that takes as input a 32-bit word and a byte, and generates a 32-bit output. We also want our function to be hard to invert. A cryptographic hash function would seem to be the ideal choice here (see Chapter 5), where we let $Y = h(X, b)$ for some hash function h, with the output truncated to 32 bits, if necessary. Then we would expect about 256 collisions for each possible Y. In fact, a CRC is sometimes mistakenly used where a cryptographic hash is required (see the discussion of WEP in Section 3.4, for example), and this may explain why a CRC was used in PKZIP. However, it is more likely that the CRC was used in the PKZIP cipher since it was already available as part of the ZIP compression routine, and it was necessary to minimize the overall size of the code.

In keeping with the spirit of PKZIP, we should replace the CRC with something that does not have much computational or coding overhead. This might preclude a sophisticated cryptographic hash function, which makes the problem more challenging (see Problem 30).

3.6   Summary

RC4, ORYX and PKZIP present interesting but very different cryptanalytic challenges. For RC4 (as used in WEP), a subtle issue in the method used to combine the IV and the long-term key leads to a devastating attack. A slight modification to the usage of RC4 renders this attack infeasible. In stark contrast, ORYX is a fundamentally flawed cipher. If known plaintext is available, the work factor to break ORYX is trivial. Not surprisingly, there is also a ciphertext-only attack on ORYX [153].

Of the three attacks considered in this chapter, the PKZIP attack is the most challenging. It is not particularly difficult to see that PKZIP has an exploitable weakness, but working through the details is not for the faint of heart.

3.7   Problems

1. Complete steps $N = 4$ through $N = 15$ of the Berlekamp–Massey Algorithm for the example in Table 3.2. Give the connection polynomial and verify that your answer is correct by generating the first 16 fills of the LFSR corresponding the your claimed connection polynomial, with initial fill 10011. Hint: The linear complexity is $L = 6$.

2. Illustrate the smallest LFSR (including the initial fill) that can generate the sequence in (3.3).

3. Suppose that $K = (k_0, k_1, \ldots)$ is a keystream bit sequence. If there exists a bit sequence $\tilde{K} = (\tilde{k}_0, \tilde{k}_1, \ldots)$ that differs in only a few elements from K and $\tilde{K}$ has a small linear complexity, why is K a cryptographically weak keystream sequence?

4. The Chan–Games Algorithm [141] is more efficient than the Berlekamp–Massey Algorithm, for the special case where the binary sequence s has period 2^n. The Chan–Games Algorithm computes the linear complexity L of s as follows:

$$a = s, \ L = 0, \ m = 2^n$$

```
while m > 1
    m = m/2
    ℓ = a₀a₁ ... aₘ₋₁
    r = aₘaₘ₊₁ ... a₂ₘ₋₁
    b = ℓ ⊕ r
    if b == 00...0 then
        a = ℓ
    else
        L = L + m
        a = b
    end if
end while
if a₀ == 1 then
    L = L + 1
end if
```

Note that ℓ is the left half of the sequence a and r is the right half. Use the Chan–Games Algorithm to determine the linear complexity of the sequence with period $s = 10011100$.

5. Recall the correlation attack discussed in Section 3.2.4. Consider the stream cipher in Figure 3.8, and suppose that Trudy recovers the con-

secutive keystream bits

$$(k_0, k_1, \ldots, k_{30}) = 0000110011001001011101100010010.$$

Determine the initial fills of registers X, Y, and Z.

6. Show that the size of the state space of the RC4 cipher is bounded by $2^{16} \cdot 256! \approx 2^{1700}$.

7. In the RC4 attack, suppose that 60 IVs of the form $(3, 255, V)$ are available. Empirically determine the probability that the key byte K_3 can be distinguished. What is the smallest number of IVs for which this probability is greater than $1/2$?

8. In (3.11) and (3.13) we showed how to recover RC4 key bytes K_3 and K_4, respectively.

   a. Assuming that key bytes K_3 through K_{n-1} have been recovered, what is the desired form of the IVs that will be used to recover K_n?
   b. For K_n what is the formula corresponding to (3.11) and (3.13)?

9. For the attack on RC4 discussed in Section 3.4, we showed that the probability that (3.11) holds is $(253/256)^{252}$. What is the probability that (3.13) holds? What is the probability that the corresponding equation holds for K_n?

10. In the discussion of the attack on RC4 keystream byte K_3 we showed that IVs of the form $(3, 255, V)$ are useful to the attacker. We also showed that IVs that are not of this form are sometimes useful to the attacker, and we gave the specific example of the $(2, 253, 0)$. Find another IV not of the form $(3, 255, V)$ that is useful in the attack on K_3.

11. The attack on RC4 discussed in this section illustrates that prepending an IV to a long-term key is insecure. In [51] it is shown that appending the IV to the long-term key is also insecure. Suggest more secure ways to employ RC4 when a long-term key is combined with an IV.

12. In the ORYX attack, suppose that the recovered bits (using the first 29 keystream bytes) are

$$(X \gg 1) = \texttt{0x9b874560b}$$
$$(A \gg 1) = \texttt{0xacd789046}$$
$$(B \gg \ell) = \texttt{0x19910954207e2}$$

and that $K_0 = \texttt{0x9f}$. Find ℓ and the initial fills of (X, A, B).

13. This problem deals with the branching that occurs in the ORYX attack.

    a. How much branching is expected at the K_1 step of the ORYX attack? Hint: After the K_0 step, there are 65,536 putative fills. At the next iteration, we test 12 extensions of each of these putative fills. How many of these 65,536 produce more than one result that is consistent with an extension of X?

    b. What is the expected branching at each of steps K_1 through K_N?

    c. Suppose that we implement the ORYX attack without branching. That is, no more than one valid extension of any given fill is retained. If this is the case, what is the probability that the solution is found?

14. When analyzing the ORYX attack, we assumed that the permutation L acts as a "random" permutation of the values $\{0, 1, 2, \ldots, 255\}$. Suppose that instead, L is the identity, that is, $L[i] = i$, for $i = 0, 1, 2, \ldots, 255$. In this case, explain why the ORYX attack given in this chapter will fail and describe an alternative attack that will succeed.

15. Discuss possible ways that the ORYX keystream generator can be modified to prevent the attack given in this chapter. Consider methods that result in a more efficient cipher than the modifications mentioned in Section 3.3.3.

16. Analyze the modified version of ORYX discussed in Section 3.3.3 for potential weaknesses. You may assume that unlimited known plaintext is available.

17. Give the PKZIP decryption routine that corresponds to the encryption routine in Table 3.11.

18. For $b = 0, 1, 2, \ldots, 255$, define

$$\mathrm{CRCtable}[b] = \mathrm{CRC}(0,b),$$

where $\mathrm{CRC}(X,b)$ is defined for the PKZIP stream cipher in Table 3.14. Show that

$$\mathrm{CRC}(X,b) = \langle X \rangle_{0\ldots23} \oplus \mathrm{CRCtable}[\langle X \rangle_{24\ldots31} \oplus b].$$

19. For $b = 0, 1, 2, \ldots, 255$, define

$$\mathrm{CRCinverse}[\langle \mathrm{CRCtable}[b] \rangle_{24\ldots31}] = (\mathrm{CRCtable}[b] \ll 8) \oplus b,$$

where $\mathrm{CRCtable}[b]$ is defined in Problem 18. Show that if

$$Y = \langle X \rangle_{0\ldots23} \oplus \mathrm{CRCtable}[\langle X \rangle_{24\ldots31} \oplus b],$$

then
$$X = (Y \ll 8) \oplus \text{CRCinverse}[\langle Y \rangle_{0...7}] \oplus b.$$

20. Consider the getKeystreamByte function of the PKZIP cipher, which appears in Table 3.12. Verify that for any value of the keystream byte k, there are precisely 64 distinct values t that yield k.

21. Verify that for 32-bit integers X and Y,
$$\langle X - Y \rangle_{0...7} = \begin{cases} \langle X \rangle_{0...7} - \langle Y \rangle_{0...7} & \text{if } X \geq Y \pmod{2^{24}} \\ \langle X \rangle_{0...7} - \langle Y \rangle_{0...7} - 1 & \text{if } X < Y \pmod{2^{24}}. \end{cases}$$

22.   a. Verify that $134{,}775{,}813^{-1} = 3{,}645{,}876{,}429 \pmod{2^{32}}$.

   b. Let $C = 134{,}775{,}813^{-1} = 3{,}645{,}876{,}429 \pmod{2^{32}}$. Show that for any byte values a and b,
$$\langle aC + b \rangle_{0...7} = \langle aC \rangle_{0...7}, \tag{3.28}$$
   where the addition is modulo 2^{32}.

   c. For which 32-bit integers C does (3.28) hold for all byte values a and b?

23. Suppose that
$$A \cdot C = B + a \pmod{2^{32}},$$
where A, B and C are 32-bit words, with $C = 3{,}645{,}876{,}429$ and a is a byte. Then what is the probability that $\langle A \cdot C \rangle_{0...7} = \langle B \rangle_{0...7}$? The motivation for this choice of C can be found in Problem 22.

24. Use the results of Problems 21 and 22, along with (3.19), to show that
$$\langle Y_{i-2} \rangle_{0...7} = \begin{cases} \langle ((Y_i - 1) \cdot C - 1) \cdot C \rangle_{0...7} - \langle \langle X_i \rangle_{24...31} \cdot C \rangle_{0...7} \\ \langle ((Y_i - 1) \cdot C - 1) \cdot C \rangle_{0...7} - \langle \langle X_i \rangle_{24...31} \cdot C \rangle_{0...7} - 1 \end{cases}$$
where the conditions that determine which half of the equation applies are analogous to those in Problem 21.

25. Suppose that A and B are randomly selected 32-bit integers. Let
$$X = A + \langle B \rangle_{24...31},$$
where the addition is taken modulo 2^{32}. What is the probability that
$$\langle X \rangle_{0...7} \neq \langle A \rangle_{0...7}?$$

26. In the PKZIP attack, show that if you are given $\langle Y_{i-1} \rangle_{0...7}$ and $\langle Y_i \rangle_{0...7}$, then the number of 32-bit values $Y_{i-1} + \langle X_{i-1} \rangle_{24...31}$ and Y_i that satisfy (3.19) is in the range of 65,534 to 65,538, inclusive.

27. In step 1 of the PKZIP attack, as specified beginning on page 114, we explain how to recover Z_{i-1} given Z_i. Give precise equations for $\langle Z_{i-1}\rangle_{0...23}$, $\langle Z_{i-1}\rangle_{24...29}$, and $\langle Z_{i-1}\rangle_{30...31}$, given Z_i.

28. As a function of x, find the precise distribution on the number of solutions a to the equation

$$x = \begin{cases} aC \\ aC + 1 \end{cases}$$

where a and x are bytes with x given, and $C = 3{,}645{,}876{,}429$. Also give the average number of solutions.

29. For the PKZIP attack, experimentally determine the expected number of surviving Z-lists when n additional keystream bytes are used in the duplicate-reduction step, for $n = 0, 1, 2, \ldots, m$, where m is at least 10,000. For each n, run at least 100 trials. Plot your results on a graph.

30. In Section 3.5.3 it is suggested that the weakest component in the PKZIP cipher is the use of the cyclic redundancy check (CRC), and we argue that a cryptographic hash function would be ideal. Suggest a possible replacement F for the CRC in PKZIP, where $Y = F(X, b)$, where X and Y are 32-bits, and b is a byte. Your function F must be computationally efficient and only require a small number of lines of code. Explain why your suggested replacement is better than the CRC used in PKZIP.

Chapter 4

Block Ciphers

Through block play, children are confronted with many mental challenges
having to do with measurement, equality, balance, shape,
spatial relationships and physical properties.
— Creativity and Play [112]

4.1 Introduction

Recall that a classic codebook cipher uses books filled with "codes" to encrypt and decrypt messages. Such codebooks have some inherent weaknesses. For example, any known plaintext immediately gives away part of the codebook. Also, information about the codebook can be obtained based on a statistical analysis of the ciphertext, in much the same way that information leaks through a simple substitution (although far more data is required to attack a respectable codebook than a simple substitution). Due to the threat of such attacks, new codebooks would have to be issued on a regular basis.

Modern block ciphers can be viewed as roughly the electronic equivalent of classic codebooks. In block ciphers, a block of n plaintext bits is encrypted to a block of n ciphertext bits. Provided that the same key is used, the same plaintext block will always be encrypted to the same plaintext block, and vice versa. This is analogous to a classic codebook, except that the "book," which would contain the binary n-tuples, is virtual in the sense that the lookups are accomplished using an algorithm that computes the required bits. That is, the entries of the codebook are computed as needed instead of being stored in an actual book.

In a block cipher, the key determines the codebook. Consequently, if we change the key, we have, in effect, switched codebooks. If the key is k bits, then the block cipher algorithm can be viewed as 2^k codebooks, indexed by the key. Therefore, by occasionally changing the key, we can avoid the classic codebook attack mentioned above.

A generic block cipher is illustrated in Figure 4.1, where P_i is the ith block of plaintext and C_i is the corresponding block of ciphertext. The inner workings of the block cipher can be complex, but when encrypting, the net effect is simply to "lookup" the ciphertext block that corresponds to the given plaintext block in the specified codebook, where the codebook is determined by the key.

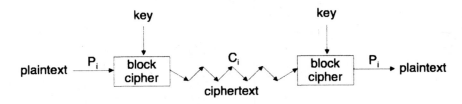

Figure 4.1: Generic block cipher.

Next, we consider some of the different ways that a block cipher can be used in practice. This further highlights the connection between modern block ciphers and codebooks. Then we discuss one popular method of block cipher design before we consider the cryptanalysis of some particular block ciphers.

4.2   Block Cipher Modes

Classic codebook ciphers often employed a so-called additive to make codebook attacks more difficult, and thereby extend the useable lifetime of the codebook. Typically, a codebook would convert words or phrases to strings of decimal digits. An additive book was filled with random string of digits. For each message, a random point in the additive book was selected, and subsequent entries in the additive book were added to the ciphertext before it was transmitted. The starting point in the additive book was usually sent in the clear (or slightly obfuscated) at the start of the message.

For modern block ciphers there is a somewhat analogous concept to the additive. But before we get to that, we consider an example to show why something like this is necessary for block ciphers.

Alice and Bob can use a modern block cipher as if it were a codebook. To do so, they must first agree on a key K, which they share and nobody else knows. This key distribution problem (which we discuss in Chapter 6) is a major issue in practice, but in this chapter, we assume that Alice and Bob know K, and nobody else knows K.

Given that Alice and Bob share the key K, then Alice can encrypt the plaintext block by block, and send the resulting ciphertext to Bob. We call this method of encrypting with a block cipher *electronic codebook* mode, or ECB mode, since it is the "electronic" equivalent of a classic codebook cipher.

When a block cipher is used in ECB mode, a problem arises that can have disastrous consequences for security. The problem is that as long as the key has not changed, the same plaintext block will be encrypted to the same ciphertext block. If this is the case, then whenever the attacker, Trudy, observes that ciphertext blocks C_i is the same as C_j, she immediately knows $P_i = P_j$. If Trudy should happen to know P_i then she knows P_j, and even if she does not know P_i, some information about the plaintext has leaked.

While this ECB issue may not seem like a serious concern, Figure 4.2 illustrates a case where it is devastating. In this example, an (uncompressed) image file has been encrypted using ECB mode. However, the encrypted file clearly does not protect the confidentiality of the data. This result occurs simply because plaintext blocks that are the identical, encrypt to the same ciphertext block, which allows patterns in the plaintext to bleed through into the ciphertext. For this reason, ECB mode should generally be avoided.

Figure 4.2: Trudy loves ECB mode [142].

An "additive" would solve the problem inherent in ECB mode, since identical plaintext blocks would then result in distinct ciphertext blocks. But is there a practical way to implement an electronic equivalent of an additive? In fact, there is a surprisingly straightforward technique that will achieve the desired result.

We define *cipher block chaining* mode, or CBC mode, as follows. Let IV be a non-secret initialization vector, which is n bits in length, where n is the size of a plaintext or ciphertext block. Then CBC encryption is defined as

$$C_i = E(P_i \oplus C_{i-1}, K), \quad \text{for} \quad i = 0, 1, 2, \ldots,$$

where the first block, C_0, requires special handling, since there is no C_{-1}. This is where we use the IV by defining $C_{-1} = \text{IV}$. It is necessary that we can decrypt, which is accomplished via

$$P_i = D(C_i, K) \oplus C_{i-1}, \quad \text{for} \quad i = 0, 1, 2, \ldots,$$

where, again, $C_{-1} = \text{IV}$. Since the IV is playing the role of a ciphertext block, it need not be secret—in practice, the IV is often sent as the first block, immediately before the first ciphertext block.

With CBC mode, if $P_i = P_j$, we almost certainly have $C_i \neq C_j$. This is the same effect that would be achieved by an additive in a classic codebook cipher. To see that this actually works, consider Figure 4.3, which shows Alice's image encrypted in CBC mode. Comparing this to Figure 4.2, the value of CBC mode is readily apparent.

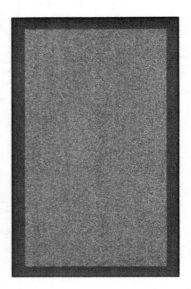

Figure 4.3: Trudy hates CBC mode [142].

CBC mode can also be used to provide data integrity. A message authentication code (MAC) consists of only the final block of CBC mode encryption, and this can be used to detect unauthorized changes to the data. Suppose Alice has plaintext blocks $P_0, P_1, \ldots, P_\ell$ and Alice and Bob share a symmetric key K. Then Alice generates a random IV and CBC "encrypts" her blocks of plaintext using this IV and the key K. She saves only the final ciphertext block C_ℓ, which is the MAC. Alice can then send C_ℓ, the IV and her plaintext message to Bob. Upon receiving the message, Bob uses the IV and the shared key K to CBC "encrypt" the received data. He compares the final ciphertext block with the received MAC, and if they agree he can be virtually certain that the data he has received is the data that Alice sent (see Problem 2). The MAC computation works because any change to a plaintext block will almost certainly propagate through the CBC encryption, resulting in a different final ciphertext block. Note that this is in stark contrast to CBC decryption, where changes do not propagate, as discussed above.

There are, in fact, many other block cipher modes.[1] One of the most useful modes is *counter* mode, or CTR mode (see Problem 3), which allows a block cipher to be used like a stream cipher [142].

4.3 Feistel Cipher

Before we dive into the cryptanalysis of specific block ciphers, we briefly consider one popular block cipher design strategy, due to Horst Feistel [70]. In a *Feistel Cipher* the plaintext block P is split into a left half L_0 and a right half R_0, that is,

$$P = (L_0, R_0).$$

Then for each round $i = 1, 2, \ldots, n$ a new left half L_i and a new right half R_i are computed as

$$L_i = R_{i-1} \tag{4.1}$$
$$R_i = L_{i-1} \oplus F(R_{i-1}, K_i) \tag{4.2}$$

where K_i is the *subkey* for round i, and F is the *round function*. The subkey K_i is derived from the key K, via a *key schedule* algorithm. The ciphertext C is the output of the final round, that is,

$$C = (L_n, R_n).$$

To decrypt, we can simply solve for L_{i-1} and R_{i-1} and run the Feistel process backwards from n to 1. More precisely, starting with $C = (L_n, R_n)$, for $i = n, n-1, \ldots, 1$, we compute

$$R_{i-1} = L_i$$
$$L_{i-1} = R_i \oplus F(R_{i-1}, K_i)$$

and the result is the corresponding plaintext $P = (L_0, R_0)$.

---

[1]But, so far as the authors are aware, there is no block cipher à la mode.

Mathematically, any round function F that outputs $n/2$ bits will work. However, it is also clear that the security of a Feistel Cipher depends on F, and not every F will result in a secure cipher. For example, $F(R_{i-1}, K_i) = R_{i-1}$ will yield an insecure cipher. One nice feature of a Feistel Cipher is that all questions of security boil down to questions about the round function F. The round function may be simple or complex, but at least the analyst knows to focus on F.

Many well-known block ciphers are Feistel Ciphers. For example, the most famous block cipher in history, the Data Encryption Standard (DES), is a Feistel Cipher. Even today, many block ciphers follow Feistel's approach, and many others (such as TEA [158]) vary only slightly from the strict definition given here. In an effort to decrease the number of rounds required, some recent block cipher designs (such as the AES) differ significantly from the standard Feistel approach.

Next, we turn our attention to Hellman's time-memory trade-off attack. This is an interesting attack method that can be applied to any block cipher. Then for the remainder of this chapter, we focus on the cryptanalysis of three specific block ciphers, namely, CMEA, Akelarre and FEAL. These three ciphers are each weak enough to be broken with a relatively small amount of work, and each attack has some interesting and noteworthy aspects.

The CMEA cipher is extremely simple, at least by block cipher standards. We discuss a chosen plaintext attack on CMEA, as well as a more realistic known plaintext attack. The known plaintext attack is particularly interesting, since it lends itself well to several algorithmic techniques that significantly improve the attack.

Akelarre combines important features from two different highly-regarded block ciphers. In spite of these "two rights," Akelarre is a "wrong" [82], since it is very weak.

FEAL is a seriously flawed cipher that, nevertheless, proved extremely important in the development of modern cryptanalysis. While there are many versions of FEAL, in this chapter we only consider the original version, now known as FEAL-4. We discuss both linear and differential cryptanalytic attacks on FEAL-4. In fact, differential cryptanalysis was originally developed to attack FEAL, and it later proved its true worth when applied to the cryptanalysis of the Data Encryption Standard (DES). In a sense, linear and differential cryptanalysis form the foundation on which modern block ciphers are constructed, since all block ciphers are designed to withstand attacks based on these two powerful techniques. Generally, these techniques are only of theoretical interest, but in the case of FEAL they yield practical attacks.

Differential cryptanalysis is also particularly well-suited for attacking hash functions. In Chapter 5, we present attacks on two well-known hash functions (MD4 and MD5) and both of these attacks rely on differential cryptanalytic techniques.

4.4   Hellman's Time-Memory Trade-Off

It usually takes a long time to find a shorter way.
— Anonymous

The objective of a time-memory trade-off (TMTO) is to do some one-time work so that each time the algorithm is executed it is more efficient. A TMTO is a general technique that can be applied to improve the performance of many types of algorithms.

In this section, we present Hellman's cryptanalytic TMTO, which was developed to attack the Data Encryption Standard (DES), but the approach will work against any block cipher. Our discussion here closely follows that given in [142].

4.4.1   Cryptanalytic TMTO

Martin Hellman describes his namesake cryptanalytic TMTO attack in [65]. Hellman's TMTO is a generic attack on a block cipher, but it is particularly effective against the Data Encryption Standard (DES) due to the small key size of 56 bits. Hellman's TMTO is a chosen plaintext attack.

Let P be a specified chosen plaintext block, and let $C = E(P, K)$ be the corresponding ciphertext block. We assume that whenever Trudy wants to attack this cipher, she can specify the plaintext block P and obtain the corresponding ciphertext block C. Trudy's goal is to recover the key K.

The most obvious way to attempt to break a cipher is an exhaustive key search. If the block cipher key K consists of k bits, then there are 2^k keys and via an exhaustive key search, Trudy would expect to find K after trying about half of the keys. Then the exhaustive key search attack has a "time" requirement of about 2^{k-1} and no "memory" (pre-computation) requirement.

Since we are assuming a known plaintext attack is possible, Trudy could instead pre-compute the ciphertext C for every possible key K for her specified chosen plaintext P. This attack requires a one-time pre-computation of 2^k encryptions and storage of these 2^k results. Then each time Trudy executes the attack, only a single table lookup is required, provided that the pre-computed list is sorted. Neglecting the one-time work, the time per attack is negligible. However, the one-time work is significantly larger than an exhaustive key search, so unless the attack is conducted many times, an exhaustive key search is more efficient.

Hellman's TMTO attack achieves a middle ground between the exhaustive key search and the massive pre-computation (and sorting) of all possible ciphertexts for a given plaintext. The TMTO attack requires some one-time work to generate a table of results (the "memory" part of the TMTO) that is then used to reduce the amount of work required (the "time" part of the TMTO) each time the attack is executed.

Suppose that Trudy wants to attack a block cipher where the block size is $n = 64$ bits and key is $k = 64$ bits. Since the key is 64 bits, there are 2^{64} distinct keys. Trudy first chooses a fixed plaintext P and she obtains the corresponding ciphertext $C = E(P, K)$. Trudy wants to recover the unknown key K.

Trudy first randomly select a 64-bit "starting point," denoted SP. She then constructs a *chain* of encryptions beginning from SP as follows. Trudy chooses a positive integer t and she successively computes

$$K_0 = SP$$
$$K_1 = E(P, SP)$$
$$K_2 = E(P, K_1)$$
$$K_3 = E(P, K_2)$$
$$\vdots$$
$$EP = K_{t-1} = E(P, K_{t-2})$$

where $EP = K_{t-1}$ is the "ending point" of the chain of encryptions of length t. Note that Trudy uses the ciphertext generated at one step as the key for the next step. Since the block size and the key size are identical, this works.

Figure 4.4 illustrates this the process of generating a chain of encryptions from SP to EP. To construct such a chain requires no knowledge of the inner workings of the block cipher. The only fact we have used here is that the block size and the key size are the same, but the process is easily modified if this is not the case.

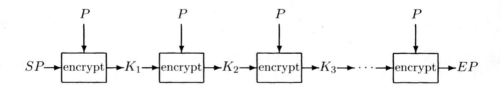

Figure 4.4: A chain of encryptions.

Another view of an encryption chain is given in Figure 4.5. Here, we have illustrated the chain as a path in the keyspace of the given block cipher.

Continuing with the example above, Trudy will generate m encryption chains, each of length t. Now suppose that Trudy computes $m = 2^{32}$ encryption chains, each of length $t = 2^{32}$, and none of the resulting chains overlap. This is unrealistic, since the chains essentially select elements of the keyspace

Figure 4.5: Chain of encryptions in the keyspace.

at random, but this assumption allows us to easily illustrate the concept behind Hellman's TMTO (below we consider a more realistic scenario). Then each of the 2^{64} keys lies within one exactly one chain. This idealized situation is illustrated in Figure 4.6.

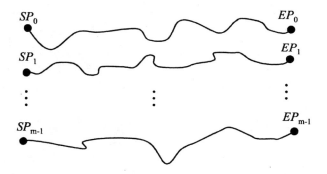

Figure 4.6: Trudy's ideal scenario.

Only the starting points and ending points of the chains are saved, that is, Trudy stores

$$(SP_0, EP_0), (SP_1, EP_1), (SP_2, EP_2), \ldots, (SP_{m-1}, EP_{m-1}).$$

For $m = 2^{32}$, the storage requirement is $2m = 2^{33}$ words, where each word is 64 bits. In general, $2m$ words must be stored, where each word is n bits. Generating the starting points and computing the corresponding end points is one-time work. The set of starting points and end points will be used each time Trudy conducts the attack to recover an unknown key K, so the pre-computation work can be amortized over the number of times the attack is conducted.

Once the pre-computation is completed, the attack is implemented as follows. Trudy chooses the same plaintext P that was used in the pre-computation phase, and she obtains the corresponding ciphertext C. To find the key K, Trudy computes an encryption chain beginning with C of maximum length t. That is, Trudy computes

$$X_0 = C$$
$$X_1 = E(P, X_0)$$
$$X_2 = E(P, X_1)$$
$$X_3 = E(P, X_2)$$

$$\vdots$$

and at each step $i = 1, 2, \ldots$ (up to a maximum of t steps), she compares X_i to each of the stored endpoints

$$EP_0, EP_1, \ldots, EP_{m-1}.$$

Since C is itself a possible key value, by our idealized assumption, C lies somewhere within exactly one chain. Suppose C is on chain j. Then for some $i \in \{0, 1, \ldots, t-1\}$, Trudy will find $X_i = EP_j$. This situation is illustrated in Figure 4.7.

Figure 4.7: Path from C to EP_j.

Once Trudy has found i and j such that $X_i = EP_j$, she can reconstruct the initial part of chain j from SP_j as

$$Y_0 = SP_j$$
$$Y_1 = E(P, Y_0)$$
$$Y_2 = E(P, Y_1)$$
$$Y_3 = E(P, Y_2)$$

$$\vdots$$

$$Y_{t-i-1} = E(P, Y_{t-i-2})$$
$$Y_{t-i} = X_0 = E(P, Y_{t-i-1}).$$

Since $C = X_0 = E(P, K)$, we have $K = Y_{t-i-1}$, as illustrated in Figure 4.8.

In this unrealistic example, the pre-computation phase of the attack requires about $tm = 2^{64}$ work. Having paid this initial price, each time Trudy executes the attack, she can expect that about 2^{31} encryptions will be required before an endpoint is found and another 2^{31} encryptions (approximately) will be needed until C is recovered from the starting point of the chain, giving a total work factor of 2^{32} per attack.

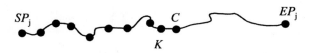

Figure 4.8: Finding K from SP_j.

If the attack is only to be executed once then an exhaustive key search, with an expected work of 2^{63}, would be more efficient. But if the attack is to be conducted many times, the pre-computation work can be amortized, since the work of 2^{32} per attack is negligible in comparison to the pre-computation.

Several refinements are possible. For example, Trudy could reduce the pre-computation work by computing chains that only cover a part of the key space. Then the probability of successfully finding an unknown key would precisely equal the percentage of the key space that is covered by chains. Necessarily, this is the way that Hellman's cryptanalytic TMTO attack works in practice.

4.4.2 Bad Chains

In reality, encryption chains are far different from the idealized case described above. Instead of obtaining chains that nicely partition the keyspace, Trudy will instead find chains that frequently merge with other chains or cycle. Chains that misbehave (from Trudy's perspective) in this way, create extra work during the labor intensive pre-computation phase, since beyond the point of a merge (or cycle), all encryptions are duplicating previous work. Merging and cycling chains are illustrated in Figure 4.9.

Figure 4.9: Bad chains.

In the pre-computation phase work is wasted due to cycling and merging. In addition, during the attack phase, cycles and merging lead to false alarms. To see why this is the case, suppose Trudy executes a TMTO attack beginning from C in Figure 4.9. Following the algorithm outlined above, she eventually arrives at the endpoint EP. She then starts from corresponding SP and reconstructs the chain that ends at EP, and she expects this to lead to the key K. In this case, she does not find K since C does not lie on the (SP, EP) chain.

If she can decrease the cycling and merging of chains, Trudy can reduce the number of false alarms, and thereby reduce the work effective factor during the pre-computation phase. To accomplish this, a "random function" F is used. With such a function, a chain is computed as

$$K_0 = SP$$
$$K_1 = F(E(P, SP))$$
$$K_2 = F(E(P, K_1))$$
$$K_3 = F(E(P, K_2))$$
$$\vdots$$
$$K_{t-1} = EP = F(E(P, K_{t-2})).$$

When $n = k$, we can choose F to be a permutation.

The advantage of using random functions is apparent if we compare Figures 4.10 and 4.11. In Figure 4.10, where no random function (or the same random) is used, once the two chains collide, they merge into a single chain. The points on the merged chains represented duplicated work which makes the pre-computation phase more expensive while not increasing the success rate in the attack phase.

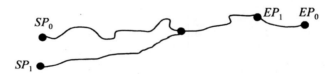

Figure 4.10: Merging chains.

On the other hand, in Figure 4.11 we see the effect of using different random functions. In this example, the functions F_0 and F_1 cause the chains to (almost certainly) diverge immediately after a collision. Consequently, with the use of different random functions, collisions can still occur, but the effects of merging and cycling are mitigated.

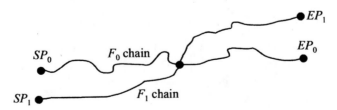

Figure 4.11: Non-merging chains.

Trudy could use a different random function for each chain, but it would be resource intensive to store all of these functions. Instead, she can obtain reasonable results by choosing r different functions, that is, we choose functions F_i, for $i = 0, 1, \ldots, r - 1$, and for each of these construct m chains, each beginning from a random starting point. As above, each chain is of length t. The set of chains that correspond to a specific function is known as a *table*. To summarize, we have r tables, m chains per table and t is the length of each chain.

The pre-computation will cover some percentage of the key space with chains. The resulting TMTO attack will find any key that lies within some chain, but it cannot recover any key that is not within at least one chain. The attack is therefore probabilistic and Trudy's objective is to maximize the probability of success for a given amount of work. This is accomplished by reducing merging and cycling as much as possible.

As above, we assume that the key length k is equal to the cipher block length n. Then the algorithm for pre-computing r tables of chains, each table having m chains, with each chain of length t, is given in Table 4.1.

Table 4.1: Algorithm to Find (SP, EP) Pairs

// Find (SP_{ij}, EP_{ij}), $i = 0, 1, \ldots, r - 1$ and $j = 0, 1, \ldots, m - 1$
findChains
    for $i = 0$ to $r - 1$
        Choose a random function F_i
        // Generate table i
        for $j = 0$ to $m - 1$
            Generate a random starting point SP_{ij}
            $K_0 = SP_{ij}$
            for $\ell = 1$ to $t - 1$
                $K_\ell = F_i(E(P, K_{\ell-1}))$
            next ℓ
            $EP_{ij} = K_{t-1}$
        next j
    next i
end findChains

The findChains algorithm in Table 4.1 finds a set of starting points and ending points for rm chains, each of length t. Consequently, at most rmt different keys could be recovered in the attack phase although, due to the inevitable cycling and merging, the actual number will be significantly less than rmt, as discussed below. If the desired key K is within one or more of the chains, then it will be found following the algorithm in Table 4.2.

The definition of the function findKey in Table 4.2 is given in Table 4.3. Note that findKey corresponds to the steps illustrated in Figure 4.8, while

Table 4.2: Algorithm to Find EP from C

```
// Given C, search for an endpoint EP
findEP(C)
    for i = 0 to r − 1
        Y = F_i(C)
        for j = 1 to t
            for ℓ = 0 to m − 1
                if Y == EP_{iℓ} then
                    found = findKey(i,ℓ,j)
                    if not found then
                        false alarm
                    else// found = K
                        return(found)
                    end if
                end if
            next ℓ
            Y = F_i(E(P,Y))
        next j
    next i
    return(key not found)
end findEP
```

the algorithm in Table 4.2 corresponds to the steps illustrated in Figure 4.7. Recall that r is the number of tables, m is the number of chains per table and t is the length of each chain. Also note that searching for a matching endpoint EP_{ij} in Table 4.2 can be made considerably more efficient if the pairs (SP_{ij}, EP_{ij}) within each table are sorted by endpoints. That is, we sort the pairs (SP_{ij}, EP_{ij}) by EP_{ij}, where $j = 0, 1, \ldots, m - 1$.

In Trudy's ideal world, all of the rmt chain elements would be distinct. If this were the case, then the chance of finding a randomly selected key would be $rmt/2^k$ (assuming $rmt \leq 2^k$; otherwise the probability would be one). Due to the merging and cycling discussed above, the real world is not so kind to Trudy (which is fortunate for Alice and Bob). While random functions help, they can only reduce the severity of the problem. Below we consider the probability of success in more detail.

For many block ciphers $k \neq n$; DES has $n = 64$ and $k = 56$, for example, while AES offers several combinations of block and key lengths. If the block length is not equal to the key length, then we cannot directly use the ciphertext C as a key K. This situation is only a minor nuisance which is easily resolved in practice by either truncating or expanding the ciphertext

Table 4.3: Algorithm to Find the Key from SP

```
// Is key K at position t − j − 1 in chain ℓ of table i?
findKey(i,ℓ,j)
      Y = SP_iℓ
      for q = 1 to t − j − 1
          Y = F_i(E(P, Y))
      next q
      K = Y
      if C = E(P, K) then
          return(K)
      else// false alarm
          return(not found)
      end if
end findKey
```

---

block as necessary. In contrast, the issue of merging and cycling chains is of fundamental importance in this TMTO attack.

4.4.3   Success Probability

What is Trudy's probability of success when she uses Hellman's TMTO attack? The fundamental problem is that keys can appear within more than one chain. Therefore, estimating the probability of success is equivalent estimating the probability of such duplication.

Perhaps the easiest[2] way to estimate the success probability for Hellman's TMTO attack is to use the classic occupancy problem, which is described nicely by Feller [49]. The details of the derivation are left as a homework problem, but the result is that Trudy's probability of successfully finding a key is approximately

$$P(\text{success}) = 1 - e^{-mtr/2^k}. \tag{4.3}$$

The probabilities given by (4.3) for various choices of mtr are given in Table 4.4. Hellman suggests choosing

$$m = t = r = 2^{k/3} \tag{4.4}$$

and, as can be seen in Table 4.4, the estimated probability of success for this choice of parameters is about 0.63.

In general, the cryptanalytic TMTO pre-computation requires mtr encryptions. The necessary storage is proportional to rm, the number of chains.

---

[2] "Easiest" is not necessarily the same as "easy."

Table 4.4: Approximate TMTO Success Probabilities

mtr	$P(\text{success})$
0	0
2^{k-5}	0.03
2^{k-4}	0.06
2^{k-3}	0.12
2^{k-2}	0.22
2^{k-1}	0.39
2^{k}	0.63
2^{k+1}	0.86
2^{k+2}	0.98
2^{k+3}	0.99
∞	1.00

If key K lies on one of the pre-computed chains then the time required when the attack is executed is about t (that is, $t/2$ steps, on average, are needed to find the matching EP and then another $t/2$ steps are required, on average, to find K). For the parameters in equation (4.4), this gives a pre-computation of 2^k encryptions, a memory requirement of $2^{2k/3}$, and a time requirement of $2^{2k/3}$. For example for DES—the cipher for which Hellman originally developed his attack—this yields a costly pre-computation of 2^{56}, but then the resulting time and memory requirements for each instance of the attack phase are both less than 2^{38}, with a high probability of success. Although the attack is only probabilistic, the probability of success is high, provided that the necessary pre-computation is feasible.

4.4.4 Distributed TMTO

Hellman's TMTO is easily adapted to a distributed attack. This version of the attack employs "distinguished points" [20]. The crucial insight is that we need not use fixed-length chains, but, instead, we can simply construct a chain until some easily distinguished point is found. For example, we can construct each chain until we obtain an output of the form

$$(x_0, x_1, \ldots, x_{s-1}, \underbrace{0, 0, \ldots, 0}_{n-s}).$$

Then each chain will, on average, be of length 2^{n-s}. In practice we would want to set a limit on the maximum length of a chain and reject any chain that exceeds the limit.

Using distinguished points, the pre-computation is similar to the case described above, except that we now retain triples

$$(SP_j, EP_j, \ell_j) \quad \text{for} \quad j = 0, 1, 2, \ldots, rm, \qquad (4.5)$$

where ℓ_j is the length of chain j (that is, the number of elements computed before a distinguished point was found). We must also keep track of the maximum length of any chain within a table; for table i, denote this as M_i.

Now suppose that r computers are available. Then each computer can search one of the r tables of chains. Computer i only needs to know the function F_i along with the ciphertext C and M_i, as well as the definition of a distinguished point. In particular, the triples in equation (4.5) do not need to be transmitted to any of the r computers, saving significant bandwidth and reducing the storage requirement on the individual computers.

Each computer then proceeds with the attack as described above, with the exception that instead of looking for a matching EP_j at each step, a distinguished point is sought. If computer i finds such a point within M_i iterations, the distinguished point is returned. Then secondary testing is necessary to determine whether the putative solution is an actual endpoint from table i or a false alarm. This secondary testing requires access to all (SP_j, EP_j, ℓ_j) triples in (4.5). Note that the overall work for secondary testing can be adjusted by selecting the definition of a distinguished point appropriately. If an endpoint is found, the process of attempting to recover K from the corresponding starting point proceeds exactly as in the non-distinguished point case discussed above.

4.4.5   TMTO Conclusions

Hellman's cryptanalytic TMTO does not rely on any particular properties of the underlying block cipher. But for the attack to be worth the effort, the keyspace must be small enough that the TMTO has a reasonable chance of success for a feasible pre-computation. Hellman's TMTO attack can be applied to any block cipher, provided there is sufficient computing power available for the initial pre-computation and enough storage to effectively deal with the tabulated results. Perhaps the most interesting aspect of this TMTO attack is that it requires no knowledge of the internal workings of the underlying block cipher.

In the remaining section of this chapter, we analyze attacks on three specific block ciphers, namely, CMEA, Akelarre, and FEAL. Each of these attacks depends heavily on the details of the underlying algorithms and it is therefore necessary to dig into the inner workings of these ciphers. While each of these ciphers is relatively weak, the attack methods differ considerably.

4.5 CMEA

PLEASE! DON'T VIOLATE THE LAW!
— TIA/EIA Standard [147]

According to United States patent 5,159,634, the Cellular Message Encryption Algorithm, or CMEA, was developed by James A. Reeds.[3] CMEA is a block cipher that was employed in the Telecommunications Industry Association (TIA) cell phone security architecture. Yes, this is the same TIA that was responsible for the deeply flawed ORYX stream cipher discussed in Chapter 3.

In this section we first describe a chosen plaintext attack on a simplified version of CMEA. Then we show that this attack can be extended to the real CMEA cipher. Finally, we discuss an interesting—and more realistic—known plaintext attack on our simplified version of CMEA and we show that this attack is also easily extended to the real CMEA cipher. The CMEA attacks presented here follow those given by Wagner, Schneier, and Kelsey in [152]. Legend has it that these attacks (or similar) originated with Greg Rose,[4] who was mysteriously forbidden from publishing his work [124].

4.5.1 CMEA Cipher

The CMEA cipher employs a 64-bit key and a variable block size, where the block size is specified in bytes. Typical block sizes are said to be two to six bytes [152].

The cipher utilizes a fixed 256-byte lookup table known as the Cave Table, which appears in Table 4.5. Contrary to what might be expected, the Cave Table is not a permutation and, in fact, only 164 distinct byte values appear. Furthermore, the distribution of the 164 values that do appear is not close to uniform: 97 of the bytes occur only once, while 44 appear twice, 21 appear three times and the remaining two both occur four times.

Given a byte that consists of hex digits x and y, let $C[xy]$ be the entry in row x and column y of the Cave Table. For example, $C[\text{0x4e}] = \text{0x09}$, since 0x09 is in row 0x4 and column 0xe of Table 4.5.

Let $K_0, K_1, \ldots, K_7$ be the eight bytes of the 64-bit CMEA key. Given the

---

[3]In 1998, Reeds deciphered Trithemius' *Steganographia*, a cryptanalytic challenge that had stood for nearly 500 years [119].

[4]This is the same Greg Rose whose work figures prominently in Section 5.4.5.

Table 4.5: Cave Table

	0	1	2	3	4	5	6	7	8	9	a	b	c	d	e	f
0	d9	23	5f	e6	ca	68	97	b0	7b	f2	0c	34	11	a5	8d	4e
1	0a	46	77	8d	10	9f	5e	62	f1	34	ec	a5	c9	b3	d8	2b
2	59	47	e3	d2	ff	ae	64	ca	15	8b	7d	38	21	bc	96	00
3	49	56	23	15	97	e4	cb	6f	f2	70	3c	88	ba	d1	0d	ae
4	e2	38	ba	44	9f	83	5d	1c	de	ab	c7	65	f1	76	09	20
5	86	bd	0a	f1	3c	a7	29	93	cb	45	5f	e8	10	74	62	de
6	b8	77	80	d1	12	26	ac	6d	e9	cf	f3	54	3a	0b	95	4e
7	b1	30	a4	96	f8	57	49	8e	05	1f	62	7c	c3	2b	da	ed
8	bb	86	0d	7a	97	13	6c	4e	51	30	e5	f2	2f	d8	c4	a9
9	91	76	f0	17	43	38	29	84	a2	db	ef	65	5e	ca	0d	bc
a	e7	fa	d8	81	6f	00	14	42	25	7c	5d	c9	9e	b6	33	ab
b	5a	6f	9b	d9	fe	71	44	c5	37	a2	88	2d	00	b6	13	ec
c	4e	96	a8	5a	b5	d7	c3	8d	3f	f2	ec	04	60	71	1b	29
d	04	79	e3	c7	1b	66	81	4a	25	9d	dc	5f	3e	b0	f8	a2
e	91	34	f6	5c	67	89	73	05	22	aa	cb	ee	bf	18	d0	4d
f	f5	36	ae	01	2f	94	c3	49	8b	bd	58	12	e0	77	6c	da

key, successively define

$$Q(x) = C[(x \oplus K_0) + K_1] + x$$
$$R(x) = C[(Q(x) \oplus K_2) + K_3] + x \qquad (4.6)$$
$$S(x) = C[(R(x) \oplus K_4) + K_5] + x$$

and, finally,

$$T(x) = C[(S(x) \oplus K_6) + K_7] + x, \qquad (4.7)$$

where x is a byte and the additions are all taken modulo 256. By the definition of T, it is apparent that $T(x) - x$ is in the Cave Table for any byte x and the same is true of $S(x) - x$, $R(x) - x$, and $Q(x) - x$. We make use of these facts—and the fact that the Cave Table is heavily biased—in the attacks discussed below.

As mentioned above, the CMEA block length is a variable number of bytes. Let n the number of bytes in the CMEA block. Then the CMEA encryption routine appears in Table 4.6.

Interestingly, the CMEA cipher is its own inverse. As a result, the encryption routine in Table 4.6 is also the decryption routine. That is, if we input the ciphertext to the algorithm, we obtain the corresponding plaintext.

Recall that the Enigma cipher is also its own inverse. For Enigma, there was a clear advantage to being self-inverse, since the same settings could be used for encryption and decryption. However, for CMEA—and modern ciphers in general—it is not clear that there is any significant advantage gained by being self-inverse.

Table 4.6: CMEA Encryption

```
// all arithmetic is mod 256 and "∨" is OR
// (c[0], c[1], . . . , c[n − 1]) = output block of ciphertext bytes
 1. (p[0], p[1], . . . , p[n − 1]) = input block of plaintext bytes
 2. z = 0
 3. for i = 0 to n − 1
 4.     k = T(z ⊕ i)
 5.     p[i] = p[i] + k
 6.     z = z + p[i]
 7. next i
 8. h = ⌊n/2⌋
 9. for i = 0 to h − 1
10.     p[i] = p[i] ⊕ (p[n − 1 − i] ∨ 1)
11. next i
12. z = 0
13. for i = 0 to n − 1
14.     k = T(z ⊕ i)
15.     z = z + p[i]
16.     c[i] = p[i] − k
17. next i
```

From the definition of CMEA in Table 4.6, we see that if the cryptanalyst, Trudy, can determine the function T, defined in 4.7, then she does not need to recover the key. The chosen plaintext attack discussed below does just that, while in the known plaintext attack, discussed further below, we recover the key. Provided that sufficient plaintext (chosen or known, as the case may be) is available, both attacks are extremely efficient.

The value $T(0)$ plays a special role in CMEA. Below, we show that in the chosen plaintext attack, once $T(0)$ is known, then $T(i)$, for $i = 1, 2, \ldots, 255$, can be recovered easily. In the known plaintext attack it is slightly more subtle, but $T(0)$ again is the linchpin of the attack. Consequently, in both of these attacks, the first priority is to determine $T(0)$.

For simplicity we restrict our attention to the case where the block size is $n = 3$ bytes. Analogous results hold for any block size.

4.5.2 SCMEA Cipher

Before attacking CMEA, we first present a slightly simplified version of the cipher, which we call simplified CMEA, or SCMEA. Our SCMEA cipher is identical to the CMEA cipher in Table 4.6 except that line 10 is replaced by

$$10.' \quad p[i] = p[i] \oplus p[n - 1 - i]$$

that is, the "$\lor 1$" has been eliminated.

Next, we present a chosen plaintext attack on SCMEA. This attack will then be extended to an effective attack on the (nonsimplified) CMEA cipher. After analyzing the chosen plaintext attack, we turn our attention to a more realistic—but more complex—known plaintext attack.

4.5.3 SCMEA Chosen Plaintext Attack

Suppose the plaintext block is of the form

$$(p_0, p_1, p_2) = ((\ell \oplus 1) - T(0), (j \oplus 2) - (\ell \oplus 1) - T(\ell), 0) \qquad (4.8)$$

for some ℓ and j. Then it is not difficult to show that the first byte of SCMEA ciphertext is

$$c_0 = (\ell \oplus 1 \oplus T(j)) - T(0). \qquad (4.9)$$

We can use this fact to develop an efficient chosen plaintext attack on the SCMEA cipher. In this attack, we first determine $T(0)$, then use $T(0)$ to obtain the remaining $T(j)$, for $j = 1, 2, \ldots, 255$.

We encrypt chosen plaintext blocks of the form

$$(p_0, p_1, p_2) = (1 - x_0, 1 - x_0, 0)$$

until we obtain a ciphertext byte c_0 that satisfies

$$c_0 = (1 \oplus x_0) - x_0 = \begin{cases} 1 & \text{if } x_0 \text{ is even} \\ 255 & \text{if } x_0 \text{ is odd.} \end{cases} \qquad (4.10)$$

Then according to (4.8) and (4.9), with $\ell = 0$ and $j = 0$, any x_0 for which (4.10) holds is consistent with $x_0 = T(0)$. Since $T(0) = T(0) - 0$, and we know that $T(x) - x$ is always in the Cave Table, we can restrict our attention to x_0 that are among the 164 distinct values that appear in the Cave Table.

Consider an x_0 for which (4.10) holds. Then x_0 is a putative value for $T(0)$. Now for each $j = 1, 2, 3, \ldots, 255$ we choose

$$(p_0, p_1, p_2) = (1 - x_0, (j \oplus 2) - x_0, 0)$$

and compute the corresponding ciphertext. If, in fact, $x_0 = T(0)$, then from (4.8) and (4.9) with $\ell = 0$, we have

$$c_0 = (1 \oplus x_j) - x_0, \qquad (4.11)$$

where $x_j = T(j)$. If (4.11) holds, we can solve for $x_j = (c_0 + x_0) \oplus 1$. Now, if it is the case that $x_0 = T(0)$, we have $x_j = T(j)$ and we know that $T(j) - j$ is in the Cave Table. Therefore, for each j, we check whether $x_j - j$ is in the Cave Table. If for any j we find $x_j - j$ is not in the Cave Table, we know that $x_0 \neq T(0)$ and we must continue to search for $T(0)$. If, on the other hand, $x_j - j$ is in the Cave Table for all j, then with high probability we have found $T(0)$.

Since there are 164 elements in the Cave Table, and since $T(0)$ must be in the Cave Table, we expect to find $T(0)$ using about 82 chosen plaintexts. Once we have determined $T(0)$, we can find all $T(j)$, for $j = 1, 2, 3, \ldots, 255$, with another 255 chosen plaintexts using (4.11). Consequently, the total chosen plaintext requirement is about 337 blocks. In addition, a small number of chosen plaintexts are required to resolve any false alarms. We give a careful analysis of these false alarms when we consider the corresponding CMEA attack below.

4.5.4 CMEA Chosen Plaintext Attack

Now consider the CMEA cipher. As in the SCMEA attack, above, we choose plaintext of the form

$$(p_0, p_1, p_2) = ((\ell \oplus 1) - T(0), (j \oplus 2) - (\ell \oplus 1) - T(\ell), 0). \qquad (4.12)$$

From the algorithm in Table 4.6, it can be shown that CMEA encryption of (4.12) yields

$$c_0 = ((\ell \oplus 1 \oplus (T(j) \vee 1)) - T(0) \qquad (4.13)$$

and

$$c_1 = (j \oplus 2) - (\ell \oplus 1) - T(\ell \oplus (T(j) \vee 1)). \qquad (4.14)$$

The corresponding equation for c_2 is slightly more complicated and somewhat more difficult to derive; see Problem 11.

Analogous to the SCMEA attack discussed above, in the CMEA attack we use (4.13) to determine whether a byte x_0 is consistent with $x_0 = T(0)$. Once we find a putative $T(0)$, we can then use (4.13) to find all putative $T(j) \vee 1$, for $j = 1, 2, \ldots, 255$. However, due to the "$\vee$" we can only determine $T(j)$ up to ambiguity in the low-order bit position. Fortunately, we can make use of (4.14) to resolve this ambiguity in the recovered $T(j)$, as discussed below. However, before we consider this issue, we first provide more details on the recovery of $T(0)$.

To find $T(0)$, we let $\ell = j = 0$ in (4.12) in which case the plaintext is

$$(p_0, p_1, p_2) = (1 - T(0), 1 - T(0), 0)$$

and, according to (4.13), (4.14), and the solution to Problem 11, the corresponding ciphertext is

$$c_0 = ((1 \oplus (T(0) \vee 1)) - T(0)$$
$$c_1 = 1 - T(T(0) \vee 1)$$
$$c_2 = T(0) - T(((1 \oplus (T(0) \vee 1)) + 1) \oplus 2).$$

We therefore encrypt chosen plaintexts of the form

$$(p_0, p_1, p_2) = (1 - x_0, 1 - x_0, 0)$$

and any of these that satisfy

$$c_0 = (1 \oplus (x_0 \vee 1)) - x_0 = \begin{cases} 0 & \text{and } x_0 \text{ is even} \\ 255 & \text{and } x_0 \text{ is odd} \end{cases}$$

are consistent with $x_0 = T(0)$. To further reduce the false alarm rate, we use the fact that if $x_0 = T(0)$ then

$$1 - c_1 - (x_0 \vee 1) \tag{4.15}$$

and

$$x_0 - c_2 - (((1 \oplus (x_0 \vee 1)) + 1) \oplus 2) \tag{4.16}$$

must both be in the Cave Table. Any false alarms that survives these tests will be discovered quickly.

After having found a putative $x_0 = T(0)$, we choose plaintext using (4.12), with $\ell = 0$ for $j = 1, 2, 3, \ldots, 255$. For each j, we recover a putative value for $x_j = T(j) \vee 1$ from (4.13). If neither $x_j - j$ nor $(x_j \oplus 1) - j$ is in the Cave Table, then we have detected a false alarm, and we discard x_0 and continue searching for $T(0)$. Assuming that $x_0 = T(0)$, then if only one of $x_j - j$ or $(x_j \oplus 1) - j$ is in the Cave Table, we have unambiguously determined $T(j)$. On the other hand, for each case where both $x_j - j$ and $(x_j \oplus 1) - j$ are in the Cave Table, the low-order bit of $T(j)$ is ambiguous.

To resolve the ambiguous low-order bit of a recovered $T(j)$, we can make use of (4.14). First, we recover all $T(j)$, for $j = 1, 2, \ldots, 255$, using $T(0)$ and the method described in the previous paragraph. We also maintain an auxiliary array, A, where $A_j = 0$ if the low-order bit of $T(j)$ is known, and $A_j = 1$ if the low-order bit of $T(j)$ is ambiguous. We can use A to resolve the ambiguous cases as follows.

Suppose that the low-order bit of $T(k)$ is ambiguous, that is, $T(k) - k$ and $(T(k) \oplus 1) - k$ are both in the Cave Table. Then we set $A_k = 1$. Now we find a t and j such that

$$k = t \oplus (T(j) \vee 1) \quad \text{and} \quad A_t = 0 \tag{4.17}$$

(that is, $T(t)$ is not ambiguous). If such a t and j are found, we then set

$$p_0 = (t \oplus 1) - T(0)$$
$$p_1 = (j \oplus 2) - (t \oplus 1) - T(t)$$
$$p_2 = 0$$

and encrypt this plaintext block using CMEA, to obtain the the corresponding ciphertext block (c_0, c_1, c_2). From (4.14), we have

$$T(t \oplus (T(j) \vee 1)) = (j \oplus 2) - (t \oplus 1) - c_1,$$

which, by our choice of t and j gives

$$T(k) = (j \oplus 2) - (t \oplus 1) - c_1.$$

There is no ambiguity in this equation, and consequently we have resolved the low-order bit of $T(k)$. Problem 14 explores the probability that this part of the attack will fail. Note that this part of the attack fails if for an ambiguous $T(k)$, we cannot find t and j satisfying (4.17).

Now we provide a careful analysis of the expected number of chosen plaintexts required in this attack. Each time we test an element in the Cave Table to see whether it is a possible $T(0)$, there is a chance of a false alarm. As noted above, letting $\ell = j = 0$ in (4.12), a plaintext of the form

$$(p_0, p_1, p_2) = (1 - T(0), 1 - T(0), 0)$$

yields

$$c_0 = \begin{cases} 0 & \text{if } T(0) \text{ is even} \\ 255 & \text{if } T(0) \text{ is odd.} \end{cases}$$

Another interesting and related property of CMEA encryption is considered in Problem 12.

Since, on average, we require 82 iterations before we can determine $T(0)$, the probability of false alarms can be approximated by a binomial distribution with $n = 81$ and $p = 1/128$. Therefore, the expected number of false alarms is about $np = 81/128 \approx 0.63$. If we include a check that both (4.15) and (4.16) are in the Cave Table, then the expected number of false alarms drops to $0.63(164/256)^2 \approx 0.258$.

Recall that 164 of the 256 elements in the Cave Table are distinct. Also, we have that $T(i) - i$ is in the Cave Table, for $i = 0, 1, 2, \ldots, 255$. Since $T(0)$ is in the Cave Table, about 82 chosen plaintexts are required before we expect to find $T(0)$. Once $T(0)$ has been recovered, one chosen plaintext is required to determine each of the remaining values $T(i)$, for $i = 1, 2, 3, \ldots, 255$. This gives a total of 337 chosen plaintexts.

However, some of the recovered $T(i)$ will be ambiguous in the low order bit. The low order bit of $T(i)$ is known if either $T(i) - i$ or $(T(i) \oplus 1) - i$

is not in the Cave Table. It can be shown (see Problem 9) that given any x in the Cave Table, the probability that $((x+i) \oplus 1) - i$ is in the Cave Table is approximately 0.6. Consequently, we expect to find about $0.6 \cdot 255 \approx 153$ ambiguous entries, and for each of these, one additional chosen plaintext is required. Note that if neither $T(i) - i$ nor $(T(i) \oplus 1) - i$ is in the Cave Table, then a false alarm has occurred, that is, the putative value of $T(0)$ is incorrect.

Assuming $x \in \{0, 1, 2, \ldots, 255\}$, is selected uniformly it can be shown (see Problem 10) that the probability that x and $x \oplus 1$ are both not in the Cave Table is about 0.11. A false alarm for $T(0)$ is detected as soon as such a value is generated. Each additional step that is needed before detecting a false alarm requires one chosen plaintext, so the expected number of chosen plaintexts per false alarm is about 9. Overall, we expect false alarms to require about $0.258 \cdot 9 \approx 2.3$ additional chosen plaintexts.

Combining these results, we find that the total expected number of chosen plaintexts is $82 + 255 + 153 + 2.3 \approx 492.3$. This accords remarkably well with the empirical data in Table 4.7, which is the average of 10^6 trials, using a randomly generated key for each trial.

Table 4.7: Chosen Plaintext Requirements

Trials	Average to Find $T(0)$	Find $T(j) \vee 1$	Average Ambiguous	Average False Alarms	Total
10^6	81.84	255	152.89	2.43	492.16

In practice, this chosen plaintext attack is likely to be unrealistic, due to the relatively large number of plaintext blocks required, and, especially, due to the fact that we must choose the plaintext. Next, we consider a known plaintext attack which is much more likely to be practical. First, we apply the attack to SCMEA, then we explain how the attack can be extended to CMEA. This known plaintext attack (for CMEA) appears in [152].

4.5.5 SCMEA Known Plaintext Attack

As with the chosen plaintext attack, above, this attack relies on the fact that $T(0)$ plays a special role in the CMEA cipher (and also in SCMEA). The known plaintext attack we describe here has two phases, a primary phase and a secondary phase, where the objective of the primary phase is to determine $T(0)$, or a small number of candidates for $T(0)$. Then in the secondary phase, we determine the key, and simultaneously eliminate any invalid putative $T(0)$ that survived the primary phase.

We briefly outline each of the two phases of the SCMEA attack before providing more details on both phases. Then we extend the attack to CMEA.

Outline of Attack

In the primary phase of the attack, we make use of the fact that if we know $T(0)$, then known plaintext–ciphertext pairs place restrictions on the possible values of other $T(j)$. In fact, we can show that each known plaintext gives us three tests that can be used to check the validity of other putative $T(j)$. If any of these tests fail, then the computed value of $T(j)$ must be incorrect, which implies that the assumed value of $T(0)$ is incorrect.

For the primary phase of the attack, we guess each possible value for $T(0)$, and use the known plaintext to deduce information about other $T(j)$ bytes. If our guess for $T(0)$ is incorrect, given sufficient known plaintext, we are highly likely to arrive at a contradiction, at which point we can eliminate our current putative $T(0)$ as a candidate for $T(0)$.

Once all possible $T(0)$ have been tested in the primary phase, we will have determined $T(0)$, or a small number of candidates for $T(0)$, depending on the number of known plaintext blocks available. We then move on to the secondary phase, where we use a combinatorial search technique known as *backtracking* [87] to recover the key. This secondary phase relies on information accumulated during the primary phase—information gleaned from the known plaintext. The success of the secondary phase depends not only on the fact that $T(j) - j$ is in the Cave Table, as can be seen from (4.7), but also on the fact that the intermediate values, $Q(j) - j$, $R(j) - j$, and $S(j) - j$, are in the Cave Table, as can be seen in (4.6).

Of course, we want to minimize the amount of known plaintext that is needed. But as we reduce the amount of known plaintext, we are increasingly likely to find additional putative values for $T(0)$ that survive the primary phase of the attack, and we are more likely to lack sufficient information to trim the keys found in the secondary phase to a sufficiently small number.

However, by using another combinatorial search technique, it is possible to further reduce the known plaintext requirement. Provided that we have uniquely determined a few $T(j)$ values in the primary phase, a *meet-in-the-middle* approach can be used to dramatically reduce the number of putative keys recovered, as compared to the simpler (and more intuitive) backtracking method mentioned in the previous paragraph. Meet-in-the-middle is a standard technique from the field of combinatorial search, where it goes by the clever name of meet-in-the-middle. When it is applicable, a meet-in-the-middle attack can essentially provide a square root improvement in the work factor, but it can be relatively complex to implement.

Next, we describe this known plaintext attack in more detail. For simplicity, we initially focus on the SCMEA cipher, then we show that the attack extends easily to CMEA—although significantly more known plaintext is required to obtain comparable results.

Primary Phase

Our first objective is to determine $T(0)$. Since $T(0)$ is in the Cave Table, $T(0)$ is limited to one of the 164 distinct bytes that appear in the Cave Table.

For each of the 164 possible choices for $T(0)$, we construct a 256×256 table A, such that $A_{i,j} = 1$ if it is possible that $T(i) = j$, and $A_{i,j} = 0$ if it is not possible that $T(i) = j$. To begin, we initialize $A_{i,j} = 1$ for all i and j. Then we make use of the restrictions inherent in the Cave Table to find impossible entries in A, that is, we find i and j for which we must have $A_{i,j} = 0$ due to the structure of the Cave Table. Finally, we use the known plaintext to mark additional impossible entries in the A table.

Denote the 164 distinct Cave Table bytes as

$$v_0, v_1, v_2, \ldots, v_{163}.$$

Since $T(j) - j$ is in the Cave Table for $j = 0, 1, 2, \ldots, 255$, we have

$$T(j) \in \{v_0 + j, v_1 + j, v_2 + j, \ldots, v_{163} + j\}.$$

This immediately places 92 zeros in row j of A. We repeat this for each row of A, so that each row has 164 ones and 92 zeros. Note that this is independent of the known plaintext or any assumption on the value of $T(0)$.

Now for a given putative $T(0)$, we can use the known plaintext to deduce additional information about various $T(j)$ and, in the process, place additional 0s in the table A. Ideally, for any incorrect choice of $T(0)$, we will arrive at a contradiction from the entries in A. In practice, it is sufficient to simply reduce the number of possible choices for $T(0)$ to a small number.

As above, we are assuming that the block size is three bytes. Denote a known 3-byte plaintext block as $P = (p_0, p_1, p_2)$ and let $C = (c_0, c_1, c_2)$ be the corresponding ciphertext block.

By carefully stepping through the SCMEA algorithm, where we are assuming a block size of $n = 3$, it can be shown that

$$c_0 = ((p_0 + T(0)) \oplus (p_2 + T((p_0 + p_1 + T(0) + T((p_0 + T(0)) \oplus 1)) \oplus 2)) - T(0),$$

which we rewrite as

$$((c_0 + T(0)) \oplus (p_0 + T(0))) - p_2$$
$$= T((p_0 + p_1 + T(0) + T((p_0 + T(0)) \oplus 1)) \oplus 2). \qquad (4.18)$$

Now if we are given a known plaintext block $P = (p_0, p_1, p_2)$ and the corresponding ciphertext byte c_0, we can use (4.18) to eliminate some potential values of $T(j)$.

For example, suppose the $(p_0, p_1, p_2) = (0xa1, 0x95, 0x71)$ and the corresponding ciphertext block has $c_0 = 0x04$. Further, suppose that for this key, we guess $T(0) = 0x34$. Then (4.18) reduces to

$$0x7c = T((0x6a + T(0xd4)) \oplus 2).$$

As noted above, there are 164 possible value for $T(0xd4)$. Once we specify one of these values for a putative $T(0xd4)$, the argument to the "outer" T function is known, as is the value of the "inner" T function.

Now let $y = (0x6a + T(0xd4)) \oplus 2$. If $A_{y,0x7c} = 0$, then this impossible entry in the table immediately implies that our guess for $T(0xd4)$ is incorrect, and we mark it as such in the A table.

For example, since 0 is in the Cave Table, we guess $T(0xd4) = 0xd4$ to see if an impossibility arises. In this case, $(0xd4 + 0x6a) \oplus 2 = 0x3c$ and we test whether $T(0x3c) = 0x7c$ is possible, based on the current A table, that is we check the value of $A_{0x3c,0x7c}$. If this is 0, we know that $T(0xd4) \neq 0xd4$ and we specify this in the A table by setting $A_{0xd4,0xd4} = 0$. We then continue to test each of the remaining 163 choices for $T(0xd4)$ in a similar manner.

If it should happen that all of the 164 possible choices for $T(0xd4)$ are impossible, then we know that our guess for $T(0)$ is incorrect and we proceed to our next guess for $T(0)$. In any case, we have almost certainly placed additional impossible entries in the A table, thereby increasing our knowledge of T, assuming that the $T(0)$ assumption is correct.

We must repeat this for each known plaintext block. Furthermore, if any new impossible entries are added to A, we must then repeat the entire process for all of the known plaintext again. This must be iterated until no changes are made to A during one entire pass through the known plaintexts.

With enough known plaintexts, we will uniquely determine $T(0)$, and in the process, we might uniquely determine additional values of $T(j)$. We will also be able to place significant restrictions on many of the $T(j)$ that have not been uniquely determined.

Unfortunately, the amount of known plaintext to uniquely determine $T(0)$ by this approach is large. However, we are not using all of the available information. Formulas analogous to (4.18) can be found for both c_1 and c_2 (see Problem 15). By using this additional information, we can dramatically reduce the known plaintext required to uniquely determine $T(0)$. Empirical estimates of the number of plaintext blocks required are summarized in Table 4.8.

Secondary Phase: Backtracking

After successful completion of the primary phase, we will have recovered $T(0)$, or a small number of candidates. We now discuss a method for determining

Table 4.8: Approximate Known Plaintext Required

Ciphertext bytes used	c_0 only	c_0 and c_1	c_0, c_1 and c_2
Known plaintext blocks	300	90	60

the key from the information accumulated to this point. For the remainder of this section, we assume that in the primary phase we uniquely determined $T(0)$; if not, we simply repeat this secondary phase for each candidate $T(0)$.

In the chosen plaintext attack, discussed above, we recovered T, without finding the key. In contrast, in the secondary phase of the known plaintext attack presented here, we recover the key, using the A table obtained in the primary phase.

From (4.7) we have

$$T(x) = C[(S(x) \oplus K_6) + K_7] + x$$

and $S(x) - x$ is an element of the Cave Table. Consequently,

$$T(x) = C[((v + x) \oplus K_6) + K_7] + x$$

for some v in the Cave Table. We select a putative (K_6, K_7), and a particular x. Then we test each v that is in the Cave Table, by computing

$$y = C[((v + x) \oplus K_6) + K_7] + x$$

and looking up the value of $A_{x,y}$. If for any x we find that every v in the Cave Table yields $A_{x,y} = 0$, then the choice of (K_6, K_7) must be incorrect. This will reduce the number of possible partial keys (K_6, K_7), with the number of survivors depending on the amount of information available in A, which, in turn, depends on the number of known plaintexts. Typical results for this secondary phase of the SCMEA attack are given in Table 4.9.

Table 4.9: Number of Surviving (K_6, K_7)

Known plaintext blocks	50	75	100	150
Partial keys (K_6, K_7)	19800	2002	42	2

For each putative (K_6, K_7), we can determine putative (K_4, K_5) values from the pair of equations

$$S(x) = C[(R(x) \oplus K_4) + K_5] + x$$
$$T(x) = C[(S(x) \oplus K_6) + K_7] + x.$$

To accomplish this, for each candidate (K_4, K_5), we compute

$$y = C[((v + x) \oplus K_4) + K_5] + x$$

and we use the putative pair (K_6, K_7) to find

$$T(x) = C[(y \oplus K_6) + K_7] + x.$$

We are now in precisely the same position as discussed above, except that here we rule out (K_4, K_5) key pairs instead of (K_6, K_7) pairs.

Suppose that we find a total of n pairs (K_6, K_7). Then for each of these we would expect to find about the same number of (K_4, K_5) pairs, since we are relying on the same A table in both cases. The attack can be extended to find putative (K_2, K_3) and putative (K_0, K_1), which enables us to obtain putative keys $(K_0, K_1, \ldots, K_7)$. The expected number of such keys is about n^4, where n is the number of (K_6, K_7) pairs. Of course, n depends on the number of known plaintext blocks available. From Table 4.9 we see that if we have 150 known plaintext blocks available, then we can expect to recover 16 putative keys. This clearly shows that the SCMEA cipher is extremely weak, and in the next section we show that these results are easily extended to CMEA—although the known plaintext requirement increases significantly.

However, 150 known plaintext bytes may be unrealistic in practice. With just 75 known plaintext blocks available, the number of putative keys would be almost 2^{44}. While this is a significant improvement over an exhaustive search, where there are 2^{64} possible keys, it is worth considering whether we can do better, particularly since the equivalent CMEA attack will require more known plaintext.

We now discuss an alternative approach to the secondary phase of this attack. This alternative is slightly more complex, but it results in a lower known plaintext requirement.

Secondary Phase: Meet-in-the-Middle

An alternative way to complete the secondary phase is a meet-in-the-middle attack, as discussed in [152]. For this attack to be practical, we must have determined $T(j)$ for at least four distinct values of j during the primary phase. This would be indicated by four rows of the A table that each contain a single one. The expected number of such rows depends on the number of known plaintext blocks available—typical numbers appear in Table 4.10. From these tabulated results, we see that this attack will be possible provided somewhat more than 50 known plaintext blocks are available. However, the attack can also be used if we do not have four uniquely determined values, provided that we have at least four rows of A, each of which has a small number of possible $T(j)$.

Table 4.10: Number of Uniquely-Determined T Elements

Known plaintext blocks	50	75	100	150
Number uniquely determined	3	6	15	45

First, we provide an intuitive description of the meet-in-the-middle attack. Then we consider a more efficient implementation.

Suppose that from the A table, we have uniquely determined $T(a)$, $T(b)$, $T(c)$, and $T(d)$, for some a, b, c, and d. Then for each of the 2^{32} choices for (K_0, K_1, K_2, K_3), we compute

$$Q(a) = C[(a \oplus K_0) + K_1] + a$$
$$R(a) = C[(Q(a) \oplus K_2) + K_3] + a$$

and similarly for b, c, and d. Then we store $R = (R(a), R(b), R(c), R(d))$ and the putative key bytes (K_0, K_1, K_2, K_3) in a row of a table M. Then M has 2^{32} rows, which we sort on R.

Next, we work backwards from the $T(a)$, $T(b)$, $T(c)$, and $T(d)$, searching for a matching R in the table. More precisely, for each $\tilde{K} = (K_4, K_5, K_6, K_7)$, we find all pairs $(S(a), R(a))$, such that

$$S(a) = C[(R(a) \oplus K_4) + K_5] + a$$
$$T(a) = C[(S(a) \oplus K_6) + K_7] + a$$

(and similarly for b, c, and d), which gives us $\tilde{R} = (R(a), R(b), R(c), R(d))$. If we find $\tilde{R}$ in the table M, then we have met-in-the-middle, and thereby found a key $K_0, K_1, \ldots, K_7$ for which $T(a)$ matches the known value a (according to the A table), and also for b, c, and d. We can then test each of these putative keys via trial decryption using known plaintext blocks.

The only tricky part of this attack is that we must invert the Cave Table entries, and this will often generate more than one possible input value. In such cases, we need to try them all. Nevertheless, by this approach, the work factor is essentially the square root of the work required for an exhaustive search. All that is needed to apply this attack is a set of four T values, which, given sufficient known plaintext, will be obtained from the primary phase.

A more clever (and more practical) approach to the meet-in-the-middle attack is given in [152]. As above, we assume that $T(a)$, $T(b)$, $T(c)$, and $T(d)$ are known. Then for each possible (K_0, K_1, K_2), we compute

$$a' = (C[(a \oplus K_0) + K_1] + a) \oplus K_2$$

and similarly for b', c', and d'. Next, we create a table M with rows of the form

$$a', b', c', d'. K_0, K_1, K_2,$$

which are indexed by the 3-byte quantity $(a' - d', b' - d', c' - d')$, where the subtractions are each mod 256. The reason for this strange choice of indexing will become clear shortly.

Note that the table M only has 2^{24} rows, so it is efficient to construct and requires minimal storage. When the table M is completed, then for each (K_4, K_5, K_6, K_7), we find a'' such that

$$R(a) = C[a''] + a$$
$$S(a) = C[(R(a) \oplus K_4) + K_5] + a$$
$$T(a) = C[(S(a) \oplus K_6) + K_7] + a$$

and similarly for b'', c'', and d''. From the definition of a', we see that

$$R(a) = C[a' + K_3] + a$$

and, therefore, we have $a'' = a' + K_3$. It follows that

$$a'' - d'' = (a' + K_3) - (d' + K_3) = a' - d'$$

and, similarly,

$$(a'' - d'', b'' - d'', c'' - d'') = (a' - d', b' - d', c' - d').$$

Consequently, we can use a'', b'', c'', and d'' to form an index into the table M corresponding to a', b', c', and d'. Furthermore, assuming that we find a match in M, we can immediately find a putative K_3 from the equation $K_3 = a'' - a'$, at which point we have recovered the entire putative key $K_0, K_1, \ldots, K_7$. We must test each putative key by trial decryption (or encryption) using the known plaintext to eliminate false alarms.

Note that the meet-in-the-middle and backtracking attacks can be combined. That is, we could use the backtracking attack to determine putative (K_6, K_7) pairs (and perhaps, also (K_4, K_5)), depending on the number of (K_6, K_7) obtained), then do the meet-in-the-middle attack restricted to these candidate partial keys.

4.5.6   CMEA Known Plaintext Attack

The known plaintext attack on CMEA is almost identical to the SCMEA known plaintext attack discussed above. In fact, once the A table has been constructed, the attacks are identical. However, the construction of the A table is slightly more complex for CMEA and it requires significantly more known plaintext.

To construct the A table for CMEA, we guess a $T(0)$ and use the restrictions inherent in the Cave Table to mark 92 entries of each row as impossible values. This is precisely the same strategy that was employed in the SCMEA attack discussed above.

For SCMEA, we used (4.18) (and analogous equations involving c_1 and c_2) to further increase the density of impossible entries in A. For CMEA, the approach is the same, except that the equation that corresponds to (4.18) is slightly more complicated. Specifically, we have

$$(c_0 + T(0)) \oplus (p_0 + T(0))$$
$$= (p_2 + T((p_0 + p_1 + T(0) + T((p_0 + T(0)) \oplus 1)) \oplus 2)) \vee 1. \quad (4.19)$$

The "$\vee\, 1$" implies that we cannot determine the low-order bit. This reduces the number of impossible values for a given amount of known plaintext, since both 0 and 1 must be tested in the low-order bit, and both must be ruled out before we can mark an entry as impossible. A similar situation holds for the equations involving c_1 and c_2. Again, once the A table has been constructed the attack is the same as the SCMEA attack described above.

It is claimed in [152] that this attack (using the meet-in-the-middle secondary phase) will succeed on CMEA provided "50 to 80" known plaintext blocks are available. Problems 16 and 17 ask for more precise empirical estimates. Using only c_0, we have found that about 420 known plaintext blocks are required to uniquely determine $T(0)$. From Table 4.8 we see that the comparable number for SCMEA is 300 blocks. Obtaining analytic results for the number of required plaintexts would be an interesting and challenging exercise.

4.5.7 More Secure CMEA?

Is it possible to slightly modify the CMEA cipher and significantly increase the security of the cipher? The attacks presented here rely heavily on the fact that the distribution of the Cave Table entries is highly skewed. Consequently, if we replace the Cave Table with a fixed permutation of the byte values, these attacks would likely fail.

There are many other possible modifications of CMEA that might yield a stronger cipher. For example, one alternative would be to make the Cave Table key-dependent. Of course, this could be combined with the previous suggestion, replacing the Cave Table with a key-dependent permutation. This would seem to greatly complicate the cryptanalysis of the CMEA cipher. It might also be interesting to consider whether it is possible to modify the cipher so that it is reasonably secure, yet the Cave Table remains as it is currently configured.

4.6   Akelarre

It was said in the trials that Akerbeltz presided over the witches' gatherings,
which happened every Monday, Wednesday and Friday.
These gatherings came to be called akelarre, the "goat meadow."
— Secret History of the Witches [33]

Akelarre is a block cipher that combines features of two strong block ciphers
with the goal of producing a more efficient strong cipher. Specifically, Akelarre uses mixed mode arithmetic, which is a primary cryptographic feature
of the highly respected IDEA cipher, and Akelarre also makes heavy use of
rotations, which are a crucial element in RC5, another highly-regarded block
cipher. By combining important elements from two strong ciphers, you might
expect that Akelarre would itself be a strong cipher. If so, you would be sadly
mistaken.

The Akelarre cipher was proposed in 1996 [3] and within a year, devastating attacks had been discovered [82]. In fact, Akelarre is an extremely weak
cipher—in spite of (or, more likely, because of) its relatively complex design.
Below, we describe a known plaintext attack, but there is also a ciphertext
only attack, which is only slightly more complex.

4.6.1   Akelarre Cipher

Akelarre is defined for any number of rounds, but its developer conjectured
that it is secure with four rounds. Amazingly, the cipher is insecure for any
number of rounds. The attack we describe is given in [82], and this attack
requires a small amount of work, regardless of the number of rounds. The
weaknesses in Akelarre are also discussed in [50].

The Akelarre block size is 128-bits. The key length can be any multiple
of 64 bits, but for simplicity, we assume here that the key size is the same
as the block length, that is, 128 bits. The difficulty of the attack does not
increase if the key size is increased.

A key schedule algorithm is used to expand the key into the required
number of 32-bit subkeys, where this number of subkeys depends on the
number of rounds. In Akelarre, the input, output, subkey and all intermediate
calculations employ 32-bit words. In particular, the 128 bit input block is
treated as four 32-bit sub-blocks, the output consists of four 32-bit sub-blocks
and all subkeys are 32 bits.

The encryption algorithm consists of an input transformation, followed
by R rounds, and, finally, an output transformation, as illustrated in Figure 4.12. The key schedule is also specified as part of the cipher algorithm.

The plaintext block first passes through the input transformation in Fig-

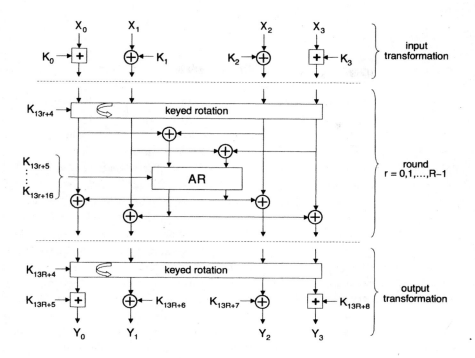

Figure 4.12: Akelarre.

ure 4.12, where mixed mode arithmetic operations are employed to combine the subkey with the four 32-bit sub-blocks of plaintext. In Figure 4.12, "$\oplus$" is XOR, while the other "plus" operation represents addition modulo 2^{32}.

The Akelarre round function is also illustrated in Figure 4.12. We use r to denote the current round, where $r = 0, 1, \ldots, R - 1$.

Each round begins with a "keyed rotation," where the right 7 bits of the 32-bit subkey K_{13r+4} are used to determine the size of the rotation. That is, $\langle K_{13r+4} \rangle_{25\ldots31}$, interpreted as an integer, is the amount that the input is rotated left. Recall that "$\lll$" is our notation for a left cyclic shift. Let (A_0, A_1, A_2, A_3) be the 128-bit input to round r (written as four 32-bit words) and let (B_0, B_1, B_2, B_3) be the output of the keyed rotation at the beginning of round r. Then

$$(B_0, B_1, B_2, B_3) = (A_0, A_1, A_2, A_3) \lll \langle K_{13r+4} \rangle_{25\ldots31}.$$

Let (T_0, T_1) be the output of the box labeled "AR" in Figure 4.12. Then for a given 128-bit block (B_0, B_1, B_2, B_3), we have

$$(T_0, T_1) = \mathrm{AR}(B_0 \oplus B_2, B_1 \oplus B_3),$$

where we have ignored the dependence on the subkey. The AR function is defined below.

Let (D_0, D_1, D_2, D_3) be the output of round r. Then given B_i and T_i as defined above, we have

$$(D_0, D_1, D_2, D_3) = (B_0 \oplus T_1, B_1 \oplus T_0, B_2 \oplus T_1, B_3 \oplus T_0).$$

The D_i are the inputs to the next round, except for the final round, where they become the inputs to the output transformation.

After R rounds, there is an output transformation, which consists of another keyed rotation, followed by XOR and addition of subkey words, as illustrated in Figure 4.12. The result of the output transformation is four 32-bit words which form the ciphertext block.

The heart of Akelarre is the addition–rotation (AR) structure, the details of which appear in Figure 4.13. One pass through the AR structure can be viewed as 14 addition–rotations, each applied to a 32-bit sub-block. Each addition consists of subkey added to the current sub-block, with the addition taken modulo 2^{32}. Each rotation affects 31 bits, as explained below, with the amount of the rotation determined by the inputs to the AR structure.

Typically, iterated block ciphers split the input in half and then operate on these halves. Since the AR structure in Akelarre operates on 32-bit quarter-blocks instead of 64-bit half-blocks, Akelarre's addition–rotations can be viewed as 14 half-rounds. Consequently, it could be argued that one pass through the AR structure is roughly equivalent to seven rounds of a typical block cipher, but this is somewhat misleading since each Akelarre addition–rotation operation is extremely simple.

In Figure 4.13, we denote the two 32-bit inputs to the AR structure as W_0 and W_1 and the output 32-bit words as Z_0 and Z_1. Note that W_1 is processed first, with the bits of W_0 used to determine the required rotations, and the resulting output is Z_1. Then W_0 is processed, with the bits of Z_1 used to determine the rotations, and the resulting output is Z_0.

The rotations in the AR structure are left rotations, but they are slightly different than the standard rotations used in the Akelarre round function and output transformation. In each AR rotation, either the low-order or the high-order bit remains fixed (as indicated by a 1 in Figure 4.13) and the remaining 31 bits (indicated by a 31) are rotated. The amount of the rotation ranges from 0 to 31 in some steps, and from 0 to 15 in other steps, depending on whether five or four bits are used to determine the rotation. For example, the first step in the AR structure consists of a left rotation of bits 0 through 30 of W_1, with the rightmost bit (bit 31 in our notation) remaining fixed and the size of the rotation determined by $\langle W_0 \rangle_{27...31}$. In our standard notation, this rotation can be written as

$$(((\langle W_1 \rangle_{0...30} \lll \langle W_0 \rangle_{27...31}), \langle W_1 \rangle_{31...31}).$$

This result is then added (modulo 2^{32}) to subkey K_{13r+5}. After six more

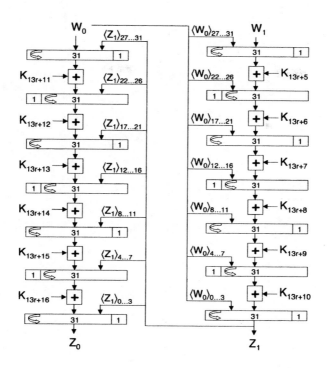

Figure 4.13: Akelarre addition–rotation structure.

steps, we obtain Z_1, which is then used to determine the rotations to apply to W_0 to generate Z_0.

The final piece of the Akelarre algorithm is the key schedule. The precise details of the key schedule are inconsistent between various documents, so we follow the algorithm given in the original Akelarre paper [3].

A diagram of the key schedule algorithm appears in Figure 4.14. The key can be any multiple of 64 bits, but, as mentioned above, we assume a 128-bit key. The key is split into 16-bit quantities which we label s_i, for $i = 0, 1, \ldots, 7$.

Define constants

$$A_0 = \texttt{0xa49ed284} \quad \text{and} \quad A_1 = \texttt{0x735203de}$$

and let

$$u_i = s_i^2 + A_0 \ (\text{mod } 2^{32}) \quad \text{and} \quad v_i = s_i^2 + A_1 \ (\text{mod } 2^{32})$$

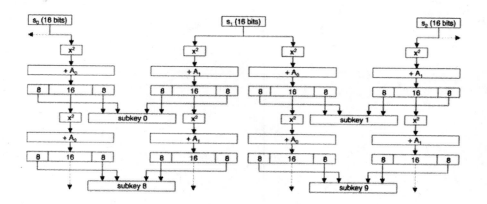

Figure 4.14: Akelarre key schedule (128-bit key).

for $i = 0, 1, \ldots, 7$. Then, for $i = 0, 1, \ldots, 7$, subkey K_i is given by

$$\langle K_i \rangle_{0\ldots7} = \langle u_i \rangle_{24\ldots31}$$
$$\langle K_i \rangle_{8\ldots15} = \langle u_i \rangle_{0\ldots7}$$
$$\langle K_i \rangle_{16\ldots23} = \langle v_{i+1} \rangle_{24\ldots31}$$
$$\langle K_i \rangle_{24\ldots31} = \langle v_{i+1} \rangle_{0\ldots7}.$$

Note that the indices on the v_i are taken modulo 8.

Next, for $i = 0, 1, \ldots, 7$, update u_i and v_i according to

$$u_i = u_m^2 + A_0 \pmod{2^{32}} \quad \text{and} \quad v_i = v_m^2 + A_1 \pmod{2^{32}},$$

where $u_m = \langle u_i \rangle_{8\ldots24}$ and $v_m = \langle v_i \rangle_{8\ldots24}$, that is, u_m consists of the middle 16 bits of the old u_i and v_m consists of the middle 16 bits of the old v_i. Then we compute subkey K_i as

$$\langle K_i \rangle_{0\ldots7} = \langle u_i \rangle_{24\ldots31}$$
$$\langle K_i \rangle_{8\ldots15} = \langle u_i \rangle_{0\ldots7}$$
$$\langle K_i \rangle_{16\ldots23} = \langle v_{i+1} \rangle_{24\ldots31}$$
$$\langle K_i \rangle_{24\ldots31} = \langle v_{i+1} \rangle_{0\ldots7}$$

for $i = 8, 9, \ldots, 15$, where, again, the index on v_i must be taken modulo 8. We continue iterating this process until subkeys K_i, for $i = 0, 1, 2, \ldots, 13R + 8$, have been computed, where R is the number of rounds.

More generally, if the key consists of n 64-bit blocks, a similar process is used except that we generate $4n$ subkeys at each level of the key schedule algorithm, until the requisite $13R + 9$ subkeys have been computed.

The precise details of the key schedule algorithm are irrelevant for the attack described below. In the attack we will determine certain subkeys, then we can recover plaintext using these subkeys without knowledge of the underlying Akelarre key.

Finally, we need to describe the decryption algorithm. Akelarre is not a Feistel Cipher, but it is designed so that the same logic can be used to encrypt and decrypt. However, unlike a Feistel Cipher where we simply need to use the subkeys in reverse order, in Akelarre, more substantial changes to the subkeys are required.

Consider a 32-bit word A. Let $x = \langle A \rangle_{25\ldots31}$, where x is interpreted as an integer, and let $y = -x \pmod{128}$. Let $\text{neg}(A)$ be the 32-bit word obtained by replacing $\langle A \rangle_{25\ldots31}$ with the the seven bits represented by y (with leading 0s included, if necessary). For example, $\text{neg}(\texttt{0xa5b5c5d5}) = \texttt{0xa5b5c5ab}$.

Now consider subkey K_{13r+4} in Figure 4.12. The rightmost seven bits of this subkey are used to determine the rotation of the 128-bit block. By using $\text{neg}(K_{13r+4})$ in place of K_{13r+4} during decryption, we can effectively undo the rotation, since a rotation of 128 is equivalent to no rotation at all.

Using this notation, the encryption subkeys and the corresponding decryption subkeys are specified in Table 4.11, where $r = 0, 1, \ldots, R - 1$, and $-X$ is to be taken modulo 2^{32}. Then the Akelarre encryption algorithm in Figure 4.12 is also the Akelarre decryption algorithm, provided the subkeys are modified as indicated in Table 4.11.

Table 4.11: Akelarre Subkeys

Transformation	Encryption Subkeys	Decryption Subkeys
Input	K_0	$-K_{13R+5}$
	K_1	K_{13R+6}
	K_2	K_{13R+7}
	K_3	$-K_{13R+8}$
Round $r = 0, 1, \ldots, R - 1$	K_{13r+4}	$\text{neg}(K_{13(R-r)+4})$
	K_{13r+5}	$K_{13(R-r-1)+5}$
	K_{13r+6}	$K_{13(R-r-1)+6}$
	$\vdots$	$\vdots$
	K_{13r+16}	$K_{13(R-r-1)+16}$
Output	K_{13R+4}	$\text{neg}(K_4)$
	K_{13R+5}	$-K_0$
	K_{13R+6}	K_1
	K_{13R+7}	K_2
	K_{13R+8}	$-K_3$

4.6.2   Akelarre Attack

The attack we discuss in this section is similar to that in [82]. This attack requires that we have a small amount of known plaintext available, and that some statistics of the plaintext are known. For example, it is sufficient if we know that the plaintext is English, or that the plaintext is ASCII. Given this information, we can recover part of the key, and we can then recover plaintext from ciphertext. The paper [82] also contains a ciphertext only attack, which is only slightly more complex than the attack presented here.

Consider a single round of Akelarre, neglecting the input and output transformations. Let r be the round number, and let $A = (A_0, A_1, A_2, A_3)$ be the input to round r, where each A_i is a 32 bit word. We denote the bits of each A_i as

$$A_i = (a_{32i}, a_{32i+1}, \ldots, a_{32i+31}),$$

that is, the bits of A are numbered consecutively from left-to-right, beginning with 0.

For a given round, let $U = (U_0, U_1, U_2, U_3)$ be the output of the keyed rotation, let $B = (B_0, B_1, B_2, B_3)$ be the output of the round and, finally, let $T = (T_0, T_1)$ the output of the AR structure. These U, B and T variables are illustrated in Figure 4.15. The individual bits of U, B and T are numbered in a similar manner as the bits of A.

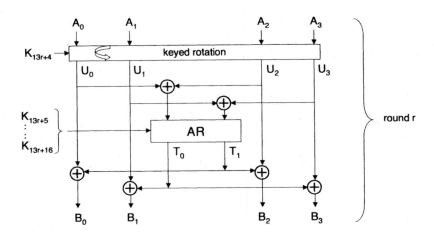

Figure 4.15: Akelarre round r.

Let ℓ be the size of the keyed rotation. Then $U = A \lll \ell$ and

$$(B_0, B_1, B_2, B_3) = (U_0 \oplus T_1, U_1 \oplus T_0, U_2 \oplus T_1, U_3 \oplus T_0).$$

It immediately follows that

$$B_0 \oplus B_2 = U_0 \oplus U_2$$
$$B_1 \oplus B_3 = U_1 \oplus U_3.$$

Note that the output of the AR structure does not appear in either of these equations. However, in this form, the equations are not particularly useful, since U is an intermediate step of the algorithm. However, if we can write B in terms of A, then perhaps we can relate the input of the round to the output, effectively bypassing the complexity of the AR structure.[5]

We have

$$U = A \lll \ell = (a_\ell, a_{\ell+1}, \ldots, a_{\ell+127}),$$

where the indices are all computed modulo 128. It follows that

$$U_0 \oplus U_2 = (a_\ell \oplus a_{\ell+64}, a_{\ell+1} \oplus a_{\ell+65}, \ldots, a_{\ell+31} \oplus a_{\ell+95})$$

and

$$U_1 \oplus U_3 = (a_{\ell+32} \oplus a_{\ell+96}, a_{\ell+33} \oplus a_{\ell+97}, \ldots, a_{\ell+63} \oplus a_{\ell+127}),$$

and, therefore,

$$(U_0 \oplus U_2, U_1 \oplus U_3) = (A_0 \oplus A_2, A_1 \oplus A_3) \lll \ell$$
$$= (A_0 \oplus A_2, A_1 \oplus A_3) \lll \ell \ (\text{mod } 64),$$

where the "mod 64" in the final term follows from the fact that

$$(A_0 \oplus A_2, A_1 \oplus A_3)$$

is only 64 bits in length. In this way, we can relate the input of a round to the output simply by

$$(B_0 \oplus B_2, B_1 \oplus B_3) = (A_0 \oplus A_2, A_1 \oplus A_3) \lll \ell \ (\text{mod } 64). \tag{4.20}$$

Since the key and the AR structure do not appear in this equation, we have, in effect, bypassed the AR structure. Furthermore, we can easily extend this through all R rounds, since the output of one round is the input to the next round.

Let ℓ_r be the size of the keyed rotation in round r, for $r = 0, 1, \ldots, R-1$, and define

$$L = \sum_{r=0}^{R-1} \ell_r.$$

---

[5]This is an example of foreshadowing.

Now let A be the 128-bit input to round 0 and let C be the output of the final round. Then A is the output of the input transformation and C is the input to the output transformation.[6] From (4.20) and Problem 19, it follows that

$$(C_0 \oplus C_2, C_1 \oplus C_3) = (A_0 \oplus A_2, A_1 \oplus A_3) \lll L \ (\text{mod } 64). \qquad (4.21)$$

In this form, we have the XOR of output bits written in terms of the XOR of input bits, with an unknown rotation L.

If Akelarre did not employ its input and output transformations, then in (4.21), A would be plaintext and C would be the corresponding ciphertext, and the ciphertext would immediately provide some information about the plaintext.

Of course, we must take the input and output transformations into account. As in Figure 4.12, we denote the plaintext block as X and the corresponding ciphertext block as Y. As above, A is the input to the first round and C is the output of the last round. Let D be the result after C passes through the keyed rotation in the output transformation, but before the key is added and XORed. Let ℓ_O be the amount of the rotation in the output transformation. Then from (4.21) we have

$$(D_0 \oplus D_2, D_1 \oplus D_3) = (A_0 \oplus A_2, A_1 \oplus A_3) \lll L' \ (\text{mod } 64), \qquad (4.22)$$

where $L' = L + \ell_O$.

Now from Figure 4.12 we have

$$A = (X_0 + K_0, X_1 \oplus K_1, X_2 \oplus K_2, X_3 + K_3)$$

and

$$D = (Y_0 - K_{13R+5}, Y_1 \oplus K_{13R+6}, Y_2 \oplus K_{13R+7}, Y_3 - K_{13R+8}).$$

Substituting these results into (4.22), we find

$$((Y_0 - K_{13R+5}) \oplus Y_2 \oplus K_{13R+7}, Y_1 \oplus K_{13R+6} \oplus (Y_3 - K_{13R+8}))$$
$$= ((X_0 + K_0) \oplus X_2 \oplus K_2, X_1 \oplus K_1 \oplus (X_3 + K_3)) \lll L' \ (\text{mod } 64), \quad (4.23)$$

which relates the plaintext X to the ciphertext Y, modulo the unknown rotation L' and the unknown subkey words K_0, K_1, K_2, K_3, K_{13R+5}, K_{13R+6}, K_{13R+7}, and K_{13R+8}.

Given sufficient known plaintext, we can solve for the unknown shift and subkey words in (4.23). Since each known plaintext yields one 64-bit equation, in principle, we can solve for the eight unknown 32-bit subkey words using

---

[6]Try saying that three times, fast.

four known plaintexts. Then one additional known plaintext will enable us to solve for the rotation, for a total requirement of five known plaintext blocks.

Suppose we have the required five known plaintexts. Then we can solve for the K_i and L' in (4.23) as follows. For each of the 64 possible choices for L', we solve for one bit at a time, beginning from the low-order bit position. It is necessary to keep track of carry bits and at some steps we must save multiple possible solutions (i.e., some branching occurs). Also, it is not possible to uniquely recover all of the subkey words using this approach. We can always recover K_0, K_2, K_{13R+5}, and K_{13R+8}, but we only determine $K_1 \oplus K_{13R+6}$ and $K_2 \oplus K_{13R+7}$, or $K_1 \oplus K_{13R+7}$ and $K_2 \oplus K_{13R+6}$, depending on the rotation L'. See Problem 20 for a slightly simplified version of this subkey recovery problem.

Once we have recovered the subkey words and the shift, we are then in a situation similar to (4.21). At this point, if we are given any ciphertext, we use the recovered subkey words to obtain the XOR of words of the corresponding plaintext. This is somewhat analogous to a one-time pad cipher where the key has been used more than once. At a minimum this leaks information about the plaintext, and it may be possible to recover the plaintext directly from the ciphertext, provided that we have sufficient information about the plaintext. In [82] it is claimed that if we simply know the plaintext is English, or random ASCII text, then it is possible to recover the plaintext.

The recovery of the plaintext from the ciphertext is considered in Problem 21, where a slightly simplified version of the problem is given. In practice, a similar approach could be used on actual Akelarre ciphertext.

4.6.3   Improved Akelarre?

It is interesting that the designers of Akelarre had great confidence in the security of the algorithm [3], primarily because it combines features found in two highly-respected crypto algorithms. Furthermore, the overall design of Akelarre is relatively complex. But since the complexity of the cipher is easily bypassed, it provides no real security. Akelarre illustrates the point that in cryptography, complexity is no substitute for careful analysis. In any case, the attack presented here highlights the fact that designing a secure cipher is a challenging and subtle art.

Akelarre is such a fundamentally flawed cipher that it is difficult to imagine a minor modification that could significantly improve its security. Virtually the entire complexity of the algorithm lies in the AR structure, which can, in effect, be bypassed. Any modification that improves the security of the algorithm would have to force the attacker to deal with the AR structure. We leave the problem of possible modifications to Akelarre as an exercise (see Problem 25).

4.7 FEAL

> ...an encipherment algorithm that has the safety equal to DES
> and is suitable for software as well as hardware implementation is needed.
> The FEAL (Fast data Encipherment ALgorithm) fills this need.
> — Fast Data Encipherment Algorithm FEAL [134]

> FEAL-4 is breakable with 5 known plaintexts in 6 minutes.
> — A New Method for Known Plaintext Attack on FEAL Cipher [98]

The Fast data Encryption ALgorithm, or FEAL, is a block cipher developed by Shimizu and Miyaguchi [134] and announced publicly in 1987. The original version of the algorithm, which is now known as FEAL-4, consists of four rounds, and it was designed to be extremely efficient, with a modest degree of security. However, devastating attacks on FEAL-4 were soon discovered, rendering the algorithm insecure for virtually any conceivable application. The developers of FEAL responded by adding more rounds—first eight rounds (FEAL-8), then a variable number of rounds (FEAL-N)—and with a larger key (FEAL-NX).

All versions of FEAL are insecure. Nevertheless, FEAL is an historically important cipher, since it spawned many developments in the field of cryptanalysis. In particular, Biham and Shamir's differential cryptanalysis [14] was specifically developed to attack FEAL. Differential cryptanalysis was then furthered honed on the Data Encryption Standard (DES), and it was ultimately discovered that DES was designed to resist such attacks. Apparently, differential cryptanalysis was known by someone involved in the development of DES (namely, the National Security Agency [140]) almost 20 years before it was, independently, rediscovered by Biham and Shamir, and it was considered a serious threat.

In the next section, we consider the original and simplest version of FEAL, now known as FEAL-4. In Section 4.7.2 we present a differential attack that can recover the 64-bit key with a work factor of about 2^{16} and only requires four pairs of chosen plaintext blocks. Similar attacks succeed against FEAL-8 (and other versions of FEAL), but the work factor is higher and the implementations are more complex.

In Section 4.7.3 we discuss the linear cryptanalysis of FEAL-4. Linear cryptanalysis was invented by Matsui [97], originally as a way to attack DES. Linear cryptanalysis is also highly effective against FEAL-4.

Today, linear and differential cryptanalysis are standard tools used to analyze all block cipher designs. These powerful techniques can be used to probe for potential weaknesses. However, neither technique is generally useful for practical attacks on ciphers. Partly, this is due to the fact that modern block ciphers are designed with linear and differential attacks in mind, but it is also due to the fact that these attacks are inherently impractical.

The primary reason for the impracticality of differential and linear cryptanalysis is that they require large amounts of chosen plaintext (differential cryptanalysis) or known plaintext (linear cryptanalysis). For example, practical attacks against DES invariably rely on an exhaustive key search to recover the 56-bit key, even though linear cryptanalytic attacks with significantly lower work factors are known. It is simply more effective in practice to pay the price of a higher work factor rather than to deal with the huge volumes of data required by these advanced cryptanalytic techniques. Also, it would generally be impractical to expect to collect huge amounts of known (or chosen) plaintext. In this regard, FEAL is an exceptional block cipher, since practical linear and differential attacks are possible. Nevertheless, even for FEAL-4, linear and differential attacks are not trivial, and considerable care is required to actually implement these attacks to recover the key.

4.7.1 FEAL-4 Cipher

There are several equivalent descriptions of the FEAL-4 cipher. In this section, we present a description that is suited for differential and linear attacks; see Problem 27 for the original description of FEAL-4.

FEAL-4 is a four-round Feistel Cipher with a block size of 64 bits and a 64-bit key [134]. In our description of the cipher, the key is expanded into six 32-bit subkeys (the original description uses twelve 16-bit subkeys). Our version of FEAL-4 appears in Figure 4.16. We ignore the key schedule algorithm, which is used to derive the subkeys from the 64-bit key, since the attacks discussed here will directly recover the subkeys. Once the subkeys have been recovered, it is straightforward to recover the original key, see [14] for the details.

The FEAL round function F is illustrated in Figure 4.17. The 32-bit input to F consists of the four bytes (x_0, x_1, x_2, x_3) and the 32-bit output is given by the four bytes (y_0, y_1, y_2, y_3). The functions G_0 and G_1 each take two bytes of input and each generates a single byte of output. These functions are defined as

$$G_0(a, b) = (a + b \ (\text{mod } 256)) \lll 2 \tag{4.24}$$

and

$$G_1(a, b) = (a + b + 1 \ (\text{mod } 256)) \lll 2, \tag{4.25}$$

where "$\lll$" is the left cyclic shift operator. For example,

$$G_1(10000010, 10010100) = (130 + 148 + 1 \ (\text{mod } 256)) \lll 2$$
$$= 23 \lll 2 = 00010111 \lll 2 = 01011100.$$

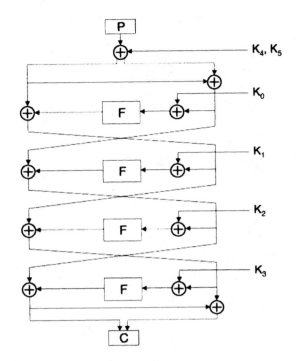

Figure 4.16: FEAL-4.

The F function in Figure 4.17 can be computed as

$$
\begin{aligned}
y_1 &= G_1(x_0 \oplus x_1, x_2 \oplus x_3) \\
y_0 &= G_0(x_0, y_1) \\
y_2 &= G_0(y_1, x_2 \oplus x_3) \\
y_3 &= G_1(y_2, x_3).
\end{aligned}
\tag{4.26}
$$

Of particular interest is the fact that y_1 and y_2 are computed from the 16 bits of $x_0 \oplus x_1$ and $x_2 \oplus x_3$. We make use of this fact in the differential attack on FEAL-4.

4.7.2 FEAL-4 Differential Attack

Differential cryptanalysis is a chosen plaintext attack, where we choose pairs of plaintext messages whose "difference" satisfies a particular property. The definition of difference can vary, depending on the attack, but for for FEAL-4, we use XOR as the difference operation. By considering the XOR of two inputs, the FEAL-4 cipher is greatly simplified. In particular, since the key is the same for the two encryptions, the XOR of the subkey effectively vanishes when considering XOR differences instead of individual encryptions.

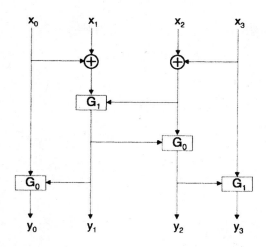

Figure 4.17: FEAL F function.

Of course, we are trying to recover the subkey, so at some point we must use our knowledge of the difference along with the individual encryptions to determine the subkeys.

A specific input difference is known as a *characteristic*. A useful characteristic will yield information about the subkey when the characteristic is pushed through several rounds of the cipher. In this way, we can recover some information about the subkey.

An example should make the process clear, but before we present our example, we must establish two facts concerning the FEAL F function. First, note the obvious fact that if we have $A_0 = A_1$, then $F(A_0) = F(A_1)$. A less obvious fact is that if

$$A_0 \oplus A_1 = \text{0x80800000},$$

then

$$F(A_0) \oplus F(A_1) = \text{0x02000000}.$$

That this holds with probability 1 is somewhat surprising, but not difficult to establish; see Problem 28. This is the crucial fact that enables the differential attack to succeed.

Now suppose we choose plaintext message P_0 at random and we then choose plaintext P_1 so that

$$P_1 = P_0 \oplus \text{0x8080000080800000}. \tag{4.27}$$

Then $P_0 \oplus P_1 = \text{0x8080000080800000}$. Since differential cryptanalysis is a chosen plaintext attack, by assumption, we have the corresponding ciphertexts, C_0 and C_1.

Let $P' = P_0 \oplus P_1$ and $C' = C_0 \oplus C_1$, and use similar notation for the intermediate steps of the FEAL-4 algorithm. Then by carefully examining the differences at the intermediate steps of FEAL-4, we obtain the results in Figure 4.18.

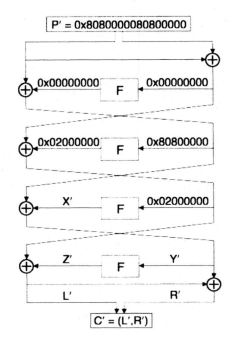

Figure 4.18: FEAL-4 differential analysis.

Note that Figure 4.18 represents the XOR of the plaintexts P_0 and P_1, as well as the XOR of the ciphertexts, and the XOR of all intermediate values. The fact that the subkeys do not appear in Figure 4.18 is not an error. The subkeys are identical for the two encryptions, and since the difference operation is XOR, the subkeys drop out of the diagram.

For any selected pair P_0 and P_1 such that $P' = $ 0x8080000080800000, Figure 4.18 holds. We now "back up" from the ciphertext to meet-in-the-middle. The ciphertexts C_0 and C_1 are known, as are C', L', and R'. From Figure 4.18 we see that

$$L' = 0x02000000 \oplus Z', \tag{4.28}$$

from which we can solve for Z'. We also have

$$R' = L' \oplus Y',$$

which allows us to solve for

$$Y' = 0x80800000 \oplus X'.$$

Also note that if we know the ciphertext $C = (L, R)$, then we compute Y as

$$Y = L \oplus R, \tag{4.29}$$

as can be seen from Figure 4.19.

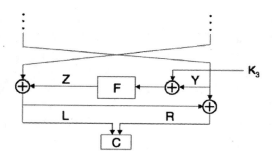

Figure 4.19: FEAL-4 last round.

We are now in a position to solve for putative values of subkey K_3. Suppose we have one pair of chosen plaintexts P_0 and P_1 that satisfy (4.27), and we have the corresponding ciphertexts C_0 and C_1. For these ciphertexts, we compute Z' from (4.28). Then we compute Y_0 and Y_1 (corresponding to C_0 and C_1, respectively) via (4.29).

There are 2^{32} possible values for subkey K_3. Denote a putative value of K_3 as $\tilde{K}_3$. We know Y_0 from (4.29). Then given $\tilde{K}_3$, we can determine $\tilde{Z}_0$ (a putative value for Z_0) and $\tilde{Z}_1$ (a putative value for Z_1). If we should find that $Z' = \tilde{Z}_0 \oplus \tilde{Z}_1$, then $\tilde{K}_3$ is a possible value for K_3 and we save it; otherwise we know that $K_3 \neq \tilde{K}_3$ and we discard this choice of $\tilde{K}_3$. Using only a single pair of chosen plaintexts, we will find many putative $\tilde{K}_3$ that pass this test, but with four pairs, we expect only the correct K_3 to survive; see Problem 29.

Following the method described in the previous paragraph, the work factor to recover K_3 is on the order of 2^{32} and four pairs of chosen plaintexts are required. However, due to the structure of the F function, it is possible to reduce this work factor to about 2^{17} as discussed below. But first we require some additional notation. As in other sections of this book, we adopt the convention that bits are numbered from left to right, beginning with 0, and we use the notation $\langle A \rangle_{i...j}$, where $j > i$, for the string of bits of length $j - i + 1$ beginning with bit i and ending with bit j of A. Let z be the all-zero byte. Then for a 32-bit word A, define

$$M(A) = M(a_0, a_1, a_2, a_3) = (z, a_0 \oplus a_1, a_2 \oplus a_3, z).$$

The improved attack to recover K_3 consists of a primary and a secondary phase. In the primary phase, for each possible $A = (z, a_0, a_1, z)$, we compute

$$Q_0 = F(M(Y_0) \oplus A) \quad \text{and} \quad Q_1 = F(M(Y_1) \oplus A).$$

From the definition of F in (4.26), we see that if $A = M(K_3)$, then

$$\langle Q_0 \oplus Q_1 \rangle_{8...23} = \langle Z' \rangle_{8...23}.$$

We can use this fact to determine a set of $A = (z, a_0, a_1, z)$ that are candidate values for $M(K_3)$. This allows us to, in effective, determines 16 bits of K_3. Using four pairs of chosen plaintexts, we expect to reduce the number of such candidates to a small number.

For the secondary phase, each survivors of the primary phase is further tested and in the process we determine the entire subkey K_3. Given a survivor $A = (z, a_0, a_1, z)$ from the primary phase, we can easily determine the full K_3 as follows. First, generate a 16-bit value $B = (b_0, b_1)$, and test a putative subkey $\tilde{K}_3 = (b_0, a_0 \oplus b_0, a_1 \oplus b_1, b_1)$ as discussed previously. That is, use $\tilde{K}_3$ as the putative subkey K_3 and compute $\tilde{Z}_0$ and $\tilde{Z}_1$, and test whether the condition $Z' = \tilde{Z}_0 \oplus \tilde{Z}_1$ holds. If so, then save $\tilde{K}_3$ as a possible K_3, otherwise we know that $K_3 \neq \tilde{K}_3$ and we select another B. In this way, we recover K_3, or a small number of candidate subkeys.

Assuming that a single chosen plaintext pair P_0 and P_1 is, used, the primary phase of this differential attack appears in Table 4.12 and the secondary phase is given in Table 4.13. However, using only a single pair of chosen plaintexts, the number of putative K_3 will be large. As mentioned above, we need to use four chosen plaintext pairs to reduce the number of putative K_3 to one (or a very small number). When more than one chosen plaintext pair is used, the primary and secondary attacks in Tables 4.12 and 4.13, respectively, both require slight modifications. In the primary phase, we want to save only those (a_0, a_1) that satisfy the necessary conditions for all plaintext and ciphertext pairs. Then in the secondary phase we will have a small number of survivors (ideally, only one) and these, again, must satisfy the necessary conditions for all of the plaintext and ciphertext pairs. The precise details of this attack are left as an exercise; see Problem 30.

After successful completion of this differential attack, we will have recovered K_3, or a small number of putative K_3 values. For simplicity, we assume a single K_3 is obtained. Now we must recover the remaining subkey values. This can be accomplished by "unzipping" the cipher to successively obtain K_2, K_1, K_0, and, finally, K_4 and K_5. With K_3 available, we can determine the input and the output to the third F function in Figure 4.16 and we can then determine K_2 in a similar manner as was used to find K_3. Once K_3 and K_2 are known, we can then effectively remove the last two rounds of the cipher and attack K_1, and so on. There are several subtle points to this attack that we leave as exercises; see Problem 31 for more details.

Before we move on to consider linear cryptanalysis, there is one issue regarding differential cryptanalysis that is worth pondering. In this differential attack on FEAL-4, the characteristic we used to determine K_3 occurs with

Table 4.12: Primary Phase of Differential Attack for K_3

```
// Characteristic is 0x8080000080800000
P_0 = random 64-bit value
P_1 = P_0 ⊕ 0x8080000080800000
// Given corresponding ciphertexts
// C_0 = (L_0, R_0) and C_1 = (L_1, R_1)
Y_0 = L_0 ⊕ R_0
Y_1 = L_1 ⊕ R_1
L' = L_0 ⊕ L_1
Z' = L' ⊕ 0x02000000
for (a_0, a_1) = (0x00, 0x00) to (0xff, 0xff)
    Q_0 = F(M(Y_0) ⊕ (0x00, a_0, a_1, 0x00))
    Q_1 = F(M(Y_1) ⊕ (0x00, a_0, a_1, 0x00))
    if ⟨Q_0 ⊕ Q_1⟩_{8...23} == ⟨Z'⟩_{8...23} then
        Save (a_0, a_1)
    end if
next (a_0, a_1)
```

probability one. Since the invention of differential cryptanalyis, block ciphers have been designed with differential attacks in mind. Consequently, differentials that occur with a high probability are unlikely to be found in practice. Nevertheless, given a differential that occurs with some positive probability p, it is still possible to determine information about the subkey. However, the smaller the value of p, the larger the number of chosen plaintexts that will be required to determine subkey bits (that is, the larger the amount of data that is required) and the higher the work factor. Ideally, the designer of a block cipher would like to make the work for any differential attack at least as high as that of an exhaustive key search.

4.7.3 FEAL-4 Linear Attack

The attack described here is similar to that given by Matsui and Yamagishi in [98], with the exception of notation and the format that we use to present the FEAL-4 cipher. There are several equivalent ways to describe FEAL-4, and we have chosen a format that is more similar to that given in the previous section than that used in [98].

For the linear cryptanalysis of FEAL-4 it is convenient to rewrite the cipher in a slightly different form than was used in the differential attack. In Figure 4.20, the subkey K_4 and K_5 appear to have migrated south, as compared to Figure 4.16. It is not difficult to show that the two formulations are equivalent, although the values of the subkeys will differ; see Problem 32.

Table 4.13: Secondary Phase of Differential Attack for K_3

```
// P_0, P_1, C_0, C_1, Y_0, Y_1, Z' as in primary
// Given list of saved (a_0, a_1) from primary
for each primary survivor (a_0, a_1)
    for (c_0, c_1) = (0x00, 0x00) to (0xff, 0xff)
        D = (c_0, a_0 ⊕ c_0, a_1 ⊕ c_1, c_1)
        Z̃_0 = F(Y_0 ⊕ D)
        Z̃_1 = F(Y_1 ⊕ D)
        if Z̃_0 ⊕ Z̃_1 == Z' then
            Save D // candidate subkey K_3
        end if
    next (c_0, c_1)
next (a_0, a_1)
```

For the linear attack, some additional notation is needed. We denote the bits of a 32-bit word X as $X = (x_0, x_1, \ldots, x_{31})$. Then let $S_{i,j}(X)$ be the XOR of bit i and bit j of X, that is, $S_{i,j}(X) = x_i \oplus x_j$. We can extend this to sum more than two bits, and we also define $S_i(X) = x_i$.

This linear attack exploits the fact that the low-order bit of $x + y$ is the same as the low-order bit of $x \oplus y$. Consequently,

$$S_7(a \oplus b) = S_7(a + b \pmod{256}) \tag{4.30}$$

so that

$$S_5 G_0(a, b) = S_5((a + b \pmod{256}) \lll 2) = S_7(a \oplus b). \tag{4.31}$$

Similarly, we have

$$S_5 G_1(a, b) = S_7(a \oplus b) \oplus 1. \tag{4.32}$$

Let X be the 32-bit input to the F function of FEAL-4, and Y the corresponding 32-bit output, where the bits are numbered 0 through 31, from left to right. Then from (4.31) and (4.32) and the formulas for F in (4.26), it is not difficult to show that

$$S_{13}(Y) = S_{7,15,23,31}(X) \oplus 1$$
$$S_5(Y) = S_{15}(Y) \oplus S_7(X)$$
$$S_{15}(Y) = S_{21}(Y) \oplus S_{23,31}(X)$$
$$S_{23}(Y) = S_{29}(Y) \oplus S_{31}(X) \oplus 1.$$

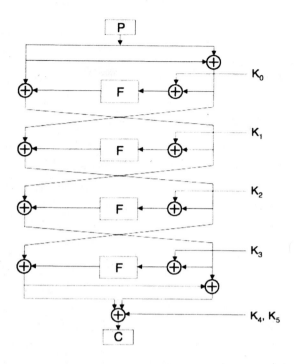

Figure 4.20: Another view of FEAL-4.

Taking all terms involving Y to the left-hand side, we find

$$S_{13}(Y) = S_{7,15,23,31}(X) \oplus 1 \tag{4.33}$$
$$S_{5,15}(Y) = S_7(X) \tag{4.34}$$
$$S_{15,21}(Y) = S_{23,31}(X) \tag{4.35}$$
$$S_{23,29}(Y) = S_{31}(X) \oplus 1. \tag{4.36}$$

Now consider the FEAL-4 diagram in Figure 4.21, which is the same as that in Figure 4.20, except that we have added labels to the intermediate steps. These labels will be used in the analysis below.

Using the notation in Figure 4.21, we have

$$S_{23,29}(L_4) = S_{23,29}(Y_3 \oplus Y_1 \oplus X_0 \oplus K_4)$$
$$= S_{23,29}(Y_3) \oplus S_{23,29}(Y_1) \oplus S_{23,29}(X_0) \oplus S_{23,29}(K_4).$$

We now expand each term on the right-hand side of this expression. First, we find

$$S_{23,29}(X_0) = S_{23,29}(L_0 \oplus R_0).$$

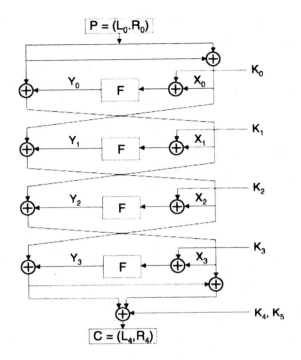

Figure 4.21: FEAL-4 intermediate steps.

Then from (4.36), we have

$$\begin{aligned}
S_{23,29}(Y_3) &= S_{31}(X_3 \oplus K_3) \oplus 1 \\
&= S_{31}(L_4 \oplus K_4 \oplus R_4 \oplus K_5 \oplus K_3) \oplus 1 \\
&= S_{31}(L_4 \oplus R_4) \oplus S_{31}(K_4 \oplus K_5 \oplus K_3) \oplus 1
\end{aligned}$$

and

$$\begin{aligned}
S_{23,29}(Y_1) &= S_{23,29}F(X_1 \oplus K_1) \\
&= S_{23,29}F(K_1 \oplus Y_0 \oplus L_0) \\
&= S_{31}(K_1) \oplus S_{31}(Y_0) \oplus S_{31}(L_0) \oplus 1
\end{aligned}$$

and we also have

$$S_{31}(Y_0) = S_{31}F(X_0 \oplus K_0) = S_{31}F(L_0 \oplus R_0 \oplus K_0).$$

Combining all of these results and rearranging terms, we obtain the expression

$$\begin{aligned}
a = S_{23,29}(L_0 \oplus R_0 \oplus L_4) &\oplus S_{31}(L_0 \oplus L_4 \oplus R_4) \\
&\oplus S_{31}F(L_0 \oplus R_0 \oplus K_0), \qquad (4.37)
\end{aligned}$$

where a is a constant bit, independent of the given plaintext and ciphertext. The precise value of a is

$$a = S_{31}(K_1 \oplus K_3 \oplus K_4 \oplus K_5) \oplus S_{23,29}(K_4),$$

but this constant is unknown in the linear attack, since we are trying to recover the subkeys. We are able to take advantage of the fact that a is constant in spite of the fact that it is unknown.

Given a set of known plaintexts and the corresponding ciphertexts, we can use (4.37) to determine bits of subkey K_0 as follows. The left-hand side of (4.37) is unknown, but it is constant. Given a known plaintext, we then know L_0, R_0, L_4, and R_4, so that the right-hand side of (4.37) is known, with the exception of K_0. We exhaust over all possible choices for K_0 and for each choice, we substitute each of our known plaintexts into (4.37). If the putative K_0 is correct, then the right-hand side of (4.37) must be constant for all of the known plaintexts. Consequently, given a sufficient number of known plaintexts, we can determine a small number of candidate values for K_0. This attack is outlined in Table 4.14.

Table 4.14: Linear Attack to Find Candidates for Subkey K_0

```
// Given (plaintext,ciphertext) pairs (P_i, C_i), i = 0, 1, 2, ..., n - 1
for K = 0 to 2^32 - 1 // putative K_0
    count[0] = count[1] = 0
    for i = 0 to n - 1
        j = bit computed in right-hand-side of (4.37)
        count[j] = count[j] + 1
    next i
    if count[0] == n or count[1] == n then
        Save K // candidate for K_0
    end if
next K
```

The attack in Table 4.14 is feasible, but we can reduce the work factor considerably. Here, we only outline this improved attack—the details are left as an exercise.

We first derive expressions analogous to those in (4.37), using (4.33), (4.34), and (4.35). Then by combining some of these, we obtain

$$
\begin{aligned}
a = S_{5,13,21}(L_0 \oplus R_0 \oplus L_4) &\oplus S_{15}(L_0 \oplus L_4 \oplus R_4) \\
&\oplus S_{15}F(L_0 \oplus R_0 \oplus K_0),
\end{aligned} \tag{4.38}
$$

where a is a fixed, but unknown, constant. Now let

$$\tilde{K}_0 = (\langle K_0 \rangle_{0...7} \oplus \langle K_0 \rangle_{8...15}, \langle K_0 \rangle_{16...23} \oplus \langle K_0 \rangle_{24...31}).$$

From the first line in (4.26), we see that $S_{15}F(L_0 \oplus R_0 \oplus K_0)$ of (4.38) depends only on the bits $\langle \tilde{K}_0 \rangle_{9...15,17...23}$. In addition, it follows from (4.30) that bits 9 and 17 of $\tilde{K}_0$ are XORed in the right-hand side of (4.38), so these bits can be taken to the left-hand side of (4.38) and treated as constant (but unknown) values. Then we are left with an expression that depends only on the twelve unknown key bits $\langle \tilde{K}_0 \rangle_{10...15,18...23}$. This allows for an exhaustive search for twelve bits of $\tilde{K}_0$. Similar expressions can be derived that allow for an extremely efficient attack to recover almost all of the bits of K_0, and the few remaining bits are easily found by a final exhaustive search. The overall work factor for this attack is far less than the 2^{32} required for the attack given in Table 4.14.

The linear crytanalytic attack on FEAL-4 described here is explored further in the problems at the end of the chapter. Specifically, Problems 33 through 35 deal with this attack.

4.7.4   Confusion and Diffusion

In his classic paper [133], Shannon discusses *confusion* and *diffusion* in the context of symmetric ciphers. These two fundamental concepts are still guiding principles of symmetric cipher design. Roughly speaking, confusion obscures the relationship between the plaintext and the ciphertext, while diffusion spreads the plaintext statistics through the ciphertext. The simple substitution and the one-time pad can be viewed as confusion-only ciphers, while transposition ciphers are of the diffusion-only variety.

Within each block, any reasonable block cipher employs both confusion and diffusion. To see, for example, where confusion and diffusion occur in FEAL-4, first note that FEAL-4 is a Feistel Cipher (see Problem 26), where the Feistel round function is simply $F(X_i \oplus K_i)$, with F illustrated in Figure 4.17, and defined in (4.26).

The FEAL-4 function F does employ both confusion and diffusion, but only to a very limited degree. The diffusion is a result of the shifting within each byte, and also the shifting of the bytes themselves (represented by the horizontal arrows in Figure 4.17). The confusion is primarily due to the XOR with the key, and, to a lesser extent, the modulo 256 addition that occurs within each G_i function. However, in FEAL-4, both the confusion and diffusion are extremely weak as evidenced by the relatively simple linear and differential attacks presented above.

Later members of the FEAL family of ciphers improved on FEAL-4, with the stronger versions having better confusion and diffusion properties, thereby making linear and differential attacks more difficult. However, attacks exist for all versions of FEAL, indicating that the cipher design itself is fundamentally flawed.

4.8 Summary

Block cipher design is relatively well understood. Consequently, it is not too difficult to design a plausible block cipher—although, by Kerckhoffs' Principle, such a cipher would not be trusted until it had received extensive peer review. For example, if we create a Feistel Cipher with a round function that has reasonable confusion and diffusion properties, and we iterate the round function a large number of times, it is likely that any attack will be nontrivial. However, things are much more challenging if we try to design a block cipher that is as efficient as possible. Two of the three ciphers discussed in this chapter are weak primarily because they were designed for extreme efficiency—Akelarre is a notable exception, since it is weak regardless of the number of rounds.

4.9 Problems

1. Suppose that we use a block cipher to encrypt according to the rule

$$C_0 = IV \oplus E(P_0, K), \ C_1 = C_0 \oplus E(P_1, K), \ C_2 = C_1 \oplus E(P_2, K), \ \ldots.$$

   What is the corresponding decryption rule? Are there any security advantages or disadvantages to this mode compared to CBC mode?

2. Suppose Alice has four blocks of plaintext, P_0, P_1, P_2, and P_3, and she computes a MAC using the key K. Alice sends the initialization vector, denoted IV, the plaintext blocks and the MAC to Bob. However, Trudy intercepts the message and replaces P_1 with X so that Bob receives IV, P_0, X, P_2, P_3, and the MAC.

   a. Precisely what does Bob compute when he attempts to verify the MAC?

   b. Show that Bob will almost certainly detect Trudy's tampering.

   c. What is the probability that Bob does not detect Trudy's tampering?

3. Counter (CTR) mode allows block ciphers to be used like stream ciphers. The CTR mode encryption formula is

$$C_i = P_i \oplus E(IV + i, K)$$

   and decryption rule us

$$P_i = C_i \oplus E(IV + i, K).$$

    a. Explain how to do random access on data encrypted using CTR mode.

    b. Explain how to do random access on data encrypted using CBC mode.

    c. Which is "better" for random access, CTR mode or CBC mode, and why?

4. Suppose that Alice and Bob always choose the same IV.

    a. Discuss one security problem this creates if CBC mode is used.

    b. Discuss one security problem this creates if CTR mode is used (see Problem 3 for a definition of CTR mode).

    c. If the same IV is always used, why is CBC mode preferable to CTR mode?

5. Consider a Feistel Cipher with four rounds. Then $P = (L_0, R_0)$ is the plaintext. What is the ciphertext $C = (L_4, R_4)$, in terms of (L_0, R_0), for each of the following round functions?

    a. $F(R_{i-1}, K_i) = X$, where X is a constant

    b. $F(R_{i-1}, K_i) = R_{i-1}$

    c. $F(R_{i-1}, K_i) = R_{i-1} \oplus K_i$

    d. $F(R_{i-1}, K_i) = R_{i-1} + K_i \pmod{2^{32}}$, where R_{i-1} and K_i are 32-bit quantities

6. Trudy wants to attack a block cipher that has a 64-bit key and 64-bit blocks. Each time she attacks this cipher, she can conduct a chosen plaintext attack and the cipher is used in ECB mode.

    a. Suppose Trudy does an exhaustive key search each time she attacks the cipher. If she conducts the attack 2^{20} times, what is the total work, the storage requirement and the success probability?

    b. Suppose Trudy pre-computes $E(P, K)$ for a selected plaintext P and every possible key K. For each attack, Trudy chooses the same plaintext P and obtains the corresponding ciphertext C. Then she simply looks up C in her pre-computed list to obtain the key K. If she again conducts the attack 2^{20} times, what is the total work, the storage requirement and the success probability?

    c. Suppose Trudy implements Hellman's TMTO attack and, as suggested in the text, she chooses $r = m = t = 2^{64/3}$. If she conducts the attack 2^{20} times, what is the total work, the storage requirement and the success probability?

7. The key size of CMEA is $k = 64$ bits and the block size n is variable. Suppose the key is restricted to 32 bits by setting all of the first 32 bits of any key equal to 0. Then, effectively, $k = 32$. Choose the block size to be $n = 32$ bits. Implement Hellman's TMTO attack on this version of the CMEA block cipher. In the TMTO attack, let $m = t = r = 2^{15}$. Empirically determine the probability of success.

8. Derive the formula in equation (4.3) for the success probability in Hellman's TMTO. Hint: See the "occupancy problem" in Feller [49].

9. Let C be the Cave Table of the CMEA cipher. Precisely determine the probability that $(x + i) \oplus 1 \in C$ for a randomly selected $x \in C$ and $i \in \{1, 2, \ldots, 255\}$.

10. Let x_i, for $i = 0, 1, 2, \ldots, 255$, be the Cave Table entries for the CMEA cipher. Show that for 28 of these, $x_i \oplus 1$ is also in the Cave Table. Consequently, for a randomly selected x in the Cave Table, the probability that $x \oplus 1$ is also in the Cave Table is about 0.11.

11. Find the value of c_2 corresponding to c_0 and c_1 in (4.13) and (4.14), respectively.

12. Consider the CMEA cipher with block size $n = 3$. Suppose that we choose plaintext blocks of the form $(p_0, p_1, p_2) = (1 - x, 1 - x, 0)$, where $x \in \{0, 1, 2, \ldots, 255\}$. Show that

  a. If x is even, then ciphertext c_0 is even.

  b. If x is odd, then ciphertext c_0 is odd.

13. For the CMEA cipher with block size $n = 3$, suppose that

$$(p_0, p_1, p_2) = (1 - T(0), 1 - T(0), 1 - T(0)).$$

  a. Apply the algorithm in Table 4.6 to determine the resulting ciphertext (c_0, c_1, c_2).

  b. Describe a chosen plaintext attack that uses this result to determine $T(0)$.

14. The purpose of this problem is to determine the probability that the attack on the CMEA cipher will succeed. Let $n = 3$ be the block size. In the CMEA attacks discussed in this chapter, we first determine a putative $T(0)$, then for each $j = 1, 2, \ldots, 255$, we attempt to recover $T(j)$. If for any j we find $x_j - j \notin C$ and $(x_j \oplus 1) - j \notin C$, then we know that the putative $T(0)$ is incorrect. If this does not occur, then we assume $T(0)$ is correct and for each j we have recovered either $T(j)$ or $T(j) \oplus 1$. Let $x_j \in \{T(j), T(j) \oplus 1\}$ be the recovered value. If $x_j - j \in C$ but

$(x_j \oplus 1) - j \notin C$, then we know that $x_j = T(j)$ and, similarly, if $(x_j \oplus 1) - j \in C$ but $x_j - j \notin C$, then we know that $x_j \oplus 1 = T(j)$. However, if $(x_j \oplus 1) - j \in C$ and $x_j - j \in C$, then we cannot immediately determine the value of $T(j)$ from x_j.

Let A be the set of $j \in \{0, 1, 2, \ldots, 255\}$ for which $T(j)$ cannot be uniquely determined. Also, let U be the set of indices for which $T(j)$ has been uniquely determined. Then $A \cup U = \{0, 1, 2, \ldots, 255\}$, and A and U are disjoint. Note that $0 \in U$.

   a. Determine $E(|A|)$ and $E(|U|)$, where $|X|$ is the cardinality of the set X, and E is the expected value. Write a program to empirically verify your results.

   b.* Let $a = |A|$ and $u = 256 - a = |U|$. Let $k \in A$. What is the probability that we can find some $\ell \in U$ and an index j such that $\ell \oplus (x_j \vee 1) = k$. Note that if no such ℓ and j can be found, the CMEA chosen plaintext attack described in this chapter cannot resolve the ambiguity in the low-order bit of $T(k)$.

15. For the SCMEA cipher, find the equations for c_1 and c_2 that correspond to the equation for c_0 in (4.18).

16. The results in Table 4.8 refer to the known plaintext attack on SCMEA. Empirically determine the analogous results for the known plaintext attack on CMEA.

17. Implement the CMEA known plaintext attack in a way that minimizes the amount of known plaintext required. Empirically determine the minimum number of known plaintext blocks required to correctly determine the key. Your results should be based on at least 1000 successful attacks. Hint: A successful attack may need to be repeated multiple times to determine the precise minimum number of known plaintext blocks required.

18. For the Akelarre cipher, let X_0, X_1, X_2, X_3 be the input to round r and Z_0, Z_1, Z_2, Z_3 be the output of round r, let $X \lll \ell$ denote a left rotation of X by ℓ. Also, let $AR(X, Y)$ be the addition–rotation structure. Recall that the inputs to the addition–rotation structure are two 32-bit words and the output consists of two 32-bit words. Next, define $(U_0, U_1, U_2, U_3) = (X_0, X_1, X_2, X_3) \lll \ell_r$, where ℓ_r is the rotation in round r, and define $(T_0, T_1) = AR(U_0 \oplus U_2, U_1 \oplus U_3)$.

   a. Show $(Z_0, Z_1, Z_2, Z_3) = (U_0 \oplus T_1, U_1 \oplus T_0, U_2 \oplus T_1, U_3 \oplus T_0)$.

   b. Show $(Z_0 \oplus Z_2, Z_1 \oplus Z_3) = (X_0 \oplus X_2, X_1 \oplus X_3) \lll \ell_r \pmod{64}$.

19. Show that rotation and XOR commute, that is, show

$$(X \oplus Y) \lll n = (X \lll n) \oplus (Y \lll n)$$

for any 32-bit words X and Y and for any rotation n.

20. A crucial step in the Akelarre attack is solving (4.23) for the subkey words. In this problem, we consider a similar equation, but to simplify the problem, we use 8-bit bytes instead of 32-bit words. Let a, b, c, d, e, f, g and h be bytes and let X and Y be 32-bit words, where $X = (x_0, x_1, x_2, x_3)$ and $Y = (y_0, y_1, y_2, y_3)$ and each x_i and y_i is a byte. Consider

$$((y_0 - e) \oplus y_2 \oplus g, y_1 \oplus f \oplus (y_3 - h))$$
$$= ((x_0 + a) \oplus x_2 \oplus c, x_1 \oplus b \oplus (x_3 + d)). \qquad (4.39)$$

Note that this equation is a 16-bit version of (4.23), with a shift of 0, and a through h playing the role of the unknown subkeys, and with X and Y playing the role of the plaintext and ciphertext, respectively. Solve for a through h, given the following five pairs of X and Y.

$$X_0 = (0x53, 0x8d, 0x86, 0x80), \ Y_0 = (0x74, 0x21, 0x9c, 0x0a)$$
$$X_1 = (0x54, 0x77, 0xd5, 0x2b), \ Y_1 = (0xf7, 0x92, 0x4d, 0xee)$$
$$X_2 = (0x21, 0x32, 0xf0, 0x7f), \ Y_2 = (0x75, 0xb9, 0x3f, 0xf0)$$
$$X_3 = (0xea, 0x75, 0xaa, 0xd3), \ Y_3 = (0x39, 0x1f, 0x22, 0x1b)$$
$$X_4 = (0x27, 0x95, 0xb7, 0x2d), \ Y_4 = (0x19, 0xbc, 0xa2, 0xc0).$$

21. Consider an equation of the form (4.39), and suppose that we know the values of a through h are given by

$$(a, b, c, d, e, f, g, h) = (0xdb, 0x2a, 0xcd, 0x43, 0xb1, 0x46, 0x07, 0x79).$$

Suppose also that we suspect that the bytes of each X consist only of lower-case ASCII characters, that is, each byte is in the range of 0x61 through 0x7a, inclusive.

a. Determine the number of four-byte X_i that are consistent with each of the following Y_i.

$$Y_0 = (0x22, 0x78, 0x9f, 0x52)$$
$$Y_1 = (0x7d, 0x3f, 0x3f, 0x00)$$
$$Y_2 = (0x1b, 0x73, 0x91, 0x4b)$$
$$Y_3 = (0x28, 0xfd, 0x8e, 0xca)$$
$$Y_4 = (0x30, 0x7b, 0x95, 0x4c)$$

b. What do these results imply about the Akelarre attack discussed in this chapter?

22. Consider an equation of the form (4.39), where all quantities are 32-bit words instead of bytes. Suppose that we know that a through d are

$$(a, b, c, d) = (\texttt{0x14dbde7d}, \texttt{0x84aec735}, \texttt{0x6d66ff01}, \texttt{0xa533ee71})$$

and e through h are

$$(e, f, g, h) = (\texttt{0xed541e0f}, \texttt{0x94c94221}, \texttt{0x94fa57bd}, \texttt{0x48d082c7}).$$

Suppose also that we suspect that the bytes of each X consist only of lower-case ASCII characters, that is, each byte is in the range of $\texttt{0x61}$ through $\texttt{0x7a}$, inclusive.

a. Determine the number of corresponding X_i that are consistent with each of the following Y_i.

$$Y_0 = (\texttt{0x241fb061}, \texttt{0x6b119143}, \texttt{0xd4021163}, \texttt{0x4f73aca9})$$
$$Y_1 = (\texttt{0x47dc28e3}, \texttt{0x424fe3bf}, \texttt{0xb4498cd8}, \texttt{0x75b4ddef})$$
$$Y_2 = (\texttt{0x1b72328c}, \texttt{0x4a05f4c8}, \texttt{0x39a9974f}, \texttt{0x72750024})$$

b. Describe a practical attack that could be used to recover a plaintext message consisting of multiple blocks, provided that you know the underlying message consists of English text, represented as ASCII.

23. The purpose of this problem is to explore the subkey recovery in the Akelarre attack. Show that in (4.23) it is possible to recover L' and either

$$K_0, K_3, K_4, K_7 \quad \text{and} \quad K_1 \oplus K_5, K_2 \oplus K_6 \qquad (4.40)$$

or

$$K_0, K_3, K_4, K_7 \quad \text{and} \quad K_1 \oplus K_6, K_2 \oplus K_5 \qquad (4.41)$$

assuming that a sufficient number of known plaintext blocks are available. In which cases do we obtain the results in (4.40) and in which cases do we obtain the results in (4.41)?

24. Suppose that $L' = 0$ in (4.23).

a. Show that

$$(X_0 + K_0) \oplus X_2 = (Y_0 - K_{13R+5}) \oplus Y_2 \oplus K_{13R+7} \oplus K_2$$
$$(X_3 + K_3) \oplus X_1 = (Y_3 - K_{13R+8}) \oplus Y_1 \oplus K_{13R+6} \oplus K_1.$$

b. Let

$$\text{RHS}_0 = (Y_0 - K_{13R+5}) \oplus Y_2 \oplus K_{13R+7} \oplus K_2$$

and

$$\text{RHS}_1 = (Y_3 - K_{13R+8}) \oplus Y_1 \oplus K_{13R+6} \oplus K_1.$$

Show that

$$(X_0, X_1, X_2, X_3) = (A, B, (A + K_0) \oplus \text{RHS}_0, (B \oplus \text{RHS}_1) - K_3),$$

where A and B can be any 32-bit words.

25. Modify the Akelarre cipher so that it is more secure. As noted in the text, any such modification must force the attacker to deal with the AR structure.

26. Show that FEAL-4 is a Feistel Cipher.

27. The original description of FEAL-4 differs from that given in this chapter. The purpose of this problem is to show that the two descriptions are equivalent. The original encryption diagram for FEAL-4 can be given as

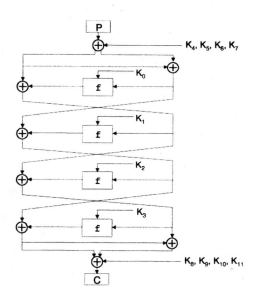

In this schematic, each subkey K_i for $i = 0, 1, 2, \ldots, 11$, is 16 bits. The diagram corresponding to the function f is

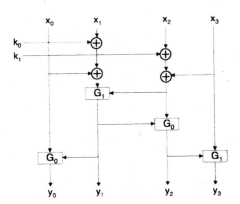

The functions G_0 and G_1 are defined in (4.24) and (4.25), respectively.

    a. Give equations for y_i, for $i = 1, 0, 2, 3$, analogous to those in (4.26).

    b. Denote the 32-bit keys in Figure 4.16 as $\tilde{K}_i$, for $i = 0, 1, 2, \ldots, 5$. Write the $\tilde{K}_i$ in terms of the 16-bit keys K_i, for $i = 0, 1, 2, \ldots, 11$, in the diagram above so that any plaintext P yields the same ciphertext C in both versions of the FEAL-4 cipher.

28. Consider the F function for the FEAL-4 cipher. This function is illustrated in Figure 4.17 and an algebraic description appears in (4.26).

    a. Show that if $A_0 \oplus A_1 = \text{0x80800000}$, then with a probability of one we have $F(A_0) \oplus F(A_1) = \text{0x02000000}$, regardless of the key.

    b. Show that if $A_0 \oplus A_1 = \text{0xa0008000}$, then with probability $1/4$, we have $F(A_0) \oplus F(A_1) = \text{0x80800000}$, regardless of the key.

29. Consider the differential attack on FEAL-4 discussed in this chapter. Determine the expected number of surviving putative values of K_3 when exactly k pairs of chosen plaintexts are used, for $k = 1, 2, 3, 4$, where each pair of chosen plaintexts satisfies (4.27).

30. A differential attack on FEAL-4 to recover the subkey K_3 is discussed in this chapter. Pseudo-code for the primary phase and secondary phase of this attack appears in Tables 4.12 and 4.13, respectively, but each of these assume that a single chosen plaintext pair is used. If available, we would use four chosen plaintext pairs in this attack. Give pseudo-code for both phases of the attack assuming that multiple chosen plaintext pairs are used.

31. In Section 4.7 a differential attack on the FEAL-4 cipher is discussed and the recovery of subkey K_3 is discussed in detail.

a. Complete the attack by giving pseudo-code to recover K_2, then K_1, then K_0, and finally, K_4 and K_5. Hint: To find K_2, use the characteristic 0xa200800022808000. Then to recover the remaining subkeys, arbitrary chosen plaintext pairs can be used.

b. The same characteristic that was used to recover K_3 cannot be used to recover K_2. Why not?

c. What is the minimum number of chosen plaintexts required to complete the attack?

32. Consider the two formulations of FEAL-4 given in Figures 4.16 and 4.20. Denote the subkeys in Figures 4.16 as $\tilde{K}_i$, for $i = 0, 1, \ldots, 5$. Show that these two formulations of FEAL-4 are equivalent by writing each subkey K_i in Figure 4.20 in terms of the subkeys $\tilde{K}_i$ in Figure 4.16.

33. In the linear cryptanalytic attack on FEAL-4, the fundamental equation (4.37) was derived from (4.36). Find the analogous equations for each of (4.33), (4.34), and (4.35).

34. Implement the linear cryptanalytic attack on FEAL-4 given in Table 4.14. Augment the attack by including the results of Problem 33.

a. Estimate the time required to exhaust over all 2^{32} choices for K_0. Specify the hardware used to obtain your timings.

b. How many known plaintexts are required to minimize the number of surviving putative K_0, and what is this minimum number of survivors?

35. Using the results of Problem 33, implement the improved linear attack on FEAL-4 discussed at the end of Section 4.7.3.

a. Describe each step of the attack and give the overall work factor. How efficient is this attack as compared to the attack in Problem 34?

b. Determine the number of known plaintext required to complete this attack.

c. Implement this attack and verify your answers to parts a and b.

36. Could you improve the linear attack on FEAL-4 if you were able to choose the plaintext, instead of just using known plaintext?

Chapter 5

Hash Functions

HASH, x. There is no definition for this word—nobody knows what hash is.
— Ambrose Bierce, *The Devil's Dictionary*

5.1 Introduction

A cryptographic *hash function*, denoted by $h(x)$, must provide all of the following.

- *Compression*: For any input x, the output $y = h(x)$ is small. In practice, cryptographic hash functions produce a fixed size output, regardless of the length of the input, with typical output lengths being in the range of 128 to 512 bits.

- *Efficiency*: It must be efficient to compute $h(x)$ for any input x. Of course, the computational effort depends on the length of x, but the work should not grow too fast, as a function of the length of x.

- *One-way*: It is computationally infeasible to invert the hash, that is, given y, we cannot find a value x such that $h(x) = y$.

- *Weak collision resistance*: Given x and $h(x)$, it is computationally infeasible to find any w, with $w \neq x$, such that $h(w) = h(x)$.

- *Strong collision resistance*: It is computationally infeasible to find any pair x and w, with $x \neq w$, such that $h(x) = h(w)$.

It might seem that there is a hierarchy among the hash function requirements, in that strong collision resistance implies weak collision resistance which implies one-way. The reality of the situation is not so simple; see Problem 1 and [130]. Also, note that the terms pre-image resistance, second pre-image resistance and collision resistance are often used for one-way, weak collision resistance and strong collision resistance, respectively.

Note that collisions do exist—lots of them—but we require that it is computationally infeasible to find any collision. If one collision is found, a hash function is considered broken. This is certainly a conservative definition of "broken", but, as we show in Section 5.4, there are legitimate real-world concerns when even one collision is known.

In hash function design, the goal is to have a large and rapid *avalanche effect*, meaning that any small change in the input should quickly propagate into a large change in the intermediate steps. This is comparable to what happens in so-called chaotic systems, where a small change in initial conditions results in a large change in the result. Another (imprecise) analogy is that a strong avalanche effect is, intuitively, the opposite of continuity [34]. For a continuous function, small changes in the input will result in small changes in the output, but for cryptographic hash functions, we want a small change in the input to result in a large change in the output. Furthermore, for a hash function, we want this large change to occur in just a few steps, since it is often possible for the attacker to, in effect, reduce the number of steps where the avalanche can occur. Reducing the effective number of hash function steps is a crucial part of the attacks covered later in this chapter.

We require so much of a cryptographic hash function that it is somewhat surprising that any exist. But, in fact, practical cryptographic hash functions do exist. The number of clever—and often not-so-intuitive—uses for cryptographic hash functions is truly amazing. Yet another surprising fact about cryptographic hash functions is how often they are not used when they should be; see the discussion of WEP in Section 3.4 for a prime example.

Next, we briefly give some background on hash functions, and we discuss two cryptographic uses for such functions. The applications mentioned here are only the tip of the iceberg when it comes to uses for hash functions. Then in the next two sections, we dive head first into hash function cryptanalysis.

A hash function provides a "fingerprint" of data, in the sense that if two files differ at all, their hash values will differ in a seemingly random way. For one thing, this allows us to make digital signatures more efficient, since we can sign the hash value, instead of the full message.[1]

Here, we adopt the notation used in [79] for public key encryption, decryption, and signing:

- Encrypt message M with Alice's public key: $C = \{M\}_{\text{Alice}}$.

- Decrypt ciphertext C with Alice's private key: $M = [C]_{\text{Alice}}$.

---

[1]Hashing is not just for efficiency—it is actually necessary for the security of many signature schemes. For example, the ElGamal signature scheme discussed in Section 6.8 is insecure if the message is not hashed before signing. In this section, we ignore the security implications of hashing before signing.

- Signing and decrypting are the same operations, so the notation for Alice signing message M is $S = [M]_{\text{Alice}}$, where S is the signed message.

Encryption and decryption are inverse operations so that

$$[\{M\}_{\text{Alice}}]_{\text{Alice}} = \{[M]_{\text{Alice}}\}_{\text{Alice}} = M.$$

Since Alice's public key is public, anyone can compute $C = \{M\}_{\text{Alice}}$. However, only Alice can compute $M = [C]_{\text{Alice}}$ or the signature $S = [M]_{\text{Alice}}$, as Alice is assumed to be in sole possession of her private key. That is, anyone can encrypt a message for Alice, but only Alice can decrypt the ciphertext. Furthermore, only Alice can sign a message but anyone can verify the signature by using Alice's public key.

Suppose that M is a message that Alice wants to sign. Then Alice could compute the signature as $S = [M]_{\text{Alice}}$ and send S and M to Bob. Suppose Bob receives S' and M', which may or may not equal S and M, respectively. Then Bob checks whether $M' = \{S'\}_{\text{Alice}}$, and, if so, he has verified the integrity of the received message. That is, Bob knows with virtual certainty that $M' = M$.

While it is also possible to provide integrity using symmetric key cryptography (see the discussion of MAC in Section 4.2 and the discussion of HMAC, below), digital signatures provide integrity and *non-repudiation*. With symmetric keys, both Alice and Bob share the key, so Alice can claim that Bob forged the integrity operation, and thereby repudiate the message. But Alice cannot repudiate a message she digitally signed, since only she has access to her private key.

However, private key operations are costly to compute and sending both S and M requires twice as much bandwidth as sending M. To reduce the bandwidth usage, Alice could instead compute $S = [h(M)]_{\text{Alice}}$ and send M and this small S to Bob. In this case, when Bob receives M' and S' he must verify that $h(M') = \{S'\}_{\text{Alice}}$. Assuming that hashing is more efficient than private key operations, we not only save bandwidth, but we also increase signing efficiency. In fact, hashing is orders of magnitude more efficient than private key operations. Consequently, this method of signing the hash of M is virtually always used in practice.

However, it is important to note that by signing the hash, the security of the signature now depends not only on the security of the public key system, but also on the security of the hash function. To see why this is so, suppose that Alice computes $S = [h(M)]_{\text{Alice}}$ and sends M and S to Bob. If Trudy can find a collision with M, that is, if Trudy can find M' such that $h(M) = h(M')$, then Trudy can replace M with M', and Bob will erroneously verify the integrity of M'.

Before considering collision attacks on particular hash functions, we mention one more cryptographic application of hashing. Suppose Alice wants to send a message M to Bob, and she wants to ensure the integrity of the message. That is, Alice wants Bob to be able to automatically check that the message he receives is the message that was actually sent. Alice has the clever idea that she will compute $y = h(M)$ and she will send y and M to Bob. Then Bob can compute the hash of the received message and compare it to y. Bob can thereby verify the integrity of the message, that is, Bob can be confident that he actually received M.

There is a serious problem with Alice's integrity scheme. If Trudy intercepts M and y, she can replace M with M', and replace y with $y' = h(M')$. Then when Bob computes the hash of the received message, it will match the received hash value, and he will not suspect that the message has been altered.

Seeing the flaw in her scheme, Alice decides instead to compute a keyed hash, that is, $y = h(M, K)$, where K is a symmetric key that Alice and Bob share and (M, K) denotes the concatenation of M and K. Then, provided that Trudy does not know K, she cannot change the message without the change (almost certainly) being detected.

To eliminate some possible attacks, Alice really should compute a so-called HMAC instead of simply appending (or prepending) the key to the message and hashing the result [142]. To understand the potential problem with appending or prepending the key, we need to delve a little deeper into the way that hash functions perform their magic.

Most cryptographic hash functions process the message in blocks through several rounds in a manner analogous to the way that block ciphers work. For the two hash functions we consider in this chapter, each round consists of several steps, with each individual step performing a relatively simple operation. The overall hash operation is similar to the way that block cipher CBC mode encryption works (see Section 4.2 for a discussion of CBC mode), since the hash function processes the current block together with the output of the previous block to generate the output for the current block. For the first block, a fixed constant is used in place of the output of the previous block (since there is no previous block), and the output from the last block is the hash value.

For the hash functions we consider, the block size is 512 bits, and the hash result is 128 bits. To hash a multi-block message, the 128-bit output of the *compression function* for block i is added[2] to the initial value for block i, and this is used as the "initial value" when compressing block $i + 1$. The output from the final block is the hash value. Also, the initial value to the first block is denoted as "IV," which is a fixed value that is specified as part of the algorithm. The process used to hash multiple blocks is illustrated

---

[2]The 128-bit blocks are treated as four 32-bit words and the addition is computed per word, modulo 2^{32}.

in Figure 5.1. This method of hashing is known as the *Merkle–Damgård construction* (or Damgård–Merkle construction, depending on who you ask). It can be shown that if the compression function is collision resistant, then so is the corresponding hash function. This is somewhat analogous to the Feistel construction for block ciphers (see Section 4.3), where the security of the resulting cipher essentially reduces to the security of the round function.

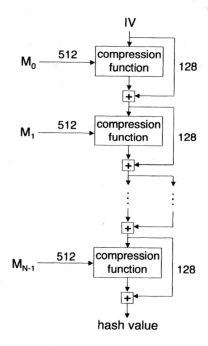

Figure 5.1: Hashing multiple blocks.

Suppose that a message consists of one 512-bit block M. Let IV be the constant initial value for the first block. Then the hash is computed as $h(M) = f(\text{IV}, M)$, where f is a known function. For the hash functions MD4 and MD5 we consider later in this chapter, the output $h(M)$ is always 128 bits, as is the initial constant IV. Then f corresponds to the compression function together with the addition operation as illustrated in Figure 5.1.

On the other hand, suppose that $M = (M_0, M_1)$ consists of exactly two 512-bit blocks. Then f is applied twice and we have[3]

$$h(M) = f(f(\text{IV}, M_0), M_1) = f(h(M_0), M_1).$$

---

[3]For both MD4 and MD5, the message is padded before hashing—even if the message is already a multiple of 512 bits. Here, we implicitly assume that the message M includes the padding.

This easily generalizes to any number of blocks, so that for a given message of the form $M = (M_0, M_1, \ldots, M_{n-1})$, we apply the function f a total of n times. It is easy to verify that

$$h(M) = f(h(M_0, M_1, \ldots, M_{n-2}), M_{n-1}).$$

One consequence of this approach to hashing is that if we have any two messages M and M' with $h(M) = h(M')$, then $h(M, X) = h(M', X)$ for any X. That is, given a collision, we can extend the colliding messages with any common value.

Now consider the keyed hash problem mentioned above. In this case, Alice wants to incorporate a key into the hash of the message M. Alice decides to compute the keyed hash of her message M as $y = h(K, M)$ and she sends y and M to Bob. Suppose that the length of (K, M) happens to be a multiple of 512 bits. Now suppose that Trudy intercepts the message and she replaces M with $M' = (M, X)$, where X consists of exactly one block. Since Trudy does not know the key K, it appears that her tampering will be detected. However, since Trudy knows $h(K, M)$, she can use the fact that

$$h(K, M') = h(K, M, X) = f(h(K, M), X)$$

to compute $y' = h(K, M')$, without knowledge of the key K. This defeats the purpose of the keyed hash.

Suppose that instead of pre-pending the key, Alice appends the key to the message before hashing. Then Alice sends $y = h(M, K)$ along with M to Bob. If it should happen that there is a collision for M, that is, if there exists some M' with $h(M') = h(M)$, then, assuming the message M is a multiple of the block length,

$$h(M, K) = f(h(M), K) = f(h(M'), K) = h(M', K).$$

In this case, Trudy can replace M with M' and the resulting keyed hash value would not need to be altered. Again, this defeats the purpose of the keyed hash.

Although this second attack is perhaps less serious than the first—since a collision must be found, in which case we consider the hash broken—both attacks are easily prevented by computing a hashed message authentication code, which is mercifully shortened to *HMAC*. In effect, the HMAC more thoroughly mixes the key into the hash value.

HMAC is defined in RFC 2104 [86] as follows. Let B be the number of bytes in a hash block. For most popular hash functions, $B = 64$. Define

$$\text{ipad} = \texttt{0x36} \text{ repeated } B \text{ times}$$

and

$$\text{opad} = \texttt{0x5C} \text{ repeated } B \text{ times}.$$

Then the HMAC of the message M is

$$\mathrm{HMAC}(M, K) = h(K \oplus \mathrm{opad}, h(K \oplus \mathrm{ipad}, M)),$$

where h is a cryptographic hash function. For the HMAC, two hashes are computed, but the outer hash is only computed over a small input, not the entire message M (which could be extremely large). An HMAC can be used to provide message integrity, as can a MAC or a digital signature. However, an HMAC has many other nifty uses as well.

Note that an HMAC can be used to detect errors that occur in transmission. However, as with any cryptographic integrity protection scheme, the HMAC provides much more than any error detection method (such as a cyclic redundancy check, or CRC) can provide. By using a cryptographic hash, the HMAC is resistant to attack by an intelligent adversary, whereas any error detection scheme can be defeated by such an adversary. See Section 3.4 and [142] for examples of the perils of using an error detection scheme when a cryptographic integrity check (such as HMAC) is required.

We note in passing that a symmetric cipher can be used as a hash function and vice versa. However, there are certain subtle issues that arise. For example, a block cipher that is used as a hash function must resist certain attacks that are not relevant when it is used as a cipher; see Problem 2.

In the next two sections we consider the cryptanalysis of the hash functions MD4 and MD5. The function MD4 was designed to be fast and in hash function design, as with most crypto, there is an inherent tradeoff between speed and security. It did not take long before fundamental weaknesses in MD4 were discovered, but it still took some time before anyone was able to produce an actual collision. We discuss Dobbertin's original attack on MD4 [42], which is a very clever and elegant piece of work.

MD5 is a much different story. After some chinks were visible in the MD4 design, it was modified and strengthened (at the expense of some speed) and the result was dubbed MD5. The hash function MD5, and its close cousin SHA-1, proceeded to become the mainstays of hashing. Recently, an MD5 collision was found due to some extraordinary cryptanalysis, which we outline in this chapter. However, the cryptanalysis of MD5 is not so elegant as that of MD4, and the attack has never been clearly explained by its inventor (or anyone else, for that matter). At the time of this writing, the kinks are still being worked out of the MD5 attack. In spite of this, many computational improvements to the original attack have been found recently. Whereas the original attack took several hours on a supercomputer, the current best attacks take about two minutes (on average) on a PC.

Another significant difference between the MD4 and MD5 attacks is that the former can be used to find a "meaningful" collision, while the latter cannot. However, we present an example that shows that both the MD4 attack and the MD5 attack create realistic security threats.

5.2   Birthdays and Hashing

> *"How many days are there in a year?"*
> *"Three hundred and sixty-five," said Alice.*
> *"And how many birthdays have you?"*
> *"One."*
> *"And if you take one from three hundred and sixty-five, what remains?"*
> *"Three hundred and sixty-four, of course."*
> *Humpty Dumpty looked doubtful.*
> *"I'd rather see that done on paper," he said.*
> *— Through the Looking Glass*

In this section we discuss the so-called birthday problem and its implications
for hashing. The birthday problem provides the necessary background for
a discussion of brute force attacks on hash functions, which are roughly the
equivalent of exhaustive key search attacks on symmetric ciphers. We also
consider a clever hashing attack that relies on the birthday problem to create
a shortcut attack for certain applications, provided the hash function employs
the Merkle–Damgård construction.

5.2.1   The Birthday Problem

Suppose that Trudy is in a room containing a total of N people (including
herself). What is the probability that at least one of the other $N - 1$ people
has the same birthday as Trudy? Assuming that birthdays are uniformly distributed among the 365 days in a year, the answer is not difficult to compute.
As with many discrete probability problems, it is easier to compute the probability of the complement and subtract the result from one. In this case, the
complement is that none of the other $N - 1$ people have the same birthday
as Trudy. For each person this probability is $364/365$, so that for all $N - 1$
people, the probability is $(364/365)^{N-1}$. Consequently, the probability we
want is

$$1 - (364/365)^{N-1}. \tag{5.1}$$

By setting (5.1) equal to $1/2$ and solving for N, we can find the number
of people that must be in a room before we expect someone to have the same
birthday as Trudy. Doing so, we find that if $N \geq 254$, then the probability
is greater than $1/2$ and we therefore expect to find someone with the same
birthday as Trudy. Intuitively, the answer should be about the number of days
in a year, and since there are 365 days in a year, the answer 254 is reasonable.
Note that in this version of the birthday problem we are comparing every
birthday to one specific birthday, namely, Trudy's. Also note that, more

generally, if there are M possible outcomes, we expect to need about M comparisons before we find a "collision".

On the other hand, suppose that we want to find the probability that any two (or more) people in a room share the same birthday, where there are N people in the room. It is again easier to compute the probability of the complement and subtract from one. Here, the complement is that all people have different birthdays, so that the desired probability is given by

$$1 - 365/365 \cdot 364/365 \cdot 363/365 \cdots (365 - N + 1)/365, \qquad (5.2)$$

provided that $N \leq 366$.

In this case, to find the number of people that must be in the room before we expect two or more to share the same birthday, we set (5.2) equal to $1/2$ and solve for N. Doing so, we find that if $N \geq 23$, then the probability in (5.2) is greater than $1/2$. That is, provided that there are at least 23 people in a room, we expect two or more to share the same birthday.

This fact is sometimes referred to as the "birthday paradox" because, at first glance, it appears paradoxical that only 23 people suffice when there are 365 days in a year. However, this result is not as paradoxical as it might seem. We are comparing every birthday to every other birthday, so with N people in the room, we are making $\binom{N}{2}$ comparisons, and once we have made about 365 comparisons, we expect to find a match. By this logic, the solution to this version of the birthday problem is the smallest value of N for which

$$\binom{N}{2} \geq 365,$$

which yields $N = 28$. This is close to the precise value of $N = 23$. As an approximation we often use $\sqrt{M}$, where M is the number of possible outcomes. For actual birthdays, $M = 365$ and we have $\sqrt{365} \approx 19$, which is indeed a good approximation to the precise result $N = 23$.

5.2.2 Birthday Attacks on Hash Functions

Recall that a cryptographic hash function must provide weak collision resistance and strong collision resistance. If we are given a particular hash value, $h(x)$ and we can find a w such that $h(w) = h(x)$ then we have "broken" the hash function, since we have violated the weak collision resistance property. The brute force attack is to randomly generate w, compute the hash and compare the result to $h(x)$, repeating until a collision is found. If the hash function h generates an n-bit output, the first version of the birthday problem discussed above implies that we will need to compute about 2^n hashes before we expect to find such a w. Therefore, for h to be considered secure, it is necessary (but not sufficient) that it is infeasible for Trudy to compute 2^n hashes. This is comparable to an exhaustive search for a cryptographic key.

If we can find a pair x and w such that $h(x) = h(w)$ then we have broken the hash h, since we have violated the strong collision resistance property. In this case, Trudy can conduct a brute force attack by randomly generating values, computing the hash, and comparing the result to all previously computed results. From the second version of the birthday problem discussed above, the number of hashes required to find a collision is about $\sqrt{2^n} = 2^{n/2}$. Consequently, a hash function that generates an n-bit output can, at best, provide a level of security comparable to a symmetric cipher with an $n/2$-bit key. In [110] the authors discuss how to use parallel computation to gain a significant improvement in this birthday attack on a hash function.

Of course, it is always possible that a cryptanalyst will find a shortcut attack. In any case, these two birthday attacks give upper bounds on the theoretical security of a hash function.

Next, we discuss two attacks that illustrate the way that these birthday attacks could be put to practical use. First we consider a generic attack on digital signatures. Then we outline a birthday attack that applies to any hash function h that employs the Merkle–Damgård construction.

5.2.3   Digital Signature Birthday Attack

The important role of hashing in the computation of digital signatures is discussed in Section 5.1, above. Recall that if M is the message that Alice wants to sign, then she computes $S = [h(M)]_{\text{Alice}}$ and sends S and M to Bob, where $[X]_{\text{Alice}}$ denotes "encryption" with Alice's private key.

Suppose that the hash function h generates an n-bit output. As discussed in [162], Trudy can, in principle, conduct a birthday attack as follows:

- Trudy selects an "evil" message E that she wants Alice to sign, but which Alice is unwilling to sign. For example, the message might state that Alice agrees to give all of the money in her bank account to Trudy.

- Trudy also creates an innocent message I that she is confident Alice is willing to sign. For example, this could be a message that appears to be routine business of the type that Alice regularly signs.

- Then Trudy generates $2^{n/2}$ variants of the innocent message by making minor editorial changes. These innocent messages, which we denote by I_i, for $i = 1, 2, \ldots, 2^{n/2}$, all have the same meaning as I, but since the messages differ, their hash values differ.

- Similarly, Trudy creates $2^{n/2}$ variants of the evil message, which we denoted by E_i, for $i = 1, 2, \ldots, 2^{n/2}$. These messages all have the same meaning as the original evil message E, but their hashes differ.

- Trudy hashes all of the evil messages E_i and all of the innocent messages I_i. By the birthday problem, she can expect to find a collision, say, $h(E_j) = h(I_k)$. Given such a collision, Trudy sends I_k to Alice, and asks Alice to sign it. Alice agrees to do so and she returns I_k and $[h(I_k)]_{\text{Alice}}$ to Trudy. Since $h(E_j) = h(I_k)$, it therefore follows that $[h(E_j)]_{\text{Alice}} = [h(I_k)]_{\text{Alice}}$ and, consequently, Trudy has effectively obtained Alice's signature on the evil message E_j.

Note that in this attack, Trudy has obtained Alice's signature on a message of Trudy's choosing without recovering Alice's private key, or attacking the underlying public key system in any way. This attack is a brute force attack on the hash function h, as it is used for computing digital signatures. To prevent this attack, it is necessary (but not sufficient) that n, the number of bits the hash function generates, is large enough so that Trudy cannot compute $2^{n/2}$ hashes.

5.2.4 Nostradamus Attack

Finally, we describe an interesting attack due to Kelsey and Kohno [80] that is applicable to any hash function that employs the Merkle-Damgård construction (see Figure 5.1, above). The hash functions MD4 and MD5 discussed later in this chapter are of this type, as are the popular SHA-1 and Tiger hashes.

Hash functions are often used in practice to prove prior knowledge or to commit to something without revealing the "something." For example, suppose that Alice, Bob and Charlie want to place sealed bids online. Since they do not trust that their bids will remain secret, neither Alice, Bob nor Charlie wants to submit their bid until the other two have submitted theirs. One possible solution to this problem is the following. First, Alice determines her bid A, Bob determines his bid B and Charlie determines his bid C. Then Alice submits $h(A)$, Bob submits $h(B)$, and Charlie submits $h(C)$. Once all three bids have been received, they are posted online, at which point Alice, Bob and Charlie can submit their respective bids, namely, A, B, and C. If the hash function h is one-way, there should be no disadvantage to submitting a bid before the other bidders. Also, if h is collision resistant, it should not be possible for Alice to change her bid once B and C have been revealed (and similarly for Bob and Charlie).[4]

Now consider the following scenario [80]. Trudy claims that she can predict the future. To prove it, on January 1, 2008 she publishes y, which she claims is $h(x)$, where x gives the final Standard and Poor's 500 (S&P 500) index[5] for December 31, 2008, along with various other predictions about events

---

[4] However, without modification, this protocol is insecure; see Problem 6.

[5] The S&P 500 is a well-known stock market index.

that will occur in 2009 and beyond. Suppose that on January 1, 2009, Trudy reveals a message x such that $y = h(x)$ and x correctly predicts the S&P 500 index for December 31, 2008, followed by a rambling set of predictions about future events that have not yet occurred.

Does this prove that Trudy can foretell the future? It would seem that by publishing y in advance, Trudy is committed to a specific x, unless she can violate the one-way property of the hash function h. It is generally much more difficult to violate the "one-way-ness" of a hash function than to find collisions. Barring any shortcut attack, if h generates an n-bit hash, then about 2^n hashes need to be computed before Trudy could expect to find a message x that hashes to a specified value y, while only about $2^{n/2}$ hashes need to be computed to find a collision. So, in the scenario outlined in the previous paragraph, it would seem that if n is sufficiently large so that it is infeasible for Trudy to compute 2^n hashes and no shortcut attack on h exists, then Trudy can legitimately claim to be the new Nostradamus.[6]

However, in [80] it is shown that Trudy can cheat, provided the hash function h uses the Merkle-Damgård construction and that Trudy is able to compute collisions. By the birthday problem, if $2^{n/2}$ is a feasible amount of work (where the hash h generates an n-bit output), Trudy can find collisions. Of course, if there is a shortcut collision attack on h, then Trudy may be able to compute collisions even more efficiently than via the birthday attack. But for the remainder of this discussion, we assume that Trudy computes collisions by the birthday attack and that $2^{n/2}$ is a feasible amount of work, while 2^n is not. Under these assumptions, we describe how Trudy can cheat.

Trudy must specify the value y in advance. Then when she knows the S&P 500 index for December 31, 2008, she wants to create a message that includes the S&P 500 result and hashes to y. More precisely, on January 1, 2009 Trudy knows the final S&P 500 index for December 31, 2008, and she sets P, the prefix, equal to this index result. Then Trudy must determine a suffix S so that $h(P, S) = y$, where y is the previously specified "hash" value. That is, the prefix P and y are specified, but Trudy is free to choose the suffix S so that $y = h(P, S)$. Of course, if Trudy can randomly 2^n suffixes S and compute the corresponding hashes, then she would expect to find one for which $y = h(P, S)$. But we assume that this is an infeasible amount of work, that is, Trudy cannot perform a brute force pre-image attack.

Kelsey and Kohno [80] describe their attack as a "herding" attack, since a specified prefix P is "herded" into the specified hash value by selecting suffixes S and computing collisions (as opposed to pre-images). Furthermore, in this attack Trudy has considerable control over S, so that it is possible for her to construct meaningful suffixes—instead of random gibberish, which

---

[6]Nostradamus (1503–1566) published numerous prophecies. His modern supporters claim that he predicted most of the major events of recent history. Ironically, Nostradamus' predictive powers seem to work best in retrospect.

might raise suspicions about her prognosticating abilities.

The attack relies on a data structure, the "diamond structure", which is essentially a cleverly constructed directed tree. An example of a small diamond structure appears in Figure 5.2. In this figure, the vertices d_{ij} represent intermediate hash values (that is, compression function results) and IV is the IV associated with the hash h (although any compression function output could be used in place of the IV in the diamond structure). The edges all represent messages, and the edges that meet at a vertex represent a compression function collision. The message blocks M_0 through M_7 can be selected arbitrarily, but the blocks M_{ij} must be chosen so that the denoted collisions occur. For example, in Figure 5.2, we have

$$d_{10} = f(d_{00}, M_{00}) = f(f(\text{IV}, M_0), M_{00})$$

and

$$d_{10} = f(d_{01}, M_{01}) = f(f(\text{IV}, M_1), M_{01}),$$

where f is the compression function of the hash h, See Figure 5.1 and the subsequent discussion for more details on the compression function f in relation to h.

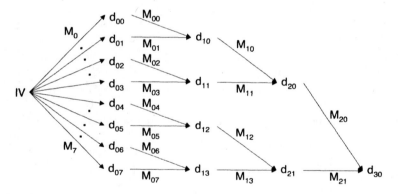

Figure 5.2: A small diamond structure.

Note that in Figure 5.1 the messages in the rightmost diamond must include any necessary padding so that d_{30} is a legitimate hash value. For hash functions such as MD4 and MD5 this is easily accomplished.

By the birthday problem we expect to find a collision within any diamond if we generate $2^{n/2} + 2^{n/2}$ messages. To see why this is the case, consider, for example, the diamond corresponding to

$$d_{10} = f(d_{00}, M_{00}) = f(d_{01}, M_{01}). \tag{5.3}$$

When determining a pair of message blocks M_{00} and M_{01} for which (5.3) holds, we only compare the hashes computed using putative M_{00} with those computed from putative M_{01} and vice versa. A collision between two hashes with different putative M_{00} values (or two different putative M_{01}) is of no use since such a collision would not yield the "diamond" that we seeks. Consequently, to generate the necessary 2^n comparisons, it is most efficient to compute $2^{n/2}$ putative M_{00} and $2^{n/2}$ putative M_{01} and compare the resulting hashes.

The "height" of the diamond structure is the number of d_{0j} elements in the directed graph. For example, the diamond structure in Figure 5.2 has a height of eight. Suppose that the height of a given diamond structure is 2^k. Then there are $2^k - 1$ diamonds, so the work required to construct the structure is, by the birthday problem, about

$$2 \cdot 2^{n/2}(2^k - 1) \approx 2^{n/2+k+1}.$$

It is claimed in [80] that this work factor can be reduced to about $2^{n/2+k/2+2}$.

Now we have the necessary machinery to describe the Nostradamus attack in detail. The attack consists of two phases. In the first phase, Trudy constructs a diamond structure and she determines the value y that she will claim as the hash of her prediction. Then in phase 2, a prefix P is given (consisting of Trudy's prediction) and Trudy must choose a suffix S so that $y = h(P, S)$.

In phase 1 of the attack, Trudy constructs a diamond structure of height 2^k and she claims that the hash of her stock market prediction is d_{k0}, the rightmost value in the diamond structure. That is, Trudy claims that $y = d_{k0}$ is the hash of x, where x includes her prediction for the closing S&P 500 index on December 31, 2008, along with other unspecified predictions for 2009 and beyond.

Then on January 1, 2009, Trudy is ready to begin phase 2 of the attack. Trudy creates the prefix P which consists of the closing S&P 500 index for December 31, 2008. She then creates a series of suffixes S', each consisting of some vague prediction of future events, and for each of these she applies the compression function of h to (P, S'). Assuming that (P, S') is a single message block, let $a' = f(IV, P, S')$, where f is the compression function of h. Trudy compares each computed a' to all 2^k of the d_{0j} and she repeats this until a match is found. Once Trudy finds such a match, she simply extends (P, S') by following the directed edges in the diamond structure until she arrives at $y = d_{k0}$. Appending the block on the traversed edges of the directed graph to (P, S'), Trudy obtains a message M that hashes to y. Most importantly, the message M contains P, the S&P 500 index for December 31, 2008, along with other predictions of future events. This is precisely what Trudy promised to deliver.

For example, suppose Figure 5.2 is Trudy's diamond structure. Further, suppose that Trudy determines S' such that $f(IV, P, S') = d_{02}$. Then

$$h(P, S', M_{02}, M_{11}, M_{20}) = y$$

and Trudy's "prediction" is the message

$$(P, S', M_{02}, M_{11}, M_{20}).$$

In [80], the authors refer to the process of following the directed path in the diamond structure as "herding" the prefix to the desired hash value.

Since the diamond structure is of height 2^k and h is an n-bit hash, the expected work for phase 2 of the attack is 2^{n-k}. As mentioned above, the claimed work for phase 1 is $2^{n/2+k/2+2}$. To minimize the total work, we set the phase 1 and phase 2 work factors equal to each other and solve for k. Doing so, we find

$$k = \frac{n-4}{3}.$$

Note that the message (P, S') is padded with k additional blocks to obtain M so that the overall message consists of $k + 1$ blocks. It would be possible to insert additional blocks, but it is probably desirable to minimize the overall size of the message.

Suppose the Nostradamus attack is applied to the MD5 hash function, which generates a 128-bit output. Then

$$k = \frac{n-4}{3} = \frac{124}{3} \approx 41,$$

which implies that the diamond structure has a height of 2^{41} and the overall work for the attack is about $2^{n-k} = 2^{87}$. While this is an enormous amount of work, it is far less than the 2^{128} work that would be required in a naïve brute force pre-image attack.

There are several possible refinements to this attack. For example, Trudy has a great deal of control over the message blocks, so that when creating the diamond structure, she can choose messages that provide meaningful predictions. That is, Trudy can use a similar approach to that discussed in Section 5.2.3, above, to make the messages meaningful.

In [80], several interesting potential applications for the Nostradamus attack are discussed. These attacks include stealing credit for an invention, editing a message without changing the hash (which has unpleasant implications for digital signatures) and random number "fixing", among many others. In effect, any application where a hash is used to commit to something is potentially susceptible to this attack.

In the remainder of this chapter, we discuss cryptanalytic attacks on two well-known hash functions, namely, MD4 and MD5. Although the MD4 attack is more efficient, both of these attacks provide highly efficient methods for generating collisions. Unlike the more generic attacks presented in this section, to understand the attacks in the next two sections, we must dig deep into the internal workings of the MD4 and MD5 hash functions.

5.3   MD4

"My dear! I really must get a thinner pencil. I can't manage this one a bit;
it writes all manner of things that I don't intend—"
— Through the Looking Glass

Message Digest 4, or MD4, is a hash algorithm proposed by Rivest in 1990.
MD4 was designed to be fast, which necessitated taking a few risks, with respect to security. By 1992 significant weaknesses had been found (although no
true collision was forthcoming) which led Rivest to produce a strengthened—
but slower—version known as MD5.

In 1998, Dobbertin [34, 41, 42] found the first true MD4 collision, and he
gave an extremely clever and efficient algorithm for generating such collisions.
Furthermore, Dobbertin demonstrated that his algorithm can be used to find
collisions that might actually matter in the real world. In this section, we
describe Dobbertin's attack on MD4. Other attacks on MD4 are now known,
but none provide as much insight into the underlying weakness of the hash
function as the attack presented here.

Part of Dobbertin's attack relies on differential cryptanalysis, while the
heart of the attack depends on finding a solution to a system of nonlinear
equations. The attack is fairly technical and involved, but the resulting algorithm is practical, with a work factor that is approximately equal to the
computation of 2^{20} MD4 hashes.

5.3.1   MD4 Algorithm

The MD4 algorithm is described by Rivest in RFC 1320 [121], where an
efficient implementation (in C) is given. Here, we only provide enough details
to implement the attack described below, and we use different notation than
is found in [121].

MD4 operates on 32-bit words. The four bytes of each word are interpreted so that the leftmost byte is the low-order (least significant) byte. That
is, a little-endian convention is followed. This is not a concern for the attack
described here, but it does become an issue if we want to construct meaningful
collisions.

Let M be the message to be hashed. The message M is padded so that
its length (in bits) is equal to 448 modulo 512, that is, the padded message
is 64 bits less than a multiple of 512. The padding consists of a single 1 bit,
followed by enough zeros to pad the message to the required length. Padding
is always used, even if the length of M happens to equal 448 mod 512. As a
result, there is at least one bit of padding, and at most 512 bits of padding.
Then the length (in bits) of the message (before padding) is appended as a

64-bit block. Padding is not a concern for the attack presented here; for the precise details, see [121].

The padded message is a multiple of 512 bits and, therefore, it is also a multiple of 32 bits. Let M be the message and N the number of 32-bit words in the (padded) message. Denote the message words as Y_i, so that $M = (Y_0, Y_1, \ldots, Y_{N-1})$. Due to the padding, N is a multiple of 16.

Define the three functions

$$F(A, B, C) = (A \wedge B) \vee (\neg A \wedge C) \qquad (5.4)$$

$$G(A, B, C) = (A \wedge B) \vee (A \wedge C) \vee (B \wedge C) \qquad (5.5)$$

$$H(A, B, C) = A \oplus B \oplus C \qquad (5.6)$$

where "$\wedge$" is the bitwise AND operation, "$\vee$" is the bitwise OR operation, "$\oplus$" is the XOR, and "$\neg A$" is the complement of A. Each of these functions has a simple interpretation. The function F uses the bits of A to select between the corresponding bits of B and C, the function G is a "majority vote" in each bit position, while H can be viewed as a bitwise parity function.

The MD4 hash algorithm appears in Table 5.1. In this algorithm, addition of 32-bit words are to be taken modulo 2^{32}.

In MD4, each 512-bit block is processed through three *rounds*, denoted as Round0, Round1, and Round2 in Table 5.1. Taken together, these three round functions and the final addition operation comprise the MD4 compression function, since they compress the 512-bit block and the 128-bit initial value into a 128-bit result. Table 5.2 shows how each of the three rounds is expanded into 16 *steps*, where the function F is used in round 0, the function G in round 1, and the function H in round 2, and "$\lll$" is a left rotation. Round i use the constant K_i, where

$$K_0 = \texttt{0x00000000}, \quad K_1 = \texttt{0x5a827999}, \quad \text{and} \quad K_2 = \texttt{0x6ed9eba1}.$$

Note that $K_0 = 0$, but we include it here to simplify some of the notation.

The three rounds give a total of 48 steps, each involving one application of F, G or H. We number these steps consecutively, from 0 through 47, where in round 0, steps 0 through 15 occur, in round 1, steps 16 through 31 occur, and round 2 consists of steps 32 through 47.

The shift for step i is denoted s_i. The values of s_i, for $i = 0, 1, \ldots, 47$, are listed in Table 5.3. In Table 5.1, the permutation of the input words is denoted by σ, that is, $W_i = X_{\sigma(i)}$. The values of $\sigma(i)$, for $i = 0, 1, 2, \ldots, 47$, are given in Table 5.4.

At step i of MD4, only the 32-bit value Q_i changes. A single MD4 step is illustrated in Figure 5.3, where

$$f_i(A, B, C) = \begin{cases} F(A, B, C) + K_0 & \text{if } 0 \le i \le 15 \\ G(A, B, C) + K_1 & \text{if } 16 \le i \le 31 \\ H(A, B, C) + K_2 & \text{if } 32 \le i \le 47. \end{cases}$$

Table 5.1: MD4 Algorithm

// $M = (Y_0, Y_1, \ldots, Y_{N-1})$, message to hash, after padding
// Each Y_i is a 32-bit word and N is a multiple of 16
MD4(M)
   // initialize $(A, B, C, D) =$ IV
   $(A, B, C, D) = (0\text{x}67452301, 0\text{xefcdab}89, 0\text{x}98\text{badcfe}, 0\text{x}10325476)$
   for $i = 0$ **to** $N/16 - 1$
      // Copy block i into X
      $X_j = Y_{16i+j}$, **for** $j = 0$ **to** 15
      // Copy X to W
      $W_j = X_{\sigma(j)}$, **for** $j = 0$ **to** 47
      // initialize Q
      $(Q_{-4}, Q_{-3}, Q_{-2}, Q_{-1}) = (A, D, C, B)$
      // Rounds 0, 1, and 2
      Round0(Q, W)
      Round1(Q, W)
      Round2(Q, W)
      // Each addition is modulo 2^{32}
      $(A, B, C, D) = (Q_{44} + Q_{-4}, Q_{47} + Q_{-1}, Q_{46} + Q_{-2}, Q_{45} + Q_{-3})$
   next i
   return A, B, C, D
end MD4

5.3.2 MD4 Attack

The attack described in this section is due to Dobbertin [42]. Our description uses different notation than the original, and we have rearranged and

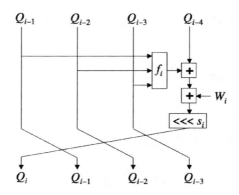

Figure 5.3: MD4 step.

Table 5.2: MD4 Rounds

Round0(Q, W)
    // steps 0 through 15
    for $i = 0$ **to** 15
        $Q_i = (Q_{i-4} + F(Q_{i-1}, Q_{i-2}, Q_{i-3}) + W_i + K_0) \lll s_i$
    next i
end Round0

Round1(Q, W)
    // steps 16 through 31
    for $i = 16$ **to** 31
        $Q_i = (Q_{i-4} + G(Q_{i-1}, Q_{i-2}, Q_{i-3}) + W_i + K_1) \lll s_i$
    next i
end Round1

Round2(Q, W)
    // steps 32 through 47
    for $i = 32$ **to** 47
        $Q_i = (Q_{i-4} + H(Q_{i-1}, Q_{i-2}, Q_{i-3}) + W_i + K_2) \lll s_i$
    next i
end Round2

---

expanded on the exposition at several points.

This attack finds two distinct 512-bit blocks that hash to the same value, thereby yielding a collision. As noted in Section 5.1, if any common bit string is appended to two colliding blocks, the resulting strings will also yield a collision.

Dobbertin's attack includes a differential phase, where we require that the pair of 512-bit inputs satisfy a certain differential property at an intermediate stage of the algorithm. When this differential property holds, then with a

Table 5.3: MD4 Shifts

Step i	0	1	2	3	4	5	6	7	8	9	10	11	12	13	14	15
Shift s_i	3	7	11	19	3	7	11	19	3	7	11	19	3	7	11	19
Step i	16	17	18	19	20	21	22	23	24	25	26	27	28	29	30	31
Shift s_i	3	5	9	13	3	5	9	13	3	5	9	13	3	5	9	13
Step i	32	33	35	35	36	37	38	39	40	41	42	43	44	45	46	47
Shift s_i	3	9	11	15	3	9	11	15	3	9	11	15	3	9	11	15

Table 5.4: MD4 Input Word Order

Step i	0	1	2	3	4	5	6	7	8	9	10	11	12	13	14	15
$\sigma(i)$	0	1	2	3	4	5	6	7	8	9	10	11	12	13	14	15
Step i	16	17	18	19	20	21	22	23	24	25	26	27	28	29	30	31
$\sigma(i)$	0	4	8	12	1	5	9	13	2	6	10	14	3	7	11	15
Step i	32	33	35	35	36	37	38	39	40	41	42	43	44	45	46	47
$\sigma(i)$	0	8	4	12	2	10	6	14	1	9	5	13	3	11	7	15

probability of about $1/2^{22}$, we obtain a collision for the full hash. The trick then is to efficiently find a sufficient number of pairs of inputs that satisfy this differential property.

After describing the differential phase of the attack, we then specify a system of nonlinear equations, any solution of which will satisfy the desired differential property. For the attack to be practical, we must be able to efficiently solve this system of equations, and we explain how to accomplish this.

There is also a third phase of the attack that connects the second phase to the initial steps of the hash algorithm. This third phase is relatively simple.

Before we dive into the computational details behind the attack, we try to motivate Dobbertin's approach to the problem. Here, we only provide a quick overview—for more details see Daum [34].

Motivation

Dobbertin's attack yields a colliding pair of messages, denoted

$$M = (X_0, X_1, \ldots, X_{15}) \text{ and } M' = (X'_0, X'_1, \ldots, X'_{15}),$$

each consisting of a single 512-bit block. The two messages are chosen to be as similar as possible with respect to the difference operation, which is defined to be subtraction modulo 2^{32}. More precisely, only one word differs between M and M', and the modular difference in that word is 1. Furthermore, the particular word where this difference occurs is chosen so that, in effect, we only need to worry about the avalanche effect for steps 12 through 19. This essentially reduces the most difficult part of the attack to just 8 of the 48 steps. Then a system of equations is derived for these 8 steps, and some clever insights make it possible to efficiently solve the resulting equations. The real beauty of Dobbertin's attack is that these equations can be solved so efficiently, that a collision can be generated in about two seconds on a PC.

While the attack does have a differential phase, the critical issue is the equation solving phase. The system of equations is solved using a method that relies on the fact that a small change in the input will usually result in a small change in the output. This, in turn, only holds because the number of steps is small, which implies that the avalanche effect is relatively small. Furthermore, it is crucial that a large number of different inputs compress to the same output, making a solution that much easier to find. In short, the attack uses a very specialized method of equation solving that takes full advantage of the structure of the MD4 hash.

Notation

Let $\text{MD4}_{i...j}(A, B, C, D, M)$ be the result of steps $i, i+1, i+2, \ldots, j$ of the MD4 hash, where the arguments (A, B, C, D) are the "initial values" at step i and M is the data array (where M consists of sixteen 32-bit words). Then $\text{MD4}_{i...j}(A, B, C, D, M)$ yields the four 32-bit words that result from applying steps i through j to the initial values (A, B, C, D), using M as the data. For example, $\text{MD4}_{14...18}(A, B, C, D, M)$ will yield the $(Q_{18}, Q_{17}, Q_{16}, Q_{15})$, the four 32-bit words that result from applying steps 14 through 18 (inclusive) using the specified initial values, and using the data array M. The only words of M that will be used in steps 14 through 18 are words 14, 15, 0, 4 and 8, respectively, as can be seen from Table 5.3. Consequently, the other words of M are irrelevant in the computation of $\text{MD4}_{14...18}(A, B, C, D, M)$.

We denote the initial values for step 0 as "IV"; that is, IV is the MD4 initialization vector. As indicated in Table 5.1, the initialization vector is

$$\text{IV} = (\text{0x67452301}, \text{0xefcdab89}, \text{0x98badcfe}, \text{0x10325476}). \qquad (5.7)$$

The attack presented here would work for any choice of IV, but we must use the IV in (5.7) to obtain an MD4 collision.

Note that even if the correct MD4 initialization vector is used,

$$\text{MD4}_{0...47}(\text{IV}, M) \neq h(M),$$

where h is the MD4 hash function, since there is a final transformation in MD4 that is not accounted for in $\text{MD4}_{0...47}(\text{IV}, X)$. This final transformation consists of adding the initial values to the output of the function and rearranging the order of the output words—see Table 5.1. The MD4 padding is also not considered in this attack. But any collision found by this attack will result in a collision for the full MD4 hash without any modification to M or M'.

Suppose

$$(Q_j, Q_{j-1}, Q_{j-2}, Q_{j-3}) = \text{MD4}_{0...j}(\text{IV}, M)$$

and

$$(Q'_j, Q'_{j-1}, Q'_{j-2}, Q'_{j-3}) = \text{MD4}_{0...j}(\text{IV}, M').$$

Then define

$$\Delta_j = (Q_j - Q'_j, Q_{j-1} - Q'_{j-1}, Q_{j-2} - Q'_{j-2}, Q_{j-3} - Q'_{j-3}),$$

where, as usual, the arithmetic is taken modulo 2^{32}.

We use 2^n to denote the 32-bit word which has decimal value $2^n \pmod{2^{32}}$, and -2^n represent $-2^n \pmod{2^{32}}$. Then, for example,

$$2^{25} = \text{0x02000000} \quad \text{and} \quad -2^5 = \text{0xffffffe0}.$$

Now we have all of the notation and machinery necessary to describe Dobbertin's clever attack, which determines two distinct 512-bit inputs, M and M', such that $\text{MD4}_{0...47}(\text{IV}, M) = \text{MD4}_{0...47}(\text{IV}, M')$. As mentioned above, this implies $h(M) = h(M')$ where h is the MD4 hash function.

Although the differential phase of Dobbertin's attack occurs last in practice, we describe it first, since it motivates the remainder of the attack. Then we work our way backwards to the start of the attack, and at each phase we consider the probability of success and the work factor.

Given a 512-bit input M, we have $M = (X_0, X_1, \ldots, X_{15})$, where each X_i is a 32-bit word. Given M, define M' by

$$X'_i = X_i \quad \text{for} \quad i \neq 12 \quad \text{and} \quad X'_{12} = X_{12} + 1. \tag{5.8}$$

As with all arithmetic operations in this section, the addition is taken modulo 2^{32}.

The input word X_{12} last appears in step 35 of the MD4 hash. Consequently, if we can find M and M' that satisfy (5.8) for which $\Delta_{35} = (0, 0, 0, 0)$, then we have found a collision. That is, if $\Delta_{35} = (0, 0, 0, 0)$ then the internal state of MD4 for inputs M and M' coincide at step 35, and all input values for steps 36 through 47 are the same, so the resulting MD4 hash values must be equal. Our goal is to find such a pair M and M'.

Given this observation concerning Δ_{35}, Dobbertin's attack consists of the following three phases.

1. First, we show that if

$$\Delta_{19} = (2^{25}, -2^5, 0, 0), \tag{5.9}$$

   then, with a probability of at least $1/2^{30}$, we obtain the desired result, that is, we have $\Delta_{35} = (0, 0, 0, 0)$. This phase is the differential attack mentioned above.

2. Then we "backup" to step 12, that is, we show how to determine initial values for step 12 that will force (5.9) to hold. This second phase of the attack requires a solution to a nonlinear system of equations.

3. Then we complete the attack by backing up further, all the way to step 0. This last phase of the attack is relatively straightforward.

At each of the three phases of the attack, some of the 32-bit words X_i of the message M are determined. When the attack has successfully completed, we will have specified a full 512-bit M and M' can be computed from (5.8). Then $M \neq M'$, but they have the same MD4 hash value and we have found the desired collision.

Steps 19 to 35

First, we describe the differential phase of the attack, which begins at step 19 and concludes at step 35. Often, differential cryptanalytic attacks use XOR as the difference operation, but here the difference is defined as subtraction modulo 2^{32}.

We assume that (5.9) is satisfied and, furthermore, that

$$G(Q_{19}, Q_{18}, Q_{17}) = G(Q'_{19}, Q'_{18}, Q'_{17}). \qquad (5.10)$$

If both of these assumptions hold, then the probabilities in Table 5.5 can be shown to hold. Recall that Q_j is the only output that changes at step j. Also, in Table 5.5, the column labeled p gives the probability that Δ_j holds, given that Δ_{j-1} holds. The i column indicates the round—and therefore whether function G, or H is used in the calculation of the corresponding row. Note that the data blocks M and M' are the same at each step, except for step 35, where $X'_{12} = X_{12} + 1$. This is indicated by the two inputs for the $j = 35$ step. The "$*$" elements in Table 5.5 indicate entries that are not relevant to the differential attack.

Consider, for example, the $j = 35$ row in Table 5.5. Assuming that the $j = 34$ row holds true, then $\Delta_{34} = (0, 0, 0, 1)$ and it follows from the definition of step 35 in Table 5.2 that

$$\begin{aligned}
Q_{35} &= (Q_{31} + H(Q_{34}, Q_{33}, Q_{32}) + X_{12} + K_2) \lll 15 \\
&= ((Q'_{31} + 1) + H(Q'_{34}, Q'_{33}, Q'_{32}) + X_{12} + K_2) \lll 15 \\
&= (Q'_{31} + H(Q'_{34}, Q'_{33}, Q'_{32}) + (X_{12} + 1) + K_2) \lll 15 \\
&= Q'_{35}
\end{aligned}$$

which implies that $\Delta_{35} = (0, 0, 0, 0)$, with probability 1. This is summarized in the $j = 35$ row of Table 5.5.

Each of the remaining probabilities in Table 5.5 can also be verified directly, although some of the counting arguments are fairly technical. In Problems 11 and 12 we outline a straightforward computational approach that can be used to determine the analogous probabilities for 8-bit words. These 8-bit probabilities are essentially identical to those obtained using 32-bit words.

The product of the probabilities in Table 5.5 is about $1/2^{30}$, which implies that if we find about 2^{30} inputs M that satisfy (5.9)—with the corresponding M' defined by (5.8)—then we can expect to obtain a pair of inputs for

Table 5.5: Differential Attack on MD4

j	ΔQ_j	ΔQ_{j-1}	ΔQ_{j-2}	ΔQ_{j-3}	i	s_j	p	Input
19	2^{25}	-2^5	0	0	*	*	*	*
20	0	2^{25}	-2^5	0	1	3	1	X_1
21	0	0	2^{25}	-2^5	1	5	1/9	X_5
22	-2^{14}	0	0	2^{25}	1	9	1/3	X_9
23	2^6	-2^{14}	0	0	1	13	1/3	X_{13}
24	0	2^6	-2^{14}	0	1	3	1/9	X_2
25	0	0	2^6	-2^{14}	1	5	1/9	X_6
26	-2^{23}	0	0	2^6	1	9	1/3	X_{10}
27	2^{19}	-2^{23}	0	0	1	13	1/3	X_{14}
28	0	2^{19}	-2^{23}	0	1	3	1/9	X_3
29	0	0	2^{19}	-2^{23}	1	5	1/9	X_7
30	-1	0	0	2^{19}	1	9	1/3	X_{11}
31	1	-1	0	0	1	13	1/3	X_{15}
32	0	1	-1	0	2	3	1/3	X_0
33	0	0	1	-1	2	9	1/3	X_8
34	0	0	0	1	2	11	1/3	X_4
35	0	0	0	0	2	15	1	$X_{12}, X_{12}+1$

which $\Delta_{35} = (0,0,0,0)$. Given such a pair, we will have found a collision and thereby have broken MD4.

Below, we show that there is a computationally efficient method to generate messages M for which the differential condition (5.9) holds. As a result, an efficient attack exists for finding collisions. In [42], it is claimed that the actual success probability of the differential phase of this MD4 attack is about $1/2^{22}$, as opposed to $1/2^{30}$, which is the probability indicated by the approximations in Table 5.5. Assuming the higher probability holds, if we can find 2^{22} data values that satisfy the initial conditions of the differential attack, then we expect to find a collision. In fact, it is easy to show empirically that the higher probability does hold.

For the differential attack in Table 5.5, there are no restrictions on M. In the remaining phases of the attack, we determine M so that $\Delta_{19} = (0,0,0,0)$ and the technical condition (5.10) holds, in which case the analysis in Table 5.5 is valid.

This completes our description of the differential phase of the attack. In the next phase of the attack, we backup to step 12 and force the necessary differential condition at step 19 to hold. This next phase is the most complex part of the attack.

Steps 12 to 19

In this phase of the attack, we consider steps 12 through 19. This is simpler than attempting to deal with steps 0 through 19 all at once. And if we can solve the problem for steps 12 through 19, then, intuitively, it should be easy to solve for steps 0 through 11, since $X_j = X_j'$ for all $j \neq 12$ and X_{12} first appears in step 12.

Table 5.6 contains the relevant information for steps 12 through 19. Here, $i = 0$ indicates that the function F is used, while $i = 1$ indicates that G is used.

Table 5.6: MD4 Steps 12 through 19

j	i	s_j	M Input	M' Input
12	0	3	X_{12}	$X_{12} + 1$
13	0	7	X_{13}	X_{13}
14	0	11	X_{14}	X_{14}
15	0	19	X_{15}	X_{15}
16	1	3	X_0	X_0
17	1	5	X_4	X_4
18	1	9	X_8	X_8
19	1	13	X_{12}	$X_{12} + 1$

To apply the differential attack in Table 5.5, it is necessary that the differential condition $\Delta_{19} = (2^{25}, -2^5, 0, 0)$ is satisfied, which means that

$$
\begin{aligned}
Q_{19} &= Q_{19}' + 2^{25} \\
Q_{18} + 2^5 &= Q_{18}' \\
Q_{17} &= Q_{17}' \\
Q_{16} &= Q_{16}'.
\end{aligned}
\tag{5.11}
$$

We want to derive equations involving Q_j and Q_j', for $j = 12, 13, \ldots, 19$. We can obtain eight equations by combining the corresponding equations in Q_j and Q_j'. For example, at step 12 we have

$$
Q_{12} = (Q_8 + F(Q_{11}, Q_{10}, Q_9) + X_{12}) \lll 3
\tag{5.12}
$$

and

$$
Q_{12}' = (Q_8' + F(Q_{11}', Q_{10}', Q_9') + X_{12}') \lll 3.
\tag{5.13}
$$

Since $X_j = X_j'$ for $j = 0, 1, 2, \ldots, 11$, and these are the only data values used in steps 0 through 11, we must have $\Delta_{11} = (0, 0, 0, 0)$, which implies that

$$
(Q_8, Q_9, Q_{10}, Q_{11}) = (Q_8', Q_9', Q_{10}', Q_{11}').
\tag{5.14}
$$

Consequently, subtracting (5.12) from (5.13) and simplifying yields

$$(Q'_{12} \lll 29) - (Q_{12} \lll 29) = 1.$$

As another example, consider step 18, where we have

$$Q_{18} = (Q_{14} + G(Q_{17}, Q_{16}, Q_{15}) + X_8) \lll 9 \qquad (5.15)$$

and

$$Q'_{18} = (Q'_{14} + G(Q'_{17}, Q'_{16}, Q'_{15}) + X_8) \lll 9. \qquad (5.16)$$

Subtracting (5.15) from (5.16) and simplifying yields

$$\begin{aligned} G(Q'_{17}, Q'_{16}, Q'_{15}) &- G(Q_{17}, Q_{16}, Q_{15}) \\ &= Q_{14} - Q'_{14} + (Q'_{18} \lll 23) - (Q_{18} \lll 23). \end{aligned}$$

Combining the corresponding equations for Q_j and Q'_j, and making use of (5.11) and (5.14), we obtain the system of equations

$$1 = (Q'_{12} \lll 29) - (Q_{12} \lll 29) \qquad (5.17)$$
$$F(Q'_{12}, Q_{11}, Q_{10}) - F(Q_{12}, Q_{11}, Q_{10}) = (Q'_{13} \lll 25) - (Q_{13} \lll 25) \qquad (5.18)$$
$$F(Q'_{13}, Q'_{12}, Q_{11}) - F(Q_{13}, Q_{12}, Q_{11}) = (Q'_{14} \lll 21) - (Q_{14} \lll 21) \qquad (5.19)$$
$$F(Q'_{14}, Q'_{13}, Q'_{12}) - F(Q_{14}, Q_{13}, Q_{12}) = (Q'_{15} \lll 13) - (Q_{15} \lll 13) \qquad (5.20)$$
$$G(Q'_{15}, Q'_{14}, Q'_{13}) - G(Q_{15}, Q_{14}, Q_{13}) = Q_{12} - Q'_{12} \qquad (5.21)$$
$$G(Q_{16}, Q'_{15}, Q'_{14}) - G(Q_{16}, Q_{15}, Q_{14}) = Q_{13} - Q'_{13} \qquad (5.22)$$
$$G(Q_{17}, Q_{16}, Q'_{15}) - G(Q_{17}, Q_{16}, Q_{15}) = Q_{14} - Q'_{14} + (Q'_{18} \lll 23)$$
$$- (Q_{18} \lll 23) \qquad (5.23)$$
$$G(Q'_{18}, Q_{17}, Q_{16}) - G(Q_{18}, Q_{17}, Q_{16}) = Q_{15} - Q'_{15} + (Q'_{19} \lll 19)$$
$$- (Q_{19} \lll 19) - 1 \qquad (5.24)$$

To solve these equations, we must find fourteen 32-bit words

$$(Q_{10}, Q_{11}, Q_{12}, Q_{13}, Q_{14}, Q_{15}, Q_{16}, Q_{17}, Q_{18}, Q_{19}, Q'_{12}, Q'_{13}, Q'_{14}, Q'_{15}) \qquad (5.25)$$

so that all of the equations (5.17) through (5.24) are satisfied. Given such a solution, then from the definition of steps 12 through 19, it is easy to verify that the desired condition on Δ_{19} will hold provided we select

$$
\begin{aligned}
X_{13} &= \text{anything} \\
X_{14} &= (Q_{14} \lll 21) - Q_{10} - F(Q_{13}, Q_{12}, Q_{11}) \\
X_{15} &= (Q_{15} \lll 13) - Q_{11} - F(Q_{14}, Q_{13}, Q_{12}) \\
X_0 &= (Q_{16} \lll 29) - Q_{12} - G(Q_{15}, Q_{14}, Q_{13}) - K_1 \\
X_4 &= (Q_{17} \lll 27) - Q_{13} - G(Q_{16}, Q_{15}, Q_{14}) - K_1 \qquad (5.26) \\
X_8 &= (Q_{18} \lll 23) - Q_{14} - G(Q_{17}, Q_{16}, Q_{15}) - K_1 \\
X_{12} &= (Q_{19} \lll 19) - Q_{15} - G(Q_{18}, Q_{17}, Q_{16}) - K_1 \\
Q_9 &= (Q_{13} \lll 25) - F(Q_{12}, Q_{11}, Q_{10}) - X_{13} \\
Q_8 &= (Q_{12} \lll 19) - F(Q_{11}, Q_{10}, Q_9) - X_{12}.
\end{aligned}
$$

That is, given a solution of the form (5.25) to the system of equations that appears in (5.17) through (5.24), if we choose X_j, for $j = 13, 14, 15, 0, 4, 8, 12$, and Q_9 and Q_8 as specified in (5.26), then we can begin at step 12 and arrive at step 19 with the necessary differential condition on Δ_{19} satisfied.[7] Consequently, this phase of the MD4 attack reduces to finding a solution to the system of equations in (5.17) through (5.24).

If we choose

$$
Q_{12} = -1 = \text{0xffffffff}, \quad Q'_{12} = 0, \quad \text{and} \quad Q_{11} = 0, \qquad (5.27)
$$

then (5.17) is satisfied, and equations (5.24), (5.23), (5.19), (5.22), and (5.18), respectively, can be rewritten as[8]

$$
\begin{aligned}
Q'_{15} &= Q_{15} - G(Q'_{18}, Q_{17}, Q_{16}) + G(Q_{18}, Q_{17}, Q_{16}) \\
&\quad + (Q'_{19} \lll 19) - (Q_{19} \lll 19) - 1 \qquad (5.28) \\
Q'_{14} &= Q_{14} - G(Q_{17}, Q_{16}, Q'_{15}) + G(Q_{17}, Q_{16}, Q_{15}) \\
&\quad + (Q'_{18} \lll 23) - (Q_{18} \lll 23) \qquad (5.29) \\
Q_{13} &= (Q_{14} \lll 21) - (Q'_{14} \lll 21) \qquad (5.30) \\
Q'_{13} &= Q_{13} - G(Q_{16}, Q'_{15}, Q'_{14}) + G(Q_{16}, Q_{15}, Q_{14}) \qquad (5.31) \\
Q_{10} &= (Q'_{13} \lll 25) - (Q_{13} \lll 25). \qquad (5.32)
\end{aligned}
$$

Most of these equations follow immediately from the corresponding equation above, but (5.30) and (5.32) require somewhat more work; see Problem 13. With the equations in this form, it is apparent that

$$
(Q_{14}, Q_{15}, Q_{16}, Q_{17}, Q_{18}, Q_{19}) \qquad (5.33)
$$

---

[7]Whew!

[8]Hopefully, we have corrected a couple of very annoying typos that appear in [42].

can be chosen arbitrarily, thereby determining

$$(Q_{10}, Q_{13}, Q'_{13}, Q'_{14}, Q'_{15}). \tag{5.34}$$

The two remaining equations, (5.21) and (5.20), can be rewritten, respectively, as

$$G(Q_{15}, Q_{14}, Q_{13}) - G(Q'_{15}, Q'_{14}, Q'_{13}) = 1 \tag{5.35}$$

$$F(Q'_{14}, Q'_{13}, 0) - F(Q_{14}, Q_{13}, -1) - (Q'_{15} \lll 13) + (Q_{15} \lll 13) = 0. \tag{5.36}$$

We refer to these as the "check" equations, and, of course, these check equations must both be satisfied before we have found a solution to the original system of equations in (5.17) through (5.24).

Finally, a solution is said to be *admissible* if it satisfies the additional constraint

$$G(Q_{19}, Q_{18}, Q_{17}) = G(Q'_{19}, Q'_{18}, Q_{17}). \tag{5.37}$$

If a solution is not admissible, then the $j = 20$ step of the differential attack in Table 5.5 will fail, so we want to restrict our attention to admissible solutions.

To solve this system we proceed as follows. First, we randomly select values for the free variables in (5.33) and substitute these into equations (5.28) through (5.32), thereby determining the values in (5.34). At this point, we have determined values for all of the variables that appear in the the check equations (5.35) and (5.36) and we can verify whether both of these required conditions hold. If so, we have found a solution to the system of equations. In this case, we can then verify whether the solution is admissible, that is, whether (5.37) holds. If the solution is admissible, then the solution is a candidate for the differential phase of the attack. If any of these three conditions fail, we can start over with another choice for the free variables in (5.28) through (5.32).

Each iteration of this process is efficient, but it appears that an inordinately large number of trials might be required before we can expect to find a solution that satisfies both of the check equations (5.35) and (5.36) and is admissible, that is, (5.37) also holds. In fact, random 32-bit words would only be expected to match with a probability of $1/2^{32}$, and if these three equations each hold with such a probability, then 2^{96} trials would be required before before a single admissible solution could be found. This would give an overall work factor much higher than an exhaustive collision search, which, by the birthday paradox, has an expected work factor of about 2^{64}.

Here, Dobbertin cleverly makes use of what he calls a "continuous approximation", that is, he uses the fact that input values for F and G that are "nearby" will generate output values that are "nearby" (see Problem 14). This reduces the work required to solve the system of equations to a very small amount, which takes less than one second on a modern PC.

Recall that the notation $\langle Y \rangle_{i...j}$ is used to represent bits i through j of Y, where the bits are numbered from left-to-right, beginning with 0. Also, we use the notation $\langle Y = 0 \rangle_{i...j}$ to denote that bits i through j of Y are all 0. Dobbertin's continuous approximation algorithm can be stated as follows:

1. Let $Q_{11} = 0$, $Q_{12} = -1$, and $Q'_{12} = 0$, as specified in (5.27).

2. Select Q_{14}, Q_{15}, Q_{16}, Q_{17}, Q_{18}, and Q_{19} at random.

3. Compute Q'_{15}, Q'_{14}, Q_{13}, Q'_{13}, and Q_{10} using (5.28) through (5.32), respectively.

4. If the check condition (5.35), holds, goto 5; otherwise goto 2.

5. At this point, all of the equations (5.28) through (5.32) are satisfied, as well as the check condition (5.35). We now find a sequence of solutions that converge to a solution that also satisfies the second check condition (5.36). Denote the values specified in step 2 as the "basic" variables and let j be the smallest index for which

$$\langle F' - F - (Q'_{15} \lll 13) + (Q_{15} \lll 13) = 0 \rangle_{j...31}, \qquad (5.38)$$

where we have let $F' = F(Q'_{14}, Q'_{13}, 0)$ and $F = F(Q_{14}, Q_{13}, -1)$. Also, we let $j = 32$ if the rightmost bit of (5.38) is not zero. If $j = 0$, then we are finished. If not, transform the solution by changing one randomly selected bit in each of the basic variables. Compute Q'_{15}, Q'_{14}, Q_{13}, Q'_{13}, and Q_{10} from (5.28) through (5.32), respectively, using these transformed values. If the first check equation (5.35) is still satisfied, and if (5.38) holds for a smaller value of j, set the basic variables equal to the transformed variables, and update j accordingly. Repeat this process until $j = 0$.

6. We have now solved the system of equations. If the solutions is admissible, that is, if the additional constraint (5.37) holds, then substitute into (5.26) to obtain the X_j values and the initial values Q_8, Q_9, Q_{10}, and Q_{11}. If the solution is not admissible, goto 2.

As mentioned above, this phase of the attack takes less than a second to complete. However, the work factor is not obvious. In the homework problems, the work factor for the various parts of this equation solving attack are estimated empirically.

For any solution found using the algorithm above, we obtain 512-bit messages M and M', with $M \neq M'$, and initial values for step 12 so that we can begin at step 12 and arrive at step 19 with the two conditions

$$\Delta_{19} = (2^{25}, -2^5, 0, 0)$$
$$G(Q_{19}, Q_{18}, Q_{17}) = G(Q'_{19}, Q'_{18}, Q_{17})$$

satisfied. Any such solution is a candidate for the differential attack discussed above. And once we find about 2^{22} such solutions, we expect that one of these will satisfy the differential condition $\Delta_{35} = (0, 0, 0, 0)$, in which case we will have found a collision. Dobbertin's algorithm, as described in this section, is extremely clever and extremely efficient.

Steps 0 to 11

Suppose that we have successfully completed the first two phases of the attack. Then we have found $(Q_8, Q_9, Q_{10}, Q_{11})$ such that

$$\text{MD4}_{12...47}(Q_8, Q_9, Q_{10}, Q_{11}, X) = \text{MD4}_{12...47}(Q_8, Q_9, Q_{10}, Q_{11}, X').$$

All that remains is to show that we can satisfy the condition

$$\text{MD4}_{0...11}(\text{IV}, X) = \text{MD4}_{0...11}(\text{IV}, X') = (Q_{11}, Q_{10}, Q_9, Q_8), \qquad (5.39)$$

where IV is the MD4 initialization vector. Recall that $X_j = X'_j$, except for $j = 12$, and that $X'_{12} = X_{12} + 1$. Also, from Table 5.4 we see that X_{12} first appears in step 12.

In the previous phases of the attack we have determined input blocks X_j, for $j = 0, 4, 8, 12, 13, 14, 15$. Therefore, we are free to choose each of the remaining X_j, that is, for $j = 1, 2, 3, 5, 6, 7, 9, 10, 11$, so that (5.39) holds. All of these X_j appear in the first 11 steps, so we will have completely determined M when this phase of the attack is completed.

The only data values that appear in (5.39) which have been previously determined are X_0, X_4, and X_8. Given the large number of free parameters (that is, the X_j values which are yet to be determined) it appears that it should be relatively easy to complete this final phase of the attack, and, in fact, that is the case.

First, we select X_1, X_2, X_3, and X_5 at random and compute the values (Q_2, Q_3, Q_4, Q_5), using the MD4 initialization vector, IV. Next, we want to select X_j, for $j = 6, 7, 9, 10, 11$, so that

$$\text{MD4}_{6...11}(Q_2, Q_3, Q_4, Q_5, X) = (Q_{11}, Q_{10}, Q_9, Q_8),$$

where $(Q_8, Q_9, Q_{10}, Q_{11})$ were found in the previous phase of the attack. Since

$$Q_{11} = (Q_7 + F(Q_{10}, Q_9, Q_8) + X_{11}) \lll 19,$$

if we select

$$X_{11} = (Q_{11} \lll 13) - Q_7 - F(Q_{10}, Q_9, Q_8)$$

we obtain the desired value for Q_{11}. Similar equations hold for X_{10} and X_9. However, X_8 was previously specified, so we are not free to select X_8 in step 8. Fortunately, all is not lost. We have

$$Q_8 = (Q_4 + F(Q_7, Q_6, Q_5) + X_8) \lll 3. \qquad (5.40)$$

From basic properties of the function F, we see that if

$$Q_7 = -1 \quad \text{and} \quad Q_6 = (Q_8 \lll 29) - Q_4 - X_8, \qquad (5.41)$$

then (5.40) holds for any X_8. We can force the conditions in (5.41) to hold by selecting

$$X_6 = (Q_6 \lll 21) - Q_2 - F(Q_5, Q_4, Q_3)$$
$$= (((Q_8 \lll 29) - Q_4 - X_8) \lll 21) - Q_2 - F(Q_5, Q_4, Q_3)$$

and

$$X_7 = (Q_7 \lll 13) - Q_3 - F(Q_6, Q_5, Q_4) = -1 - Q_3 - F(Q_6, Q_5, Q_4).$$

To summarize, given $(Q_8, Q_9, Q_{10}, Q_{11})$, we select X_1, X_2, X_3, and X_5 at random. Then by setting

$$Q_6 = (Q_8 \lll 29) - Q_4 - X_8$$
$$Q_7 = -1$$
$$X_6 = (((Q_8 \lll 29) - Q_4 - X_8) \lll 21) - Q_2 - F(Q_5, Q_4, Q_3)$$
$$X_7 = Q_7 - Q_3 - F(Q_6, Q_5, Q_4)$$
$$X_9 = (Q_9 \lll 25) - Q_5 - F(Q_8, Q_7, Q_6)$$
$$X_{10} = (Q_{10} \lll 21) - Q_6 - F(Q_9, Q_8, Q_7)$$
$$X_{11} = (Q_{11} \lll 13) - Q_7 - F(Q_{10}, Q_9, Q_8)$$

we are assured that

$$(Q_{11}, Q_{10}, Q_9, Q_8) = \text{MD4}_{0\ldots11}(\text{IV}, X),$$

where $(Q_8, Q_9, Q_{10}, Q_{11})$ were computed in the previous phase of the attack. This solution can then be tested to see whether the condition $\Delta_{35} = (0, 0, 0, 0)$ is satisfied, and, if so, we have found a collision.

All Together Now

Here, we describe the complete MD4 collision attack. Recall that $X'_j = X_j$, for $j \neq 12$, and $X'_{12} = X_{12} + 1$, so if we determine $M = (X_0, X_1, \ldots, X_{15})$, we will also have determined $M' = (X'_0, X'_1, \ldots, X'_{15})$. Therefore, we ignore M' in this description.

The attack proceeds as follows:

1. Find $(Q_8, Q_9, Q_{10}, Q_{11})$ and X_j, for $j = 0, 4, 8, 12, 13, 14, 15$ as specified in the section labeled **Steps 12 to 19**, above. This phase of the attack also determines the initial values required in the next phase of the attack, namely, $(Q_{16}, Q_{17}, Q_{18}, Q_{19})$ and $(Q'_{16}, Q'_{17}, Q'_{18}, Q'_{19})$.

2. Complete the attack described in the section labeled **Steps 0 to 11**, above. In this phase, X_j, for $j = 1, 2, 3, 5$ are selected at random, and X_j, for $j = 6, 7, 9, 10, 11$ are determined.

3. Check whether the differential condition in the section labeled **Steps 19 to 35**, above, is satisfied. That is, compute

$$\Delta_{35} = (Q_{35}, Q_{34}, Q_{33}, Q_{32}) - (Q'_{35}, Q'_{34}, Q'_{33}, Q'_{32})$$

and if $\Delta_{35} = (0, 0, 0, 0)$ we have found a collision; if not goto 2.

There are several ways to improve the efficiency of this attack, the most significant of which involves number 3, above. Instead of computing all the way from step 20 to step 35 before checking the validity of the result, we can instead check at each intermediate step $j = 21, 22, 23, \ldots$ whether the corresponding Δ_j condition in Table 5.5 holds. Given the probabilities in the table, the vast majority of trials will terminate within a few steps. With this modification, the attack is so efficient that other improvements are probably not worth the additional effort.

Notice that the continuous approximation phase of the attack only needs to be completed once per collision. Dobbertin's equation solving method is so efficient that the overall work factor for the attack is dominated by the testing of the differential condition in number 3, above. Empirically, it can be shown that about 2^{22} iterations are required before we expect to find a collision. This gives an overall work factor equivalent to the computation of about 2^{20} MD4 hashes; see Problem 17.

5.3.3   A Meaningful Collision

In [42], Dobbertin gives a meaningful collision that was generated with a modified version of his attack. The two messages in Figure 5.4 yield a collision, where each "*" represents a "random" bytes. The attacker might claim that these random-looking bytes are present for security purposes, but these bytes would actually be selected so that the resulting messages generate the same MD4 hash values; see Problem 19 for more details of this particular collision.

If MD4 were used in practice, the attack illustrated in Figure 5.4 would be a serious issue. Since MD4 is not used today, the attack is not a practical concern, but it does illustrate the dangers inherent from meaningful collisions.

Below, we consider a collision attack on MD5—a hash function which is widely used in practice. However, the MD5 attack is far costlier and more restrictive than this MD4 attack presented here. Consequently, it is unclear whether any meaningful MD5 collision could ever be constructed using such an attack. For this reason, it is often claimed that the collision attack on MD5 is of little consequence in the real world. However, after we present the

```
*******************
CONTRACT

At the price of $176,495 Alf Blowfish
sells his house to Ann Bonidea ...
```

```
*******************
CONTRACT

At the price of $276,495 Alf Blowfish
sells his house to Ann Bonidea ...
```

Figure 5.4: MD4 collision [42].

MD5 attack, we give an example that shows how a meaningless collision can be used to break security in a very meaningful way.

5.4 MD5

> "I can't explain myself, I'm afraid, Sir," said Alice,
> "because I'm not myself, you see."
> — Alice in Wonderland

Message Digest 5, or MD5, is a strengthened version of MD4. Like MD4, the MD5 hash was invented by Rivest [122]. Also, MD5 was obviously used as the model for SHA-1, since they share many common features. It is undoubtedly the case that MD5 and SHA-1 are the two most widely used hash algorithms today, but use of MD5 will certainly decline over time, since it is now considered broken. At the time of this writing, it appears certain that SHA-1 will soon share the same fate as MD5.

5.4.1 MD5 Algorithm

MD5 is similar to MD4 and in this section, we often refer to our previous discussion of MD4. It is important to read Section 5.3 carefully before attempting this section, since both the operation of MD4 and various aspects of the MD4 attack will be referenced here.

Define the four functions

$$F(A, B, C) = (A \wedge B) \vee (\neg A \wedge C) \qquad (5.42)$$

$$G(A, B, C) = (A \wedge C) \vee (B \wedge \neg C) \qquad (5.43)$$

$$H(A, B, C) = A \oplus B \oplus C \qquad (5.44)$$

$$I(A, B, C) = B \oplus (A \vee \neg C) \qquad (5.45)$$

where A, B and C are 32-bit words, "$\wedge$" is the AND operation, "$\vee$" is the OR operation, "$\oplus$" is the XOR, and "$\neg A$" is the complement of A.

The MD5 algorithm pads the message using the same method as MD4. As in the MD4 attack, the padding is not important for the attack we discuss here. And, as with MD4, the MD5 hash operates on 512-bit blocks of data, with the 128-bit output of one block being used as the initial value for the next block. The IV used in MD5 is the same as that used in MD4, which appears in (5.7) in Section 5.3.

The MD5 algorithm is given in Table 5.7 and the four MD5 round functions are given in Table 5.8. Here, we number the steps consecutively from 0 to 63, with the ith output denoted by Q_i. These Q values correspond to the A, B, C and D values in [122].

Each step of MD5 has its own additive constant. We denote the constant for step i as K_i. Although these constants play no role in the attack, for completeness, the K_i are given in the Appendix in Table A-1. The shift for step i is denoted s_i and the values of s_i are listed in Table 5.9.

In Table 5.7, the permutation applied to the input blocks is denoted by σ, that is, $W_i = X_{\sigma(i)}$. The values of $\sigma(i)$, for $i = 0, 1, 2, \ldots, 63$, are given in Table 5.10.

The significant differences between MD4 and MD5 are the following [122]:

1. MD5 has four rounds, whereas MD4 has only three. Consequently, the MD5 compression function includes 64 steps, whereas the MD4 compression function has 48 steps.

2. Each step of MD5 has a unique additive constant, whereas each round of MD4 uses a fixed constant.

3. The function G in the second round of MD5 is less symmetric than the G function in MD4.

4. Each step of MD5 adds the result of the previous step, which is not the case with MD4. The stated purpose of this modification is to produce a faster avalanche effect.

5. In MD5, the order in which input words are accessed in the second and third rounds is less similar to each other than is the case in MD4.

Table 5.7: MD5 Algorithm

// $M = (Y_0, Y_1, \ldots, Y_{N-1})$, message to hash, after padding
// Each Y_i is a 32-bit word and N is a multiple of 16
MD5(M)
    // initialize $(A, B, C, D) = $ IV
    $(A, B, C, D) = (\texttt{0x67452301}, \texttt{0xefcdab89}, \texttt{0x98badcfe}, \texttt{0x10325476})$
    for $i = 0$ to $N/16 - 1$
        // Copy block i into X
        $X_j = Y_{16i+j}$, for $j = 0$ to 15
        // Copy X to W
        $W_j = X_{\sigma(j)}$, for $j = 0$ to 63
        // initialize Q
        $(Q_{-4}, Q_{-3}, Q_{-2}, Q_{-1}) = (A, D, C, B)$
        // Rounds 0, 1, 2 and 3
        Round0(Q, W)
        Round1(Q, W)
        Round2(Q, W)
        Round3(Q, W)
        // Each addition is modulo 2^{32}
        $(A, B, C, D) = (Q_{60} + Q_{-4}, Q_{63} + Q_{-1}, Q_{62} + Q_{-2}, Q_{61} + Q_{-3})$
    next i
    return A, B, C, D
end MD5

---

6. It is claimed in [122] (without further explanation) that in MD5, "the shift amounts in each round have been approximately optimized, to yield a faster 'avalanche effect'." Also, the shifts employed in each round of MD5 are distinct, which is not the case in MD4.

A single MD5 step is illustrated in Figure 5.5, where

$$f_i(A, B, C) = \begin{cases} F(A, B, C) & \text{if } 0 \leq i \leq 15 \\ G(A, B, C) & \text{if } 16 \leq i \leq 31 \\ H(A, B, C) & \text{if } 32 \leq i \leq 47 \\ I(A, B, C) & \text{if } 48 \leq i \leq 63. \end{cases}$$

It may be instructive to compare Figure 5.5 to a step of the MD4 algorithm, which is illustrated in Figure 5.3.

As in the MD4 attack of Section 5.3, here we denote rounds i through j of the MD5 function as MD5$_{i\ldots j}(A, B, C, D, M)$, where (A, B, C, D) are the "initial values" at step i and M is a 512-bit input block. Similar to MD4, we have

$$\text{MD5}_{0\ldots 63}(\text{IV}, M) \neq h(M),$$

Table 5.8: MD5 Rounds

$Round0(Q, W)$
    // steps 0 through 15
    for $i = 0$ **to** 15
        $Q_i = Q_{i-1} + ((Q_{i-4} + F(Q_{i-1}, Q_{i-2}, Q_{i-3}) + W_i + K_i) \lll s_i)$
    next i
end Round0

$Round1(Q, W)$
    // steps 16 through 31
    for $i = 16$ **to** 31
        $Q_i = Q_{i-1} + ((Q_{i-4} + G(Q_{i-1}, Q_{i-2}, Q_{i-3}) + W_i + K_i) \lll s_i)$
    next i
end Round1

$Round2(Q, W)$
    // steps 32 through 47
    for $i = 32$ **to** 47
        $Q_i = Q_{i-1} + ((Q_{i-4} + H(Q_{i-1}, Q_{i-2}, Q_{i-3}) + W_i + K_i) \lll s_i)$
    next i
end Round2

$Round3(Q, W)$
    // steps 48 through 63
    for $i = 48$ **to** 63
        $Q_i = Q_{i-1} + ((Q_{i-4} + I(Q_{i-1}, Q_{i-2}, Q_{i-3}) + W_i + K_i) \lll s_i)$
    next i
end Round3

---

where h is the MD5 hash function. In other words, the hash value is not just the output of this function, since there is a final transformation and the message is padded. Next, we consider the final transformation; for details on the padding, see Section 5.3.

Define

$$f(\text{IV}, M) = (Q_{60}, Q_{63}, Q_{62}, Q_{61}) + \text{IV},$$

where $(Q_{63}, Q_{62}, Q_{61}, Q_{60}) = \text{MD5}_{0\ldots63}(\text{IV}, M)$ and the addition is computed modulo 2^{32}, per 32-bit word. Then f is the MD5 compression function. If we hash a message $M = (M_0, M_1)$ consisting of two 512-bit blocks, we have

$$h(M) = f(f(\text{IV}, M_0), M_1).$$

In effect, $f(\text{IV}, M_0)$ acts as the IV for the second iteration of the compression

Table 5.9: MD5 Shifts

Step i	0	1	2	3	4	5	6	7	8	9	10	11	12	13	14	15
Shift s_i	7	12	17	22	7	12	17	22	7	12	17	22	7	12	17	22
Step i	16	17	18	19	20	21	22	23	24	25	26	27	28	29	30	31
Shift s_i	5	9	14	20	5	9	14	20	5	9	14	20	5	9	14	20
Step i	32	33	35	35	36	37	38	39	40	41	42	43	44	45	46	47
Shift s_i	4	11	16	23	4	11	16	23	4	11	16	23	4	11	16	23
Step i	48	49	50	51	52	53	54	55	56	57	58	58	60	61	62	63
Shift s_i	6	10	15	21	6	10	15	21	6	10	15	21	6	10	15	21

Table 5.10: MD5 Input Word Order

Step i	0	1	2	3	4	5	6	7	8	9	10	11	12	13	14	15
$\sigma(i)$	0	1	2	3	4	5	6	7	8	9	10	11	12	13	14	15
Step i	16	17	18	19	20	21	22	23	24	25	26	27	28	29	30	31
$\sigma(i)$	1	6	11	0	5	10	15	4	9	14	3	8	13	2	7	12
Step i	32	33	35	35	36	37	38	39	40	41	42	43	44	45	46	47
$\sigma(i)$	5	8	11	14	1	4	7	10	13	0	3	6	9	12	15	2
Step i	48	49	50	51	52	53	54	55	56	57	58	58	60	61	62	63
$\sigma(i)$	0	7	14	5	12	3	10	1	8	15	6	13	4	11	2	9

function f. Figure 5.1 illustrates the general case.

At this point we have the necessary notation and background to begin discussing the MD5 attack. The MD4 attack in the previous section finds two 512-bit blocks that have the same MD4 hash value. The MD5 attack presented here, which is due to Wang [157], finds a pair of 1024-bit messages that have the same MD5 hash value. We denote the two 1024-bit messages as $M' = (M_0', M_1')$ and $M = (M_0, M_1)$, where each M_i' and M_i is a 512-bit block. As with MD4, each 512-bit block consists of 16 words, where each word is 32 bits.

Initially, Wang gave a collision [155, 156] without providing any explanation of the underlying technique. This lack of information led to an impressive attempt to reverse engineer the "Chinese method" [64]. Incredibly, this reverse engineering was successful enough that it yielded a more efficient attack [81] than Wang's, and it has provided the basis for subsequent improvements in the attack.

The Chinese team did eventually release some details of their attack [157]. Minor flaws and incremental improvements have been reported by various

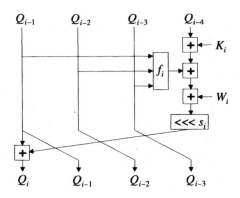

Figure 5.5: MD5 step.

authors in subsequent papers [94, 127, 161]. To date, the most thorough and insightful description of the MD5 attack methodology was published by Daum in his PhD dissertation [34].[9]

Below, we describe the MD5 attack which originally appeared in [157]. As mentioned above, this attack can be used to efficiently find a pair of 1024-bit messages whose MD5 hashes are the same. But before giving details of the attack, we first present some background and motivation. This background material relies primarily on information in Wang's paper [157] and in Daum's PhD dissertation [34].

A Note on Notation

Unfortunately, everyone who writes about Wang's attack seems to have their own pet notation. Even more unfortunately, we are no exception. Our notation is closest to that in [16], with the only major difference being that we number bits from left-to-right—in our notation, the high-order (leftmost) bit is bit 0, while the low-order (rightmost) bit of a 32-bit word is bit number 31. As noted above, we denote the step outputs for a message block as Q_0 through Q_{63}, with the IV consisting of $Q_{-4}, Q_{-1}, Q_{-2}, Q_{-3}$. In contrast, in several papers, including [81, 144], the IV is denoted $Q_{-3}, Q_0, Q_{-1}, Q_{-2}$ and the computed outputs are Q_1 through Q_{64} (but, as if to further confuse matters, these authors number the message words 0 through 63).

The papers of Wang [155, 156, 157] and various other authors, use a completely different numbering of the outputs. Instead of Q_j, the outputs are denoted as a_j, b_j, c_j, or d_j, where $j = 1, 2, \ldots, 16$ (or, in some cases, $j = 0, 1, \ldots, 15$) depending on the round. While this is more consistent with

---

[9]Daum's work was supervised by Hans Dobbertin, whose MD4 attack is discussed in Section 5.3.2.

the notation used in the original description of MD5 [122], it is awkward for analysis of the algorithm. Strangely, Wang numbers the bits of 32-bit words from 1 to 32 (right-to-left). Some authors use δ for the modular difference and Δ for the XOR difference, while we use Δ for the modular difference. The bottom line is that considerable care must be taken when attempting to analyze results culled from a variety of papers, since it is not a trivial task to translate the results into a consistent notation.

5.4.2 A Precise Differential

Wang's MD5 attack is a differential attack. Recall that Dobbertin's MD4 attack [42] uses subtraction modulo 2^{32} as the difference operator. Wang's attack uses this same modular difference for inputs. However, some parts of the MD5 attack require more detailed information than modular subtraction provides, so a "kind of precise differential" [157] is also employed. This differential combines modular subtractions with information on the precise location of the bit differences. In effect, this precise differential includes both a modular difference and an XOR difference, and also provides additional information beyond what these two standard differentials provide.

To motivate this precise differential, consider the pair of bytes given by $y' = 00010101$ and $y = 00000101$ and another pair of bytes $z' = 00100101$ and $z = 00010101$. Then

$$y' - y = z' - z = 00010000 = 2^4,$$

which implies that with respect to the modular difference, these two pairs are indistinguishable. However, in the MD5 attack, we must distinguish between cases such as these, and to do so, we need more information than modular subtraction can provide. To this end, we employ a differential that includes modular subtraction along with an explicit specification of the bit positions that differ between the two terms.

While an XOR difference specifies the bit positions that differ, we actually require even more information than modular subtraction and the XOR together can provide. Specifically, we need to know whether the difference in each bit position corresponds to a $+1$ or -1 in the modular difference, and this level of detail is not provided by the XOR.

Let $y = (y_0, y_1, \ldots, y_7)$ and $y' = (y'_0, y'_1, \ldots, y'_7)$, where each y_i and y'_i is a bit. Using the same example as above, we have

$$y' - y = 00010101 - 00000101 = 2^4$$

and

$$y' \oplus y = 00010101 \oplus 00000101 = 00010000.$$

In this case, the nonzero bit in the XOR difference occurs since $y_3' = 1$ and $y_3 = 0$. However, the same XOR difference in bit 3 would result if $y_3' = 0$ and $y_3 = 1$. For Wang's attack, we need to distinguish between cases such as these. To do so, we use a "signed" difference that is essentially a signed version of the XOR difference. That is, when there is a 1 in bit i of the XOR difference, we put a "+" if $y_i' = 1$ and $y_i = 0$ and we put a "−" if $y_i' = 0$ and $y_i = 1$. We use a "." to indicate those bits that are 0 in the XOR difference, which simply means that $y_i' = y_i$. We use the notation ∇y this signed difference.[10] As in the MD4 attack, we denote the modular difference as Δy. Then for $y' = 00010101$ and $y = 00000101$ and we have $\Delta y = 2^4$ and ∇y is given by "...+....".

Now consider

$$z' - z = 00100101 - 00010101 = 2^4. \tag{5.46}$$

In this case we have

$$z' \oplus z = 00100101 \oplus 00010101 = 00110000,$$

and hence ∇z is "..+−....", since $z_2' - z_2 = 1 - 0$ and $z_3' - z_3 = 0 - 1$.

From ∇x, the XOR difference is easily computed. In addition, Problem 21 shows that ∇x determines the modular difference. Consequently, all of the relevant difference information is contained in ∇x. However, for convenience we retain the modular difference.

We refer to Wang's precise differential as the *signed differential*. This differential provides more information than the modular and XOR differential combined, and, therefore, it allows us to have correspondingly greater control over the results at each step. However, it is important to realize that there is still a great deal of freedom in choosing values that satisfy a given signed differential. Consider, for example, 8-bit bytes y' and y. Then the modular difference is $y' - y \pmod{2^8}$. Suppose ∇y is specified. Then for each "+" in ∇y, the corresponding bit of y' must be 1, and the corresponding bit of y must be 0. Similarly, for each "−" in ∇y, the corresponding bit of y' must be 0, and the corresponding bit of y must be 1. But for any bit position that is not a 1 in $y' \oplus y$ the bits of y' and y must agree, and the value of the bits in each such position is arbitrary. That is, we have one bit of freedom for each "." in ∇y, and no freedom whatsoever for each "+" and "−".

To make this more concrete, suppose we require that ∇z be "..+−....". Then z' and z in (5.46) satisfy this requirement, as do each of the pairs

$$(z_0', z_0) = (10100101, 10010101)$$
$$(z_1', z_1) = (11100000, 11010000)$$
$$(z_2', z_2) = (11101111, 11011111)$$

---

[10]The symbol "∇" is usually pronounced as "nabla" or "del", but feel free to call it "upside-down triangle" if you prefer.

and many others. The point here is that while the signed differential is more restrictive than either a modular difference or an XOR difference (or a combination of the two), it still allows for considerable freedom in the choice of values that satisfy a given differential.

5.4.3 Outline of Wang's Attack

Here, we attempt to provide some motivation for Wang's attack. However, it appears that the actual development of the attack was essentially ad hoc.[11] Consequently, the motivation is not always clear, but Daum [34] has pulled together enough threads to provide a plausible explanation for much of the reasoning that most likely went into the development of the attack. The remainder of this section draws primarily on material found in Daum's dissertation [34].

Below, we distinguish between input differences and output differences. Input differences are modular differences between input words of messages M' and M, whereas output differences are differences between corresponding intermediate values, Q_i' and Q_i. The output difference operator is the signed difference discussed above, which is more restrictive than the modular difference or the XOR difference, but offers correspondingly greater control.

Recall that Dobbertin's MD4 attack discussed in Section 5.3.2 includes a differential phase, but the attack is primarily based on a clever equation solving technique. In the differential phase of Dobbertin's attack, the input modular difference is specified, but the output differences are not highly constrained. This is crucial since the continuous approximation technique (the equation solving phase) makes heavy use of the fact that the output values can be altered.

In contrast, Wang's MD5 attack is more of a "pure" differential attack. Wang's attack completely specifies the input differences. In addition, Wang places significant constraints on the output differences—in fact, the output differences are much more tightly constrained than the input differences, since the signed difference is applied to the outputs.

At a high level, Wang's attack can be viewed as consisting of two phases. First, appropriate input and output differential patterns must be found. Then the computational part of the attack consists of finding messages that satisfy the given patterns. These two phases can be further broken down as follows:

1. Specify an input differential pattern that behaves nicely in the later rounds. Here, the modular difference is used.

2. Specify an output differential pattern that is easily satisfied in the early rounds. For the output differential, the more restrictive signed differ-

---

[11]Wang's approach has also been described as "intuitive" and "done by hand" by other baffled authors.

ence is used. This is the part of the attack that is most shrouded in mystery, but we provide some hints on the methodology, below. In any case, finding useful difference patterns is obviously extremely challenging, since all MD5 attacks to date are based on Wang's lone differential patterns.

3. Given the differential patterns, derive a set of sufficient conditions on the outputs (along with a few necessary conditions on intermediate values). Provided all of these conditions are met, the differential path will hold and we will therefore obtain a collision.

4. Finally, we must determine a pair of 1024-bit messages for which all of the sufficient conditions are satisfied. This is the computational part of the attack and Wang's approach for solving it consists of the following.

    (a) Generate a random 512-bit message M_0.

    (b) Use "single-step modifications" (as described below) to modify M_0 so that all of the sufficient conditions in the early steps are forced to hold. This is accomplished via a direct modification of message words, and it can be done in a way that preserves the input differential conditions and any previously satisfied conditions.

    (c) Use "multi-step modifications" (as outlined below) to force some of the sufficient conditions in the middle steps for M_0 to hold. This a more complex modification technique than the single step modification. The difficulty arises since we must satisfy the differential conditions while maintaining all previously-satisfied sufficient conditions.

    (d) Check the conditions for all of the remaining steps. If any of these conditions are not satisfied, goto 4b. These remaining sufficient conditions are satisfied probabilistically, that is, the attack is iterated until all of these probabilistic sufficient conditions hold. These iterations can be done efficiently and, since the input differential was chosen to behave nicely in the later steps, the probability of success is relatively high.

    (e) Once M_0 has been found, generate a random 512-bit message M_1.

    (f) Use single-step modifications to modify M_1 so that all of the conditions for the early steps are satisfied. Note that the initial values for M_1 are not the MD5 initial values. Instead, the MD5 output from processing M_0 must be used for the initial values.

    (g) Use multi-step modifications to force the sufficient conditions in the middle steps for M_1 to hold.

    (h) Check the conditions for all of the remaining steps. If any of these conditions are not satisfied, goto 4f.

(i) Compute $M_0' = M_0 + \Delta M_0$ and $M_1' = M_1 + \Delta M_1$. The precise values of ΔM_0 and ΔM_1 are specified by the input differential. For Wang's differential, these values are given in the next section.

(j) The MD5 hash of message $M = (M_0, M_1)$ is equal to the MD5 hash of the message $M' = (M_0', M_1')$.

See Problem 25 for one simple improvement to the computational phase of the attack as described here.

For Wang's differential, the work factor for the computational part of the attack is dominated by finding M_0. The work factor for finding M_0 is on the order of 2^n MD5 hashes, where n is the number of conditions for M_0 that are not satisfied by the modification techniques mentioned above (and described in more detail, below). As originally implemented by Wang, the computational phase had a work factor significantly greater than 2^{40}. Subsequent improvements have steadily lowered the work factor and, to date, the best claimed work factor is on the order of about $2^{32.25}$ MD5 hashes [144]. It is possible that this will be reduced further by incremental improvements to Wang's attack.

Below, we discuss each part of the attack, with the emphasis on the computational aspects. But before diving into the details, we mention an interesting insight due to Daum [34]. Suppose we have an MD-like hash function that only has three rounds—such as MD4 but not MD5. Then we would expect to find a collision using Wang's technique, since, roughly speaking, the input differential can be selected so that the third round conditions hold, single-step modifications can then be used to ensures that the first round conditions hold, and, finally, multi-step modifications can ensure that the second round conditions hold. However, MD5 has four rounds, so some special property of MD5 must be exploited to make Wang's attack succeed. We briefly consider this "special feature" after discussing the attack outlined above.

5.4.4 Wang's MD5 Differentials

Here, we describe the theoretical part of Wang's attack—at least we attempt to do so. This is the least well-understood part of the attack, and Wang has provided little information, which has led many people to conjecture on possible motivations for the attack. We give Wang's differentials and attack, then we consider some of the explanations offered by cryptographers who have attempted to analyze Wang's methodology.

Input Differential Pattern

Denote the MD5 initialization vector as $IV = (A, B, C, D)$ and denote the initialization vector for the second block (assuming that M_0 is the first block) as $IV_1 = (AA, BB, CC, DD)$. Note that

$$IV_1 = (AA, BB, CC, DD) = (Q_{60}, Q_{63}, Q_{62}, Q_{61}) + (A, B, C, D),$$

where

$$(Q_{63}, Q_{62}, Q_{61}, Q_{60}) = MD5_{0...63}(IV, M_0).$$

Then the hash value of (M_0, M_1) is given by

$$h = (\hat{Q}_{60}, \hat{Q}_{63}, \hat{Q}_{62}, \hat{Q}_{61}) + (AA, BB, CC, DD),$$

where $(\hat{Q}_{63}, \hat{Q}_{62}, \hat{Q}_{61}, \hat{Q}_{60}) = MD5_{0...63}(IV_1, M_1)$. Define IV_1' and h' similarly using M_0' and M_1'.

For Wang's attack, the input modular differences are specified as

$$\Delta M_0 = M_0' - M_0 = (0, 0, 0, 0, 2^{31}, 0, 0, 0, 0, 0, 0, 2^{15}, 0, 0, 2^{31}, 0) \qquad (5.47)$$

$$\Delta M_1 = M_1' - M_1 = (0, 0, 0, 0, 2^{31}, 0, 0, 0, 0, 0, 0, -2^{15}, 0, 0, 2^{31}, 0). \qquad (5.48)$$

That is, messages M_0 and M_0' differ only in words 4, 11, and 14, and M_1 and M_1' also differ in the same words—with the differences being the same as for the first pair of blocks, except at word 11.

We also require that

$$\Delta IV_1 = IV_1' - IV_1 = (2^{31}, 2^{25} + 2^{31}, 2^{25} + 2^{31}, 2^{25} + 2^{31})$$
$$\Delta h = h' - h = (0, 0, 0, 0).$$

The idea here is that if we can specify the initial value for the second block (more precisely, the value of ΔIV_1), then we can construct a collision in the second block. In this way, we hope to force the Δh condition to hold, which simply states that we have found a collision.

Output Differential Pattern

Wang's output differential corresponding to the input differentials in (5.47) and (5.48) appear in the Appendix in Tables A-2, A-3, A-4, and A-5. The columns in Tables A-2 and A-3 have the following meaning: The j column specifies the step, "Output" refers to the output when processing M_0, W_j is the data element used at the given step, ΔW_j is the modular difference between the input for M_0' and M_0, ΔOutput is the modular difference in the outputs for M_0' and M_0 (the output is Q_j in all but the last four rounds), and ∇Output is the signed differential term corresponding to the modular difference ΔOutput. Note that in these tables we use a compact notation for sums of powers of two which is also used in Table 5.11 and defined on page 239. In Tables A-4 and A-5, the columns have the same meaning as those appearing in Tables A-2 and A-3.

Both the modular difference and the XOR difference are easily computed from the signed difference. Consequently, the ΔOutput column is not strictly necessary in Table A-2, A-3, A-4, or A-5. However, it is convenient to have the modular difference available.

Derivation of Differentials

Wang has not provided much information about several crucial points in her attack, and from the brief descriptions provided, it appears that her approach was largely intuitive. But that has not prevented people from offering various theories as to how the differential patterns were derived.

To date, the most ambitious attempt to analyze the "Chinese method" has been provided by Daum [34], who also gives many interesting ideas for analyzing hash functions in general. Although Daum's analysis of Wang's method is indeed interesting, he focuses primarily on MD4, not the more complex MD5, and in some cases it is not obvious how the techniques translate to MD5. In contrast to Daum's relatively exhaustive approach, Black, Cochran, and Highland [16] provide a brief, analysis and conjecture on possible motivations for some aspects of the attack. Here, we attempt to summarize the crucial points of the attack, primarily following Daum.

First, it is interesting to consider the development of attacks on ciphers in the MD4 family—which includes MD5. Dobbertin applied the method he used to attack MD4 to MD5. He had considerable success against MD5, as indicated by the discussion in [34]. However, Dobbertin was unable to obtain a collision for the full MD5 hash function. Dobbertin's technique is based on modular differences and equation solving.

Chabaud and Joux [27] had success against SHA-0 using XOR differences. In their method, the analysis is accomplished by approximating the nonlinear parts of the hash by XOR. This technique is somewhat analogous to what is done in the linear cryptanalysis of block ciphers.

Wang's attack [157] on MD5 uses the modular difference for inputs and the "more precise" signed differences for outputs. In this way, Wang has considerable control over the outputs, yet she is still able to work with the actual step functions, not approximations. Another important feature of Wang's attack is that the colliding messages she finds consist of two message blocks. In this way, the attack on the second block becomes, in effect, a chosen IV attack.

But the real magic in Wang's attack lies in the selection of the difference patterns. Apparently, the input differences were selected so as to behave nicely in the later rounds. More precisely, Wang takes advantage of the fact that an output difference of 2^{31} "is propagated from step to step with probability 1 in the third round and with probability $1/2$ per step in a large part of the fourth round" [34]. In fact, this is precisely the "special property" of MD5 alluded to in Section 5.4.3 that allows Wang's method—which would be expected to work on any three-round MD-like hash—to succeed on the four-round MD5 hash.

The choice of the output differences is the greater mystery. Perhaps the best that can be done is to analyze the bit differences, as per [64], in an effort to gain some insight into the Wang's approach. We delve into this analysis below.

There is no known method for automatically generating useful difference patterns. Daum [34] suggests building a "tree of difference patterns", including both input and output differences. Specifying the input difference pattern would limit the branching to something more manageable, but the the tree must still be pruned since the growth is exponential. However, most branches would have low probabilities. so a cost function that incorporates probability could be used for pruning. The suggestion is to use use a meet-in-the-middle approach to find "inner" collisions, that is, collisions after a few steps. Then, presumably, these inner collisions could be strung together to create a collision for an entire message block. However, Daum's approach has not yet produced a useful difference pattern, and neither has any other approach other than Wang's intuition—at least not yet.

In spite of the fact that the mechanics behind Wang's attack are now relatively well-understood, and several incremental improvements in the attack have been made, nobody has been able to produce a different useful differential pattern. This is perhaps the strongest indication of the extreme cleverness that underlies Wang's attack, even if Wang herself cannot fully explain it.

5.4.5   Reverse Engineering Wang's Attack

As mentioned above, when Wang's team initially revealed an MD5 collision, they provided virtually no information on how the collision was obtained. This led Hawkes, Paddon, and Rose [64] to do some extremely detailed detective work, based entirely on the one published collision. This work is interesting in its own right, but it is also significant since the most efficient attacks are based on this work, not on the limited details provided by Wang. Amazingly, this reverse engineering effort discovered useful information on the computational part of the attack that was apparently unknown to Wang's team. In addition, this analysis provides the best hope of obtaining additional insight into the construction of output differentials.

In [64], the authors began with the only MD5 collision known at that time, and carefully analyzed the intermediate values (the outputs) that are generated when these two inputs are hashed. By carefully analyzing the differential conditions at each step, they were able to derive conditions on the the outputs and thereby obtain a set of conditions that, if satisfied, will yield a collision. Remarkably, this reverse-engineering work is the basis for all of the fast MD5 collision attacks developed to date. Here, we only consider the first few steps for the first message block M_0.

Conditions on T_j

In this section, we use the notation

$$T_j = F(Q_{j-1}, Q_{j-2}, Q_{j-3}) + Q_{j-4} + K_j + W_j$$
$$R_j = T_j \lll s_j$$
$$Q_j = Q_{j-1} + R_j$$

which is valid for the first round, $j = 0, 1, \ldots, 15$, since the function F is specified. Here, each Q_j, K_j, W_j, and s_j are identical to those given in the description of the MD5 algorithm as presented above, and the initial values are denoted Q_{-4}, Q_{-3}, Q_{-2}, and Q_{-1}.

Define Δ to be the modular difference operator, $\Delta X = X' - X$, where the difference is taken modulo 2^{32}. For $j = 0, 1, \ldots, 15$, we have

$$\Delta T_j = \Delta F(Q_{j-1}, Q_{j-2}, Q_{j-3}) + \Delta Q_{j-4} + \Delta W_j \qquad (5.49)$$
$$\Delta R_j \approx (\Delta T_j) \lll s_j \qquad (5.50)$$
$$\Delta Q_j = \Delta Q_{j-1} + \Delta R_j \qquad (5.51)$$

where the approximation in the second line holds with a high probability (see Problem 23) and

$$\Delta F(Q_{j-1}, Q_{j-2}, Q_{j-3}) = F(Q'_{j-1}, Q'_{j-2}, Q'_{j-3}) - F(Q_{j-1}, Q_{j-2}, Q_{j-3}).$$

We use ΔF_j as shorthand for $\Delta F(Q_j, Q_{j-1}, Q_{j-2})$.

Using the only MD5 collision available at the time, the authors of [64] computed ΔQ_j, ΔF_j, ΔT_j, and ΔR_j for each j. Then they were able to derive conditions on the the bits of ΔT_j that ensure the desired differential path will hold. These conditions for the first round of the message block M_0 are summarized in Table 5.11. To save space, in Table 5.11 and in the remainder of this section, we put "+" on top of n to indicate 2^n, "$-$" to indicate -2^n and "$\pm$" to indicate that the number could be 2^n or -2^n. Then, for example,

$$(\overset{\pm}{31}\ \overset{+}{23}\ \overset{-}{6}) = \pm 2^{31} + 2^{23} - 2^6.$$

This compact notation appears in several MD5 papers.

Next, we analyze the first few rows of Table 5.11 in some detail to determine conditions on T_j that will ensure the rotation yields the desired effect. The rotation requires careful analysis. For example, suppose $T' = 2^{20}$ and $T = 2^{19}$ and $s = 10$. Then $\Delta T = 2^{19}$ and

$$(\Delta T) \lll s = (T' - T) \lll s = (T' \lll s) - (T \lll s) = 2^{29}.$$

Table 5.11: First Round of M_0 [64]

step j	ΔQ_j	ΔF_{j-1}	ΔW_j	ΔT_j	s_j	ΔR_j
0–3	0	0	0	0	—	0
4	$\overset{-}{6}$	0	$\overset{-}{31}$	$\overset{-}{31}$	7	$\overset{-}{6}$
5	$\overset{\pm}{31}\,\overset{+}{23}\,\overset{-}{6}$	$\overset{+}{19}\,\overset{+}{11}$	0	$\overset{+}{19}\,\overset{+}{11}$	12	$\overset{+}{31}\,\overset{+}{23}$
6	$\overset{-}{27}\,\overset{+}{23}\,\overset{-}{6}\,\overset{-}{0}$	$\overset{-}{14}\,\overset{-}{10}$	0	$\overset{-}{15}\,\overset{+}{14}\,\overset{-}{10}$	17	$\overset{+}{31}\,\overset{-}{27}\,\overset{-}{0}$
7	$\overset{-}{23}\,\overset{-}{17}\,\overset{-}{15}\,\overset{+}{0}$	$\overset{-}{27}\,\overset{-}{25}\,\overset{+}{16}\,\overset{+}{10}\,\overset{+}{5}\,\overset{-}{2}$	0	$\overset{-}{27}\,\overset{-}{25}\,\overset{+}{16}\,\overset{+}{10}\,\overset{+}{5}\,\overset{-}{2}$	22	$\overset{+}{27}\,\overset{-}{24}\,\overset{-}{17}\,\overset{-}{15}\,\overset{+}{6}\,\overset{+}{1}$
8	$\overset{\pm}{31}\,\overset{-}{6}\,\overset{+}{0}$	$\overset{\pm}{31}\,\overset{-}{24}\,\overset{+}{16}\,\overset{+}{10}\,\overset{+}{8}\,\overset{+}{6}$	0	$\overset{-}{31}\,\overset{-}{24}\,\overset{+}{16}\,\overset{+}{10}\,\overset{+}{8}$	7	$\overset{-}{31}\,\overset{+}{23}\,\overset{+}{17}\,\overset{+}{15}\,\overset{-}{6}$
9	$\overset{+}{31}\,\overset{+}{12}$	$\overset{\pm}{31}\,\overset{+}{26}\,\overset{-}{23}\,\overset{-}{20}\,\overset{+}{6}\,\overset{+}{0}$	0	$\overset{+}{26}\,\overset{-}{20}\,\overset{+}{0}$	12	$\overset{+}{12}\,\overset{-}{6}\,\overset{-}{0}$
10	$\overset{+}{31}\,\overset{+}{30}$	$\overset{-}{23}\,\overset{+}{13}\,\overset{+}{6}\,\overset{+}{0}$	0	$\overset{-}{27}\,\overset{+}{13}$	17	$\overset{+}{30}\,\overset{+}{12}$
11	$\overset{+}{31}\,\overset{-}{13}\,\overset{-}{7}$	$\overset{-}{8}\,\overset{-}{0}$	$\overset{+}{15}$	$\overset{-}{23}\,\overset{-}{17}\,\overset{-}{8}$	22	$\overset{-}{30}\,\overset{-}{13}\,\overset{-}{7}$
12	$\overset{+}{31}\,\overset{+}{24}$	$\overset{+}{31}\,\overset{+}{17}\,\overset{+}{7}$	0	$\overset{+}{17}\,\overset{+}{6}\,\overset{+}{0}$	7	$\overset{+}{24}\,\overset{+}{13}\,\overset{+}{7}$
13	$\overset{+}{31}$	$\overset{+}{31}\,\overset{-}{13}$	0	$\overset{-}{12}$	12	24
14	$\overset{+}{31}\,\overset{-}{15}\,\overset{+}{3}$	$\overset{+}{31}\,\overset{+}{18}$	$\overset{-}{31}$	$\overset{-}{30}\,\overset{+}{18}$	17	$\overset{-}{15}\,\overset{+}{3}$
15	$\overset{+}{31}\,\overset{-}{29}$	$\overset{+}{31}\,\overset{+}{25}$	0	$\overset{+}{25}\,\overset{+}{13}\,\overset{-}{7}$	22	$\overset{-}{29}\,\overset{+}{15}\,\overset{-}{3}$

In this example, the difference and rotation commute, that is, it does not matter whether the difference or rotation is applied first. But this is not always the case. Consider, for example, $T' = 2^{22}$ and $T = 2^{21} + 2^{20} + 2^{19}$. Then, as in the previous example, $\Delta T = 2^{19}$, and hence for $s = 10$,

$$(\Delta T) \lll s = 2^{29},$$

but

$$(T' \lll s) - (T \lll s) = 2^0 - (2^{31} + 2^{30} + 2^{29}) = 2^{29} + 1.$$

Now consider another example involving negative numbers. Suppose that we have $T' = 2^{19}$ and $T = 2^{20}$ and $s = 10$. Then

$$(\Delta T) \lll s = (T' \lll s) - (T \lll s) = -2^{29}.$$

However, if $s = 17$,

$$(\Delta T) \lll s = -2^5$$

but

$$(T' \lll s) - (T \lll s) = 2^4 - 2^5 = -2^4.$$

These examples illustrate that when ΔT is specified, we can still obtain different values for $\Delta R = \Delta T \lll s$ by placing various restrictions on T. In particular, it is possible to specify T so that bits propagate via the left rotation into lower-order bit positions, regardless of the magnitude of the rotation s. This fact can be used to determine conditions on T_j that must be satisfied for the required differential path to hold.

Next, we outline a few steps in the process whereby restrictions on T_j are deduced from a given collision. But first note that $-2^{31} = 2^{31}$ (mod 2^{32}) always holds and, modulo 2^{32}, we also have $2^{31} + 2^{31} = 0$. We make use of these facts below.

Now consider the second row of Table 5.11 (step 4). From the known collision we find $\Delta Q_3 = 0$, for $\Delta Q_4 = -2^6$. From (5.51), we have

$$\Delta Q_4 = \Delta Q_3 + \Delta R_4 = -2^6,$$

which implies that with high probability

$$\Delta R_4 = (\Delta T_4 \lll 7) = -2^6.$$

Since $\Delta T_4 = T_4' - T_4 = -2^{31}$, the condition $\langle T_4 = 1 \rangle_0$ is sufficient to ensure that $\Delta T_4 = -2^{31}$. As in the MD4 attack, here we use the notation $\langle Y = a \rangle_i$ to indicate that bit i of Y is a, and $\langle Y = a \rangle_{i...j}$ denotes that bits i through j of Y are all set to a.

Step 5 is also reasonably straightforward to analyze. In this step, we have $\Delta T_5 = 2^{19} + 2^{11}$. Also, we have

$$\Delta Q_4 = -2^6 \quad \text{and} \quad \Delta Q_5 = \pm 2^{31} + 2^{23} - 2^6,$$

and it follows that

$$\Delta R_5 = \Delta Q_5 - \Delta Q_4 = \pm 2^{31} + 2^{23}.$$

Since $s_5 = 12$, we want

$$\Delta R_5 = \Delta T_5 \lll 12 = \pm 2^{31} + 2^{23},$$

which holds provided that $\Delta T_5 = 2^{19} + 2^{11}$ does not propagate into higher-order bit positions. For example, we cannot have $\Delta T_5 = 2^{20} - 2^{19} + 2^{11}$, since this would cause bits to "wrap around" after the shift by 12, resulting in an incorrect value for ΔR_5. We see that the condition $\langle T_5 = 0 \rangle_{12}$ is necessary, as is a more complex condition that will restrict borrows; see [64] for details on this latter condition.

For step 6, the situation is slightly more complicated. At this step, we have $\Delta T_6 = -2^{14} - 2^{10}$. Since we have $s_6 = 17$, we want

$$\Delta R_6 = \Delta T_6 \lll 17 = \Delta Q_6 - \Delta Q_5 = \pm 2^{31} - 2^{27} - 2^0.$$

But if we simply rotate $\Delta T_6 = -2^{14} - 2^{10}$ by 17, we obtain $-2^{31} - 2^{27}$, which is not the desired result. In this case, we must rewrite ΔT_6 so that a bit wraps around into the low-order position after the rotation. This is easily accomplished by rewriting ΔT_6 as

$$\Delta T_6 = -2^{15} + 2^{14} - 2^{10}.$$

Among other conditions, this implies we must have $\langle T_6 = 0 \rangle_{17}$; again, see [64] for more details on the additional restrictions.

Continuing in this manner, it is possible to obtain a set of conditions on the T_j that must be met for the differential to hold. These conditions are specified in excruciating detail in [64]. It is interesting to note that prior to Stevens' work [144], these conditions were not used directly in the collision-finding attack. We briefly discuss Stevens' implementation of Wang's attack after analyzing the outputs.

Conditions on Q_j

Next, we consider conditions on the outputs, that is, the Q_j. These are the conditions that all attacks to date attempt to satisfy—the more of these conditions that can be satisfied deterministically, the more efficient the resulting attack will be. For this analysis, we again restrict our attention to the first few rounds.

To analyze the output differences, we require a difference operator that is more "precise" than either the modular difference or the XOR difference. Here, we use the signed difference, ∇X, discussed above. Recall that this difference operation provides more information than the modular difference and the XOR difference combined.

We consider 32-bit words so that, for example, if

$$X' = \text{0x02000020} \quad \text{and} \quad X = \text{0x80000000},$$

then ∇X is given by

$$\text{``-.....+. ....+.....''}.$$

For all steps of the MD5 collision provided by Wang, the authors of [64] computed the values of ΔQ_j and ∇Q_j. In Table 5.12 we have reproduced these results for the first round of M_0, translated into our notation. Of course, this MD5 collision was generated using Wang's method, so an analysis of this collision should provide clues as to Wang's approach.

Also, for this same MD5 collision, the authors of [64] found the values of ΔF_j and ∇F_j for all steps. In Table 5.13 we have reproduced these results for the first round. The results in Table 5.13 were computed from the same MD5 collision that was used to generate the data in Table 5.12.

Here, we only consider the first round, where the function F is used. Recall that

$$F(A, B, C) = (A \wedge B) \vee (\neg A \wedge C).$$

Table 5.12: First Round Output Differences [64]

j	ΔQ_j	∇Q_j
0-3	0	....
4	$\overset{-}{6}$	....-++++++ ++++++++ ++......
5	$\overset{\pm\ +\ -}{31\ 23\ 6}$	±....... +....... ....-......
6	$\overset{-\ +\ -\ -}{27\ 23\ 6\ 0}$	±+++++-- -....... ....-+++ ++-+++++
7	$\overset{-\ -\ -\ +}{23\ 17\ 15\ 0}$	.... -..-+++- +....... ....+
8	$\overset{\pm\ -\ +}{31\ 6\ 0}$	±....... ....- ++....+-
9	$\overset{\pm\ +}{31\ 12}$	±....... ....+-.... ....
10	$\overset{\pm\ +}{31\ 30}$	±+...... ....
11	$\overset{\pm\ -\ -\ -}{31\ 13\ 7}$	±....... ....-+++ +++....- +.......
12	$\overset{\pm\ +}{31\ 24}$	±.....+- ....
13	$\overset{\pm}{31}$	±....... ....
14	$\overset{\pm\ -\ +}{31\ 15\ 3}$	±....... .... -....... ....+...

This function uses the bits of A to choose between the corresponding bits of B and C. That is, if bit i of A is 1, then bit i of $F(A, B, C)$ is bit i of B; otherwise, bit i of $F(A, B, C)$ is bit i of C. Using the information in Tables 5.12 and 5.13, and the definition of F, we can derive conditions on the bits of the Q_j.

For $j \leq 3$ we have $\Delta Q_j = \Delta Q_{j-1} = \Delta Q_{j-2} = 0$ which implies $\Delta F_j = 0$, that is, $F_j = F_j'$. Using the notation defined above, it follows that ∇F_j is

$$``........ \quad .... \quad .... \quad ...."$$

for $j \leq 3$. This imposes no restrictions on the corresponding Q_j. Consequently, no conditions are imposed on any Q_j based on the analysis of steps 0 through 3.

Now consider F_4. In this case, the attacker has $\Delta Q_2 = \Delta Q_3 = 0$ and $\Delta Q_4 = -2^6$, and wants to obtain $\Delta F_4 = 2^{19} + 2^{11}$. From the collision results in Tables 5.12 and 5.13, the relevant information for F_4 is collected in Table 5.14.

From ∇Q_4 in Table 5.14, it immediately follows that

$$\langle Q_4 = 1 \rangle_9 \quad \text{and} \quad \langle Q_4 = 0 \rangle_{10\ldots25}.$$

We refer to bits $9, 10, \ldots, 25$ as the "nonconstant" bits of Q_4, while the remaining bits are the "constant" bits of Q_4. That is, $Q_4' = Q_4$ on the constant bits, while $Q_4' \neq Q_4$ on the nonconstant bits.

Table 5.13: First Round F_j Differences [64]

j	ΔF_j	∇F_j
0-3	0	....
4	$\overset{+}{19}\ \overset{+}{11}$	....+... ....+... ....
5	$\overset{-}{14}\ \overset{-}{10}$	....-++++++ +.++++.. ....
6	$\overset{-}{27}\ \overset{-}{25}\ \overset{+}{16}\ \overset{+}{10}\ \overset{+}{5}\ \overset{-}{2}$	.....-.- ....+ .....+.. ..+..-..
7	$\overset{\pm}{31}\ \overset{-}{24}\ \overset{+}{16}\ \overset{+}{10}\ \overset{+}{8}\ \overset{-}{6}$	±......- ....+ .....+.+ .+......
8	$\overset{\pm}{31}\ \overset{+}{26}\ \overset{-}{23}\ \overset{-}{20}\ \overset{+}{6}\ \overset{+}{0}$	±....+.. -..-.... ....+.....+
9	$\overset{-}{23}\ \overset{+}{13}\ \overset{+}{6}\ \overset{+}{0}$	.... -....... ..+..... .+.....+
10	$\overset{-}{8}\ \overset{-}{0}$	....- ....-
11	$\overset{\pm}{31}\ \overset{+}{17}\ \overset{+}{7}$	±....... ....+--. .... +.......
12	$\overset{\pm}{31}\ \overset{-}{13}$	±....... ....-+++ +++..... ....
13	$\overset{\pm}{31}\ \overset{+}{18}$	±....... .....+.. ....
14	$\overset{\pm}{31}\ \overset{+}{25}$	±.....+. ....

Table 5.14: F_4 Computation

	Δ	∇
Q_2	0	....
Q_3	0	....
Q_4	$\overset{-}{6}$	....-++++++ +++++++++ ++......
F_4	$\overset{+}{19}\ \overset{+}{11}$	....+... ....+... ....

First, we consider the constant bits of Q_4. The function $F(Q_4, Q_3, Q_2)$ selects the bits of Q_3 or Q_2 based on the bits of Q_4. From ∇Q_4, we have $\langle Q_4 = Q_4' \rangle_{0...8,26...31}$ and for each of these bits of Q_4 it follows that:

- If $\langle Q_4 = 1 \rangle_j$, then $\langle F_4 = Q_3 \rangle_j$ and $\langle F_4' = Q_3' \rangle_j$.

- If $\langle Q_4 = 0 \rangle_j$, then $\langle F_4 = Q_2 \rangle_j$ and $\langle F_4' = Q_2' \rangle_j$.

Since $Q_2 = Q_2'$ and $Q_3 = Q_3'$, we have $\langle F_4' = F_4 \rangle_j$ for each constant bit j. From Table 5.14 we see that this is the desired condition, since each of the constant bits of Q_4 is also a constant bit of F_4. Consequently, the desired conditions on F_4 are met, and no restrictions on Q_j are implied.

Next, we deal with the nonconstant bits of Q_4. Note that ∇Q_4, which appears in Table 5.14, immediately implies

$$\langle Q_4 = 0 \rangle_{10...25} \quad \text{and} \quad \langle Q_4 = 1 \rangle_9.$$

Also, on the nonconstant bits of Q_4, we have:

- If $\langle Q_4 = 1 \rangle_j$, then $\langle F_4 = Q_3 \rangle_j$ and $\langle F'_4 = Q'_2 \rangle_j$.

- If $\langle Q_4 = 0 \rangle_j$, then $\langle F_4 = Q_2 \rangle_j$ and $\langle F'_4 = Q'_3 \rangle_j$.

For ∇F_4 in Table 5.14 to hold, it is necessary that $\langle F'_4 = F_4 \rangle_{10,11,13...19,21...25}$. But, we have $\langle Q'_4 = 1 \rangle_{10,11,13...19,21...25}$ so that $\langle F'_4 = Q'_3 \rangle_{10,11,13...19,21...25}$. Since $\langle Q_4 = 0 \rangle_{10,11,13...19,21...25}$ it follows that $\langle F_4 = Q_2 \rangle_{10,11,13...19,21...25}$. Furthermore, since $Q_3 = Q'_3$, for the ∇F_4 condition to hold for bits 10, 11, 13 through 19 and bits 21 through 25, the conditions

$$\langle Q_3 = Q_2 \rangle_{10,11,13...19,21...25}$$

are sufficient.

We still must consider the nonconstant bits in positions 12 and 20. Here, we require that $\langle F'_4 = 1 \rangle_{12,20}$ and $\langle F_4 = 0 \rangle_{12,20}$. From ∇Q_4 it follows that $\langle Q'_4 = 1 \rangle_{12,20}$ and $\langle Q_4 = 0 \rangle_{12,20}$, which implies that $\langle F'_4 = Q'_3 \rangle_{12,20}$ and $\langle F_4 = Q_2 \rangle_{12,20}$. Since $Q'_3 = Q_3$, the desired condition on F_4 holds provided that

$$\langle Q_3 = 1 \rangle_{12,20} \quad \text{and} \quad \langle Q_2 = 0 \rangle_{12,20}.$$

Finally, we have to deal with bit 9. From ∇Q_4 we have $\langle Q'_4 = 0 \rangle_9$ and $\langle Q_4 = 1 \rangle_9$ which implies $\langle F'_4 = Q'_2 \rangle_9$ and $\langle F_4 = Q_3 \rangle_9$. From ∇F_4, the desired condition is $\langle F'_4 = F_4 \rangle_9$. Since $Q_2 = Q'_2$, the required condition here is

$$\langle Q_2 = Q_3 \rangle_9.$$

All of the conditions derived at step 4 are listed in Table 5.15.

Table 5.15: Step 4 Conditions

$\langle Q_4 = 0 \rangle_{10...,25}$
$\langle Q_4 = 1 \rangle_9$
$\langle Q_3 = 1 \rangle_{12,20}$
$\langle Q_2 = 0 \rangle_{12,20}$
$\langle Q_2 = Q_3 \rangle_{10,11,13...19,21...25}$

Next, we analyze one more step in this process. Note that all of the steps for both message blocks are analyzed in [64].

From Tables 5.12 and 5.13, we have extracted the relevant information for step 5 and collected it in Table 5.16. In this case, the attacker knows that $\Delta Q_3 = 0$, $\Delta Q_4 = -2^6$ and $\Delta Q_5 = \pm 2^{31} + 2^{23} - 2^6$, and he wants to ensure $\Delta F_5 = -2^{14} - 2^{10}$.

Table 5.16: F_5 Computation

	Δ	∇
Q_3	0	`........ ........ ........ ........`
Q_4	$\bar{6}$	`........ .-++++++ ++++++++ ++......`
Q_5	$\overset{\pm\ +\ -}{31\ 23\ 6}$	`±....... +....... ........ .-......`
F_5	$\overline{14}\ \overline{10}$	`........ .-++++++ +.++++.. ........`

From ∇Q_5, we have $\langle Q_5 = 0 \rangle_8$ and $\langle Q_5 = 1 \rangle_{25}$. Here, no restriction is implied on $\langle Q_5 \rangle_0$ (although we do obtain a restriction on this bit in the analysis below).

Now consider the constant bits of Q_5, that is, those bits where $Q'_5 = Q_5$. From Table 5.16, we have $\langle Q'_5 = Q_5 \rangle_{1...7,9...24,26...31}$. The function F_5 selects between the bits of Q_4 and Q_3, depending on the corresponding bits of Q_5, with Q_3 selected if the bit of Q_5 is 0, and Q_4 selected if the bit of Q_5 is 1. The analogous statement holds for F'_5 on the constant bits of Q_5.

From Table 5.16, we see that the desired condition on ∇F_5 is given by $\langle \nabla F_5 = \nabla Q_4 \rangle_{9...16,18...21}$ and this will hold provided F'_5 selects Q'_4 and F_5 selects Q_4 on these bits. Since we have $\langle Q'_5 = Q_5 \rangle_{9...16,18...21}$, (i.e., these bits are among the constant bits of Q_5) this will hold true provided that we have $\langle Q_5 = 1 \rangle_{9...16,18...21}$. Also, $\langle \nabla F_5 = \nabla Q_3 \rangle_{17,22,23,24}$ and this holds provided F'_5 selects Q'_3 and F_5 selects Q_3. Since these are also among the constant bits of Q_5, we require that $\langle Q_5 = 0 \rangle_{17,22,23,24}$.

For the remaining constant bits of Q_5 we want $\langle F'_5 = F_5 \rangle_j$. But each such constant bit of Q_5 is also a constant bits of Q_4 and Q_3, that is, $\langle Q'_4 = Q_4 \rangle_j$ and $\langle Q'_3 = Q_3 \rangle_j$. Consequently, on these bits it does not matter which bits are selected, and therefore, no additional restrictions are implied.

Now consider the nonconstant bits of Q_5, that is, $\langle Q_5 \rangle_{0,8,25}$. Since we have $\langle Q'_5 = 1 \rangle_8$ and $\langle Q_5 = 0 \rangle_8$, it follows that $\langle F'_5 = Q'_4 \rangle_8$ and $\langle F_5 = Q_3 \rangle_8$. From Table 5.16, the desired condition here is $\langle F'_5 = F_5 \rangle_8$. Since $\langle Q'_4 = Q_4 \rangle_8$, we require that $\langle Q_4 = Q_3 \rangle_8$.

Also, we want $\langle F'_5 = F_5 \rangle_{25}$. From ∇Q_5 in Table 5.16 we have the conditions $\langle Q'_5 = 0 \rangle_{25}$ and $\langle Q_5 = 1 \rangle_{25}$. Therefore, $\langle F'_5 = Q'_3 \rangle_{25}$ and $\langle F_5 = Q_4 \rangle_{25}$. Since we have $\langle Q_3 = Q'_3 \rangle_{25}$, this yields the condition $\langle Q_3 = Q_4 \rangle_{25}$. However, from ∇Q_4 in Table 5.16, we have $\langle Q_4 = 0 \rangle_{25}$ (which was already noted, above), and, consequently, the new condition here is $\langle Q_3 = 0 \rangle_{25}$.

Finally, we have $\langle Q'_5 \neq Q_5 \rangle_0$ and we want to ensure that $\langle F'_5 = F_5 \rangle_0$. Since $\langle Q'_3 = Q_3 \rangle_0$ and $\langle Q'_4 = Q_4 \rangle_0$, the desired condition will hold provided that $\langle Q_4 = Q_3 \rangle_0$. In Table 5.17 we list all of the conditions derived based on this analysis of the constant and nonconstant bits in step 5.

Table 5.17: Step 5 Conditions

$$
\begin{array}{l}
\langle Q_5 = 1 \rangle_{9\ldots16,18\ldots21,25} \\
\langle Q_5 = 0 \rangle_{8,17,22,23,24} \\
\langle Q_3 = 0 \rangle_{25} \\
\langle Q_4 = Q_3 \rangle_{0,8}
\end{array}
$$

Continuing in this manner, it is possible to obtain a set of conditions on the outputs Q_j. If these conditions are all satisfied, then a collision will result. Each such condition can be expected to hold, at random, with a probability of about $1/2$. Based on the examples presented here, it is apparent that there will be a large number of conditions that must be satisfied. In fact, there are over 300 conditions on the first message block that must be satisfied. If the attacker simply generates random messages and checks whether the conditions are met, the "attack" would be much worse than the birthday attack.

Fortunately, all conditions that occur in the first round (that is, within the first 16 steps) can be satisfied simply by directly modifying the message words. In addition, some conditions in later steps can be satisfied by a more complex modification procedure. It is critically important that the differential has been constructed so that the number of conditions is large in the early steps, but very small in the later steps. In this way, the number of conditions that can be satisfied deterministically is large, while the number that must be satisfied probabilistically—which determines the work factor of the attack—is much smaller.

The work presented in [64] (and outlined above) can be used to develop an efficient attack to find MD5 collisions, as suggested in the previous paragraph. The idea behind the attack is straightforward. First, we choose the message words so that all of the conditions on Q_j, for $j = 0, 1, \ldots, 15$, are satisfied using a "single-step modification" technique (as explained below). Then we use a "multi-step modification" technique, due to Wang, whereby some of the conditions on Q_j for $j > 15$ can be forced to hold, while all of the conditions on the Q_j, for $j \leq 15$, still hold (this is outlined below). Then we test all of the remaining Q_j conditions. If all of these are satisfied, then we have found a collision; if not, we generate another candidate message that satisfies all of the deterministic conditions (that is, the conditions in the early steps) and again test the probabilistic conditions (that is, the conditions in the later steps), and we repeat this until a collision is found.

The Q_j conditions that are satisfied probabilistically each hold with a probability of about $1/2$. Consequently, the work factor for the attack is determined by the number of conditions that must be satisfied probabilistically.

Of course, this entire process needs to be repeated for both message blocks, M_0 and M_1. With some refinements, this is the path that all of the MD5 collision attacks have followed up to the time of this writing.

All improvements in the collision attack to date revolve around providing a way to deterministically satisfy more conditions by choosing the message block appropriately, thereby reducing the number of conditions that must be satisfied probabilistically. Before leaving this part of the attack, we show that it is also possible to force some of the conditions on the T_j to hold, that is, some of the T_j conditions can be satisfied deterministically.

Stevens [144] observes that

$$Q_j - Q_{j-1} = R_j = T_j \lll s_j$$

and he notes that this opens the possibility of specifying conditions on Q_j and Q_{j-1} that will force conditions on T_j to hold. For example, above we derived the condition $\langle T_4 = 1 \rangle_0$. Since $r_4 = 7$, we have $\langle T_4 \rangle_0 = \langle R_4 \rangle_{25}$ and from the analysis above, $\langle Q_4 = 0 \rangle_{25}$. $\langle Q_4 = 0 \rangle_{25}$ and $\langle Q_4 = 1 \rangle_{26}$. With the additional conditions $\langle Q_3 = 1 \rangle_{27}$, $\langle Q_3 = 1 \rangle_{26}$ and $\langle Q_4 = 0 \rangle_{25}$, we are assured that $\langle R_4 = 1 \rangle_{25}$, and hence $\langle T_4 = 1 \rangle_0$, as desired. To see that this is the case, note that the subtraction is given by

$$
\begin{array}{lll}
\ldots 010 \ldots & \longleftrightarrow & \langle Q_4 \rangle_{25,26,27} \\
- \ldots 011 \ldots & \longleftrightarrow & \langle Q_3 \rangle_{25,26,27} \\
\hline
\ldots 11\text{x} \ldots & \longleftrightarrow & \langle R_4 \rangle_{25,26,27}
\end{array}
$$

where $\langle R_4 = 1 \rangle_{25}$ follows since a borrow from higher-order bit positions must occur.

Continuing in this manner, Stevens [144] is able to derive conditions that force several of the T_j conditions to hold. This work yields the fastest MD5 attack as of the time of this writing. Using a typical modern PC, Stevens' attack takes about two minutes, on average, to find a collision. We give Stevens' algorithm, below.

The conditions for the first message block, as specified by Stevens' attack, are given in the Appendix in Tables A-6 and A-7. For Q_j, a "^" indicates that the specified bit must agree with the corresponding bit of Q_{j-1}, while a "!" indicates that the specified bit must not agree with the corresponding bit of Q_{j-1}. On the other hand, a "." indicates that there is no restriction on that particular bit.

The corresponding tables for the second message block M_1 are due to Klima [81] and these tables can also be found in [144]. For completeness, we reproduce these in the Appendix in Tables A-8 and A-9. The attack to find the first message block, M_0, is more costly than the attack for the second message block, M_1, so the overall work is dominated by finding a 512-bit message block satisfying the conditions in Tables A-6 and A-7.

Single-step Modification

The idea behind the single-step modification technique (also known as single-message modification) is straightforward. We simply use the fact that each of the 16 message words appears once in the first 16 steps, and the fact that by modifying a message word W_j, we can change the output Q_j. An example should make the process clear.

As mentioned in the previous section, we first select the message block at random. Then we use the single-step modification technique to force all of the conditions on Q_j to hold, for $j = 0, 1, \ldots, 15$, by modifying the message words. Next, we show precisely how this works, but first note that if

$$M_0 = (X_0, X_1, \ldots, X_{15}),$$

then from Table 5.10 we have $W_i = X_i$, for $i = 0, 1, \ldots, 15$.

Suppose that we have randomly selected $\tilde{M}_0 = (\tilde{X}_0, \tilde{X}_1, \ldots, \tilde{X}_{15})$ as the first message block. Let $\tilde{W}_i$, for $i = 0, 1, \ldots, 63$ be the corresponding input words to the MD5 algorithm. Our goal is to modify $\tilde{M}_0$ to obtain a message block $M_0 = (X_0, X_1, \ldots, X_{15})$ for which all of the first round output conditions hold, that is, all of the conditions on Q_i for $i < 16$ hold.

Now suppose that we have already found X_0 and X_1 and consider step 2. Recall that the IV is denoted $Q_{-4}, Q_{-1}, Q_{-2}, Q_{-3}$. Then using $\tilde{M}_0$, we compute

$$\tilde{Q}_2 = Q_1 + (f_1 + Q_{-2} + \tilde{W}_2 + K_2) \lll s_2, \qquad (5.52)$$

where $f_1 = F(Q_1, Q_0, Q_{-1})$. We want to transform $\tilde{Q}_2$ to Q_2 so that the conditions in the Q_2 row of Table A-6 hold, namely, $\langle Q_2 = 0 \rangle_{12,20,25}$. For each $i = 0, 1, \ldots, 31$, let E_i be the 32-bit word defined by

$$\langle E_i = 1 \rangle_i \quad \text{and} \quad \langle E_i = 0 \rangle_j \quad \text{for} \quad j \neq i, \qquad (5.53)$$

that is, E_i is 0 except for bit i, which is 1. Then we have $E_i = 2^{31-i}$. Denote the bits of $\tilde{Q}_2$ as

$$\tilde{Q}_2 = (q_0, q_1, q_2, \ldots, q_{31}).$$

Let $D = -q_{12} E_{12} - q_{20} E_{20} - q_{25} E_{25}$. Then the desired conditions on Q_2 are satisfied by letting

$$Q_2 = \tilde{Q}_2 + D. \qquad (5.54)$$

Now suppose that we replace $\tilde{W}_2$ in (5.52) with the value of W_2 for which

$$Q_2 = Q_1 + (f_1 + Q_{-2} + W_2 + K_2) \lll s_2.$$

Then this value W_2 can be determined algebraically. Doing so, we find

$$W_2 = ((Q_2 - Q_1) \ggg s_2) - f_1 - Q_{-2} - K_2. \qquad (5.55)$$

From (5.54), we see that Q_2 is known, and all other terms on the right-hand-side of (5.55) are known, so we have determined W_2. Then letting $X_2 = W_2$, we obtain Q_2 which satisfies the required output conditions at step 2.

After repeating a similar process for each of steps 0 through 15, we will have determined a message $M_0 = (X_0, X_1, \ldots, X_{15})$ for which all of the output conditions in these steps hold. We could then simply test the remaining conditions and if all hold, we have found a collision. If any condition beyond step 15 does not hold, then we could select a new random $\tilde{M}_0$ and repeat the entire process. Since each condition is expected to hold at random with a probability of about $1/2$, this yields an attack with a work factor on the order of 2^c, where c is the number of conditions in steps 16 through 63.

Using only single-step modifications provides a feasible shortcut attack. However, it is possible to further reduce the work factor by using the multi-step modification technique described in the next section.

Multi-step Modification

Wang's multi-step modifications (also known as multi-message modifications) make it possible to satisfy some of the conditions in steps beyond 15. It is critical that when we satisfy conditions by this approach, we do not violate the output conditions from previous steps. This makes the multi-step modification more complex than the single-step modifications.

There are actually several multi-step modification techniques, some of which are very convoluted, and some of which are not entirely deterministic, that is, the condition can fail with some small probability. Here, we describe the simplest example of a multi-step modification. The paper [16] discusses some other multi-step modifications, while Daum [34] provides a good description of several such techniques.

Let $\tilde{M}_0 = (\tilde{X}_0, \tilde{X}_1, \ldots, \tilde{X}_{15})$ be the message block M_0 after single-step modifications. Consider step 16, where we want the output condition specified by $\langle Q_{16} = 0 \rangle_0$ to hold (see the Q_{16} row of Table A-6). We have

$$\tilde{Q}_{16} = Q_{15} + (f_{15} + Q_{12} + \tilde{W}_{16} + K_{16}) \lll s_{16},$$

where $\tilde{W}_{16} = \tilde{X}_1$ and $f_{15} = G(Q_{15}, Q_{14}, Q_{13})$.

Let $\tilde{Q}_{16} = (q_0, q_1, \ldots, q_{31})$ and define $D = -q_0 E_0$, where E_i is given in (5.53). Then it is easy to verify that $Q_{16} = \tilde{Q}_{16} + D$ will satisfy the required condition at step 16. As with the single-step modification, we replace $\tilde{W}_{16}$ with W_{16} so that

$$Q_{16} = Q_{15} + (f_{15} + Q_{12} + W_{16} + K_{16}) \lll s_{16}.$$

Solving, we find

$$W_{16} = ((Q_{16} - Q_{15}) \ggg s_{16}) - f_{15} - Q_{12} - K_{16}.$$

Since $W_{16} = X_1$, we must ensure that all of the conditions in the first round involving X_1 still hold. Since Q_i, for $i = 1, 2, 3, 4, 5$, also depend on X_1, we must carefully consider each of these steps. However, since no conditions were previously specified on Q_1, the $i = 1$ case is not a concern.

We have determined a new input at step 16, namely, $W_{16} = X_1$. From the single-step modification, we have

$$Q_1 = Q_0 + (f_0 + Q_{-3} + \tilde{X}_1 + K_1) \lll s_1.$$

Now compute

$$Z = Q_0 + (f_0 + Q_{-3} + X_1 + K_1) \lll s_1,$$

that is, Z is the new Q_1 that results from the modified X_1 computed in step 16. Since no conditions were specified on Q_1, we will not violate any previous conditions by letting $Q_1 = Z$.

Next, recall that

$$Q_2 = Z + (f_1(Q_1, Q_0, Q_{-1}) + Q_{-2} + \tilde{X}_2 + K_2) \lll s_2.$$

Using the same approach as the single-step modification, we choose X_2 so that

$$Q_2 = Z + (f_1(Z, Q_0, Q_{-1}) + Q_{-2} + X_2 + K_2) \lll s_2,$$

which implies that

$$X_2 = ((Q_2 - Z) \ggg s_2) - f_1(Z, Q_0, Q_{-1}) - Q_{-2} - K_2.$$

Observe that by selecting X_2 in this way, the modification we made when selecting X_1, as required for step 16, will not affect any of the output conditions from step 2. That is, all of the conditions on Q_2 that hold as a result of the single-step modifications still hold true.

Similarly, we choose

$$X_3 = ((Q_3 - Q_2) \ggg s_3) - f_2(Q_2, Z, Q_0) - Q_{-1} - K_3$$

and

$$X_4 = ((Q_4 - Q_3) \ggg s_4) - f_3(Q_3, Q_2, Z) - Q_0 - K_4$$

and, finally,

$$X_5 = ((Q_5 - Q_4) \ggg s_5) - f_4(Q_4, Q_3, Q_2) - Z - K_5.$$

Since Z (the new Q_1) is not used in the calculation of any other Q_i, no other X_i must be modified.

The bottom line here is that we now have deterministically satisfied the conditions on step 16, while maintaining all of the conditions on steps 0 through 15 that resulted from the single-step modifications. The multi-step modification considered here is the simplest case. Several other methods have been developed in an effort to slightly reduce the work factor of Wang's attack. The evolution of Wang's attack seems to have reached the point where the attack is so efficient (about two minutes for Stevens [144] implementation) and the difficulty and complexity of finding improved multi-step modifications is now so high—and many of the more advanced modification techniques only hold probabilistically—that it appears likely that further improvement along these lines will be incremental, at best.

5.4.6 Stevens' Implementation of Wang's Attack

Stevens [144] gives the algorithm in Table 5.18 for finding a message block M_0 satisfying Wang's differential conditions. This attack is based on the set of output conditions given in Tables A-6 and A-7, which appear in the Appendix.

Table 5.18: Efficient Algorithm to Find M_0

```
// Find M_0 = (X_0, X_1, ..., X_15), where "all M_0 conditions" refers to:
//     all Table A-7 conditions,
//     all IV conditions for M_1 (see Table A-8),
//     both ⟨T_21 = 0⟩_14 and ⟨T_33 = 0⟩_16
Find M_0
    repeat
        Choose Q_0, Q_2, Q_3. ..., Q_15 satisfying conditions in Table A-6
        Compute X_0, X_6, X_7, ..., X_15
        repeat
            Choose Q_16 satisfying conditions
            Compute X_1 using j = 16
            Compute Q_1 and X_2, X_3, X_4, X_5
            Compute Q_17, Q_18, Q_19, Q_20
        until Q_16, Q_17, ..., Q_20 satisfy conditions in Table A-6
        for (Q_8, Q_9) consistent with X_11
            Compute X_8, X_9, X_10, X_12, X_13
            Compute Q_21, Q_22, ..., Q_63
            if all M_0 conditions are satisfied then
                return M
            end if
        next (Q_8, Q_9)
    until all M_0 conditions are satisfied
end Find M_0
```

Stevens also presents an efficient algorithm for the second block, M_1, which we give in Table 5.19. This is identical to the algorithm given by Klima in [81]. However, finding M_0 dominates the overall collision-finding work, so all efforts to improve Wang's attack have been focused on the first message block, M_0.

Table 5.19: Efficient Algorithm to Find M_1

```
// Find M₁ = (X₀, X₁, ..., X₁₅), where "all M₁ conditions" refers to:
//     all Table A-9 conditions,
//     both ⟨T₂₁ = 0⟩₁₄ and ⟨T₃₃ = 0⟩₁₆
Find M₁
    repeat
        Choose Q₁, Q₂, ..., Q₁₅ satisfying conditions in Table A-8
        Compute X₄, X₅, ..., X₁₄
        repeat
            Choose Q₀ satisfying conditions
            Compute X₀, X₁, X₂, X₃, X₄
            Compute Q₁₆, Q₁₇, Q₁₈, Q₁₉, Q₂₀
        until Q₁₆, Q₁₇, ..., Q₂₀ satisfy conditions in Table A-8
        for (Q₈, Q₉) consistent with X₁₁
            Compute X₈, X₉, X₁₀, X₁₂, X₁₃
            Compute Q₂₁, Q₂₂, ..., Q₆₃
            if all M₁ conditions are satisfied then
                return M
            end if
        next (Q₈, Q₉)
    until all M₁ conditions are satisfied
end Find M₁
```

5.4.7   A Practical Attack

It is sometimes claimed that most hash collision attacks are of little or no practical significance. For the MD5 attack, it is presently not possible to produce arbitrary collisions, so it seems highly improbable that a meaningful collision can be constructed. However, there are cases where an apparently useless collision can be used to create a security vulnerability. Here, we consider one such scenario; see Daum and Lucks [35] for the original description of this clever attack.

Suppose that Alice wants to digitally sign the letter of "recommendation" shown in Figure 5.6, which is in the form of a postscript file, `rec.ps`. Alice carefully reads the letter, which was created by her new secretary, Trudy, then Alice digitally signs it. As usual, the signature is computed by first hashing the file and the resulting hash value is signed. Suppose that the MD5 hash function is used in this signing operation. In this case, Alice computes

$$S = [h(\texttt{rec.ps})]_{\text{Alice}},$$

where h is the MD5 hash, and $[M]_{\text{Alice}}$ denotes the digital signature of M using Alice's private key. Then S and the original letter, $\texttt{rec.ps}$, can be sent to the intended recipient, who can verify the signature using Alice's public key.

To Whom it May Concern:

Tom Austin and Ying Zhang have demonstrated decent programming ability. They should do OK in any programming position, provided that the work is not too complex, and that the position does not require any independent thought or initiative.

However, I think they like to steal office supplies, so I would keep a close eye on them. Also, their basic hygiene is somewhat lacking so I would recommend that you have them telecommute.

Sincerely,

Alice

Figure 5.6: Recommendation letter.

Now consider the letter in Figure 5.7, which was printed from the file $\texttt{auth.ps}$. This letter is obviously much different than the letter in Figure 5.6, but, incredibly, the files $\texttt{auth.ps}$ and $\texttt{rec.ps}$ have the same MD5 hash values. For the specific files used in this example,

$$h(\texttt{rec.ps}) = h(\texttt{auth.ps}) = \texttt{0xc3261825f024565d0731fa07ed660f22},$$

where h is the MD5 hash.

How can these two very different letters have the same MD5 hash? After all, in the MD5 collision attack discussed above, the colliding messages are almost identical, with the precise bit difference per 512-bit message block specified by (5.47) and (5.48). It would seem that these two messages could not possibly have been generated using the MD5 attack outlined above.

In fact, the messages in Figures 5.6 and 5.7 were not directly generated using the attack above and, furthermore, the printed text from these two letters does not yield an MD5 collision. The identical hash values of the two files—as distinct from the actual displayed text—is made possible by the fact that postscript has a conditional statement, which enables Trudy to include

---

To Bank of America:

Tom Austin and Ying Zhang are authorized access to all of my account information and may make withdrawals or deposits.

Sincerely,

Alice

Figure 5.7: Authorization letter.

the text of both letters in both postscript files. Trudy can use a "meaningless" MD5 collision to force the hashes of the two files to be the same, even though the hashes of the actual printed text is not the same. To see how this works, we need to examine the postscript inside these files.

Figure 5.8 contains excerpts of rec.ps. These excerpts have been slightly modified for clarity. Also, "⊔" represents a blank space inserted so that the header information is precisely 64 bytes.

The postscript conditional statement is of the form

$$(X)(Y)\texttt{eq}\{T_0\}\{T_1\}\texttt{ifelse}$$

where T_0 is processed if the text X is identical to Y and T_1 is processed otherwise. Let W be the first 64 bytes of the file in Figure 5.8. Then W consists of all bytes up to and including the opening "(" in "$(X)(Y)\texttt{eq}\{$". Now let $Z = \text{MD5}_{0\ldots63}(\text{IV}, W)$, that is, Z is the result of compressing the initial block of the file. Using the MD5 attack discussed above, we find a collision where Z is used as the IV (the MD5 attack can be modified to work for any IV). Denote the resulting pair of 1024-byte values as M and M'.

Let L be the file obtained by letting $X = Y = M$ in Figure 5.8, and let L' be the file obtained by by letting $X = M'$ and $Y = M$ in Figure 5.8. Then for the file L, the two strings before the "eq" are identical (since both are M), which causes the postscript interpreter to only display (or print) the text in Figure 5.6. On the other hand, in the file L' the two strings before the "eq" differ and therefore the else condition holds, which implies that only the text in Figure 5.7 will be visible when the file is processed through postscript. Furthermore, the MD5 hashes of the files L and L' are identical. This follows from the fact that M and M' have the same MD5 hash (since the initial block is W for both files), and from the fact that all bits after X are identical in both L and L'. Letting rec.ps $= L$ and auth.ps $= L'$ yields the results displayed in Figures 5.6 and 5.7, with the two files having identical MD5 hashes.

```
%!PS-Adobe-1.0
%%BoundingBox:   0 0 612 792␣␣␣␣␣␣␣␣␣␣␣␣␣␣␣␣␣␣␣␣␣(X)(Y)eq{
/Times-Roman findfont 20 scalefont setfont
25 450 moveto (To Whom it May Concern:)  show
25 400 moveto
(Tom Austin and Ying Zhang have demonstrated...
         ⋮
(Sincerely,)
show
25 150 moveto
(Alice)
show
}{/Times-Roman findfont 20 scalefont setfont
25 450 moveto (To Bank of America:)  show
25 400 moveto
(Tom Austin and Ying Zhang are authorized access...
         ⋮
(Sincerely,)
show
25 250 moveto
(Alice)
show
}ifelse
showpage
```

Figure 5.8: Postscript file.

Of course, anyone who examines either of the postscript files in a text editor will quickly realize that something is amiss. But the whole point of a cryptographic integrity check is that integrity problems can be detected automatically, without human intervention. To detect this particular attack automatically is possible, but to deal with all possible attacks of this type would be a challenge. Consequently, this attack is a realistic threat and it nicely illustrates that there is a potential risk when any hash collision is known, whether or not the collision itself is meaningful.

5.5   Summary

For many years, it seems that hash functions had been largely ignored by cryptographers. But with the successful attack on MD5, and similar results for SHA-1 pending, hash functions have moved from a sleepy cryptographic backwater to the forefront of research. It is likely that new hashing techniques that thwart differential attacks like those described in this chapter will soon emerge. This might occur through the usual research process, or there might be an organized "bake off" similar to the process that produced the Advanced Encryption Standard (AES).

Finally, we note that MD5 and SHA-1 are not only the two most widely-used hash functions, but they are also very similar in design. This was probably not a major issue when both hash functions were considered secure, but when MD5 was broken, it became clear that this lack of "genetic diversity" in hashing was a potential problem. It is worth noting that public key cryptography suffers from a similar lack of diversity. Today, almost all of the public key cryptosystems used in practice rely on the difficulty of factoring or the difficulty of the discrete log problem (or the elliptic curve equivalents). If a significant shortcut is found for either of these problems, it would leave a gaping hole in the realm of public key cryptography, which would be far more severe than the temporary turmoil in the world of hashing that was created by Wang's MD5 attack.

5.6   Problems

1. Justify the following statements regarding cryptographic hash functions.

   a. Strong collision resistance implies weak collision resistance.

   b. Strong collision resistance does not imply one-way.

2. Suppose that we have a block cipher, where $C = E(P, K)$, and want to use this block cipher as a hash function. Let X be a specified constant and let M be a message consisting of a single block, where the block size is the size of the key in the block cipher. Define the hash of M as $Y = E(X, M)$.

   a. Assuming that the underlying block cipher is secure, verify that this hash function satisfies all of the requirements of a hash function as listed at the start of this chapter.

   b. Extend the definition of this hash so that messages of any length can be hashed.

   c. Why must a block cipher used in this way be resistant to a "chosen key" attack? Hint: Suppose that if we are given plaintext P, we can find two keys K_0 and K_1 such that $E(P, K_0) = E(P, K_1)$. Show that this block cipher is insecure for use as a hash function.

3. Suppose that a hash function h has M different possible outputs. In Section 5.2 we showed that about M hashes must be computed before we expect to find a w such that $h(w) = h(x)$. In terms of M, precisely how many hashes must we compute before we expect to find such a w?

4. Suppose that a hash function h has M different possible outputs. In Section 5.2 we showed that about $\sqrt{M}$ hashes must be computed before we expect to find a collision, that is, before we can expect to find x and w such that $h(x) = h(w)$. In terms of M, give an explicit and simple formula that is more accurate than $\sqrt{M}$ for the number of hashes that must be computed before we expect to find such a x and w?

5. How could the digital signature attack discussed in Section 5.2.3 be prevented?

6. Recall the online bid scheme discussed in Section 5.2.4.

   a. Describe a forward search attack (see Section 6.5.1 for a definition) against this scheme.

   b. Describe a simple modification to this scheme that will prevent a forward search attack

7. The Nostradamus attack is discussed in Section 5.2.4. We showed that to apply this attack to MD5, which generates a 128-bit hash, the diamond structure has a height of 2^{41} and the work factor is on the order of 2^{87}.

   a. What is the height of the diamond structure and what is the work factor to apply this attack to the Bobcat hash, which generates a 48-bit output (Bobcat is a "toy" hash function discussed in [142])?

   b. What is the height of the diamond structure and what is the work factor to apply this attack to the SHA-1 hash, which generates a 160-bit output?

   c. What is the height of the diamond structure and what is the work factor to apply this attack to the Tiger hash, which generates a 192-bit output?

8. Suppose that the Nostradamus attack in Section 5.2.4 uses the diamond structure in Figure 5.2. Then the "predicted" hash value is $y = d_{30}$. If $f(\text{IV}, P, S') = d_{05}$, what is the resulting message M, in terms of P, S' and M_{ij}, such that $h(M) = y$?

9. Write computer programs to verify the following, where a, b and c are 8-bit bytes (as opposed to the 32-bit words used in MD4).

   a. For $F(a, b, c) = (a \wedge b) \vee (\neg a \wedge c)$,

      i. $F(a, b, c) = F(\neg a, b, c)$ if and only if $b = c$

      ii. $F(a, b, c) = F(a, \neg b, c)$ if and only if $a = \texttt{0x00}$

      iii. $F(a, b, c) = F(a, b, \neg c)$ if and only if $a = \texttt{0xff}$.

b. For $G(a, b, c) = (a \wedge b) \vee (a \wedge c) \vee (b \wedge c)$,

   i. $G(a, b, c) = G(\neg a, b, c)$ if and only if $b = c$

   ii. $G(a, b, c) = G(a, \neg b, c)$ if and only if $a = c$

   iii. $G(a, b, c) = G(a, b, \neg c)$ if and only if $a = b$.

c. For $H(a, b, c) = a \oplus b \oplus c$,

   i. $H(a, b, c) = \neg H(\neg a, b, c) = \neg H(a, \neg b, c) = \neg H(a, b, \neg c)$

   ii. $H(a, b, c) = H(\neg a, \neg b, c) = H(\neg a, b, \neg c) = H(a, \neg b, \neg c)$.

10. Recall that for the differential attack on MD4 (which is outlined in Table 5.5), the only difference between M and M' is in word X_{12}, and $X'_{12} = X_{12} + 1$. Assuming that a similar attack could succeed using a different word, why would it make sense to focus the attack on word 12?

11. Show that the following statements are true, where "steps" refer to the steps of the differential attack on MD4, as given in Table 5.5. Also, G and H are defined in (5.5) and (5.6), respectively.

a. To verify steps 22, 23, 26, 27, 30, and 31 it is sufficient to show that

$$G(X, Y, Z) = G(X, Y, Z + (\pm 1 \ll n)),$$

with a probability of about $p = 1/3$ for any $n \in \{0, 1, 2, \ldots, 31\}$.

b. To verify steps 24, 25, 28 and 29 it is sufficient to show that

$$G(X, Y, Z) = G(X, Y + (\pm 1 \ll n), Z + (\mp 1 \ll m)),$$

with a probability of about $p = 1/9$ for any $n, m \in \{0, 1, 2, \ldots, 31\}$ with $n \neq m$.

c. To verify steps 32 and 33 it is sufficient to show that

$$H(X, Y, Z) = H(X, Y + 1, Z - 1),$$

with a probability of about $p = 1/3$.

d. To verify steps 34 it is sufficient to show that

$$H(X, Y, Z) = H(X, Y, Z + 1) - 1,$$

with a probability of about $p = 1/3$.

12. Consider the formulas given in Problem 11. Suppose that we replace the 32-bit words X, Y, and Z with 8-bit bytes x, y and z. Then we can compute the probabilities exactly. Write a computer program to verify the claimed probability in each part of Problem 11 using 8-bit words instead of 32-bit words.

13. Verify equations (5.30) and (5.32).

14. The continuous approximation phase of the MD4 attack relies on the fact that for the functions F and G in (5.4) and (5.5), nearby inputs produce nearby outputs. Suppose that the 32-bit words A, B and C are replaced with 8-bit bytes a, b and c. Furthermore, suppose that a' differs from a in exactly one randomly selected bit position, b' differs from b in exactly one randomly selected bit position, and c' differs from c in exactly one randomly selected bit position. Write computer programs to answer the following.

   a. Find the probability that $F(a,b,c)$ and $F(a',b',c')$ differ in exactly k bit positions, for $k = 0,1,2,\ldots,8$.

   b. Find the probability that $G(a,b,c)$ and $G(a',b',c')$ differ in exactly k bit positions, for $k = 0,1,2,\ldots,8$.

   c. Find the probability that $H(a,b,c)$ and $H(a',b',c')$ differ in exactly k bit positions, for $k = 0,1,2,\ldots,8$, where H is defined in (5.6).

15. Implement the continuous approximation equation solving phase of the MD4 attack. Use your program to provide empirical estimates of the following.

   a. How many iterations, on average, are required before the check condition in (5.35) holds?

   b. In the continuous approximation, on average, how many iterations are required before the solution converges? That is, given a solution to (5.35), how many iterations are needed before (5.36) is satisfied?

   c. The continuous approximation can sometimes fail to converge. Using a cutoff of 100,000 iterations, what is the probability that the continuous approximation fails to converge?

   d. How many nonadmissible solutions are computed, on average, before one admissible solution is found?

16. Write a program to implement the differential phase of the MD4 attack. Use your program to empirically estimate the probabilities that appear in Table 5.5.

17. Dobbertin [42] claims that the probability of success of the differential phase of the MD4 attack is $1/2^{22}$. Assuming this is the case, show that the work factor for Dobbertin's attack is roughly equivalent to the computation of 2^{20} MD4 hashes.

18. Approximately how many MD4 collisions can be found using Dobbertin's attack?

19. Let $M = (X_0, X_1, \ldots, X_{15})$, where

$$
\begin{array}{ll}
X_0 = \texttt{0x9074449b}, & X_1 = \texttt{0x1089fc26}, \\
X_2 = \texttt{0x8bf37fa2}, & X_3 = \texttt{0x1d630daf}, \\
X_4 = \texttt{0x63247e24}, & X_5 = \texttt{0x4e4f430a}, \\
X_6 = \texttt{0x43415254}, & X_7 = \texttt{0x410a0a54}, \\
X_8 = \texttt{0x68742074}, & X_9 = \texttt{0x72702065}, \\
X_{10} = \texttt{0x20656369}, & X_{11} = \texttt{0x2420666f}, \\
X_{12} = \texttt{0x2c363731}, & X_{13} = \texttt{0x20353934}, \\
X_{14} = \texttt{0x20666c41}, & X_{15} = \texttt{0x776f6c42}.
\end{array}
$$

a. Compute the MD4 hash of M.

b. Let M' be the same as M, with the exception that X_{12} is replaced by $X'_{12} = X_{12} + 1$, that is, $X'_{12} = \texttt{0x2c363732}$. Compute the MD4 hash of M'.

c. Interpret M and M' as ASCII text, where the byte order of each X_i is little endian. Then, for example, X_6 consists of the bytes

$$(\texttt{0x54}, \texttt{0x52}, \texttt{0x41}, \texttt{0x43})$$

which represents the ASCII text "TRAC".

20. Let

$$F(A, B, C) = (A \wedge B) \vee (\neg A \wedge C)$$

and

$$\tilde{F}(A, B, C) = (A \wedge B) \oplus (\neg A \wedge C).$$

Suppose that A, B and C are 32-bit words selected at random. Then what is the probability that $F(A, B, C) = \tilde{F}(A, B, C)$?

21. In Section 5.4.2 we described Wang's "precise differential," which we denoted by ∇X. Given 32-bit words X' and X, let $U = X' \wedge \neg X$ and $L = \neg X' \wedge X$. Then it is easy to see that $X' \oplus X = U \oplus L$.

a. Show that for U and L defined in this way,

$$X' - X = U - L \pmod{2^{32}}. \tag{5.56}$$

b. Given $U = (u_0, u_1, \ldots, u_{31})$, $L = (\ell_0, \ell_1, \ldots, \ell_{31})$ and X' and X as defined above, define a string $S = (s_0, s_1, \ldots, s_{31})$ with a "+" in precisely those positions j where $u_j = 0$, a "−" in precisely those positions where $\ell_j = 0$, and a "." in all other positions. Show that $S = \nabla X$.

   c. Verify that (5.56) holds for every line in Tables A-2, A-3, A-4, and A-5, that is, show that

$$\Delta \text{Output} = U - L \pmod{2^{32}},$$

where U and L are determined from the ∇Output. That is, U has a 1 in each position where there is a "+" in ∇Output and 0 elsewhere, and L has a 0 in each position where there is a "−" in ∇Output and 0 elsewhere.

22. This problem deals with some properties of cyclic rotations with respect to the signed differential.

   a. Verify that

$$((2^1 + 2^6 - 2^{15} - 2^{17} - 2^{24} + 2^{27}) \ggg 22)$$
$$= -1 - 2^2 - 2^5 + 2^8 + 2^{11} + 2^{16} - 2^{25} - 2^{27}.$$

   b. Suppose that we have $X' - X = U - L$, where $U = X' \wedge \neg X$, and $L = \neg X' \wedge X$. Then, in addition to the differences being equal, we have $X' \oplus X = U \oplus L$, each 1 in U corresponds to a 1 in X' and a 0 in X, each 1 in L corresponds to a 1 in X and a 0 in X', and U and L are "disjoint", in the sense that $U \wedge L = 0$. Given such X', X, U and L, verify that

$$(X' \lll n) - (X \lll n) = (U \lll n) - (L \lll n).$$

Either prove this in general, or verify that it holds for all choices of 1-byte values and for all $n = 0, 1, 2, \ldots, 7$.

   c. Let X', X, U and L be as in part b. Let $Z = X' - X$. Give an example for which

$$(Z \lll n) \neq (U \lll n) - (L \lll n).$$

23. Let x and y be randomly selected bytes. For each $k = 0, 1, 2, \ldots, 7$, what is the probability p_k that

$$(x - y) \ggg k = (x \ggg k) - (y \ggg k),$$

where the subtraction is taken modulo 256?

24. This problem analyzes some issues related to the MD5 single-step modifications technique.

a. Let X and Y be 32-bit words and $n \in \{0, 1, 2, \ldots, 31\}$ and compute

$$Z = X + (Y \lll n) \pmod{2^{32}}.$$

Denote the bits of Z as $(z_0, z_1, \ldots, z_{31})$. Let $i_0, i_1, \ldots, i_k$ be a set of k distinct elements of the set $\{0, 1, 2, \ldots, 31\}$. Let E_i be the byte that is all 0, except for a 1 in bit i. Then $E_i = 2^{31-i}$. Let

$$A = (Z - z_{i_0} E_{i_0} - z_{i_1} E_{i_1} - \cdots - z_{i_k} E_{i_k}) \pmod{2^{32}} \qquad (5.57)$$

and

$$\tilde{Y} = ((A - Z) \ggg n) + Y \pmod{2^{32}}.$$

Show that $\tilde{Z} = X + (\tilde{Y} \lll n) \pmod{2^{32}}$ has zero bits in positions $i_0, i_1, \ldots, i_k$. Either prove this in general, or show that it holds for all 1-byte values, with n and k modified accordingly.

b. Suppose that we want to force some bits of $\tilde{Z}$ to be 1 instead of 0. How can be accomplish this by modifying (5.57)?

25. Consider the MD5 attack, as described in this chapter. Suppose we are trying to find a collision for the first message block M_0. When we test the probabilistic conditions, and the test fails, why does it suffice to only modify the last two words of M_0 instead of computing an entirely new M_0?

26. This problem asks you to demonstrate that a meaningless MD5 collision can be used in a meaningful attack.

a. Verify that the following two 1024-bit messages (given in hexadecimal) differ, specify the bit positions where the messages differ, and verify that the two messages have the same MD5 hash value.

```
d1 31 dd 02 c5 e6 ee c4     69 3d 9a 06 98 af f9 5c
2f ca b5 87 12 46 7e ab     40 04 58 3e b8 fb 7f 89
55 ad 34 06 09 f4 b3 02     83 e4 88 83 25 71 41 5a
08 51 25 e8 f7 cd c9 9f     d9 1d bd f2 80 37 3c 5b
96 0b 1d d1 dc 41 7b 9c     e4 d8 97 f4 5a 65 55 d5
35 73 9a c7 f0 eb fd 0c     30 29 f1 66 d1 09 b1 8f
75 27 7f 79 30 d5 5c eb     22 e8 ad ba 79 cc 15 5c
ed 74 cb dd 5f c5 d3 6d     b1 9b 0a d8 35 cc a7 e3
```

and

```
d1 31 dd 02 c5 e6 ee c4     69 3d 9a 06 98 af f9 5c
2f ca b5 07 12 46 7e ab     40 04 58 3e b8 fb 7f 89
55 ad 34 06 09 f4 b3 02     83 e4 88 83 25 f1 41 5a
08 51 25 e8 f7 cd c9 9f     d9 1d bd 72 80 37 3c 5b
96 0b 1d d1 dc 41 7b 9c     e4 d8 97 f4 5a 65 55 d5
35 73 9a 47 f0 eb fd 0c     30 29 f1 66 d1 09 b1 8f
75 27 7f 79 30 d5 5c eb     22 e8 ad ba 79 4c 15 5c
ed 74 cb dd 5f c5 d3 6d     b1 9b 0a 58 35 cc a7 e3
```

b. Use the collision in part a to construct two files that display very different text when viewed or printed, yet have identical MD5 hashes. Hint: Mimic the attack outlined in Section 5.4.7.

27. In Section 5.4.5 we determined conditions on T_5 and T_6 that must be met for Wang's MD5 attack to succeed. Perform a similar analysis to determine conditions on T_7.

28. In Section 5.4.5 we analyzed steps four and five of the MD5 hash to determine conditions on the Q_j that must be met for Wang's MD5 attack to succeed. Perform a similar analysis for step six.

Chapter 6

Public Key Systems

It is generally regarded as self-evident, that, in order to prevent an interceptor
from understanding a message which is intelligible to the authorised recipient,
it is necessary to have some initial information known to the sender
and to the recipient but kept secret from the interceptor....
This report demonstrates that this secret information
is not theoretically necessary....
— James Ellis [45]

6.1 Introduction

All of the cryptosystems discussed in previous chapters are examples of *symmetric key* ciphers. In this type of system, both parties use a common key to encrypt and decrypt messages. In *public key cryptography*, each user has a *key pair* consisting of a *public key* and a *private key*. Not surprisingly, Alice's public key is public, while Alice's private key is known only to Alice. Anyone can use Alice's public key (since it is public) to send encrypted messages to her, but only she can decrypt such messages since only she has the corresponding private key. Whereas symmetric key cryptography has been used since antiquity, public key cryptography came into being in the 1970s. Perhaps the most remarkable thing about public key crypto is that it exists at all.

A public key cryptosystem is based on a "trap door one-way function." The security of a public key cipher rests on this function, which is easy to compute in one direction but difficult to compute in the other direction. Furthermore, the trap door feature ensures that an attacker cannot obtain information about the secret decryption key from knowledge of the public encryption key. Examples of trap door one-way functions used in public key cryptography include factoring (RSA), discrete logarithms (Diffie–Hellman), and finding the nearest codeword in a linear binary code (McEliece). Finding a trap door one-way function suitable for use in a public key cryptosystem is not an easy task. Consequently, the number of sensible public key cryptosystems is far smaller than the number of strong symmetric cipher systems.

Digital signatures can also be implemented using public key cryptography. Alice can digitally sign a message by "encrypting" it with her private key. Then, anyone can "decrypt" the message using Alice's public key, thereby verifying that only Alice could have signed the message. In fact, the ability to create digital signatures is a very useful feature of public key cryptography, for which there is no analog in the realm of symmetric ciphers.

Alice's digital signature is similar to her handwritten signature in the sense that only she can create it, but, in principle, anyone can verify whether or not the signature is Alice's. However, digital signatures offer some significant advantages over handwritten signatures. For example, when correctly implemented, a digital signature cannot be forged, in stark contrast to a handwritten signature. Also, a digital signature is tied directly to the signed document. Whereas a handwritten signature can be photocopied onto different documents, a digital signature cannot be duplicated in such a manner.

As discussed in Section 5.1, digital signatures provide integrity. That is, if Alice signs a message M, the recipient can automatically verify that the received message is the message that was actually sent. Another important property of digital signatures is that they provide *non-repudiation*. When Alice digitally signs a message, it guarantees that she actually signed the message and she cannot later claim that she did not do so. That is, Alice cannot repudiate the signature. While it is possible to provide integrity using symmetric key cryptography, it is not possible to achieve non-repudiation using symmetric keys. This follows from the fact that Alice's private key is known only to Alice. On the other hand, if Alice wants to communicate with Bob using a symmetric key, the key must be known to both Alice and Bob. Since Bob has the symmetric key, he can do anything with the key that Alice can do. Consequently, if Alice "signs" with the symmetric key, she can later repudiate the signature, claiming that Bob forged her signature. Although Bob knows that he did not "sign" for Alice, he cannot prove it.

In this chapter, we examine several public key systems, including the Merkle–Hellman knapsack cipher, the Diffie–Hellman and Arithmetica key exchange protocols, the RSA, Rabin and NTRU public key cryptosystems, and the ElGamal signature scheme. All of these systems have played (and in some instances, continue to play) an important role in the fascinating field of public key cryptography.

Our primary goal in this chapter is to introduce the variety of public key systems and to emphasize some of the relatively subtle mathematical issues that arise in public key cryptography. In keeping with the theme of the book, we present these math issues as "attacks," although many of the attacks discussed in this chapter would never be a serious threat in practice. However, the attacks on the Merkle–Hellman knapsack discussed in the next section, and some of the attacks on NTRU mentioned in Section 6.7 are exceptions, since these raise serious cryptanalytic issues. However, the coverage of these attacks is less detailed than those presented in previous chapters. Chapter 7 is more in tune with the previous chapters of the book, since it contains a more in-depth treatment of a few cryptanalytic attacks on public key systems.

6.2 Merkle–Hellman Knapsack

Every private in the French army carries a Field Marshal wand in his knapsack.
— Napoleon Bonaparte

The Merkle–Hellman knapsack cryptosystem [100] was one of the first proposed public key cryptosystems. This cipher utilizes a few elementary, but nonetheless clever mathematical ideas. Because of its historical significance and since it is easy to understand, we examine it first. The cipher is based on a mathematical problem which is known to be NP-complete [55].

The subset sum or *knapsack problem* can be stated as follows: Given a set of r weights

$$W = (w_0, w_1, \ldots, w_{r-1})$$

and a sum X, find $x_0, x_1, \ldots, x_{r-1}$, where each $x_i \in \{0, 1\}$, so that

$$X = x_0 w_0 + x_1 w_1 + \cdots + x_{r-1} w_{r-1},$$

provided that this is possible. Note that the x_i simply select a subset of the weights.

For example, suppose that the weights are $W = (4, 3, 9, 1, 12, 17, 19, 23)$ and the given sum is $X = 35$. Then, a solution to the subset problem exists and is given by $x = (01011010)$, since

$$0 \cdot 4 + 1 \cdot 3 + 0 \cdot 9 + 1 \cdot 1 + 1 \cdot 12 + 0 \cdot 17 + 1 \cdot 19 + 0 \cdot 23 = 35.$$

For this set of weights, if $X = 6$, the problem does not have a solution.

While the general knapsack problem is NP-complete, a special type of knapsack known as a *superincreasing knapsack* can be solved efficiently. A superincreasing knapsack is a set W that, when ordered from least to greatest, has the property that each weight is greater than the sum of all the previous weights. For example,

$$W = (2, 3, 6, 13, 29, 55, 112, 220) \tag{6.1}$$

is a superincreasing knapsack.

It is straightforward to solve a superincreasing knapsack problem. For example, suppose that we are given the set of weights in (6.1) and the sum $X = 76$. Since X is less than 112, we must have $x_7 = x_6 = 0$. Then, since $X > 55$ and we have $2 + 3 + 6 + 13 + 29 < 55$, it must be the case that $x_5 = 1$. That is, if we do not select the weight 55, then we cannot possibly reach the desired sum, since the sum of all remaining weights is less than 55, due to the superincreasing property.

Now, let $X_1 = X - 55 = 21$. Since $13 < X_1 < 29$, we must have that $x_4 = 0$ and $x_3 = 1$. Continuing in this manner, we find $x = (10110100)$ which is easily verified to be correct since $76 = 2 + 6 + 13 + 55$. This process yields an efficient (linear time) algorithm to solve any superincreasing knapsack problem.

Merkle and Hellman's [100] idea was to disguise a superincreasing knapsack S through the use of a mathematical transformation to make it look like an arbitrary knapsack T. The disguised knapsack T is made public by Alice and T acts as Alice's public key. When Alice receives a ciphertext, she applies the inverse of the transformation to convert the problem back to the superincreasing case. Alice decrypts by solving the resulting superincreasing knapsack problem. Without knowledge of the transformation, it would appear that a cryptanalyst must solve a general knapsack, which is a hard problem. However, there is a shortcut attack, which we describe below. But first we discuss the the knapsack cryptosystem in more detail.

To create her public and private keys, Alice first chooses a superincreasing knapsack $S = (s_0, s_1, \ldots, s_{r-1})$. To convert S into T, she also chooses a conversion factor m and a modulus n, where $\gcd(m, n) = 1$ and n is greater than the sum of all elements of S. The transformed knapsack is computed as

$$T = (s_0 m \ (\mathrm{mod}\ n), s_1 m \ (\mathrm{mod}\ n), \ldots, s_{r-1} m \ (\mathrm{mod}\ n))$$

and T is made public. Alice's private key consists of S and $m^{-1} \ (\mathrm{mod}\ n)$. Suppose Bob wants to send a message of r bits to Alice. Bob first converts his plaintext into a binary block B. He then uses the 1 bits of B to select the elements of T, which are then summed to give the ciphertext block C. Alice recovers the plaintext B, by using the private key to compute $Cm^{-1} \ (\mathrm{mod}\ n)$, and solves using her superincreasing knapsack. To encrypt longer messages, multiple blocks are encrypted.

To make things more concrete, consider the following example. Suppose that Alice chooses the superincreasing knapsack

$$S = (2, 3, 7, 14, 30, 57, 120, 251),$$

along with $m = 41$ and modulus $n = 491$. To transform S into a general knapsack T, Alice performs the following computations

$$2m = 2 \cdot 41 = 82 \ (\text{mod} \ 491)$$
$$3m = 3 \cdot 41 = 123 \ (\text{mod} \ 491)$$
$$7m = 7 \cdot 41 = 287 \ (\text{mod} \ 491)$$
$$14m = 14 \cdot 41 = 83 \ (\text{mod} \ 491)$$
$$30m = 30 \cdot 41 = 248 \ (\text{mod} \ 491)$$
$$57m = 57 \cdot 41 = 373 \ (\text{mod} \ 491)$$
$$120m = 120 \cdot 41 = 10 \ (\text{mod} \ 491)$$
$$251m = 251 \cdot 41 = 471 \ (\text{mod} \ 491).$$

Then Alice's public key is

$$T = (82, 123, 287, 83, 248, 373, 10, 471).$$

Alice's private key consists of

$$S = (2, 3, 7, 14, 30, 57, 120, 251)$$

and

$$m^{-1} \ (\text{mod} \ n) = 41^{-1} \ (\text{mod} \ 491) = 12.$$

Now, suppose that Bob wants to encrypt the message $M = 150$ for Alice. He first converts 150 to binary, that is 10010110. He then uses the 1 bits to select the elements of T that are summed to give the ciphertext. In this example, Bob computes the ciphertext

$$C = 82 + 83 + 373 + 10 = 548$$

and sends C to Alice. To decrypt this ciphertext, Alice uses her private key to compute

$$Cm^{-1} \ (\text{mod} \ n) = 548 \cdot 12 \ (\text{mod} \ 491) = 193.$$

She then solves the superincreasing knapsack S for 193 and she recovers the message in binary 10010110 or, in decimal, $M = 150$.

That this decryption process works can be verified by using elementary properties of modular arithmetic. In the particular example considered above, we have

$$548m^{-1} = 82m^{-1} + 83m^{-1} + 37m^{-1} + 10m^{-1}$$
$$= 2mm^{-1} + 14mm^{-1} + 57mm^{-1} + 120mm^{-1}$$
$$= 2 + 14 + 57 + 120$$
$$= 193 \ (\text{mod} \ 491).$$

In general, due to the linearity of the process used to convert from the superincreasing knapsack S into the public key knapsack T, knowledge of m^{-1} makes it easy to convert the ciphertext to the superincreasing case. Without Alice's private key, $(S, m^{-1} \pmod{n})$, the attacker Trudy needs to find a subset of T which sums to the ciphertext value C. This appears to be a general knapsack problem, which is intractable.

By converting the superincreasing knapsack into the general knapsack through the use of modular arithmetic, a trapdoor is introduced into the knapsack. Without m, it is not clear how to find the conversion factor m^{-1}. The one-way feature results from the fact that it is easy to encrypt with the general knapsack, but it is (hopefully) difficult to decrypt without the private key. But with the private key, the problem can be converted into a superincreasing knapsack, which is easy to solve and thus enables the intended recipient to easily decrypt.

However, this cryptosystem was shown to be insecure by Shamir [132] in 1983. It turns out that the "general knapsack" (the public-key) which arises in the Merkle–Hellman cryptosystem is not general enough. Instead, it is a highly structured case of the knapsack and Shamir's lattice reduction attack is able to take advantage of this fact. Shamir's ingenious method of attack is dicussed in the next section.

6.2.1   Lattice-Reduction Attack

Lattice reduction is a powerful technique which can be used to solve many different types of combinatorial problems. We first describe the lattice reduction method, as discussed in [142], and then illustrate how it can be used to attack the Merkle–Hellman knapsack cryptosystem. Some elementary linear algebra is used in this section; see the Appendix for an overview of the necessary linear algebra.

Consider, for example, the vectors

$$c_0 = \begin{bmatrix} -1 \\ 1 \end{bmatrix} \quad \text{and} \quad c_1 = \begin{bmatrix} 1 \\ 2 \end{bmatrix}.$$

Since c_0 and c_1 are linearly independent, any point in the plane can be uniquely represented by $\alpha_0 c_0 + \alpha_1 c_1$, where α_0 and α_1 are real numbers. If we restrict the coefficients to integers, that is, we require that α_0 and α_1 are integers, then we obtain a *lattice* consisting of discrete points in the plane. Figure 6.1 illustrates the lattice spanned by c_0 and c_1. In general, a lattice $\mathcal{L}$ is the set of all linear combinations of a set of column vectors c_i with integer coefficients.

Given an $m \times n$ matrix A and an $m \times 1$ matrix B, suppose we want to find a solution U to the matrix equation $AU = B$, with the restriction that U consists entirely of 0s and 1s. If U is a solution to $AU = B$, then the block

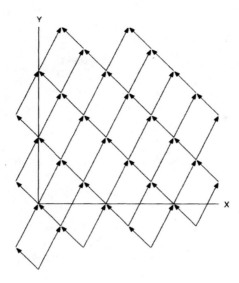

Figure 6.1: A lattice in the plane.

matrix equation

$$MV = \begin{bmatrix} I_{n \times n} & 0_{n \times 1} \\ A_{m \times n} & -B_{m \times 1} \end{bmatrix} \begin{bmatrix} U_{n \times 1} \\ 1_{1 \times 1} \end{bmatrix} = \begin{bmatrix} U_{n \times 1} \\ 0_{m \times 1} \end{bmatrix} = W \qquad (6.2)$$

holds true, since $MV = W$ is equivalent to $U = U$ and $AU - B = 0$. Consequently, finding a solution V to the block matrix equation $MV = W$ is equivalent to finding a solution U to the original matrix equation $AU = B$. Note that the columns of M are linearly independent, since the $n \times n$ identity matrix appears in the upper left and the final column begins with n zeros.

Let $c_0, c_1, c_2, \ldots, c_n$ be the $n + 1$ columns of the matrix M in (6.2) and let $v_0, v_1, v_2, \ldots, v_n$ be the elements of V. Then

$$W = v_0 c_0 + v_1 c_1 + \cdots + v_n c_n. \qquad (6.3)$$

We have $MV = W$, where

$$W = \begin{bmatrix} u_0 \\ u_1 \\ \vdots \\ u_{n-1} \\ 0 \\ \vdots \\ 0 \end{bmatrix} = \begin{bmatrix} U \\ \vec{0} \end{bmatrix} \qquad (6.4)$$

and we want to determine U. Instead of solving linear equations to obtain V, we will find U by determining W. Note that because of (6.3), W is in the lattice $\mathcal{L}$, spanned by the columns of M.

The Euclidean length of a vector $Y = [y_0, y_1, \ldots, y_{n+m-1}]^T$ is

$$\|Y\| = \sqrt{y_0^2 + y_1^2 + \cdots + y_{n+m-1}^2}.$$

However, the length of a vector W in (6.4) is

$$\|W\| = \sqrt{u_0^2 + u_1^2 + \cdots + u_{n-1}^2} \leq \sqrt{n},$$

which is much "shorter" than a typical vector in $\mathcal{L}$. Furthermore, W has a very special form, since its first n entries consist of 0s and 1s with its last m entries being all 0. Is it possible to take advantage of this special structure to find W?

In 1982, Lenstra, Lenstra and Lovàsz [91] discovered the so-called LLL Algorithm, which provides an efficient method to find short vectors in a lattice. In Table 6.1, we give an outline of their algorithm in pseudo-code, where GS(M) refers to the Gram–Schmidt process, which returns an orthonormal basis for the subspace spanned by the columns of M. The Gram–Schmidt process appears in Table 6.2. Note that a small number of lines of pseudo-code suffices to specify the entire LLL Algorithm.

With clever insight, Shamir [132] realized that lattice reduction could be used to attack the Merkle–Hellman knapsack cryptosystem. Suppose that Bob's public knapsack is given by $T = (t_0, t_1, \ldots, t_{r-1})$, and Alice sends Bob a ciphertext block C, encrypted with Bob's public knapsack. Since the attacker, Trudy, knows the public knapsack T and C, she can break the system if she is able to solve the matrix equation $TU = C$, where U is an $r \times 1$ column matrix consisting of 0s and 1s.

Trudy can rewrite the matrix equation $TU = C$ in block matrix form as

$$MV = \begin{bmatrix} I_{r \times r} & 0_{r \times 1} \\ T_{1 \times r} & -C_{1 \times 1} \end{bmatrix} \begin{bmatrix} U_{r \times 1} \\ 1_{1 \times 1} \end{bmatrix} = \begin{bmatrix} U_{r \times 1} \\ 0_{1 \times 1} \end{bmatrix} = W$$

and apply the LLL Algorithm to the matrix M. The resulting short vectors which are obtained can be checked to see if they have the special form required of W, which is a column vector where the first r entries are all 0 or 1 and last entry is 0. The LLL Algorithm will not always produce the desired vector and therefore, the attack is not always successful. However, in practice, the lattice reduction attack is highly effective against the original Merkle–Hellman knapsack.

To illustrate the lattice reduction attack, suppose Alice constructs her knapsack key pair from the superincreasing knapsack

$$S = (s_0, s_1, \ldots, s_7) = (2, 3, 7, 14, 30, 57, 120, 251),$$

Table 6.1: LLL Algorithm

```
// find short vectors in the lattice spanned
// by the columns of M = (b₀, b₁, . . . , bₙ)
repeat
    (X, Y) = GS(M)
    for j = 1 to n
        for i = j − 1 to 0
            if |yᵢⱼ| > 1/2 then
                bⱼ = bⱼ − ⌊yᵢⱼ + 1/2⌋bᵢ
            end if
        next i
    next j
    (X, Y) = GS(M)
    for j = 0 to n − 1
        if ‖xⱼ₊₁ + yⱼ,ⱼ₊₁xⱼ‖² < ¾‖xⱼ‖² then
            swap(bⱼ, bⱼ₊₁)
            goto abc
        end if
    next j
    return(M)
abc:    continue
forever
```

with $m = 41$ and modulus $n = 491$. Then, $m^{-1} = 12 \pmod{491}$. The corresponding general knapsack T is obtained by computing $t_i = 41 s_i \pmod{491}$, for $i = 0, 1, 2, \ldots, 7$, which was found above to be

$$T = (t_0, t_1, \ldots, t_7) = (82, 123, 287, 83, 248, 373, 10, 471).$$

Alice's knapsack key pair is defined by

$$\text{Public key: } T$$

and

$$\text{Private key: } S \text{ and } m^{-1} \pmod{n}.$$

Suppose Bob wants to encrypt the message $M = 10010110$ for Alice. Then, as discussed above, Bob computes

$$1 \cdot t_0 + 0 \cdot t_1 + 0 \cdot t_2 + 1 \cdot t_3 + 0 \cdot t_4 + 1 \cdot t_5 + 1 \cdot t_6 + 0 \cdot t_7 = 548$$

and sends ciphertext $C = 548$ to Alice.

Table 6.2: Gram–Schmidt Process

```
// Gram–Schmidt M = (b₀, b₁, ..., bₙ)
GS(M)
     x₀ = b₀
     for j = 1 to n
         xⱼ = bⱼ
         for i = 0 to j − 1
             yᵢⱼ = (xᵢ · bⱼ)/||xᵢ||²
             xⱼ = xⱼ − yᵢⱼxᵢ
         next i
     next j
     return(X, Y)
end GS
```

Now, suppose that Trudy wants to recover the plaintext that corresponds to ciphertext $C = 548$. Since Trudy knows the public key T and ciphertext $C = 548$, she needs to find a set of u_i, for $i = 0, 1, \ldots, 7$, with the restriction that each $u_i \in \{0, 1\}$. and

$$82u_0 + 123u_1 + 287u_2 + 83u_3 + 248u_4 + 373u_5 + 10u_6 + 471u_7 = 548.$$

This can be written as the matrix equation

$$T \cdot U = 548,$$

where T is Alice's public knapsack and $U = (u_0, u_1, \ldots, u_7)$, and the a_i are unknown, but each must be either 0 or 1. This is of the form $AU = B$ (as discussed above), so Trudy rewrites the matrix equation as $MV = W$ and applies the LLL Algorithm to M. In this case, Trudy finds

$$M = \begin{bmatrix} I_{8\times8} & 0_{8\times1} \\ T_{1\times8} & -C_{1\times1} \end{bmatrix} = \begin{bmatrix} 1 & 0 & 0 & 0 & 0 & 0 & 0 & 0 & 0 \\ 0 & 1 & 0 & 0 & 0 & 0 & 0 & 0 & 0 \\ 0 & 0 & 1 & 0 & 0 & 0 & 0 & 0 & 0 \\ 0 & 0 & 0 & 1 & 0 & 0 & 0 & 0 & 0 \\ 0 & 0 & 0 & 0 & 1 & 0 & 0 & 0 & 0 \\ 0 & 0 & 0 & 0 & 0 & 1 & 0 & 0 & 0 \\ 0 & 0 & 0 & 0 & 0 & 0 & 1 & 0 & 0 \\ 0 & 0 & 0 & 0 & 0 & 0 & 0 & 1 & 0 \\ 82 & 123 & 287 & 83 & 248 & 373 & 10 & 471 & -548 \end{bmatrix}.$$

The LLL Algorithm outputs a matrix M', consisting of short vectors in the lattice spanned by the columns of the matrix M. In this example, LLL yields

$$M' = \begin{bmatrix} -1 & -1 & 0 & 1 & 0 & 1 & 0 & 0 & 1 \\ 0 & -1 & 1 & 0 & 1 & -1 & 0 & 0 & 0 \\ 0 & 1 & -1 & 0 & 0 & 0 & -1 & 1 & 2 \\ 1 & -1 & -1 & 1 & 0 & -1 & 0 & -1 & 0 \\ 0 & 0 & 1 & 0 & -2 & -1 & 0 & 1 & 0 \\ 0 & 0 & 0 & 1 & 1 & 1 & 1 & -1 & 1 \\ 0 & 0 & 0 & 1 & 0 & 0 & -1 & 0 & -1 \\ 0 & 0 & 0 & 0 & 0 & 0 & 1 & 1 & -1 \\ 1 & -1 & 1 & 0 & 0 & 1 & -1 & 2 & 0 \end{bmatrix}.$$

The entries in the fourth column of M' have the correct form to be a solution to this knapsack problem. Therefore, Trudy obtains the putative solution

$$U = (1, 0, 0, 1, 0, 1, 1, 0).$$

Using the public key and ciphertext $C = 548$, she can easily verify that U is indeed the original plaintext sent by Bob.

6.2.2 Knapsack Conclusion

Much research has been done on the knapsack problem since the Merkle–Hellman cryptosystem was broken. Several different knapsack variants have been created and some of these appear to yield secure cryptosystems. However, people have been reluctant to use these systems, since "knapsack" continues to be equated with "broken," even to this day. For more information on knapsack cryptosystems, see [37, 89, 109].

6.3 Diffie–Hellman Key Exchange

> *[If] you look right under the center of a streetlight,*
> *you don't find anything that wasn't known before.*
> *If you look out into the darkness, you don't discover anything,*
> *cause you can't see anything.*
> *So you're always working at the edge of the streetlight,*
> *trying to find your keys.*
> — Whitfield Diffie

In symmetric key cryptography, both parties use a common key to encrypt and decrypt messages. However, when using such a system, there is a critical issue that needs to be dealt with, that is, how can Alice and Bob agree upon a key? Can this be accomplished in a secure manner over a public channel?

These and related questions were on the minds of Diffie, Hellman and Merkle during the 1970s. At the time, there was no solution in sight for this vexing *key distribution problem.*

In 1976, Diffie and Hellman published their seminal paper [38] which made the case that public key cryptography should be possible and proposed the Diffie–Hellman key exchange protocol as a solution to the key distribution problem; see also [120]. Ironically, the first to discover Diffie–Hellman was actually Malcolm Williamson of GCHQ (roughly, the British equivalent of NSA) [93]. However, this does nothing to diminish the accomplishment of Diffie and Hellman, since Williamson's work was classified.

The Diffie–Hellman key exchange, as illustrated in Figure 6.2, operates in the following way. Let p be a large prime and g an integer, where $2 \leq g \leq p-2$. Both the prime p and *generator* g are publicly known. Alice chooses a random number a, where $1 \leq a \leq p - 2$ and calculates $\alpha = g^a \pmod{p}$. She then sends α to Bob. The number a is private, that is, a is known only to Alice. Bob also chooses a random number b, where $1 \leq b \leq p - 2$ and calculates $\beta = g^b \pmod{p}$ and sends β to Alice. The number b is private, known only to Bob. Alice then calculates

$$\beta^a \pmod{p} = (g^b)^a \pmod{p} = g^{ab} \pmod{p}$$

and Bob computes

$$\alpha^b \pmod{p} = (g^a)^b \pmod{p} = g^{ab} \pmod{p}.$$

Alice and Bob now share $g^{ab} \pmod{p}$, which can be used as a symmetric key.

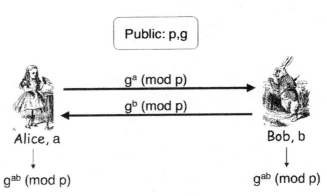

Figure 6.2: Diffie–Hellman key exchange.

Trudy sees $g^a \pmod{p}$ and $g^b \pmod{p}$ and she breaks the key exchange protocol if she can find $g^{ab} \pmod{p}$. To do so, it appears that she must find a from $g^a \pmod{p}$ or b from $g^b \pmod{p}$. Therefore, the strength of the Diffie–Hellman key exchange protocol is believed to depend on the computational complexity of solving the *discrete logarithm* problem. That is, there is no efficient solution to the problem of finding y given x^y (mod p), the base x and the modulus p.

Suppose, for example, we want to solve the equation $2^x = 9$ (mod 11). Since the numbers are so small, this is easy to solve by exhaustively searching through all of the possible exponents. We see that

$$2^0 = 1 \ (\text{mod } 11)$$
$$2^1 = 2 \ (\text{mod } 11)$$
$$2^2 = 4 \ (\text{mod } 11)$$
$$2^3 = 8 \ (\text{mod } 11)$$
$$2^4 = 16 = 5 \ (\text{mod } 11)$$
$$2^5 = 5 \cdot 2 = 10 \ (\text{mod } 11)$$
$$2^6 = 10 \cdot 2 = 9 \ (\text{mod } 11)$$

and, therefore, $x = 6$ is the desired solution. However, for large p, an exhaustive search is not feasible. Although there are some efficient methods for solving certain classes of discrete logarithm problems, there is no known efficient algorithm for solving $g^x = t$ (mod p) for x in general, where g, t and p are given. Some of the current discrete log algorithms are analyzed in Section 7.3.

6.3.1 Man-in-the-Middle Attack

The Diffie–Hellman key exchange is subject to a *man-in-the-middle attack* if there is no procedure to authenticate the participants during the key exchange. Suppose that Trudy wants to read messages that are being sent between Alice and Bob, where Alice and Bob use the Diffie–Hellman key exchange. First, Trudy chooses an exponent t. She then intercepts g^a (mod p) and g^b (mod p) and sends g^t (mod p) to Alice and Bob. At this point, Alice believes g^t (mod p) came from Bob, and Bob believes g^t (mod p) came from Alice. Now Trudy computes $K_A = (g^a)^t$ (mod p) and $K_B = (g^b)^t$ (mod p). Alice, not realizing that Trudy is in the middle, follows the Diffie–Hellman protocol and computes K_A. Similarly, Bob computes K_B. Then when Alice sends a message to Bob (encrypted with K_A), Trudy can intercept it, decrypt it and re-encrypt it (or encrypt a different message) with K_B before sending it on to Bob. In this manner, Trudy can read (and alter, if she so desires) all messages between Alice and Bob, and neither Alice nor Bob will suspect that there is any problem. Figure 6.3 illustrates this man-in-the-middle attack.

The man-in-the-middle attack on the Diffie–Hellman key exchange can be prevented provided the parties are properly authenticated. For example, an authentication protocol that uses digital signatures would assure Alice and

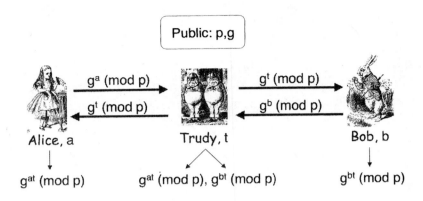

Figure 6.3: Man-in-the-middle attack on Diffie–Hellman.

Bob that the received messages originated from the correct person. Since Trudy cannot forge Alice's or Bob's signatures, her man-in-the-middle attack would be thwarted. In addition, such a protocol will prevent a replay attack.

There are several ways to prevent the man-in-the-middle attack on Diffie–Hellman. For example, the *Station-to-Station* protocol, devised by Diffie, van Oorschot and Wiener [39], could be used for authentication purposes. Problem 3 gives a simple example illustrating a technique that prevents the man-in-the-middle attack.

6.3.2   Diffie–Hellman Conclusion

Diffie–Hellman provides an elegant solution to one of the most challenging problems in all of cryptography—the so-called *key establishment problem* (or key distribution problem), that is, how to securely agree on a shared symmetric key. Prior to the development of public key cryptography, the most common method of key establishment was via a human courier. Obviously, this was not a desirable situation.

Care must be taken when using Diffie–Hellman, since the man-in-the-middle attack is a serious threat. But the man-in-the-middle attack can be prevented in many important applications. Consequently, the Diffie–Hellman key exchange is one of the most useful—and widely used—public key cryptosystems.

Diffie–Hellman is used, for example, in the IPSec protocol to provide *perfect forward secrecy* (PFS); see Problem 4. To achieve PFS, an *ephemeral Diffie–Hellman key exchange* is used. In some situations, Diffie–Hellman can be used to make a weak PIN-based or password-based authentication protocol relatively secure; see [11] and Problem 5 for more details.

6.4 Arithmetica Key Exchange

> To divide a cube into two other cubes,
> a fourth power or in general any power whatever into two powers
> of the same denomination above the second is impossible,
> and I have assuredly found an admirable proof of this,
> but the margin is too narrow to contain it.
> — in the margin of Pierre de Fermat's
> copy of Diophantus' *Arithmetica*

Arithmetica is a relatively new key exchange mechanism which was invented in 1999 by Anshel, Anshel, and Goldfeld [5]. Although it serves the same purpose as the Diffie–Hellman key exchange, Arithmetica uses an entirely different approach than Diffie–Hellman. The Arithmetica key exchange relies on some of the most sophisticated mathematics that we discuss in this book. However, the reader should not feel intimidated since the basic ideas underlying the system are relatively easy to understand. We assume that the reader is familiar with the basic notion of a group. Section A-2 in the Appendix provides enough group theory background to understand all of the material in this section.

The material in this section is a little more abstract than most of the other sections in this book, so we begin with some examples. Along the way, relevant definitions and concepts will be introduced. For our first example, consider the set G consisting of all finite *words* using the alphabet

$$\{1_G, a, b, a^{-1}, b^{-1}\}. \tag{6.5}$$

Typical elements of G include

$$abaab^{-1}b^{-1},\ bba^{-1}a1_Gba,\ bbbb,\ aba^{-1}b^{-1},\ a,\ b^{-1},\ 1_G. \tag{6.6}$$

The letter 1_G can be thought of as the *empty word* in G. Here, it is important to note that the order in which letters appear in a word matters so that, for example, ab and ba are two different words in G. When working with elements of G, we use exponent notation and its properties. Consequently, the elements in (6.6) can be rewritten as

$$aba^2b^{-2},\ b^3a,\ b^4,\ aba^{-1}b^{-1},\ a,\ b^{-1},\ 1_G,$$

respectively. A binary operation "$*$", which is the concatenation operator, can be defined on G. For example,

$$aba^2b^{-2} * b^3a = aba^2b^{-2}b^3a = aba^2ba.$$

The set G of all finite words using the alphabet in (6.5), along with the concatenation operator "$*$", is a *group* (see Section A-2 in the Appendix). In fact, this group is known as the *free group on two generators* and it is denoted by

$$G = \langle a, b \rangle. \tag{6.7}$$

The elements a and b are the *generators* of G, since all non-empty words in G are formed using a and b (along with a^{-1} and b^{-1}). The term "free" refers to the fact that there are no *relations* between a, b, a^{-1}, and b^{-1}. For example, ab cannot be written as, say, ba.

We can impose relations on $G = \langle a, b \rangle$. For example, consider the set G as in (6.7) with the concatenation operator "$*$" (as in our first example), along with the relations

$$abab^{-1}a^{-1}b^{-1} = 1_G, \ a^2 = 1_G, \ b^2 = 1_G.$$

Then the identity element 1_G can be expressed in an infinite number of ways, including

$$1_G = a^2, \ 1_G = b^2, \ 1_G = abab^{-1}a^{-1}b^{-1}, \ \text{and} \ 1_G = a^3baba^{-1}b,$$

and concatenation between words in G can be rewritten, as dictated by the relations. For example,

$$aba^{-1} * ab = ab1_Gb = ab^2 = a1_G = a.$$

Our set G, along with concatenation operator "$*$" and these relations, is also a group. Let us denote this group as

$$S_3 = \langle a, b \mid abab^{-1}a^{-1}b^{-1}, a^2, b^2 \rangle.$$

This notation gives a *finite presentation* of the group S_3, which is a well-known symmetric group. It is important to note that a group G may have many different finite presentations. For example, Problem 6 asks the reader to show that

$$S_3 = \langle x, y \mid x^3, y^2, (xy)^2 \rangle.$$

Sometimes, the relations in a finite presentation can be used to rewrite every possible word into a canonical form. For example, using the finite presentation $S_3 = \langle x, y \mid x^3, y^2, (xy)^2 \rangle$, we see that the element $xyxy = 1_{S_3}$ can be rewritten as $x^{-1}(xyxy) = x^{-1} \cdot 1_{S_3}$, which simplifies to $yxy = x^{-1}(x^3)$, which, in turn, simplifies to $yxy = x^2$ and, finally, $yx = x^2y$. Using the fact that $yx = x^2y$, along with the fact that $x^3 = y^2 = 1_{S_3}$, we can write every word in S_3 in the form x^iy^j, where $i \in \{0, 1, 2\}$ and $j \in \{0, 1\}$. Consequently, the group S_3 can be viewed as the set of elements $\{1_{S_3}, x, x^2, y, xy, x^2y\}$, together with the binary operation of concatenation, and subject to the relations $x^3 = y^2 = xyxy = 1_{S_3}$.

We are now ready to give a description of Arithmetica. Suppose that Alice and Bob want to establish a symmetric key. A finitely presented, infinite non-abelian group G is made public. Alice and Bob create their public keys to be subgroups of G, say,

$$S_A = \langle s_0, s_1, \ldots, s_{n-1} \rangle \quad \text{and} \quad S_B = \langle t_0, t_1, \ldots t_{m-1} \rangle,$$

respectively, and these are made public knowledge. The subgroups S_A and S_B can be thought of as being the sets of all formal words in the alphabets s_i and t_j respectively, with the binary operation of concatenation, subject to the relations of G. Alice and Bob select their private keys

$$a = s_{\sigma(0)}^{i_0} \cdots s_{\sigma(n-1)}^{i_{n-1}} \in S_A \quad \text{and} \quad b = t_{\tau(0)}^{j_0} \cdots t_{\tau(m-1)}^{j_{m-1}} \in S_B,$$

respectively.

Then Alice computes the set of elements $\{a^{-1}t_0 a, \ldots, a^{-1}t_{m-1}a\}$ and sends the result to Bob. Bob computes the set $\{b^{-1}s_0 b, \ldots, b^{-1}s_{n-1}b\}$ and sends it to Alice. Before transmission, each of these sets are rewritten (using the specified relations) so as to obscure the private keys a and b. With the information received from Bob, Alice is able to compute $b^{-1}ab$ since

$$b^{-1}ab = b^{-1}s_{\sigma(0)}^{i_0} \cdots s_{\sigma(n-1)}^{i_{n-1}}b$$

$$= b^{-1}s_{\sigma(0)}^{i_0}bb^{-1}s_{\sigma(1)}^{i_1}b \cdots b^{-1}s_{\sigma(n-1)}^{i_{n-1}}b$$

$$= (b^{-1}s_{\sigma(0)}b)^{i_0} \cdots (b^{-1}s_{\sigma(n-1)}b)^{i_{n-1}}.$$

Similarly, Bob can compute $a^{-1}ba$. Using their respective private keys, Alice and Bob each compute $a^{-1}b^{-1}ab$, which can serve as a shared symmetric key.

Although this seems very complicated, in fact it really is not, as a simplified example will illustrate. Suppose Alice and Bob decide to establish a common key, using the Arithmetica key exchange. They first select a group, say,

$$G = \langle x, y \mid x^4, y^2, yxyx \rangle$$

and make it public. Alice chooses her public key to be

$$S_A = \langle s_0, s_1 \rangle = \langle x^2, y \rangle = \{1_G, x^2, y, x^2 y\}$$

and Bob chooses his public key to be

$$S_B = \langle t_0 \rangle = \langle x \rangle = \{1_G, x, x^2, x^3\},$$

which are also made public. Now, Alice generates her private key

$$a = (x^2)^2 \cdot (y)^{-1} = x^4 y^{-1} = 1_G \cdot y^{-1} = y^{-1}$$

and Bob generates his private key

$$b = (x)^3 = x^3.$$

Next, Alice computes $a^{-1}t_0a = y^{-1}xy$ and rewrites it as yxy. She then sends $\{yxy\}$ to Bob. In a similar manner. Bob computes (and rewrites)

$$b^{-1}s_0b = x^{-3}x^2x^3 = x^2 = x^{-2}$$

and

$$b^{-1}s_1b = x^{-3}yx^3 = xyx^3 = x \cdot x^{-3}y = x^{-2}y = x^2y.$$

He then sends $\{x^{-2}, x^2y\}$ to Alice.

To establish a common key. Alice computes

$$b^{-1}ab = (x^{-2})^2(x^2y)^{-1} = (x^2)^2(y^{-1}x^{-2})$$
$$= x^4y^{-1}x^{-2} = 1_G \cdot y^{-1}x^{-2} = yx^2 = x^2y.$$

Finally, she computes $a^{-1}(b^{-1}ab) = (y^{-1})^{-1}(x^2y) = yx^2y = x^2$. Similarly, Bob computes

$$a^{-1}ba = (yxy)^3 = yxy \cdot yxy \cdot yxy$$
$$= yxy^2xy^2xy = yx \cdot 1_G \cdot x \cdot 1_G \cdot xy$$
$$= yx^3y = x.$$

Bob then computes the value $a^{-1}b^{-1}a = (a^{-1}ba)^{-1} = x^{-1}$, which he uses to obtain the shared secret $(a^{-1}b^{-1}a)b = x^{-1} \cdot x^3 = x^2$. Alice and Bob can then compute a shared symmetric key based on this shared secret.

In our example, a small finite non-abelian group was used to illustrate the ideas underlying Arithmetica. In a real-world implementation of Arithmetica, G, S_A, and S_B are chosen to be infinite non-abelian groups, each having a large number of generators.

Before outlining an attack on Arithmetica, we mention some important observations concerning the algorithm. First, the security of Arithmetica is based on the computational complexity of the *conjugacy problem*. For a finitely represented group G, there is no known efficient algorithm to solve the following problem: Given two words x and y in G, does there exist a word $g \in G$ so that $y = g^{-1}xg$? If the attacker Trudy is able to efficiently solve the conjugacy problem, she would be able to recover the private keys a and b by solving the associated systems of conjugacy equations (from S_A and S_B).

Also in the Arithmetica key exchange, it is very likely that the established key will be written in different ways for Alice and Bob. Therefore, it is necessary to extract an identical element from the common key $a^{-1}b^{-1}ab$. One way to do this is if every element in G can be put into a unique canonical form. If this is the case, then Alice and Bob simply convert their shared key into canonical form. In [15], Birman, Ko, and Lee showed that for the *braid groups*, there is a polynomial-time algorithm for converting the group elements into a canonical form. Furthermore, the conjugacy problem is seemingly intractable for this class of groups. Consequently, a braid group is often used in the implementation of Arithmetica.

6.4.1 Hughes–Tannenbaum Length Attack

It is somewhat ironic that the necessity of being able to convert the group elements into a canonical form in Arithmetica also opens the door to an attack on the system. Introduced by Hughes and Tannenbaum [69], the basic idea of the attack on Arithmetica (and other similar systems) is that group elements with long lengths—which is well-defined since every element has a canonical form—have a higher probability of not combining with other factors. This allows an attacker to recover information about the shared secret. Here, we give a very brief description of the length attack on Arithmetica.

For any element $w \in G$, define the *length* of w to be

$$\ell(w) = |k_0| + |k_1| + \cdots + |k_{N-1}|,$$

where

$$w = g_{i_0}^{k_0} g_{i_1}^{k_1} \cdots g_{i_{N-1}}^{k_{N-1}}$$

is in canonical form. Then for any two words $x, y \in G$, we see that the lengths satisfy $\ell(xy) \leq \ell(x) + \ell(y)$. If some of the parts of x and y cancel, then it may be that the length of xy is much shorter than the sum of the lengths of x and y.

As above, let

$$a \in S_A = \langle s_0, s_1, \ldots, s_{n-1} \rangle$$

be Alice's private key. For purposes of this discussion, we assume that the factors s_i have lengths which are large, relative to the length of a. From Bob's public key,

$$S_B = \langle t_0, t_1, \ldots, t_{m-1} \rangle,$$

Alice computes $u_r = a^{-1} t_r a$, for $r = 0, 1, \ldots, m-1$, and transmits these to Bob. The attacker Trudy performs the length attack by repeatedly computing

$$\ell(s_i^{\pm 1}(u_r) s_i^{\mp 1}).$$

If she finds that

$$\ell(s_i^{\pm 1}(u_r) s_i^{\mp 1}) < \ell(u_r),$$

Trudy infers that $s_i^{\mp 1}$ is a factor of a on the left—not with certainty, but with some positive probability. Once a factor is recovered, the attack is similarly applied again to recover another factor of a and this process is repeated to recover all of a, with some positive probability. The length attack is effective when the $\ell(s_i)$ are large. Experimental evidence [5] suggests that if the generators $s_0, s_1, \ldots, s_{n-1}$ are each of length less than ten (for the Artin generators of the braid group G) then the length attack is thwarted. This attack is very new and is the subject of ongoing research.

6.4.2 Arithmetica Conclusion

In comparison to many of the cryptosystems discussed in this book, Arithmetica uses some very sophisticated mathematics. However, it is not particularly unusual in the world of public key cryptography, where advanced mathematics plays a significant role in the design and analysis of cryptosystems. For example, ongoing research in elliptic curve cryptography, group-based cryptosystems and lattice-based encryption schemes illustrate this point. The interested reader is directed to [17, 84. 102], respectively, for more information on these mathematically sophisticated types of cryptosystems. Undoubtedly, advanced mathematics will play a central role in the design and analysis of future public key cryptosystems.

6.5 RSA

> Using RSA in the manner I used for this example
> would result in a system that would be no harder to break
> than those famous quotation puzzles in the Sunday paper.
> — Ben Goren [60]

In 1973, Clifford Cocks, a cryptologist in the British government agency GCHQ, wrote an internal document describing a practical public key cryptosystem [93]. This was a significant accomplishment as Cocks had found an appropriate mathematical one-way function for such a cryptosystem. Its security was based on the idea that factoring an integer into its prime divisors is a computationally difficult task. In 1978, Rivest, Shamir, and Adelman [123] published their ground-breaking paper, stunning the cryptographic community at large. Essentially, their paper rediscovered Cocks' cryptosystem, which had been classified five years earlier by the British government. Of course, this does nothing to diminish Rivest, Shamir, and Adelman's discovery, since it was accomplished independently of Cock's work.

In the RSA cryptosystem, Alice's public–private key pair is generated as follows: First, generate two large distinct primes, p and q, and let $N = pq$. Then, choose e so that $\gcd(e, \phi(N)) = 1$ and let $d = e^{-1} \pmod{\phi(N)}$, where $\phi(N)$ denotes the Euler phi function (this function is defined in Section A-2 of the Appendix). Alice's public key is (e, N) and her private key is d. Below, we make use of the fact that $\phi(N) = (p-1)(q-1)$.

To send a message, an agreed-upon protocol for converting text into a sequence of positive integers (each less than N) must first be established. The public key (e, N) is made public and used to send messages to Alice. Only Alice knows her private decryption key d. Encryption of a message M is accomplished by $C = M^e \pmod{N}$ and decryption of the ciphertext C is $M = C^d \pmod{N}$.

Why does this work? To verify that RSA works, we must show that for any integer M, where $1 \le M < N$, we have $(M^e)^d \pmod{N} = M$. First, if $\gcd(M, N) = 1$, then

$$(M^e)^d = M^{ed} = M^{1+k\phi(N)} = M(M^{\phi(N)})^k \pmod{N}.$$

By Euler's Theorem, which appears in Section A-2 of the Appendix, we have $M^{\phi(N)} = 1 \pmod{N}$ so that

$$M(M^{\phi(N)})^k = M \cdot 1^k \pmod{N} = M \pmod{N},$$

as desired. On the other hand, if $\gcd(M, N) = p$, then

$$
\begin{aligned}
(M^e)^d &= M^{1+k\phi(N)} \\
&= M^{1+(p-1)(q-1)k} \\
&= M(M^{q-1})^{k(p-1)} \\
&= M(1)^{k(p-1)} = M \pmod{q},
\end{aligned}
$$

again, by Euler's Theorem. Also note that in this case, $M = 0 \pmod{p}$, which implies $(M^e)^d = 0 \pmod{p}$. It follows that $(M^e)^d = M \pmod{N}$; see Problem 14.

In the next section, we consider some mathematical and implementation issues related to RSA. Then in Chapter 7 we discuss implementation-related attacks on RSA.

6.5.1 Mathematical Issues

There is large body of literature focusing on the cryptanalysis of RSA. An excellent source of information is Boneh's survey [19]. In this section, we mention a few mathematical issues related to the security of RSA. Our intent is to illustrate some of the issues that can lead to attacks on flawed implementations of RSA.

First, we mention a generic attack that applies to public key systems (and hash functions in some situations) but not to symmetric ciphers. We state the attack in the context of RSA, but it applies to other public key cryptosystems as well.

Suppose that Alice encrypts the secret message

$$M = \text{``Attack at dawn''}$$

using Bob's public key (e, N), that is, she computes $C = M^e \pmod{N}$, and she sends C to Bob. Suppose Trudy intercepts C. Since Bob's public key is public, Trudy can try to guess messages M' and for each guess compute the putative ciphertext $C' = (M')^e \pmod{N}$. If Trudy ever finds a message M' for which $C' = C$, then Trudy knows that $M' = M$ and she has broken the RSA encryption.

This method of attacking public key encryption is known as a *forward search*. It does not apply to symmetric ciphers, since Alice and Bob's shared symmetric key would not be available to Trudy, so she could not try to encrypt likely messages. Obviously, for both symmetric key and public key cryptography, the size of the key space must be large enough to prevent a brute-force exhaustive search. However, the forward search attack shows that for public key encryption, the size of the plaintext space must be sufficiently large that an attacker cannot simply try to encrypt all likely messages. In practice, it is easy to prevent the forward search attack by padding messages with a sufficient number of random bits, thereby increasing the size of the plaintext space.

RSA is also susceptible to a chosen ciphertext attack in the following sense. Suppose that Alice will decrypt an innocent-looking ciphertext of Trudy's choosing and return the result to Trudy. Then Trudy can recover the plaintext for any ciphertext that was encrypted with Alice's public key; see Problem 13.

An interesting mathematical fact regarding RSA is that the factors p and q of N are easily obtained if we know $\phi(N)$. To see why this is so, suppose that $\phi(N)$ is known, where $N = pq$ with $q < p$. Then

$$\phi(N) = (p-1)(q-1) = pq - (p+q) + 1 = N - (p+q) + 1$$

and this implies

$$p + q = N - \phi(N) + 1. \tag{6.8}$$

Also,

$$(p+q)^2 = p^2 + 2pq + q^2 = p^2 - 2pq + q^2 + 4pq = (p-q)^2 + 4N,$$

which implies

$$p - q = \sqrt{(p+q)^2 - 4N}. \tag{6.9}$$

From (6.8) and (6.9), we can easily compute

$$p = \frac{(p+q) + (p-q)}{2} \quad \text{and} \quad q = \frac{(p+q) - (p-q)}{2},$$

and we have factored N.

In addition, if $\phi(N)$ is known, the private key d is easily recovered by using the Euclidean Algorithm (see Section A-2 in the Appendix), since the encryption exponent e is public knowledge. Since d is the multiplicative inverse of e modulo $\phi(N)$, the process to determine d is precisely the same as that used in the construction of the key pair.

Clearly, the numbers p, q and d must be "large," so as to prevent a brute-force attack, but what other properties should they (and e) have? When constructing the modulus N, the prime numbers p and q need to be chosen carefully. A *strong prime* p is a prime number such that $p - 1$ has a large prime factor r, $p + 1$ has a large prime factor, and $r - 1$ has a large prime factor. Strong primes p and q should always be used in any implementation of RSA to thwart the factorization of N through the use of *Pollard's $p - 1$ Algorithm* [21].

If the modulus N is misused, then RSA is easily compromised. Suppose that (e_j, N) are the RSA public keys of j parties. That is, each user has the same modulus N, but a different public encryption exponents e_j (and, therefore, different private decryption exponent d_j). With the knowledge of a single private decryption exponent d_j, we can efficiently factor N, as explained below. Then the Euclidean Algorithm can then be used to recover all of the other decryption keys.

Given a decryption exponent d and the corresponding public key (e, N), we can determine the factors of N as follows [19]. First, we compute the number $k = de - 1$. Because of the way d and e are constructed, we know that k is a multiple of $\phi(N)$, say, $k = \ell\phi(N)$ for some ℓ. Since $\phi(N)$ is even, so is k. Then $k = 2^t r$, for some odd r and $t \geq 1$. By a similar argument as that used above to show that the RSA algorithm works, we have

$$g^k = g^{\ell\phi(N)} = 1 \ (\mathrm{mod} \ N)$$

for every $g \in \{1, 2, \ldots, N - 1\}$ and, therefore, $g^{k/2}$ is a square root of unity, modulo N, that is, $(g^{k/2})^2 = 1 \ (\mathrm{mod} \ N)$. The number 1 has four square roots, modulo $N = pq$. Two of these square roots are ± 1 and the other two (which can be found using the Chinese Remainder Theorem—see Section A-2 in the Appendix), are $\pm x$, where x satisfies the conditions $x = 1 \ (\mathrm{mod} \ p)$ and $x = -1 \ (\mathrm{mod} \ q)$. Using either one of these last two square roots, the factorization of N is revealed by computing $\gcd(x-1, N)$.[1] A straightforward argument [19] shows that if $g \in \{1, 2, \ldots, N - 1\}$ is chosen at random, then with probability at least $1/2$ one of the elements in the sequence

$$g^{k/2}, g^{k/4}, \ldots, g^{k/2^t} \ (\mathrm{mod} \ N)$$

---

[1] See Section 7.2.2 for an explanation of why this technique yields the desired factorization.

is a square root of unity that reveals the factorization of N. All elements in the sequence can be efficiently computed in time on the order of n^3, where we have $n = \log_2 N$, that is, n is the number of bits in the binary representation of N.

If a small decryption exponent is used, then an attack due to Wiener [159] can break RSA. Let $N = pq$, where p and q are primes with $q < p < 2q$ and suppose that the decryption exponent satisfies $d < \frac{1}{3}N^{1/4}$. Wiener showed that under these conditions, there is an efficient algorithm for computing d, assuming that the public key (e, N) is known.

A common small encryption exponent e can be (and often is) used. That is, all users can share the same encryption exponent e, but have different N and d. Often, $e = 3$ or $e = 2^{16} + 1$ are used in practice, since these values make public key operations extremely efficient.[2] But this efficiency does not carry over to the corresponding private key operations.

Suppose that Alice wishes to send the same message M to Bob, Carol and Dave, whose respective public keys are $(3, N_i)$, for $i = 0, 1, 2$. We assume that $\gcd(N_i, N_j) = 1$ for $i \neq j$, since otherwise an attacker could factor N_i and N_j by simply computing $\gcd(N_i, N_j)$. Given this scenario, Alice sends $C_0 = M^3 \pmod{N_0}$ to Bob, $C_1 = M^3 \pmod{N_1}$ to Carol and $C_2 = M^3 \pmod{N_2}$ to Dave. If Trudy is eavesdropping and obtains C_0, C_1 and C_2, then she can use the Chinese Remainder Theorem to compute $M^3 \pmod{N_0 N_1 N_2}$. Since $M^3 < N_0 N_1 N_2$, Trudy can obtain M by simply computing the ordinary (non-modular) cube root of M^3 (see Problem 16). In practice, this cube root attack (and analogous attacks when a common encryption exponent other than $e = 3$ is used) is easily prevented by padding the message M. Provided that, as numbers, we have $M > N^{1/3}$, the cube root attack will not succeed.

6.5.2 RSA Conclusion

RSA has proven to be remarkably robust. Having been carefully scrutinized by many researchers, it has remained secure since its invention more than three decades ago [19]. Timing attacks represent the only publicly-known practical attacks on sound implementations of RSA, and these do not result from any weakness in the underlying algorithms, and, furthermore, there are straightforward defenses against such attacks.

The RSA algorithm is the "gold standard" in public key cryptography. Unlike other more specialized systems, it provides both encryption and signatures. The algorithm is also widely deployed and freely available (the patents

---

[2] Recently, Bleichenbacher has shown that if $e = 3$ is used, a simple signature forgery attack exists against certain incorrect implementations of RSA. For this reason, it is generally recommended to avoid using $e = 3$ as an encryption exponent.

have expired). For example, most secure transactions on the Internet use the Secure Socket Layer (SSL), which uses RSA.

Undoubtedly it is for these reasons that RSA is the de facto standard in public key cryptography. Baring some major breakthrough in factoring, or some unexpected attack by other means, RSA appears certain to remain a de-facto standard for the foreseeable future.

6.6 Rabin Cipher

> *And one of the elders saith unto me...*
> *the Root of David, hath prevailed to open the book,*
> *and to loose the seven seals thereof.*
> — Revelation 5:5

As we saw in Section 6.5, solving the factoring problem breaks RSA. Although it is generally believed that the most efficient possible way to break RSA is by factoring the modulus, no proof of this is known. Rabin [118] proposed a cryptosystem where the underlying encryption algorithm is provably as difficult to break as the factorization of large numbers.

In Rabin's clever (and simple) cryptosystem, Alice's public and private keys are generated in the following way: Let $N = pq$, where p and q are distinct primes. Although the scheme works for arbitrary primes, to simplify the exposition we will assume that $p = 3$ (mod 4) and $q = 3$ (mod 4). Alice's public key is N and her private key consists of p and q.

An agreed-upon protocol for converting text into a sequence of positive integers (each less than N) is established. Then to encrypt message M, compute $C = M^2$ (mod N). Decryption is accomplished by the computation of square roots of the ciphertext C modulo N, one of which yields the message M.

How does Alice compute the square roots of ciphertext C modulo N? We first examine the case where we want to compute the square roots of C modulo a prime p. The case where $C = 0$ (mod p) is trivial, so we assume that $C \neq 0$ (mod p). Then we set $y = C^{(p+1)/4}$ (mod p), and by Euler's Theorem, $C^{p-1} = 1$ (mod p), and therefore,

$$y^4 = C^{p+1} = C^2 C^{p-1} = C^2 \text{ (mod } p).$$

This implies

$$y^4 - C^2 = (y^2 - C)(y^2 + C) = 0 \text{ (mod } p),$$

and hence $y^2 = \pm C$ (see Problem 17). From this, we deduce that C is a square modulo p or that $-C$ is a square modulo p, but not both (see Problems 18 and 19). In the case where C is a square modulo p, the square roots of C are $\pm y$; otherwise, the square roots of $-C$ modulo p are $\pm y$.

For example, suppose we want to find the square roots of 3 (mod 11). Since $(p+1)/4 = 3$, we have

$$y = 3^{(p+1)/4} = 3^3 = 27 = 5 \ (\text{mod } 11).$$

So, either ± 5 are the square roots of 3 (mod 11) or ± 5 are the square roots of -3 (mod 11), but not both. In this particular example, it is easily verified that $(\pm 5)^2 = 3$ (mod 11).

Now we consider the computation of square roots, modulo N, where, as usual, $N = pq$. In this slightly more complicated situation, we begin with a concrete example. Suppose that we want to solve $x^2 = 16$ (mod 33). Any solution of this equation satisfies $x^2 = 16 + 3(11)k$ and, in addition, $x^2 = 16 = 1$ (mod 3) and $x^2 = 16 = 5$ (mod 11). Using the method described in the previous paragraph, we find that ± 1 are the square roots of 1 (mod 3) and that ± 4 are the square roots of 5 (mod 11). These can be combined in any of four ways:

$$x = 4 \ (\text{mod } 11) \quad \text{and} \quad x = 1 \ (\text{mod } 3)$$
$$x = 4 \ (\text{mod } 11) \quad \text{and} \quad x = -1 \ (\text{mod } 3)$$
$$x = -4 \ (\text{mod } 11) \quad \text{and} \quad x = 1 \ (\text{mod } 3)$$
$$x = -4 \ (\text{mod } 11) \quad \text{and} \quad x = -1 \ (\text{mod } 3).$$

Using the Euclidean Algorithm, we find integers r and s so that $11r + 3s = 1$. In this case, we see that

$$11 = 3 \cdot 3 + 2$$
$$3 = 2 \cdot 1 + 1$$
$$2 = 1 \cdot 2 + 0.$$

By back-substituting, we find $11(-1) + 3(4) = 1$. The Chinese Remainder Theorem provides the unique solution (mod pq) for the system

$$x = a \ (\text{mod } p)$$
$$x = b \ (\text{mod } q) \tag{6.10}$$

namely, $x = bpr + aqs$, where $pr + qs = 1$. So, in our example, we have $p = 11$, $q = 3$, $r = -1$ and $s = 4$. Therefore, the unique solution to the system

$$x = 4 \ (\text{mod } 11)$$
$$x = 1 \ (\text{mod } 3)$$

is $x = (1)(11)(-1) + (4)(3)(4) = -11 + 48 = 37 = 4$ (mod 33). In a similar fashion, we find that the solutions to the other three systems are given by $x = 26$ (mod 33), $x = 7$ (mod 33) and $x = 29$ (mod 33), respectively, and we have that the square roots of 16 (mod 33) are 4, 7, 26, and 29.

In summary, to compute square roots of C (mod N), we first compute the square roots of C, modulo p and q. Then all systems of the form (6.10), where a is a square root of C (mod p) and b is a square root of C (mod q) are created. Using the Chinese Remainder Theorem, solutions to these systems are found. These solutions are the square roots of C (mod N).

Once the square roots of C (mod N) have been computed, Alice needs to decide which one of the square roots corresponds to the original plaintext M. If the message is written in some natural language, it is easy for her to choose the right one. In the case where the message is less structured, the sender might add a header to the message. Such additional information would allow Alice to easily determine the correct square root of C.

6.6.1 Chosen Ciphertext Attack

If the attacker Trudy is able to compute square roots modulo N, then she can factor N and thereby break the Rabin cryptosystem. To see why this is the case, consider the modulus $N = pq$, where $p > 2$ and $q > 2$ are distinct primes. Let u and v be square roots of C (mod N), and assume that $u \neq \pm v$. It is easily verified that either $p = \gcd(u+v, N)$ or $q = \gcd(u+v, N)$ as follows. Since $u^2 = v^2 = C$ (mod N), we have that N divides $(u^2 - v^2) = (u+v)(u-v)$. But, N does not divide $u + v$ and N does not divide $u - v$. Therefore, from the Euclidean Algorithm, we compute $\gcd(u+v, N)$ which is one of the prime factors of N.

This fact allows Trudy to perform the following chosen ciphertext attack on the Rabin cryptosystem. Suppose that Trudy has access to Alice's decryption machine (as a black box). Trudy chooses M, where $0 < M < N$ and computes $C = M^2$ (mod N). She then uses Alice's decryption machine to decrypt C, yielding y. The probability that $M \neq \pm y$ (mod N) is 1/2, and if this is the case, Trudy finds the prime factors of N and is able to read all messages sent to Alice; see Problem 23.

By applying some appropriate message preprocessing, this attack can be thwarted. For example, *optimal asymmetric encryption padding* (OAEP) [10] is a padding scheme that can be used to encode a message before asymmetric encryption is applied. Through the use of such a scheme, two goals are achieved. First, an element of randomness is introduced, which converts a deterministic encryption scheme into a probabilistic one. Secondly, partial decryption of ciphertexts is made more difficult.

The OAEP scheme works as follows [36]. Here, we assume that binary strings of length n are used by the bijective trapdoor function f of a cryptosystem. Along with this, OAEP utilizes a pseudorandom bit generator G that maps k-bit strings to ℓ-bit strings and a hash function h mapping ℓ-bit strings to k-bit strings, where $n = k + \ell$.

To encrypt a message $M \in \{0.1\}^{\ell}$, a random bit string $r \in \{0,1\}^{k}$ is first chosen. Then, we set

$$x = (M \oplus G(r)) \parallel (r \oplus h(M \oplus G(r))),$$

where the "$\parallel$" indicates concatenation and "$\oplus$" denotes the bitwise XOR operator. Finally, $C = f(x)$ is computed. The first ℓ bits of x, that is, $M \oplus G(r)$, are obtained from the mixing of M and the pseudorandom bits $G(r)$. The last k bits of x arise from the mixing of random seed r and masked $h(M \oplus G(r))$. Therefore, a single message M can (and will) yield different ciphertexts, given different random bit strings r.

To decrypt ciphertext C, we use f^{-1}, the same pseudorandom bit generator G, and the same hash function h as above. First, we compute $f^{-1}(C)$ which is of the form $a \parallel b$, where the length of a is ℓ and the length of b is k. Next, we compute $r = h(a) \oplus b$. Then to recover the original message M, we use the fact that

$$M = M \oplus G(r) \oplus G(r) = M \oplus G(r) \oplus G(h(a) \oplus b) = a \oplus G(r).$$

In order for attacker Trudy to recover plaintext M from ciphertext $C = f(x)$, she must determine all of the bits of x from C. She needs the first ℓ bits to compute $h(a)$ and the last k bits to get r. Consequently, partial decryption of ciphertexts (by exploiting some partial knowledge of x) is made more difficult.

6.6.2 Rabin Cryptosystem Conclusion

Although the Rabin cryptosystem is effective and it was developed shortly after RSA, it has never enjoyed anything like the popularity of RSA. Perhaps, this is because only one of the four possible decrypts of a ciphertext corresponds to the plaintext. However, this issue is easily resolved.[3]

It is easily verified that the security of the Rabin cryptosystem is equivalent to factoring, while this is not known to be the case for RSA. Consequently, it is conceivable that RSA could be compromised without solving the factoring problem. Viewed in this light, it is not unreasonable to argue that the Rabin cryptosystem rests on a somewhat more secure foundation than RSA. Of course, to date, the most significant general attack on RSA is to factor the modulus. So, in a practical sense, the security of RSA and Rabin are indistinguishable today. Without an overwhelming reason to abandon the gold standard of RSA, it is unlikely that the Rabin cryptosystem will gain a more significant following in the public key arena.

---

[3]RSA was patented (the patents have now expired) and promoted by RSA Security, Inc. In contrast, the Rabin cipher had no comparable corporate backing.

6.7   NTRU Cipher

> "That's a great deal to make one word mean,"
> Alice said in a thoughtful tone.
> "When I make a word do a lot of work like that,"
> said Humpty Dumpty, "I always pay it extra."
> — Through the Looking Glass

Relative to many other public key cryptosystems, the NTRU cipher, rumored to stand for "Nth-degree TRUncated polynomial ring" or "Number Theorists aRe Us," is young. Invented in 1995 by Hoffstein, Pipher, and Silverman [68], it is somewhat more complicated than RSA or the Rabin cryptosystem. The security of NTRU derives from the difficulty of a certain factoring problem in a polynomial ring. We have more to say about this below, but first we describe the NTRU system and give an example.

The NTRU cipher depends on three positive integer parameters (N, p, q) and four sets of polynomials of degree $N - 1$ with integer coefficients. The sets of polynomials are denoted L_f, L_g, L_r, and L_m. The parameters p and q are chosen so that $\gcd(p, q) = 1$ and $q > p$, where q must be much larger than p.

All of the NTRU polynomials are in the set of truncated polynomials of degree $N - 1$ having integer coefficients. That is, an NTRU polynomial is of the form

$$a(x) = a_0 + a_1 x + a_2 x^2 + \cdots + a_{N-2} x^{N-2} + a_{N-1} x^{N-1},$$

where the a_i are integers (taken modulo p or q, depending on the specific polynomial). Polynomials are added in the usual way. Multiplication is perfomed modulo $x^N - 1$, meaning that polynomials are multiplied in the usual way, but x^N is replaced by 1, x^{N+1} is replaced by x, x^{N+2} is replaced by x^2 and so on. We use the symbol "$\star$" to denote this type of polynomial multiplication. In mathematical terms, all of the NTRU polynomials are in the quotient ring

$$R = \frac{Z[x]}{(x^N - 1)}.$$

The message space L_m consists of all polynomials in R modulo p. Assuming that p is odd, we define the message space as

$$L_m = \{M(x) \in R \mid \text{all coefficients of } M \text{ lie in } [-(p-1)/2, (p-1)/2]\}.$$

As a notational convenience, let $L(d_0, d_1)$ be the set of polynomials in R with d_0 coefficients that are $+1$ and d_1 coefficents that are -1, and all remaining coefficients are 0. For example,

$$-1 + x^2 + x^3 - x^5 + x^9 \in L(3, 2),$$

since the nonzero coefficients consists of three $+1$s and two -1s.

Given the NTRU parameters (N, p, q), we must select three additional parameters, denoted d_f, d_g, and d, which should be selected from the recommended NTRU parameters (the current set of recommended parameters can be found at [108]). These additional parameters are used to define the sets of polynomials

$$L_f = L(d_f, d_f - 1), \quad L_g = L(d_g, d_g), \quad \text{and} \quad L_r = L(d, d).$$

Now Alice generates her NTRU key pair as follows. She first chooses two polynomials $f(x)$ and $g(x)$, where $f(x) \in L_f$ and $f(x)$ is invertible modulo p and modulo q, and $g(x) \in L_g$. She can find a suitable $f(x)$ using the algorithm in Table 6.3 [137].

Table 6.3: Algorithm to Find Inverse Polynomial

```
// Input: polynomial a(x), prime p
// Output: b(x) = a(x)⁻¹ in (Z/pZ)[x]/(xᴺ − 1)
// Initialization
k = 0, b(x) = 1, c(x) = 0, f(x) = a(x), g(x) = xᴺ − 1
// find inverse
repeat
    while f₀ = 0
        f(x) = f(x)/x
        c(x) = c(x) ⋆ x
        k = k + 1
    end while
    if deg(f) = 0 then
        b(x) = f₀⁻¹b(x) (mod p)
        return xᴺ⁻ᵏb(x) mod (xᴺ − 1)
    end if
    if deg(f) < deg(g) then
        swap(f, g)
        swap(b, c)
    end if
    u = f₀g₀⁻¹ (mod p)
    f(x) = f(x) − u ⋆ g(x) (mod p)
    b(x) = b(x) − u ⋆ c(x) (mod p)
forever
```

Denote the inverses of $f(x)$ modulo p and q as $f_p(x)$ and $f_q(x)$ respectively, so that

$$f_p(x) \star f(x) = 1 \ (\text{mod } p) \quad \text{and} \quad f_q(x) \star f(x) = 1 \ (\text{mod } q).$$

Then Alice's public key is the polynomial $h(x) = pf_q(x) \star g(x)$ (mod q). The ploynomial $h(x)$, along with the parameters N, p, and q, are made public. Alice's private key consists of the polynomials $f(x)$ and $f_p(x)$. To summarize, we have

$$\text{Public key: } h(x)$$

$$\text{Private key: } (f(x), f_p(x))$$

where $h(x) = pf_q(x) \star g(x)$ (mod q) and $f(x) \star f_q(x) = 1$ (mod q).

Bob encrypts a message for Alice as follows. Bob first selects a polynomial $M(x) \in L_m$ that represents the plaintext message. Recall that the coefficients of the message ploynomial $M(x)$ are in the range $-(p-1)/2$ and $(p-1)/2$ and that q is much larger than p. Consequently, the message $M(x)$ can be viewed as a "small" polynomial modulo q, in the sense that the vector of coefficients has small Euclidean length.

Bob then chooses a random "blinding" polynomial $r(x) \in L_r$ and uses Alice's public key to compute the ciphertext message $C(x)$ (also a polynomial) as

$$C(x) = r(x) \star h(x) + M(x) \text{ (mod } q),$$

which he sends to Alice.

To decrypt Bob's message, Alice computes

$$a(x) = f(x) \star C(x) = f(x) \star r(x) \star h(x) + f(x) \star M(x) \text{ (mod } q).$$

The coefficients of $a(x)$ are chosen to be in the interval $-q/2$ to $q/2$ (it is crucial that the coefficients be taken in this interval before the next step in the decryption). Then Alice computes $b(x) = a(x)$ (mod p). Although it is not obvious, Alice recovers the message $M(x)$ by computing

$$f_p(x) \star b(x) \text{ (mod } p).$$

Below we give an intuitive explanation why NTRU decryption works, but first we give an example.

To illustrate the NTRU algorithm, we use the example found at [108]. Suppose that we select NTRU parameters $N = 11$, $q = 32$, $p = 3$, and the sets of polynomials $L_f = L(4,3)$, $L_g = L(3,3)$, and $L_r = L(3,3)$. Then to generate her private key, Alice selects a polynomial $f(x) \in L_f$, that is, a polynomial of degree ten with four $+1$ coefficients and three -1 coefficients, and all remaining coefficients set to 0. She also chooses a polynomial $g(x)$, where $g(x) \in L_g$. Suppose that the selected polynomial are

$$f(x) = -1 + x + x^2 - x^4 + x^6 + x^9 - x^{10} \in L_f$$
$$g(x) = -1 + x^2 + x^3 + x^5 - x^8 - x^{10} \in L_g.$$

Next, Alice computes $f_p(x)$ and $f_q(x)$, the inverses of $f(x)$ modulo p and q, respectively. Using the algorithm in Table 6.3, she finds

$$f_p(x) = 1 + 2x + 2x^3 + 2x^4 + x^5 + 2x^7 + x^8 + 2x^9$$
$$f_q(x) = 5 + 9x + 6x^2 + 16x^3 + 4x^4 + 15x^5 + 16x^6 + 22x^7$$
$$+ 20x^8 + 18x^9 + 30x^{10}.$$

Alice's private key consists of the pair of polynomials $(f(x), f_p(x))$. To generate her public key $h(x)$, Alice computes

$$h(x) = pf_q(x) \star g(x)$$
$$= 8 + 25x + 22x^2 + 20x^3 + 12x^4 + 24x^5 + 15x^6$$
$$+ 19x^7 + 12x^8 + 19x^9 + 16x^{10} \pmod{32}.$$

Now, suppose that Bob wants to send the message

$$M(x) = -1 + x^3 - x^4 - x^8 + x^9 + x^{10} \in L_m$$

to Alice. He first chooses a random blinding polynomial $r(x)$ of degree ten (or less) with three $+1$ coefficients and three -1 coefficients, say,

$$r(x) = -1 + x^2 + x^3 + x^4 - x^5 - x^7 \in L_r.$$

Bob computes the ciphertext polynomial $C(x)$ as

$$C(x) = r(x) \star h(x) + M(x)$$
$$= 14 + 11x + 26x^2 + 24x^3 + 14x^4 + 16x^5 + 30x^6$$
$$+ 7x^7 + 25x^8 + 6x^9 + 19x^{10} \pmod{32},$$

which he sends to Alice.

When Alice receives the ciphertext polynomial $C(x)$ from Bob, she uses her private key $f(x)$ to compute

$$a(x) = f(x) \star C(x)$$
$$= 3 - 7x - 10x^2 - 11x^3 + 10x^4 + 7x^5 + 6x^6$$
$$+ 7x^7 + 5x^8 - 3x^9 - 7x^{10} \pmod{32},$$

where the coefficients of $a(x)$ have been chosen to lie between $-q/2$ and $q/2$ (in this example, from -15 to $+16$). Alice then reduces the coefficients of $a(x)$ modulo $p = 3$ to obtain

$$b(x) = -x - x^2 + x^3 + x^4 + x^5 + x^7 - x^8 - x^{10} \pmod{3}.$$

She finds the plaintext message M by computing

$$f_p(x) \star b(x) = -1 + x^3 - x^4 - x^8 + x^9 + x^{10} \pmod{3}.$$

Why does NTRU work? Consider $C(x) = r(x) \star h(x) + M(x) \pmod{q}$, where $h(x)$ is, say, Alice's public key. Recall that $h(x) = pf_q(x) \star g(x) \pmod{q}$. For the first step in the decryption, Alice computes

$$
\begin{aligned}
a(x) = f(x) \star C(x) &= f(x) \star r(x) \star h(x) + f(x) \star M(x) \pmod{q} \\
&= pf(x) \star r(x) \star f_q(x) \star g(x) + f(x) \star M(x) \pmod{q} \\
&= pr(x) \star g(x) + f(x) \star M(x) \pmod{q}.
\end{aligned}
$$

The polynomials $r(x)$, $g(x)$, $f(x)$, and $M(x)$ all have coefficients that are small, relative to q. Therefore, the polynomial $pr(x) \star g(x) + f(x) \star M(x)$ (not taken modulo q) is most likely the same as the polynomial

$$pr(x) \star g(x) + f(x) \star M(x) \pmod{q}.$$

If this is the case, the "mod q" in the computation of $a(x)$ has no effect and it follows that

$$b(x) = a(x) \pmod{p} = f(x) \star M(x) \pmod{p},$$

as desired. Then since $f_p(x) \star f(x) = 1 \pmod{p}$, Alice can easily recover the plaintext $M(x)$ from $b(x)$. However, if $pr(x) \star g(x) + f(x) \star M(x)$ (not taken modulo q) does not equal the polynomial $pr(x) \star g(x) + f(x) \star M(x) \pmod{q}$, then the decryption can fail. Therefore, the NTRU decryption process is probabilistic—although it does succeed with a very high probability for appropriately chosen parameters.

Before considering attacks, we briefly discuss the underlying hard problem that is the basis for the security of NTRU. The NTRU public key is the polynomial $h(x)$, where

$$h(x) = pf_q(x) \star g(x) \pmod{q}$$

and the corresponding private key consists of the pair of polynomials $f(x)$ and $f_q(x)$, where $f(x) \star f_q(x) = 1 \pmod{q}$. Note that this implies

$$h(x) \star f(x) = pg(x) \pmod{q}.$$

If the attacker, Trudy, can determine $f(x)$ or $f_q(x)$ from $h(x)$, she can recover the private key and thereby break NTRU.

We have

$$h(x) = h_0 + h_1 x + h_2 x^2 + \cdots + h_{N-1} x^{N-1},$$

with $f(x)$ and $g(x)$ defined similarly. Let f be the column vector of coefficients of $f(x)$ and g the coefficients of $g(x)$, also given as a column vector. Next, define the $N \times N$ matrix

$$
H = \begin{bmatrix}
h_0 & h_{N-1} & h_{N-2} & \cdots & h_1 \\
h_1 & h_0 & h_{N-1} & \cdots & h_2 \\
\vdots & & \ddots & & \vdots \\
h_{N-1} & h_{N-2} & h_{N-3} & \cdots & h_0
\end{bmatrix}.
$$

Then by the definition of "$\star$", we have

$$Hf = pg \pmod{q}.$$

We can now state the problem of recovering $f(x)$ from $h(x)$ as a lattice reduction problem. Given the public key $h(x)$, we have the block matrix equation

$$MV = \left[\begin{array}{cc} I_{N \times N} & 0_{N \times N} \\ H_{N \times N} & qI_{N \times N} \end{array} \right] \left[\begin{array}{c} f \\ s \end{array} \right] = \left[\begin{array}{c} f \\ pg \end{array} \right] = W \pmod{q}, \qquad (6.11)$$

where V and W are unknown. This block matrix equation simply states that $f = f$ and $Hf + qs = pg \pmod{q}$. From this latter equation it follows that $Hf = pg \pmod{q}$, regardless of s. Since H only depends on the public key $h(x)$, if we can determine V or W, then we can break NTRU. But W is in the lattice spanned by the columns of M (note that, due to the identity matrices on the diagonal, the columns of M are linearly independent). Furthermore, W has a very special form, since it is a "short" vector in the lattice (recall that both $f(x)$ and $g(x)$ are chosen to be small relative to q), and the elements of W consist of a known number of $+1$s, -1s, and 0s (as determined by the parameters d_f and d_g).

This lattice reduction problem is very similar to that used to successfully attack the knapsack; see Section 6.2. Therefore, we could use lattice reduction techniques, such as the LLL Algorithm in an attempt to break NTRU. However, the NTRU lattice problem is believed to be very difficult to solve, and no efficient algorithms are known. In fact, the security of the NTRU cipher is intentionally based on the difficulty of this particular lattice reduction problem. It is somewhat ironic that the very technique that leads to a devastating attack on the knapsack can, in a slightly modified setting, become the basis for constructing a public key system.

It is worth noting that there is one significant difference between the NTRU lattice problem in (6.11) and the knapsack lattice problem considered in Section 6.2. The successful knapsack attack breaks a single message, but it does not enable the attacker to recover the private key. However, in (6.11) we are trying to recover the private key from the public key, and, intuitively, this should be a much harder problem. So it might seem to be unfair to compare this NTRU lattice problem to the knapsack lattice problem. It is possible to give a lattice reduction attack on a single NTRU message, which is more analogous to the knapsack setting. However, the NTRU lattice reduction attack is intractable (as far as is known), even in this seemingly simpler case [101].

The primary claim to fame for NTRU is its efficiency—the encryption, decryption, and the key generation process are all very fast by public key standards. The inventors of NTRU claim that when comparing a moderate NTRU security level to RSA with a 512-bit modulus, NTRU is approximately 5.9 times faster for encryption, 14.4 times faster for decryption and 5.0 times faster during key creation [68]. In addition, when comparing the highest NTRU security level to RSA with a 1024 bit RSA modulus, it is claimed that NTRU is the same speed for encryption, 3.2 times faster for decryption, and 5.3 times faster for key creation. For this reason alone, NTRU might be an attractive cryptosystem to use in resource constrained environments such as embedded systems.

NTRU is somewhat unique since there have been several published attacks, but yet the cipher is not considered broken. In the next sections, we briefly outline a few attacks against NTRU. Some of these attacks have led to modifications in the suggested parameters for NTRU.

6.7.1   Meet-in-the-Middle Attack

The NTRU cipher is susceptible to a meet-in-the-middle attack. Andrew Odlyzko first pointed out that if a polynomial $s(x)$ is chosen from a space with 2^n elements, then a brute-force search can be conducted on a space of size $2^{n/2}$ to recover $s(x)$. His argument was then adapted by Silverman in [136], where it is shown that if the private key $f(x)$ is chosen from a space of 2^n elements, then the security level of NTRU is $2^{n/2}$. Here, we outline how this attack works.

Let N, q, d_f, $f(x)$, $g(x)$, and $h(x)$ be defined as above. To illustrate the attack, we assume that N and d_f are even. The modifications to the attack for odd values are straightforward. All polynomials are expressed as ascending sums of powers of x. Let k and ℓ be positive integers chosen by the attacker, Trudy, so that

$$(q/2^\ell)^k > \binom{N/2}{d_f/2}\binom{N/2 - d_f/2}{d_f/2 - 1},$$

where the left-hand side of the inequality is much greater than the right-hand side (by, say, a factor of 100).

Let the symbol "$\|$" denote concatenation. Trudy searches for the private key $f(x)$, where $f(x) \in L(d_f, d_f - 1)$ is of the form $f_0(x) \| f_1(x)$, and $f_0(x)$ (of length $N/2$) has $d_f/2$ coefficients of $+1$ and $d_f/2$ coefficients of -1 (and the rest, zeros) and $f_1(x)$ (of length $N/2$) has $d_f/2$ ones, $d_f/2 - 1$ negative ones (and the rest, zeros). She wants to find $f_0(x)$ and $f_1(x)$ such that

$$(f_0(x) \| f_1(x)) \star h(x) = f(x) \star h(x) = g(x) \pmod{q}$$

has coefficients in $\{-1, 0, 1\}$. If this is the case, then $g(x) \pmod{q}$ is of the correct form and therefore $f_0(x) \| f_1(x)$ is a candidate for the private key.

First, Trudy lists the polynomials $f_0(x)$, which are of length $N/2$. We identify these polynomials with the length-N vectors formed by appending $N/2$ zeros. This requires

$$\binom{N/2}{d_f/2}\binom{N/2 - d_f/2}{d_f/2}$$

steps and is done in the following manner. The $f_0(x)$ polynomials are stored in bins based on the first k coordinates of $f_0(x) \star h(x) \pmod{q}$. To form the bins, divide the interval $[0, q-1]$ into subintervals of length 2^ℓ and call this set of subintervals I, that is, the set I is composed of the subintervals

$$I_j = [2^\ell j, 2^\ell(j+1) + 1], \quad \text{where} \ \ 0 \le j < q/2^\ell.$$

A bin is a k-tuple of intervals chosen from I. If the first k coordinates of $f_0(x) \star h(x) \pmod{q}$ are, respectively, $(a_0, a_1, \ldots, a_{k-1})$, then $f_0(x)$ is stored in bin $(I_0, \ldots, I_{k-1})$, where $a_i \in I_i$, for $i = 0, 1, \ldots, k-1$. Note that the storage location of an $f_0(x)$ depends only on its first k coordinates and therefore, a bin may contain multiple $f_1(x)$ polynomials.

In a similar manner, Trudy lists the polynomials $f_1(x)$, which are also of length $N/2$. In this case, we identify the polynomials with the length-N vectors formed by prepending $N/2$ zeros. This requires

$$\binom{N/2}{d_f/2}\binom{N/2 - d_f/2}{d_f/2 - 1}$$

steps. The $f_1(x)$ polynomials are stored in bins based the first k coordinates of each polynomial $-f_1(x) \star h(x) \pmod{q}$. However the bins which are formed for the $f_1(x)$ polynomials are slightly larger than the $f_0(x)$ bins. More precisely, let J be the set of subintervals

$$J_j = [2^\ell j - 1, 2^\ell(j+1) - 1], \quad \text{where} \ \ 0 \le j < q/2^\ell.$$

The subintervals J_j overlap, so some $f_1(x)$ polynomials will go into more than one bin.

Finally, Trudy finds the non-empty, overlapping $f_0(x)$ and $f_1(x)$ bins. In this case, for each

$$f_0(x) \in (I_{i_0}, \ldots, I_{i_{k-1}}) \quad \text{and} \quad f_1(x) \in (J_{j_0}, \ldots, J_{j_{k-1}}),$$

it is very likely that $(f_0(x) \ \| \ f_1(x)) \star h(x) \pmod{q}$ has coefficients in $\{-1, 0, 1\}$. Therefore, $f_0(x) \ \| \ f_1(x)$ is a candidate for the private key $f(x)$, which follows from the fact that $(f_0(x) \ \| \ f_1(x)) \star h(x) \pmod{q}$ is of the correct form.

A few remarks might help to clarify the attack. Although the private key $f(x)$ may not have the property that half of its ones (that is, $d_f/2$ of its ones) fall in the first $N/2$ bits, there is at least one rotation of $f(x)$ which has this property and any rotation of $f(x)$ can serve as the private key (see Problem 26). In [136], it is assumed that $f(x)$ is chosen with d_f ones and $N - d_f$ zeros and some technical conditions on $g(x)$ are satisfied. Under these conditions, Silverman showed that the time required for the attack is on the order of

$$\text{time} \approx \sqrt{d_f} \left(\frac{q}{2^\ell} \right)^k$$

and that the storage necessary for the bins is on the order of $2(q/2^\ell)^{2k}$. Furthermore, Silverman provides experimental results for various values of N, q, d_f, k, and ℓ.

6.7.2 Multiple Transmission Attack

Suppose that Trudy conducts a denial-of-service attack on Alice. During this time, Bob sends Alice an NTRU encrypted message using her public key $h(x)$. Because of Trudy's attack, his message never reaches Alice. Since Bob is not aware of Trudy's attack, he assumes that the message was lost and he resends the same message, again using Alice's public key $h(x)$, but a different blinding polynomial $r(x)$. Suppose that this scenario is repeated a few more times, with Bob sending the same message $M(x)$ to Alice n times, using the same public key $h(x)$ but each time using a different $r(x)$, where the ith choice of $r(x)$ is denoted $r_i(x)$.

Under this scenario, Trudy can attack NTRU. The outline of the attack is as follows. Trudy intercepts the encrypted messages

$$C_i(x) = r_i(x) \star h(x) + M(x) \; (\text{mod } q), \quad \text{for } i = 0, 1, \ldots, n.$$

Assuming that $h^{-1}(x) \; (\text{mod } q)$ exists, she then computes

$$C_i(x) - C_0(x) = pr_i(x) \star h(x) - pr_0(x) \star h(x) \; (\text{mod } q)$$
$$= p(r_i(x) - r_0(x)) \star h(x) \; (\text{mod } q),$$

for $i = 1, 2, \ldots, n$, and Trudy thereby obtains

$$z_i(x) = p^{-1}(C_i(x) - C_0(x)) \star h^{-1}(x) \; (\text{mod } q)$$
$$= r_i(x) - r_0(x) \; (\text{mod } q),$$

for $i = 1, 2, \ldots, n$. Trudy reduces the coefficients of $z_i(x)$ so that they lie between $-q/2$ and $q/2$. Since the coefficients of the $r_i(x)$ are small (relative to q), she recovers $r_i(x) - r_0(x)$, for most (if not all) $i = 1, 2, \ldots, n$. From this, many (if not all) of the coefficients of $r_0(x)$ can be obtained (see Problem 28). If Trudy can recover enough of $r_0(x)$ in this way, then she can recover the remaining coefficients by brute force. Once $r_0(x)$ is known, Trudy computes $C_0(x) - r_0(x) \star h(x) \; (\text{mod } q)$ and thereby recovers the message $M(x)$.

6.7.3   Chosen Ciphertext Attack

In 2000, Jaulmes and Joux [73] developed a clever chosen-ciphertext attack on NTRU. Their discovery resulted in changes to the recommended parameter sets by NTRU Cryptosystems, Inc. Since the attack also is effective on OAEP-like padding, which was originally proposed for use with NTRU, other padding methods are now used with NTRU. For our overview of the attack, we will reference the NTRU parameter sets given in [138] and reproduced here in Table 6.4.

Table 6.4: Previous Recommended NTRU Parameters

Case	N	p	q	L_f	L_g	L_r
A	107	3	64	$L(15,14)$	$L(12,12)$	$L(5,5)$
B	167	3	128	$L(61,60)$	$L(20,20)$	$L(18,18)$
C	263	3	128	$L(50,49)$	$L(24,24)$	$L(16,16)$
D	503	3	256	$L(216,215)$	$L(72,72)$	$L(55,55)$

Recall that the NTRU decryption process consists of first computing

$$
\begin{aligned}
a(x) &= f(x) \star M(x) \\
&= f(x) \star r(x) \star h(x) + f(x) \star M(x) \ (\text{mod } q) \\
&= f(x) \star pr(x) \star f_q(x) \star g(x) + f(x) \star M(x) \ (\text{mod } q) \\
&= pr(x) \star g(x) + f(x) \star M(x) \ (\text{mod } q),
\end{aligned}
$$

followed by $f_p(x) \star a(x) \ (\text{mod } p)$ which usually yields the plaintext message $M(x)$. For appropriate parameter choices, the coefficients of the polynomial $pr(x) \star g(x) + f(x) \star M(x)$ lie in the range $-q/2$ and $q/2$. Consequently, the polynomial $pr \star g(x) + f(x) \star M(x) \ (\text{mod } q)$ is the same as the true (non-modular) polynomial, that is, the mod q has no effect. The idea of Jaulmes and Joux's chosen-ciphertext attack is to construct ciphertexts, which result in intermediate polynomials whose modular values differ from the true values.

For example, suppose Trudy chooses a ciphertext polynomial which is of the form $C(x) = yh(x) + y$, where y is an integer and $h(x)$ is Alice's public key. The NTRU decryption algorithm yields

$$
\begin{aligned}
a(x) &= f(x) \star C(x) = f(x) \star yh(x) + yf(x) \ (\text{mod } q) \\
&= yf(x) \star h(x) + yf(x) \ (\text{mod } q) \\
&= yg(x) + yf(x) \ (\text{mod } q),
\end{aligned}
$$

where $f(x)$ and $g(x)$ both have coefficients in $\{0,1,-1\}$. It follows that the polynomial $yg(x) + yf(x)$ has coefficients in $\{0, y, -y, 2y, -2y\}$. If Trudy has chosen y so that $y < q/2$ and $2y > q/2$, then the decryption process reduces only the coefficients equal to $\pm 2y$ modulo q and these coefficients are selected so as to lie between $-q/2$ and $q/2$. Now suppose that a single coefficient of $a(x)$ is $\pm 2y$, say, $a_i = +2y$. Then $a(x) \pmod q = yg(x) + yf(x) - qx^i$, and the final decrypted output is

$$f_p(x) \star a(x) = yf_p(x) \star g(x) + y - f_p(x) \star qx^i \pmod{p}.$$

Furthermore, if Trudy chose y to be a multiple of p, then the final decrypted output collapses to

$$z(x) = -f_p(x) \star qx^i = -qf_p(x) \star x^i \pmod{p}.$$

Trudy then recovers Alice's private key $f(x)$ by computing

$$f(x) = -qx^i \star z^{-1}(x) \pmod{p}.$$

In general, the polynomial $yf(x) + yg(x)$ may have none or several co-efficients equal to $\pm 2y$. In these cases, the above attack would not work. However, this chosen-ciphertext attack can be generalized and it can be practical, even for stronger security parameters [138].

The *intersection polynomial* $w(x)$ of polynomials $u(x)$ and $v(x)$ is defined to be

$$w(x) = w_0 + w_1 x + w_2 x^2 + \cdots + w_{N-1} x^{N-1},$$

where

$$w_i = \begin{cases} 1 & \text{if } u_i = v_i = 1 \\ -1 & \text{if } u_i = v_i = -1 \\ 0 & \text{otherwise.} \end{cases}$$

We say that polynomials $u(x)$ and $v(x)$ have a *collision* when they have the same non-zero coefficient in a corresponding term.

In the attack discussed above, the intersection polynomial of $f(x)$ and $g(x)$ was the polynomial $w(x) = x^i$, that is, $f(x)$ and $g(x)$ had one collision. Using the security parameters corresponding to $N = 107$ in Table 6.4, Jaulmes and Joux found that the probability of one collision occurring between $f(x)$ and $g(x)$ was 0.13. Therefore, for this particular choice of parameters, the chosen ciphertext attack using $C(x) = yh(x) + y$ is successful approximately thirteen percent of the time and, in these instances, it easily recovers $f(x)$.

For higher security parameters, the number of expected collisions between $f(x)$ and $g(x)$ is too high and Alice's private key $f(x)$ cannot be recovered in this manner when using the chosen ciphertext $C(x) = yh(x) + y$. In these cases, chosen ciphertext messages of the form

$$z(x) = yh(x)x^{i_0} + \cdots + yh(x)x^{i_{t-1}} + yx^{j_0} + \cdots + yx^{j_{s-1}},$$

where y is a multiple of p with

$$(t + s - 1)y < q/2 \quad \text{and} \quad (t + s)y > q/2$$

can be used to attack NTRU. The numbers t and s are chosen so that the average number of collisions between

$$\sum_{\ell=0}^{t-1} g \star x^{i_\ell} \quad \text{and} \quad \sum_{\ell=0}^{s-1} f \star x^{j_\ell}$$

is approximately one. Jaulmes and Joux give the heuristic approximation of the number of collisions as

$$\frac{2d_f^s d_g^t}{N^{t+s-1}}.$$

When this number is near one, appropriate values for t and s have been determined for the chosen-ciphertext attack. In [73], the authors present an example of complete key recovery, using the highest security set of parameters described in [138]. They also provide estimated running times for different sets of parameters using different values of t, s, and y.

Although we will not discuss it here, Jaulmes and Joux also shows that this attack can be modified so that it is effective against OAEP-like padding within NTRU. One way to thwart this chosen-ciphertext attack is to use other padding methods as described in [54].

6.7.4   NTRU Conclusion

Like any respectable cryptosystem, NTRU has been under close scrutiny since its invention. As attacks and weaknesses have been discovered, the implementation—as well as the recommended security parameters N, p, q, L_f, L_g, and L_r—have evolved over time. In fact, NTRU encryption is now in its third major revision, due to viable attacks on earlier versions.[4]

Of course, Kerckhoffs' Principle dictates that a cryptosystem must be subject to extensive investigation. However, the evolution of NTRU is in stark contrast to, say, RSA, which has undergone no significant revisions since its invention. Given these track records, it could be argued that RSA likely rests on a sounder foundation than NTRU. Nevertheless, there are no known weaknesses in the current version of NTRU encryption [101].

In any case, it appears that NTRU is a cryptosystem with a future, in contrast to many other proposed public key systems—although a cynic might argue that this has as much to do with patents and the heavy corporate backing NTRU has received than with any inherent technical superiority. Time will tell whether the current version of NTRU proves more durable than its predecessors.

---

[4]Note that these revisions are much more significant than simply increasing the size of the parameters.

6.8 ElGamal Signature Scheme

> *Drink nothing without seeing it; sign nothing without reading it.*
> — Spanish Proverb

Public key cryptography can be used to create digital signatures. If properly implemented, when Bob receives a message digitally signed by Alice, he is assured that it was composed by Alice—assuming that Alice's private key is private.

Several different digital signature schemes have been proposed. For example, RSA can be used for signing by simply using the private key to "encrypt" and the public key to verify the signature. ElGamal is another signature scheme, which we discuss in this section.

In this section, we employ the public key notation defined previously in Section 5.1. That is, we use the following notation:

- Encrypt message M with Alice's public key: $C = \{M\}_{\text{Alice}}$.

- Decrypt ciphertext C with Alice's private key: $M = [C]_{\text{Alice}}$.

- Signing and decrypting are the same operations, so the notation for Alice signing message M is $S = [M]_{\text{Alice}}$, where S is the signed message.

Encryption and decryption are inverse operations so that

$$[\{M\}_{\text{Alice}}]_{\text{Alice}} = \{[M]_{\text{Alice}}\}_{\text{Alice}} = M.$$

It is important to remember that only Alice can sign since the signature requires Alice's private key. However, anyone can verify Alice's signature, since that is a public key operation.

We can define *confidentiality* as "no unauthorized reading" and *integrity* as "no unauthorized writing" [142]. By using Bob's public key, Alice can send encrypted messages to Bob and be assured of confidentiality. For integrity, Alice can use a digital signature, as discussed in Section 5.1. Both integrity and confidentiality can be achieved by using symmetric key cryptography, but a digital signature also provides non-repudiation, which cannot be achieved with symmetric keys.

How can Alice have confidentiality, integrity and non-repudiation using a public key cryptosystem? There are two natural strategies which Alice might use to accomplish this, that is, she can sign the message M and then encrypt the result before sending it to Bob or she can encrypt M and then sign the result before sending it to Bob.

Using scenarios found in [142], we will show that both of these strategies have potential pitfalls. First, suppose that Alice and Bob are romantically involved. Alice decides to send the message

$$M = \text{``I love you''}$$

to Bob. Using sign and encrypt, she sends Bob

$$\{[M]_{\text{Alice}}\}_{\text{Bob}}.$$

Not long after, Alice and Bob have an argument and Bob, in an act of spite, decrypts the signed message to obtain $[M]_{\text{Alice}}$ and re-encrypts it as

$$\{[M]_{\text{Alice}}\}_{\text{Charlie}}$$

before sending it on to Charlie. Upon reading the message, Charlie thinks that Alice is in love with him, causing great embarrassment for both Alice and Charlie.

Having learned her lesson, Alice vows to never sign and encrypt again. Instead, she will encrypt and then sign. Some time later, after Alice and Bob have resolved their earlier dispute, Alice discovers a solution to a difficult math problem and she wants to inform Bob. This time, her message is

$$M = \text{``Factoring is easy and I have assuredly found an admirable}$$
$$\text{algorithm, but the margin is too narrow to contain it.''}$$

which she then encrypts and signs

$$[\{M\}_{\text{Bob}}]_{\text{Alice}}$$

before sending to Bob.

However, Charlie, who is still angry with both Alice and Bob, has set himself up as a man-in-the-middle and he is able to intercept all traffic between Alice and Bob. Charlie uses Alice's public key to compute $\{M\}_{\text{Bob}}$, which he then signs

$$[\{M\}_{\text{Bob}}]_{\text{Charlie}}$$

and sends to Bob. When Bob receives the message, he verifies Charlie's signature and assumes that Charlie has made this astounding discovery. Bob immediately promotes Charlie. Note that in this scenario Charlie cannot read the message, but, regardless of the message, he can at least cause confusion.

In the first scenario, Charlie can be certain that Alice signed the message. However, Charlie does not know who encrypted the message (since encryption is a public key operation) and he cannot know whether or not he was the intended recipient of the original message.

In the second scenario, Bob can be certain that Charlie signed the message. However, this does not imply that Charlie encrypted the message (since encryption is a public key operation), or even that Charlie knows the content of the message.

In both of these scenarios, the public key operations were exploited, which illustrates a fundamental issue in public key cryptography, namely, that anyone can encrypt a message and anyone can verify a signature. The underlying problem in both scenarios is that the recipient is making assumptions about digital signatures that are not valid.

Now, let us examine the ElGamal signature scheme [44]. As with Diffie–Hellman, the security of ElGamal rests on the presumed intractability of the discrete logarithm problem.

Suppose that Alice wants to create a digital signature to protect the integrity of messages that she sends to Bob. To generate her private and public keys, Alice chooses a large prime p and a base s, where $2 \leq s \leq p - 2$. She then chooses a private key a, where $2 \leq a \leq p - 2$, and she computes $\alpha = s^a \pmod{p}$. Alice makes the triple (p, s, α) public.

Now suppose that Alice wants to sign a message $M \in \{0, 1, \ldots, p-1\}$. She first selects a random session key k, with $1 \leq k \leq p-2$ and $\gcd(k, p-1) = 1$. Alice then uses k to compute

$$r = s^k \pmod{p} \quad \text{and} \quad t = k^{-1}(M - ra) \pmod{(p-1)}.$$

The signed message consists of the triple (M, r, t), which Alice sends to Bob.

When Bob receives (M, r, t), he checks to see whether $1 \leq r \leq p-1$. If not, the signature is rejected. If this test is passed, Bob computes $v = s^M \pmod{p}$ and $w = \alpha^r \cdot r^t \pmod{p}$. If $v = w \pmod{p}$, the signed message is accepted and otherwise it is rejected.

Why does the ElGamal signature scheme work? Is this scheme secure? To answer the first question, suppose that Alice signs the message (M, r, t) as described above. Then we have $v = w \pmod{p}$, where

$$v = s^M \pmod{p} \quad \text{and} \quad w = \alpha^r \cdot r^t \pmod{p},$$

which follows from

$$
\begin{aligned}
w = \alpha^r \cdot r^t \pmod{p} &= (s^a)^r (s^k)^t \pmod{p} \\
&= s^{ra} \cdot s^{kk^{-1}(M-ra)} \pmod{p} \\
&= s^M \pmod{p} \\
&= v \pmod{p}.
\end{aligned}
$$

If the attacker Trudy is able to compute discrete logarithms efficiently, then she would be able to recover Alice's private key a from α. In order for Trudy to forge Alice's signature on a message M, she would need to find elements r and t such that $s^M = \alpha^r \cdot r^t$. It is not known whether this problem is equivalent to the computation of discrete logarithms. However, no efficient algorithm for this problem is known.

6.8.1   Mathematical Issues

As in the RSA cryptosystem, some care needs to be taken when using the
ElGamal signature scheme. We now give an overview of some mathematical
issues that arise with ElGamal.

If all of the prime factors of $p - 1$ are small, then there is an efficient
algorithm for computing discrete logarithms [83]. Consequently, at least one
of the prime factors of $p - 1$ must be "large."

Alice should use a "good" random number generator to create k. If Trudy
is able to guess k for a signed message (M, r, t), then she is able to compute $ra = M - kt \pmod{(p-1)}$. Since it is very likely that $\gcd(r, p - 1) = 1$,
Trudy can then readily obtain Alice's secret key a (see Problem 32).

Alice must use a different session key k for each signed message. To see
why this is the case, suppose Alice uses k to sign messages M and M', where
$M \neq M'$. Then Trudy can compute $t - t' = k^{-1}(M - M') \pmod{(p-1)}$ and,
thereby obtain k, since

$$k = (M - M')(t - t')^{-1} \pmod{(p-1)}.$$

Once Trudy has k, she can obtain Alice's secret key a (see Problem 33).

As with most other signature schemes, Alice should hash her message
and sign the hashed value. This is not just a matter of efficiency—if Alice
signs the message instead of its hash, Trudy can forge Alice's signature on a
message (see Problem 31). That is, Trudy can construct a message M and
valid signature (M, r, t). To accomplish this, Trudy first chooses b and c,
where $\gcd(c, p - 1) = 1$. She then sets $r = s^b \alpha^c \pmod{p}$ and computes the
value $t = -rc^{-1} \pmod{(p-1)}$. Finally, $M = -rbc^{-1} \pmod{(p-1)}$ yields a
valid signed message (M, r, t), since

$$\alpha^r \cdot r^t \pmod{p} = (s^a)^r \cdot (s^b \alpha^c)^{-rc^{-1}} \pmod{p}$$

$$= (s^{ar}) \cdot (s^b \cdot s^{ac})^{-rc^{-1}} \pmod{p}$$

$$= (s^{ar})(s^{-brc^{-1}})(s^{-ar}) \pmod{p}$$

$$= s^{-rbc^{-1}} \pmod{p}$$

$$= s^M \pmod{p}.$$

6.8.2   ElGamal Signature Conclusion

Since its invention, the ElGamal signature scheme has generated continued
interest within the cryptologic community. Research on the cryptosystem,
as well as real-world usage of ElGamal, continue to this day. In addition,
the ideas underlying ElGamal form the basis of other important signature
schemes such as the Digital Signature Standard (DSS) and the Schnorr signature scheme.

6.9   Summary

In this chapter, we briefly considered seven public key cryptosystems. The Merkle–Hellman knapsack provides a nice introduction to public key cryptography. After giving an overview of this cryptosystem, we presented Shamir's ingeniuous lattice-reduction attack on the knapsack. This attack clearly shows that the Merkle–Hellman knapsack is insecure and it also highlights the difficulty of finding secure trap door one-way functions for use in public key cryptography.

The Diffie–Hellman key exchange was then examined, along with a man-in-the-middle attack on the system. Our overview of the recently introduced Arithmetica key exchange illustrates the role of sophisticated mathematics in the design of public key cryptosystems. We also briefly described the heuristic (and probabilistic) length attack of Hughes and Tannenbaum on Arithmetica.

The de facto standard in public key cryptography, RSA, was presented. A few mathematical issues related to RSA were considered. The important practical issue of implementation attacks on RSA is discussed in some detail in Chapter 7.

The Rabin cryptosystem and an easily thwarted chosen ciphertext attack were discussed. The Rabin cipher is at least as secure as RSA, since breaking Rabin is mathematically equivalent to solving the factoring problem, and this is not known to be the case for RSA.

We then consider the NTRU cipher and we mentioned several attacks on it. Lastly, the ElGamal signature scheme was studied and some implementation issues were discussed.

6.10   Problems

1. Suppose that the published Diffie–Hellman prime and generator are given by $p = 37$ and $g = 6$, respectively. If Alice sends Bob the number $\alpha = 36$ and Bob sends $\beta = 31$ to Alice, find the key on which they agreed. What makes the recovery of this key so easy? From Alice and Bob's viewpoint, what would be a better choice of g?

2. In the Diffie–Hellman key exchange, g is chosen so that $2 \le g \le p - 2$. Why is $g = p - 1$ not a good choice?

3. In the text we mentioned that digital signatures can be used to prevent the man-in-the-middle attack on Diffie–Hellman. Suppose that Alice and Bob already share a symmetric key K before they begin the Diffie–Hellman procedure. Draw a diagram to illustrate a simple method Alice and Bob can use to prevent a man-in-the-middle attack.

4. Suppose that Alice and Bob each have a public–private key pair, and Alice and Bob encrypt all communications to and from each other. Trudy records all encrypted messages between Alice and Bob. Later, Trudy breaks into Alice and Bob's computers and steals Alice's private key and Bob's private key. If Trudy cannot decrypt the messages that she previously recorded, we say that Alice and Bob have perfect forward secrecy (PFS). Explain how Alice and Bob can use Diffie–Hellman to attain perfect forward secrecy. Hint: Use an *ephemeral Diffie–Hellman* exchange, where Alice forgets her secret exponent a after she no longer needs it and Bob forgets his secret exponent b after he no longer needs it. You must also prevent a man-in-the-middle attack.

5. Suppose that Alice and Bob share a 4-digit PIN,. Consider the authentication protocol below, where R_A is a random *challenge*, (or *nonce*) selected by Alice, and R_B is a random challenge selected by Bob. The *response* is $h(\text{"Bob"}, R_A, \text{PIN})$, which is sent in message two and is intended to authenticate Bob to Alice, since the creator of the message must know the PIN, and the nonce R_A prevents a replay attack. Similarly, message three is intended to authenticate Alice to Bob. However, if Trudy observes, say, the first two messages, she can do an offline PIN cracking attack. That is, Trudy can simply try each possible 4-digit PIN and easily determine Alice and Bob's shared PIN.

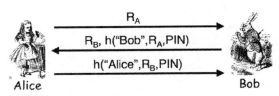

a. Slightly modify the protocol to make it resistant to an offline PIN-cracking attack. Note that Alice and Bob only share a PIN and no public/private key pairs are available. Hint: Use Diffie–Hellman, while preventing a man-in-the-middle attack.

b. Why are the identifiers "Bob" and "Alice" necessary in the second and third messages, respectively?

6. For S_3, the symmetric group on three elements, the underlying set consists of the permutations on three elements. Show that S_3 has the following finite presentation:

$$S_3 = \langle x, y \mid x^3, y^2, (xy)^2 \rangle.$$

7. Show that S_3 (see Problem 6) can be interpreted as the set of rigid motions of an equilateral triangle in 3-space.

8. Is the Arithmetica key exchange susceptible to a man-in-the-middle attack? Why or why not?

9. Use the Euclidean Algorithm to find the greatest common divisor of 12,345 and 67,890.

10. Suppose 1500 soldiers arrive in training camp. A few soldiers desert the camp. The drill sergeants divide the remaining soldiers into groups of five and discover that there is one left over. When they divide them into groups of seven, there are three left over, and when they divide them into groups of eleven, there are again three left over. Determine the number of deserters.

11. In the RSA cryptosystem, it is possible that $M = C$, that is, the plaintext and the ciphertext are identical. For modulus $N = 3127$ and encryption exponent $e = 17$, find a message M that encrypts to itself.

12. Suppose that Bob uses the following variant of RSA: He chooses N and two encryption exponents e_1 and e_2. He asks Alice to encrypt her message M to him by first computing $C_1 = M^{e_1} \pmod{N}$, then encrypting C_1 to get $C_2 = C_1^{e_2} \pmod{N}$. Alice then sends C_2 to Bob. Does this double encryption increase the security over single encryption? Why or why not?

13. Alice uses RSA to receive a single ciphertext C (encrypted using her public key), corresponding to plaintext M from Bob. To tease her nemesis, Alice challenges Trudy to recover M. Alice sends C to Trudy and agrees to decrypt one ciphertext from Trudy, as long as it is not C, and return the result. Is it possible for Trudy to recover M?

14. Suppose $N = pq$ with p and q prime. Let e be the corresponding RSA public encryption exponent and d the private decryption exponent. Use the fact that

$$(M^e)^d = M \pmod{p} \quad \text{and} \quad (M^e)^d = M \pmod{q}$$

to show that

$$(M^e)^d = M \pmod{N}.$$

15. Let (e_1, N) and (e_2, N) be the RSA public keys of Alice and Bob, respectively. Using the attack discussed in Section 6.5.1 beginning on page 287, write a computer program to show that Alice can read encrypted messages which are sent to Bob (and vice-versa).

16. Construct a specific example that illustrates the cube root attack discussed in Section 6.5.1. Does this mean that a small encryption exponent e should never be used in RSA? Why or why not?

17. Let p be prime. Suppose that a and b are integers with $ab = 0 \pmod{p}$. Show that either $a = 0 \pmod{p}$ or $b = 0 \pmod{p}$.

18. Let $p = 3 \pmod{4}$ be prime. Show that $x^2 = -1 \pmod{p}$ has no solutions. Hint: Suppose that x exists. Raise both sides to the power $(p-1)/2$ and use Euler's Theorem.

19. Let $p = 3 \pmod{4}$ be prime. Using Problem 18, show that $x^2 = \pm y$ cannot occur simultaneously. Hint: Assume that $y = a^2 \pmod{p}$ and that $-y = b^2 \pmod{p}$ and reach a contradiction.

20. For the Rabin cryptosystem, write a computer program to calculate the square roots of C, modulo a prime p. Assume that $p = 3 \pmod{4}$.

21. Let $N = pq$, where p and q are distinct primes. Give an example to show that if p divides C and q does not divide C, then there are two (and not four) distinct square roots of C in Z_N.

22. Set up a Rabin encryption scheme for Alice, by generating a public–private key pair. Playing the role of Bob, choose a suitable plaintext and encrypt it. Now, playing the role of Alice, decrypt the ciphertext message.

23. Construct an example that illustrates a chosen-ciphertext attack on the Rabin cryptosystem, as discussed in Section 6.6.1.

24. In the NTRU cipher, the encryption and decryption processes use the associative, commutative and distributive properties of "+" and "$\star$". Verify that these properties are valid in

$$R = \frac{Z[X]}{(X^N - 1)}.$$

25. For NTRU, write a computer program to perform the operations of addition and multiplication, mod $(X^N - 1)$, in R. Use your program to verify the first example given in Section 6.7.

26. In NTRU, suppose that (f, g) is Alice's secret key which she uses for decryption. Show that Alice can also use $(f/x^i, g/x^i)$ to decrypt messages.

27. In the NTRU cipher, Alice must keep both f and g secret. Suppose that Trudy discovers g. How can she use this knowledge to decrypt messages sent to Alice?

28. Consider the multiple transmission attack against NTRU discussed in Section 6.7.2. Suppose that each r_i is a polynomial of degree four or less and

$$r_1(x) - r_0(x) = -1 + x - 2x^3 + x^4$$
$$r_2(x) - r_0(x) = x + x^2$$
$$r_3(x) - r_0(x) = -2 + x + 2x^2 - x^3 + x^4.$$

   a. Determine as many coefficients of $r_0(x)$ as you can.

   b. Give a general procedure for determining the coefficients of $r_0(x)$ from a set of polynomials of the form $r_i(x) - r_0(x)$.

29. Suppose we select NTRU parameters are $N = 11$, $q = 32$, $p = 7$, and the sets of polynomials are given by $L_f = L(4,3)$, $L_g = L(3,3)$, and $L_r = L(3,3)$. Suppose Alice chooses

$$f(x) = -1 + x + x^2 - x^4 + x^6 + x^9 - x^{10} \in L_f$$
$$g(x) = -1 + x^2 + x^3 + x^5 - x^8 - x^{10} \in L_g.$$

Then

$$f_q(x) = 5 + 9x + 6x^2 + 16x^3 + 4x^4 + 15x^5 + 16x^6 + 22x^7$$
$$+ 20x^8 + 18x^9 + 30x^{10}.$$

Recall that NTRU decryption does not always succeed.

   a. Use the algorithm in Table 6.3 to find $f_p(x)$. Give Alice's public and private keys.

   b. Give an example of a message $M_0(x) \in L_m$, and the corresponding ciphertext $C_0(x)$ obtained by encrypting $M_0(x)$ with Alice's public key, such that $C_0(x)$ decrypts to $M_0(x)$ using Alice's private key.

   c. If possible, give a message $M_1(x) \in L_m$, and the corresponding ciphertext $C_1(x)$ obtained by encrypting $M_1(x)$ with Alice's public key, such that $C_1(x)$ does not decrypt to $M_1(x)$ using Alice's private key.

30. Write a computer program to implement the meet-in-the-middle attack on the NTRU cipher. To verify that your program is working, it should output the recovered key as well as the approximate number of operations performed and computation time.

31. Set up an ElGamal signature scheme for Alice.

   a. Assume that Alice pre-processes her messages with a hash function before signing them. Generate an ElGamal signed message from Alice. Playing the role of Bob, verify the signed message.

b. Now, assume that Alice does not pre-process her messages before signing them. Playing the role of the attacker Trudy, forge a signed message.

32. If Trudy can guess the session key k in the ElGamal signature scheme, she can recover Alice's secret key a. Construct a specific example that illustrates this implementation attack, as discussed in Section 6.8.1.

33. In the ElGamal signature scheme, a different session key must be used for each signed message. If k is used to sign multiple messages, then an implementation attack can be initiated, as described in Section 6.8.1. Construct an example to illustrate this attack.

Chapter 7

Public Key Attacks

There is always more spirit in attack than in defence.
— Titus Livius

7.1 Introduction

In this chapter, we cover some attacks on public key systems in detail. The most widely used public key cryptosystems rely on the difficulty of factoring (RSA) and the discrete log problem (Diffie–Hellman and ElGamal). So we first discuss factoring algorithms and algorithms for solving the discrete log problem. These represent fundamental attacks on the underpinnings of the most widely used public key systems. These attacks are roughly the public key equivalents of an exhaustive key search attack on a symmetric cipher.

Then we present a fascinating set of attacks on RSA that are, in a sense, the polar opposite of factoring, since these do not directly attack the RSA algorithm. Instead, these attacks take advantage of implementation issues that, under some circumstances, allow an attacker to recover the private key without breaking the RSA algorithm per se. First, we discuss three different timing attacks on RSA. These attacks are examples of *side-channel attacks*, where an attacker gains information about an underlying computation which, in turn, leaks information about the key. Such attacks have dramatically changed the nature of cryptanalysis and the development of cryptography in general.

We also discuss a devastating *glitching attack* on RSA, where a single induced error can enable an attacker to recover the private key. This attack, which is an example of a *fault induction* attack [107], is amazing and amazingly simple.

Implementation attacks have more than proven their value in the cryptanalysis of smartcards. In fact, in any scenario where the attacker has physical access to the crypto device holding the key, such attacks are a serious threat. Consequently, these attacks are certain to play a role in the emerging field of trusted computing [4, 48]. A practical timing attack has recently been developed which can be used to recover an RSA private key from a Web server [22]. This particular attack is covered in Section 7.4.

7.2   Factoring Algorithms

> *The obvious mathematical breakthrough*
> *would be development of an easy way to factor large prime numbers.*
> — Bill Gates [56]

The RSA public key cryptosystem is the "gold standard" by which all other public key systems are measured. The security of RSA is thought to rest squarely on the difficulty of factoring large integers.[1] More precisely, given N, where $N = pq$, with p and q prime, if we can determine p or q, then we can break RSA. Consequently, a tremendous amount of effort has been devoted to developing efficient factoring methods.

In this section we consider several integer factorization methods. First, we briefly discuss the obvious approach, that is, trial division by numbers up to $\sqrt{N}$. Then we present Dixon's Algorithm, followed by the quadratic sieve, which is a refinement of Dixon's Algorithm. Like trial division, these algorithms are guaranteed to find the factors of N, provided enough computing power is available. The quadratic sieve is the best available factoring algorithm for numbers having about 110 decimal digits or less, and it has been used to successfully factor numbers with about 130 decimal digits. For integers with more than about 110 decimal digits, the number field sieve reigns supreme, and we briefly mention this more complex factoring method at the end of this section.

7.2.1   Trial Division

Given a composite integer N, one obvious way to factor it is to simply try to divide it by each of the numbers

$$2, 3, 5, 7, 9, 11, \ldots, \lfloor \sqrt{N} \rfloor.$$

Any of these that divides N is a factor. The work required is on the order of $\sqrt{N}/2$.

---

[1]In contrast to RSA, the security of the Rabin cryptosystem is easily proven to be equivalent to factoring.

We can improve on this simple method by only testing the prime numbers up to $\sqrt{N}$, instead of testing all odd integers. In this case, the work factor is on the order of $\pi(\sqrt{N})$, where $\pi(x)$ is the function that counts the number of primes less than or equal to x, assuming we can efficiently generate the required primes. For large N, the approximation $\pi(N) \approx N/\ln(N)$ holds. Consequently, the work to factor N by trial division is, at best, on the order of $N/\ln(N)$.

7.2.2 Dixon's Algorithm

Suppose we want to factor the integer N. If we find integers x and y such that $N = x^2 - y^2$, then $N = (x - y)(x + y)$ and we have found factors of N. More generally, suppose we can find x and y such that $x^2 - y^2$ is a multiple of N, that is,

$$x^2 = y^2 \ (\text{mod} \ N). \tag{7.1}$$

Then $x^2 - y^2 = kN$ for some $k \neq 0$, so that $(x - y)(x + y) = kN$, which implies that N divides the product $(x - y)(x + y)$. If we are unlucky, we could have $x - y = k$ and $x + y = N$ (or vice versa), but with a probability of at least $1/2$ we can obtain a factor of N [40]. If this is the case, then $\gcd(N, x - y)$ and $\gcd(N, x + y)$ reveal factors of N.

For example, since $100 = 9 \ (\text{mod} \ 91)$, we have $10^2 = 3^2 \ (\text{mod} \ 91)$ and hence

$$(10 - 3)(10 + 3) = (7)(13) = 0 \ (\text{mod} \ 91).$$

Since $91 = 7 \cdot 13$, we have obtained the factors of 91. However, in general we must compute $\gcd(x - y, N)$ or $\gcd(x + y, N)$ to obtain a factor of N. To see that the gcd is necessary, consider $34^2 = 8^2 \ (\text{mod} \ 91)$. In this example, we have $26 \cdot 42 = 0 \ (\text{mod} \ 91)$ and the factors of 91 are found by computing $\gcd(26, 91) = 13$ and $\gcd(42, 91) = 7$.

Since the gcd is easy to compute (using the Euclidean Algorithm), we can factor N provided we can find x and y satisfying (7.1). But finding such x and y is difficult. We can relax these conditions somewhat, thereby making it easier to find the required pair of values. For example,

$$41^2 = 32 \ (\text{mod} \ 1649) \ \text{ and } \ 43^2 = 200 \ (\text{mod} \ 1649) \tag{7.2}$$

and neither 32 nor 200 is a square. However, if we multiply these two equations, we find

$$41^2 \cdot 43^2 = 32 \cdot 200 = 6400 \ (\text{mod} \ 1649), \tag{7.3}$$

which yields

$$(41 \cdot 43)^2 = 80^2 \ (\text{mod} \ 1649),$$

and we have obtained the much-coveted congruence of squares. We have that $41 \cdot 43 = 114 \ (\text{mod} \ 1649)$ and $114 - 80 = 34$. In this example, we find a factor of 1649 from the gcd computation $\gcd(34, 1649) = 17$. It is easily verified that $1649 = 17 \cdot 97$.

In (7.3), we combined two nonsquares to obtain a square. To see why this works in this particular case, note that

$$32 = 2^5 \cdot 5^0 \quad \text{and} \quad 200 = 2^3 \cdot 5^2,$$

so that the product is given by

$$32 \cdot 200 = 2^8 \cdot 5^2 = (2^4 \cdot 5^1)^2 = 80^2.$$

This example illustrates that we can obtain a perfect square from non-square congruence relations such as those in (7.2). To find these perfect squares, we only need to concern ourselves with the powers in the prime factorization of the relations under consideration. Also, by properties of exponentiation, the corresponding powers add when we multiply terms. Furthermore, any time we multiply terms and all of the resulting powers are even, we obtain a perfect square. Consequently, we only need to be concerned with whether the powers are even or odd, that is, we only need to know the powers modulo 2.

We can associate each number with a vector of the powers in its prime factorization, and we obtain a perfect square by multiplying corresponding terms whenever the sum of these vectors contain only even numbers. In the example above we have

$$32 \to \begin{bmatrix} 5 \\ 0 \end{bmatrix} = \begin{bmatrix} 1 \\ 0 \end{bmatrix} \pmod{2},$$

where the numbers in the vector represent the powers of the prime factors 2 and 5, respectively, in the prime decomposition of 32. Similarly,

$$200 \to \begin{bmatrix} 3 \\ 2 \end{bmatrix} = \begin{bmatrix} 1 \\ 0 \end{bmatrix} \pmod{2}.$$

The product therefore satisfies

$$32 \cdot 200 \to \begin{bmatrix} 8 \\ 2 \end{bmatrix} = \begin{bmatrix} 0 \\ 0 \end{bmatrix} \pmod{2}.$$

Since the powers are all even, we know that $32 \cdot 200$ is a perfect square modulo 1649. Furthermore, from (7.2), we know that this square is equal to $(41 \cdot 43)^2 \pmod{1649}$, giving us the desired congruence of squares. While the actual powers are required to determine the value that is squared (80 in this example), to determine whether or not we have a congruence of squares, we only require the mod 2 vectors of powers.

We can multiply any number of relations to obtain a perfect square. Also, the number of distinct primes in the factorizations of the numbers under consideration determines the size of the vectors. Since we ultimately want to factor large numbers, it is imperative that we keep the vectors small. Consequently, we will choose a bound B and a set of primes, where each prime is less than B. This set of primes is our *factor base*. While all primes in the factor base are less than B, generally not every such prime will be included in the factor base (see Problem 7).

A number that factors completely over the given factor base is said to be *B-smooth*. Smooth relations (or, more precisely, B-smooth relations) are those relations that factor completely over the factor base. By restricting our attention to B-smooth relations, we restrict the size of the vectors of powers. The fewer elements in the factor base, the smaller the vectors that we need to deal with (which is good), but the harder it is to find B-smooth values (which is bad).

An example should illustrate the idea. Suppose we want to factor the integer $N = 1829$ and we choose $B = 15$, as in the example given in [92]. Since we want numbers with small factors, it is advantageous to deal with modular numbers between $-N/2$ and $N/2$, instead of in the range 0 to $N-1$. This creates a slight complication, since we must include -1 in our factor base, but this is easily managed. In this example, $B = 15$ and we take

$$-1, 2, 3, 5, 7, 11, 13$$

as our factor base.

Now we could simply select a random r and check whether $r^2 \pmod{N}$ is B-smooth, repeating this until we have obtained a sufficient number of B-smooth values. Instead, we use a slightly more systematic approach. We select the values $\lfloor \sqrt{kN} \rfloor$ and $\lceil \sqrt{kN} \rceil$, for $k = 1, 2, 3, 4$, and test whether the square of each, modulo 1829, is B-smooth. For this example we obtain

$$42^2 = 1764 = -65 = -1 \cdot 5 \cdot 13 \pmod{1829}$$
$$43^2 = 20 = 2^2 \cdot 5 \pmod{1829}$$
$$60^2 = 1771 = -58 = -1 \cdot 2 \cdot 29 \pmod{1829}$$
$$61^2 = 63 = 3^2 \cdot 7 \pmod{1829}$$
$$74^2 = 1818 = -11 = -1 \cdot 11 \pmod{1829}$$
$$75^2 = 138 = 2 \cdot 3 \cdot 23 \pmod{1829}$$
$$85^2 = 1738 = -91 = -1 \cdot 7 \cdot 13 \pmod{1829}$$
$$86^2 = 80 = 2^4 \cdot 5 \pmod{1829}.$$

All of these values are B-smooth except for 60^2 and 75^2, giving us six useful relations.

For each of the six B-smooth values we obtain a mod 2 vector of of length seven, where the first entry represents the sign bit (1 represents "$-$", while 0 represents "+") and the remaining positions correspond to the factor base elements $2, 3, 5, 7, 11$, and 13, respectively. In this case, we have

$$42^2 = -65 \rightarrow \begin{bmatrix} 1 \\ 0 \\ 0 \\ 1 \\ 0 \\ 0 \\ 1 \end{bmatrix}, \; 43^2 = 20 \rightarrow \begin{bmatrix} 0 \\ 0 \\ 0 \\ 1 \\ 0 \\ 0 \\ 0 \end{bmatrix}, \; 61^2 = 63 \rightarrow \begin{bmatrix} 0 \\ 0 \\ 0 \\ 0 \\ 1 \\ 0 \\ 0 \end{bmatrix} \quad (7.4)$$

and

$$74^2 = -11 \rightarrow \begin{bmatrix} 1 \\ 0 \\ 0 \\ 0 \\ 0 \\ 1 \\ 0 \end{bmatrix}, \; 85^2 = -91 \rightarrow \begin{bmatrix} 1 \\ 0 \\ 0 \\ 0 \\ 1 \\ 0 \\ 1 \end{bmatrix}, \; 86^2 = 80 \rightarrow \begin{bmatrix} 0 \\ 0 \\ 0 \\ 1 \\ 0 \\ 0 \\ 0 \end{bmatrix}. \quad (7.5)$$

Any combination of these vectors that sum to the zero vector, modulo 2, will yield the desired modular squares and, with high probability, a factor of N. Note that the sign bits must also sum to 0 modulo 2, since an even number of sign bits imply that the product is positive. In this example, we can sum the vectors corresponding to 42^2, 43^2, 61^2, and 85^2, modulo 2, to obtain the zero vector, since

$$\begin{bmatrix} 1 \\ 0 \\ 0 \\ 1 \\ 0 \\ 0 \\ 1 \end{bmatrix} \oplus \begin{bmatrix} 0 \\ 0 \\ 0 \\ 1 \\ 0 \\ 0 \\ 0 \end{bmatrix} \oplus \begin{bmatrix} 0 \\ 0 \\ 0 \\ 0 \\ 1 \\ 0 \\ 0 \end{bmatrix} \oplus \begin{bmatrix} 1 \\ 0 \\ 0 \\ 0 \\ 1 \\ 0 \\ 1 \end{bmatrix} = \begin{bmatrix} 0 \\ 0 \\ 0 \\ 0 \\ 0 \\ 0 \\ 0 \end{bmatrix}.$$

This yields the congruence

$$\begin{aligned} 42^2 \cdot 43^2 \cdot 61^2 \cdot 85^2 &= (-65) \cdot 20 \cdot 63 \cdot (-91) \\ &= (-1 \cdot 5 \cdot 13) \cdot (2^2 \cdot 5) \cdot (3^2 \cdot 7) \cdot (-1 \cdot 7 \cdot 13) \\ &= 2^2 \cdot 3^2 \cdot 5^2 \cdot 7^2 \cdot 13^2 \pmod{1829}, \end{aligned}$$

which can be rewritten as

$$(42 \cdot 43 \cdot 61 \cdot 85)^2 = (2 \cdot 3 \cdot 5 \cdot 7 \cdot 13)^2 \pmod{1829}.$$

This simplifies to

$$1459^2 = 901^2 \pmod{1829}$$

and, since $1459 - 901 = 558$, we determine the factor 31 of 1829 via the calculation of $\gcd(558, 1829) = 31$, which can be computed efficiently using the Euclidean Algorithm. It is easily verified that $1829 = 59 \cdot 31$.

This example raises a few questions. For example, can we be sure of obtaining a solution? And, if so, how many relations are required before we can be certain of obtaining a solution? These questions can be answered positively with some basic linear algebra.

While in the example above we found a solution by simply "eyeballing" the vectors in (7.4) and (7.5), a more systematic approach is possible. Let M be the matrix with columns given by the vectors in (7.4) and (7.5). Then a solution is given by any vector x satisfying $Mx = 0 \pmod 2$, that is the 1s in x determine which of the vectors in (7.4) and (7.5) to sum to obtain a mod 2 sum equal to the 0 vector. In linear algebra terms, we seek a linear combination of the columns of M that sum to 0, that is, we seek a linearly dependent set of columns. In the example above, we want to find a solution $(x_0, x_1, \ldots, x_5)$ to the matrix equation

$$\begin{bmatrix} 1 & 0 & 0 & 1 & 1 & 0 \\ 0 & 0 & 0 & 0 & 0 & 0 \\ 0 & 0 & 0 & 0 & 0 & 0 \\ 1 & 1 & 0 & 0 & 0 & 1 \\ 0 & 0 & 1 & 0 & 1 & 0 \\ 0 & 0 & 0 & 1 & 0 & 0 \\ 1 & 0 & 0 & 0 & 1 & 0 \end{bmatrix} \begin{bmatrix} x_0 \\ x_1 \\ x_2 \\ x_3 \\ x_4 \\ x_5 \end{bmatrix} = \begin{bmatrix} 0 \\ 0 \\ 0 \\ 0 \\ 0 \\ 0 \\ 0 \end{bmatrix} \pmod 2.$$

In general, if n is the number of elements in the factor base (including -1), then n is also the number of elements in each column vector, and, therefore, the matrix M has n rows. It is a theorem from linear algebra that if there are at least $n + 1$ columns in M, then we can find a linearly dependent collection of the columns. Furthermore, this can be done efficiently using standard techniques from linear algebra. This implies that with with $n + 1$ or more B-smooth relations, we will obtain a congruence of squares and thereby, with a high probability, a factor of N. Note that in the example above, $n = 7$ and we only had six relations. In this case, we were lucky since we did find a solution, although we lacked a sufficient number of relations to be guaranteed of doing so.

In effect, we have reduced the problem of factoring to the problem of finding a sufficient number of B-smooth relations and then solving a system of linear equations, modulo 2. Dixon's Algorithm, as given in Table 7.1, uses a very simple approach to find the necessary B-smooth relations, while the

Table 7.1: Outline of Dixon's Algorithm

// Given integer N, find a nontrivial factor
Select B and factor base of primes less than B
$n =$ number of elements in factor base (including -1)
// Find relations
$m = 0$
while $m \leq n$
    $y = r^2 \pmod{N}$ // r can be selected at random
    if y factors completely over the factor base **then**
        Save mod 2 exponent vector of y
        Save r^2 and y
        $m = m + 1$
    end if
end while
// Solve the linear system
$M =$ matrix of mod 2 exponent vectors
Solve $Mx = 0 \pmod{2}$ for vector $x = (x_0, x_1, \ldots, x_n)$
$I = \{i \mid x_i = 1\}$
We have congruence of squares: $\prod_I r_i^2 = \prod_I y_i \pmod{N}$
Compute required gcd and check for nontrivial factor of N

---

quadratic sieve (discussed in Section 7.2.3) uses a more efficient but more complex approach.

It is worth emphasizing that by increasing B, we can find B-smooth relations more easily, but the size of the vectors will increase, making the resulting linear algebra problem more difficult to solve. Determining an optimal B is challenging since it depends, among other things, on the efficiency of the implementation of the various steps of the algorithm. Another interesting feature of this factoring algorithm is that the problem of finding B-smooth relations is reasonably parallel, since given k different computers, each can test a disjoint subset of random values r for B-smoothness. However, the linear equation solving is not parallel.

In the next section we describe the quadratic sieve factoring algorithm, which is a refinement of Dixon's Algorithm. The quadratic sieve is the fastest known algorithm for factoring large integers up to about 110 to 115 decimal digits. Beyond that point, the number field sieve is superior. We briefly mention the number field sieve before leaving the topic of factoring. Then in Section 7.3 we consider algorithms for solving the discrete log problem. Some of these discrete log algorithms use similar techniques to the factoring algorithms considered below.

7.2.3   Quadratic Sieve

The quadratic sieve (QS) factoring algorithm is essentially Dixon's Algorithm on steroids. In particular, finding B-smooth relations is beefed up in QS as compared to the more-or-less random approach followed in Dixon's Algorithm. In both algorithms, the linear algebra is identical, so here we ignore the linear algebra phase. In this section, we assume that the reader is familiar with Dixon's Algorithm, as presented in Section 7.2.2.

As in Dixon's Algorithm, we first choose a bound B and a factor base containing primes less than B. Given this factor base, we must find a sufficient number of B-smooth relations.

Define the polynomial

$$Q(x) = (\lfloor \sqrt{N} \rfloor + x)^2 - N. \tag{7.6}$$

We use this quadratic polynomial to generate the values to be tested for B-smoothness. The word "quadratic" in quadratic sieve comes from the fact that $Q(x)$ is a quadratic polynomial.

To obtain smooth relations, we choose an interval containing 0, say, $[-M, M]$, and for every integer $x \in [-M, M]$ we compute $y = Q(x)$. Then, modulo N, we have $y = \tilde{x}^2$, where $\tilde{x} = \lfloor \sqrt{N} \rfloor + x$. Consequently, we are in the same situation as with Dixon's Algorithm, that is, we test whether y is B-smooth and, if so, we save the mod 2 exponent vector for the linear equation solving phase. The advantage of QS over Dixon's Algorithm arises from the fact that we can sieve, as described below. Sieving greatly reduces the work factor.

A variety of tricks are used to speed up the relation-finding part of the QS algorithm—the most significant of these is a sieving method. That is, the QS algorithm utilizes a method whereby the smooth numbers eventually "fall through" while the non-smooth numbers are filtered out. The process is somewhat analogous to the sieve of Eratosthenes [25], which is used to find all primes less than a given bound. Before discussing the sieve used in the QS algorithm, we review the sieve of Eratosthenes.

Suppose that we want to find all primes less than 31. First, we list all of the numbers 2 through 30:

$$
\begin{array}{cccccccccc}
& 2 & 3 & 4 & 5 & 6 & 7 & 8 & 9 & 10 \\
11 & 12 & 13 & 14 & 15 & 16 & 17 & 18 & 19 & 20 \\
21 & 22 & 23 & 24 & 25 & 26 & 27 & 28 & 29 & 30.
\end{array}
\tag{7.7}
$$

Then we cross out every other number beginning with 4, since all of these have a factor of 2. Next, we cross out every third number beginning with 6, since these all have a factor of 3, and so on. At each step, the smallest number not yet considered that has not been crossed out must be prime, and we remove all factors of that number from the list.

For the numbers in (7.7), we begin by marking every number in the list that has a factor of 2 (other than 2 itself). This is easily accomplished by simply marking every other number with "—", beginning from 4, to obtain

$$
\begin{array}{cccccccccc}
2 & 3 & \cancel{4} & 5 & \cancel{6} & 7 & \cancel{8} & 9 & \cancel{10} \\
11 & \cancel{12} & 13 & \cancel{14} & 15 & \cancel{16} & 17 & \cancel{18} & 19 & \cancel{20} \\
21 & \cancel{22} & 23 & \cancel{24} & 25 & \cancel{26} & 27 & \cancel{28} & 29 & \cancel{30}.
\end{array}
$$

The next unmarked number after 2, which is 3, must be prime. To remove all numbers with a factor of 3 (other than 3 itself), we mark every third number, beginning from 6, with "/" to obtain

$$
\begin{array}{cccccccccc}
2 & 3 & 4 & 5 & \cancel{6} & 7 & 8 & \cancel{9} & 10 \\
11 & \cancel{12} & 13 & 14 & \cancel{15} & 16 & 17 & \cancel{18} & 19 & 20 \\
\cancel{21} & 22 & 23 & \cancel{24} & 25 & 26 & \cancel{27} & 28 & 29 & \cancel{30}.
\end{array}
$$

The next unmarked number, 5, must be prime, so we mark every fifth number beginning from 10 with "\", giving

$$
\begin{array}{cccccccccc}
2 & 3 & 4 & 5 & \cancel{6} & 7 & 8 & \cancel{9} & \cancel{10} \\
11 & \cancel{12} & 13 & 14 & \cancel{15} & 16 & 17 & \cancel{18} & 19 & \cancel{20} \\
\cancel{21} & 22 & 23 & \cancel{24} & \cancel{25} & 26 & \cancel{27} & 28 & 29 & \cancel{30}.
\end{array}
$$

Continuing, we mark numbers having a factor of 7 with "|",

$$
\begin{array}{cccccccccc}
2 & 3 & 4 & 5 & \cancel{6} & 7 & 8 & \cancel{9} & \cancel{10} \\
11 & \cancel{12} & 13 & \cancel{14} & \cancel{15} & 16 & 17 & \cancel{18} & 19 & \cancel{20} \\
\cancel{21} & 22 & 23 & \cancel{24} & \cancel{25} & 26 & \cancel{27} & \cancel{28} & 29 & \cancel{30}
\end{array}
$$

and numbers having a factor of 11 are marked with "‖",

$$
\begin{array}{cccccccccc}
2 & 3 & 4 & 5 & \cancel{6} & 7 & 8 & \cancel{9} & \cancel{10} \\
11 & \cancel{12} & 13 & \cancel{14} & \cancel{15} & 16 & 17 & \cancel{18} & 19 & \cancel{20} \\
\cancel{21} & \cancel{22} & 23 & \cancel{24} & \cancel{25} & 26 & \cancel{27} & \cancel{28} & 29 & \cancel{30}
\end{array}
$$

and, finally, numbers with a factor of 13 are marked with "∩",

$$
\begin{array}{cccccccccc}
2 & 3 & 4 & 5 & \cancel{6} & 7 & 8 & \cancel{9} & \cancel{10} \\
11 & \cancel{12} & 13 & \cancel{14} & \cancel{15} & 16 & 17 & \cancel{18} & 19 & \cancel{20} \\
\cancel{21} & \cancel{22} & 23 & \cancel{24} & \cancel{25} & \cancel{26} & \cancel{27} & \cancel{28} & 29 & \cancel{30}.
\end{array}
$$

(7.8)

Since the next unmarked number is 17, which is greater than $30/2$, we are finished. The primes less than 31, namely,

$$2, 3, 5, 7, 11, 13, 17, 19, 23, 29$$

have passed through the "sieve."

While the sieve of Eratosthenes gives us the primes, it also provides considerable information on the non-primes in the list, since the marks through any given number tell us the prime factors of the number. However, the marks do not tell us the power to which a given prime factor occurs. For example, in (7.8), the number 24 is marked with "—" and "/", so we know that it is divisible by 2 (due to the "—") and 3 (due to the "/"), but from this information we do not know that 24 has a factor of 2^3.

Now suppose that instead of crossing out the numbers, we divide out the factors (here, we also divide the prime by itself). Then, beginning again from

$$
\begin{array}{cccccccccc}
2 & 3 & 4 & 5 & 6 & 7 & 8 & 9 & 10 \\
11 & 12 & 13 & 14 & 15 & 16 & 17 & 18 & 19 & 20 \\
21 & 22 & 23 & 24 & 25 & 26 & 27 & 28 & 29 & 30
\end{array}
$$

after dividing every other number by 2, beginning from 2, we have

$$
\begin{array}{cccccccccc}
\underline{1} & 3 & \underline{2} & 5 & \underline{3} & 7 & \underline{4} & 9 & \underline{5} \\
11 & \underline{6} & 13 & \underline{7} & 15 & \underline{8} & 17 & \underline{9} & 19 & \underline{10} \\
21 & \underline{11} & 23 & \underline{12} & 25 & \underline{13} & 27 & \underline{14} & 29 & \underline{15}
\end{array}
$$

where the numbers that were divided by 2 at this step are underlined. Next, we divide every third number by 3, beginning with 3 (again, underlining the numbers that were divided at this step), to obtain

$$
\begin{array}{cccccccccc}
1 & \underline{1} & 2 & 5 & \underline{1} & 7 & 4 & \underline{3} & 5 \\
11 & \underline{2} & 13 & 7 & \underline{5} & 8 & 17 & \underline{3} & 19 & 10 \\
\underline{7} & 11 & 23 & \underline{4} & 25 & 13 & \underline{9} & 14 & 29 & \underline{5}.
\end{array}
$$

Then we divide every fifth number by 5, beginning with 5,

$$
\begin{array}{cccccccccc}
1 & 1 & 2 & \underline{1} & 1 & 7 & 4 & 3 & \underline{1} \\
11 & 2 & 13 & 7 & \underline{1} & 8 & 17 & 3 & 19 & \underline{2} \\
7 & 11 & 23 & 4 & \underline{5} & 13 & 9 & 14 & 29 & \underline{1}.
\end{array}
$$

Dividing every seventh number by 7 yields

$$
\begin{array}{cccccccccc}
1 & 1 & 2 & 1 & 1 & \underline{1} & 4 & 3 & 1 \\
11 & 2 & 13 & \underline{1} & 1 & 8 & 17 & 3 & 19 & 2 \\
\underline{1} & 11 & 23 & 4 & 5 & 13 & 9 & \underline{2} & 29 & 1
\end{array}
$$

and suppose that we stop at this point. Then the numbers that correspond to the positions now occupied by the 1s in this array are 7-smooth, that is, they have no prime factors greater than 7. However, some of the numbers that correspond to non-1s are also 7-smooth, such as 28, which is represented by the number 2 in the last row. The problem here is that we need to divide by the highest prime power at each step, which slightly complicates the sieving. This is essentially the principle—with some significant computational refinements—that is followed in the QS algorithm to obtain B-smooth relations.

It is costly to test each candidate $Q(x)$ for B-smoothness by trial division. Suppose that we find that the prime p, where p is in the factor base, divides $Q(x)$. Then it is easy to verify that p also divides $Q(x + kp)$, for any $k \neq 0$ (see Problem 6). That is, once we determine that $Q(x)$ is divisible by p, we know that Q of each of the following

$$\ldots, x - 2p, x - p, x, x + p, x + 2p, \ldots$$

is also divisible by p, so we can save the work of testing whether each of these Q values is divisible by p. By repeating this for other choices of x and other primes in the factor base, we can eventually "sieve" out the B-smooth integers in the interval $[-M, M]$. This process is somewhat analogous to the sieve of Eratosthenes, as discussed above. This sieving process is where the "sieve" in quadratic sieve comes from.

Sieving in the most costly part of the QS algorithm, and several tricks are used to speed up the process. For example, suppose $y = Q(x)$ is divisible by p. Then $y = 0 \pmod{p}$ and from the definition of Q, we have

$$(x + \lfloor \sqrt{N} \rfloor)^2 = N \pmod{p}. \tag{7.9}$$

Therefore, given p in our factor base, we can compute the square roots of $N \pmod{p}$, say, s_p and $p - s_p$, and use these to immediately determine the sequence of values of $x \in [-M, M]$ such that the corresponding $Q(x)$ are divisible by p. Since there exists an efficient algorithm (the Shanks–Tonelli Algorithm [131]) for finding the square roots implied by (7.9), this approach is efficient.

The actual sieving could proceed as follows. Create an array containing the values $Q(x)$, for $x = -M, -M + 1, \ldots, -1, 0, 1, \ldots, M - 1, M$. For the first prime p in the factor base, generate the sequence of $x \in [-M, M]$ that are divisible by p, as described in the previous paragraph. For each of these, we know that the corresponding array element is divisible by p, so determine the highest power of p that divides the array element, and store this power, reduced modulo 2, in a vector of powers corresponding to the given array element. Also divide the array element by this highest power of p. Repeat this process for each of the remaining primes p in the factor base.

When we have completed the sieving, those array elements that are 1 will have factored completely over the factor base, and these are precisely the B-smooth elements. Retain the vectors of powers mod 2 for the B-smooth elements and discard all remaining elements and vectors. These retained vectors of powers will be used in the linear algebra phase, precisely as described for Dixon's Algorithm in Section 7.2.2 above. Provided we have found enough B-smooth elements, we will obtain a solution to the linear equations, and with high probability this will yield the factors of N.

There are some fairly obvious improvements to the sieving process as we have described it. However, there are also several not-so-obvious, but critically important improvements that are used in practice. Most significantly, it is possible to use an inexpensive approximate "logarithm" calculation to avoid the costly division operations [99]. The results are only approximate, so that the survivors of the sieving that have been reduced to "small" values will require secondary testing to determine whether they are actually B-smooth. It is also possible to use a similar technique to avoid the costly process of determining the highest power of p that divides a given value.

We want to restrict the sieving interval $[-M, M]$ to be small, so that the resulting Q values are more likely to have small factors (and therefore to be B-smooth). In practice, it is difficult to obtain enough smooth relations using only the polynomial $Q(x)$ as defined in (7.6). Therefore, multiple quadratic polynomials of the form $Q(x) = (ax+b)^2 - N$ are used. This variant is given the name *multiple polynomial quadratic sieve* (MPQS) to distinguish it from the regular quadratic sieve. Certain choices of the parameters a and b will give better results; see [115].

Note that in the sieving process as we have described it, we only retain the powers modulo 2. This is sufficient for the linear algebra phase of the attack, but, as with Dixon's Algorithm, once a congruence of squares has been found, it is necessary to know the actual factorization of the elements. Since all of these are B-smooth, we know the factors are small and, therefore, Pollard's Rho Algorithm [32] can be used to factor these numbers, since this algorithm is particularly efficient at finding small factors.

In summary, the QS algorithm can be viewed as an improved version of Dixon's Algorithm. The speedup due to sieving is significant and with multiple polynomials, the sieving interval $[-M, M]$ can be made much smaller. This leads to a better parallel implementation where each processor sieves over the entire interval, but with a different polynomial. Recent factoring attacks have made use of the parallelizability of the sieving phase by distributing the work over a large number of computers (which is relatively easy, thanks to the Internet) and then gathering the exponent vectors before doing the equation solving phase on a supercomputer.

7.2.4 Factoring Conclusions

Currently, the *number field sieve* is the best available algorithm for factoring integers having more than 110 decimal digits or so. While the quadratic sieve is relatively straightforward, the number field sieve relies on some advanced mathematics. For a brief and readable introduction to both of the quadratic sieve and the number field sieve, see [116].

Finally, we mention the work factor of factoring. Recall that for trial division as described above, the work to factor N is on the order of $N/\ln(N)$, For the quadratic sieve, the work factor is on the order of $e^{(\ln N)^{1/2}(\ln \ln N)^{1/2}}$. For the number field sieve, the work factor is on the order of $e^{c(\ln N)^{1/3}(\ln \ln N)^{2/3}}$, where $c \approx 1.9223$. Note that the dominant term of $(\ln N)^{1/2}$ in the work factor for the quadratic sieve has been reduced to $(\ln N)^{1/3}$ in the number field sieve. However, the relatively large constant c in the number field sieve is the reason that the quadratic sieve is faster for N below a threshold of about 110 decimal digits.

We consider these functions for the work factors a little more closely. First, note that the number of bits in N is $x = \log_2 N$. Since we measure the work required to break a symmetric cipher in terms of bits, it appears that x is the "right" parameter for measuring the work required to break a public system. Up to constant factors, we can rewrite the work factor functions as in Table 7.2, where $f(x)$ is the work factor for an integer N, with $x = \log_2 N$. The final column in Table 7.2 gives the logarithm, base 2, of the work factor $f(x)$.

Table 7.2: Work Factors for Factoring $N = 2^x$

Factoring Method	$f(x)$	$\log_2 f(x)$
Trial division	$2^x/x$	$x - \log_2 x$
Quadratic sieve	$2^{x^{1/2}(\log_2 x)^{1/2}}$	$x^{1/2}(\log_2 x)^{1/2}$
Number field sieve	$2^{1.9223\, x^{1/3}(\log_2 x)^{2/3}}$	$1.9223\, x^{1/3}(\log_2 x)^{2/3}$

In Figure 7.1 we have plotted the function

$$x - \log_2 x,$$

which is the logarithm (base 2) of the work factor for trial division, alongside the functions

$$x^{1/2}(\log_2 x)^{1/2}$$

and

$$1.9223\, x^{1/3}(\log_2 x)^{2/3},$$

which represent the logarithm (base 2) of the work factors for the quadratic sieve and the number field sieve, respectively. These same functions appear in the final column of Table 7.2. The work factor for trial division is exponential in x, while work factors for the two sieving methods are said to be subexponential. A subexponential algorithm has a work factors that is asymptotically better than any fully exponential algorithm, but slower than any polynomial-time algorithm [99]. The dominant term in the quadratic sieve work factor function is $x^{1/2}$, while the dominant term for the number field sieve is $x^{1/3}$. However, due to the larger constant, the number field sieve function is larger than the quadratic sieve function for small x. But, regardless of constants, these functions are both smaller than any polynomial in x for sufficiently large values of x. This is precisely what it means for an algorithm to have a subexponential work factor.

It is instructive to compare the results in Table 7.2 with the work required for an exhaustive key search attack on a symmetric cipher. Consider a symmetric cipher with an x-bit key. Then an exhaustive key search has an expected work factor of 2^{x-1} and taking the logarithm, base 2, gives $x - 1$. From Table 7.2, we see that factoring is asymptotically easier than an exhaustive key search (provided one of the sieving methods is used), regardless of any constants that are involved. This implies that to obtain a comparable level of security for, say, RSA as is provided by a secure symmetric cipher, the RSA modulus N must have far more bits then the corresponding symmetric key; see Problem 8.

Note that the quadratic sieve is superior to the number field sieve for integers N up to about 390 bits, and from that point on, the number field sieve has the lower work factor. Since a 390-bit integer has about 117 decimal digits, this is consistent with the often stated claim that the quadratic sieve is more efficient for factoring large integers up to about 115 decimal digits. Also, from Figure 7.1 we can roughly compare the number of bits in a the key of a secure symmetric cipher to the number of bits in an RSA modulus. For example, a 390-bit RSA modulus requires about the same amount of work to factor (and thereby recover the private key) as an exhaustive search to recover a 60-bit symmetric key.

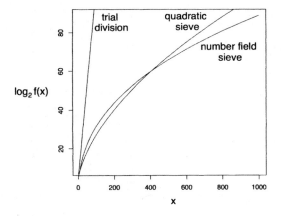

Figure 7.1: Comparison of factoring algorithms.

7.3   Discrete Log Algorithms

> In pioneer days they used oxen for heavy pulling,
> and when one ox couldn't budge a log,
> they didn't try to grow a larger ox.
> — G. Hopper

The security of the Diffie–Hellman key exchange and the ElGamal signature scheme are believed to rest on the difficulty of the discrete logarithm problem. That is, given p, g and g^a (mod p), where a is unknown, if we can determine a, then we can break Diffie–Hellman and ElGamal.

In this section, we give a brief overview of three methods of solving the discrete log problem. First, we present the naïve method of *trial multiplication*, which is the analog of trial division for the factoring problem (factoring is discussed in Section 7.2). Then we discuss the *baby-step giant-step* method, which is a fairly straightforward time-memory trade-off (TMTO) extension of trial multiplication. Finally, we discuss the *index calculus*, which is roughly the discrete log analog of Dixon's Algorithm for integer factorization. Variations of the index calculus algorithm are the most efficient known algorithms for solving the discrete log problem that arises in Diffie–Hellman and other public key systems.

7.3.1   Trial Multiplication

Suppose we are given a generator g, a prime p and g^a (mod p), and we want to determine a. We can compute the sequence

$$g^2 \text{ (mod } p), \ g^3 \text{ (mod } p), \ g^4 \text{ (mod } p), \ \ldots$$

until we find g^a (mod p). As mentioned above, this method of solving the discrete log problem is essentially the analog of trial division for factoring.

For example, suppose we are given $g = 3$, $p = 101$, and we want to find the exponent a such that g^a (mod p) = 94. Then we would compute

$$3^2 \text{ (mod } 101) = 9$$
$$3^3 \text{ (mod } 101) = 27$$
$$3^4 \text{ (mod } 101) = 81$$
$$3^5 \text{ (mod } 101) = 41$$
$$\vdots \qquad \qquad \vdots$$
$$3^{11} \text{ (mod } 101) = 94.$$

Alternatively, we could begin at g^k (mod p), for any given k. In any case, the expected number of multiplications is about $p/2$.

7.3.2 Baby-Step Giant-Step

The baby-step giant-step algorithm provides an improvement over trial multiplication based on a time-memory trade-off [99]. Again, we are given a generator g, a prime p and $x = g^a \pmod{p}$, and we want to determine a. First, we select $m = \left\lceil \sqrt{p-1} \right\rceil$. Then we have $a = im + j$ for some $i \in \{0, 1, \ldots, m-1\}$ and $j \in \{0, 1, \ldots, m-1\}$. For this choice of i and j, it follows that

$$x = g^a \pmod{p} = g^{im+j} \pmod{p}$$

and therefore

$$g^j = xg^{-im} \pmod{p}. \tag{7.10}$$

If we can determine i and j so that (7.10) holds, then, since $a = im + j$, we have found a. To determine a we proceed as follows. Given $x = g^a \pmod{p}$, we compute $xg^{-im} \pmod{p}$ for $i = 0, 1, \ldots, m-1$ (recall that g and p are public and m is known). Then for each $j = 0, 1, \ldots, m-1$, we compute $g^j \pmod{p}$ and compare the result to all of the computed $xg^{-im} \pmod{p}$ values. When we find a match, we have found i and j such that (7.10) is satisfied and, therefore, we have recovered a. Note that in this algorithm, the $g^j \pmod{p}$ represent the "baby steps," while the $xg^{-im} \pmod{p}$ are the "giant steps."

An example should clarify the algorithm. Suppose that $g = 3$, $p = 101$ and we want to solve for the discrete log of $x = g^a \pmod{p} = 37$. Then we select $m = \sqrt{100} = 10$ and note that $g^{-m} = 3^{-10} = 14 \pmod{p}$. Next, we compute

$$xg^{-im} = 37 \cdot 3^{-10i} = 37 \cdot 14^i \pmod{101},$$

for $i = 0, 1, 2, \ldots, m-1$, and save the results in a table. This phase of the computation is summarized in Table 7.3.

Table 7.3: Example Giant-Step Computation

giant step i	0	1	2	3	4	5	6	7	8	9
$3^{-10i} \pmod{101}$	1	14	95	17	36	100	87	6	84	65
$37 \cdot 3^{-10i} \pmod{101}$	37	13	81	23	19	64	88	20	78	82

Next, we compute $3^j \pmod{101}$, for $j = 0, 1, \ldots, 9$, until we obtain a value that appears in the third row of Table 7.3. For $j = 0, 1, 2, 3$ we do not find such a match, but for $j = 4$ we have $3^4 = 81 \pmod{101}$ which appears in the third row of the $i = 2$ column in Table 7.3. Consequently, (7.10) holds with $m = 10$, $i = 2$, and $j = 4$, that is,

$$3^4 = 37 \cdot 3^{-2 \cdot 10} \pmod{101}.$$

Therefore, $3^{24} = 37 \pmod{101}$ and we have solved this particular discrete log problem.

In general, for the giant-step phase, we compute about $\sqrt{p}$ values and store these in our table. Then in the baby-step phase, after trying about $\sqrt{p}/2$ choices for j we expect to have found a solution. Assuming the table lookups do not carry any cost (the table could be sorted or a hash table used), this algorithm requires about $1.5\sqrt{p}$ multiplications and it also requires storage (or space) of about $\sqrt{p}$. Assuming the storage requirement is feasible, this is a significant improvement over the naïve method of trial multiplication, but still an exponential work factor.

7.3.3 Index Calculus

As above, we are given the generator g, a prime p, and $x = g^a \pmod{p}$, and we want to find a. Analogous to Dixon's factoring algorithm, we first select a bound B and a factor base of primes less than B. Then we pre-compute the discrete logarithms to the base g of the elements in the factor base and we save the logarithms of these elements. These logarithms of the factor base can be found efficiently by solving a system of linear equations; see Problem 11.

Once the logarithms of the elements in the factor base are known, the attack is straightforward. We have $x = g^a \pmod{p}$, and we want to find a. Let $\{p_0, p_1, \ldots, p_{n-1}\}$ be the set of primes in the factor base. We randomly select $k \in \{0, 1, 2, \ldots, p-2\}$ and compute $y = x \cdot g^k \pmod{p}$ until we find a y that factors completely over the factor base. Given such a y we have

$$y = x \cdot g^k = p_0^{d_0} \cdot p_1^{d_1} \cdot p_2^{d_2} \cdots p_{n-1}^{d_{n-1}} \pmod{p},$$

where each $d_i \geq 0$. Taking $\log_g$ on both sides and simplifying, we find

$$
\begin{aligned}
a = \log_g x = (d_0 \log_g p_0 + d_1 \log_g p_1 \\
+ \cdots + d_{n-1} \log_g p_{n-1} - k) \pmod{p-1}.
\end{aligned} \tag{7.11}
$$

Assuming that the logarithms of the elements in the factor base are known, we have determined a. Note that the mod $p-1$ in (7.11) follows from Fermat's Little Theorem, which is given in Appendix A-2 and, for example, in [25].

An example should clarify the algorithm. Suppose $g = 3$, $p = 101$ and we are given $x = 3^a = 94 \pmod{101}$ and we want to determine a. As our factor base we choose the set of primes $\{2, 3, 5, 7\}$ and by solving a system of linear equations (see Problem 11), we determine

$$\log_3 2 = 29, \ \log_3 3 = 1, \ \log_3 5 = 96, \ \log_3 7 = 61.$$

Next, we randomly select k until we obtain a value $94 \cdot 3^k \pmod{101}$ which factors completely over the factor base. For example, if we choose $k = 10$ then

$$94 \cdot 3^{10} = 50 \pmod{101}. \tag{7.12}$$

and $50 = 2 \cdot 5^2$ factors over our factor base. Taking logarithms of both sides of (7.12) yields

$$\log_3 94 = \log_3 2 + 2 \log_3 5 - 10 \pmod{100}.$$

Substituting the values for the logarithms of the primes in the factor base, we have

$$\log_3 94 = 29 + 192 - 10 = 11 \pmod{100},$$

which implies that $3^{11} = 94 \pmod{101}$. Then $a = 11$ and we have solved this particular discrete log problem.

The index calculus provides the most efficient method for solving a general discrete log problem. The work factor for the index calculus is subexponential; more precisely, the work is on the order of $e^{(\ln p)^{1/2}(\ln \ln p)^{1/2}}$. The form of this work factor is the same as that given for the quadratic sieve factoring method in Section 7.2.4, which is, perhaps, not surprising since both rely on finding smooth integers. For more information on the index calculus, a good source is [99].

7.3.4   Discrete Log Conclusions

There are many parallels between the discrete log algorithms discussed in this section and the factoring algorithms in Section 7.2. In particular, Dixon's factoring algorithm and the index calculus discrete log algorithm have many similarities. Both algorithms have an equation finding phase and a linear algebra phase.

For properly chosen parameters, the costliest part of the index calculus algorithm is solving for the logarithms of the elements in the factor base. As with Dixon's Algorithm, the equation finding part of the index calculus algorithm can be distributed among multiple processors, but the linear algebra part cannot.

There exists another class of algorithms for factoring and discrete logarithm which are known as collision search techniques. The best general collision search method is Pollard's Rho Algorithm [32]. However, collision search algorithms have an exponential work factor, while the quadratic sieve and index calculus are subexponential (see Section 7.2.4 for a discussion of the work factor for the quadratic sieve).

Finally, it is worth noting that there is no analog of the quadratic sieve or index calculus for elliptic curve cryptosystems since, for elliptic curves, there is no analog of a factor base. Consequently, collision search is the best available technique for breaking systems based on elliptic curves, and this is why smaller parameters sizes can be used with elliptic curve cryptosystems without sacrificing security.

7.4   RSA Implementation Attacks

Timing is everything.
— Anonymous

If factoring and discrete log algorithms represent classical attacks on public key systems, then the attacks in this section are strictly "punk rock." The attacks discussed here do not follow the usual cryptanalytic approach of analyzing the underlying crypto algorithm for weaknesses. Instead, the cryptanalyst looks for any weak link in the overall implementation that might allow information about the private key to leak.

First, we discuss three different timing attacks. By exploiting small timing differences that occur in specific methods of modular exponentiation, the attacker can gain information about the private key. Then we consider a "glitching" attack, where the attacker induces an error in a computation (for example, by abusing a smartcard). For a particular method of modular exponentiation, a single induced error can enable an attacker to easily recover the private key. Both timing and glitching attacks are practical and it is therefore critical that cryptosystems are built to resist such attacks.

It is important to emphasize that the attacks discussed in this section do not exploit any inherent weakness in the RSA algorithm itself. Instead, these attacks exploit specific implementation issues that allow information to leak out—with potentially devastating consequences.

7.4.1   Timing Attacks

At one time, it was widely believed that if RSA was implemented correctly, the only realistic way to attack it was by factoring the modulus. In 1996 Paul Kocher [85] surprised the crypto world when he demonstrated a practical side-channel attack on RSA.

A side channel is an unintended source of information. In the crypto context, side channels sometimes leak information about a computation, which in turn reveals information about the key. For example, careful measurements of the amount of current used by smartcards have been used to recover keys.

Kocher's side-channel attack on RSA is based on a careful timing of various cryptographic operations. Using selected inputs, he was able to recover the private keys from smartcards which used a relatively simple method of modular exponentiation. Kocher conjectured that his technique could also be used in settings where the modular exponentiation was computed using more efficient means, but other researchers soon discovered this was not the case.

Schindler [129] was able to develop a timing attack that succeeds when modular exponentiation is computed in a more optimized fashion than the case where Kocher's attack applies. Brumley and Boneh [22] have pushed Schindler's results much further, developing a successful timing attack against the highly optimized RSA implementation in OpenSSL. This attack is sufficiently robust that it can be conducted over a network, illustrating that timing attacks are a serious threat to real-world RSA implementations.

In this section we discuss Kocher's attack, Schindler's attack, and the Brumley–Boneh attack. We also consider defenses against timing attacks. But first, we introduce the techniques used to compute modular exponentiation which are employed in efficient implementations of RSA. Specifically, we discuss repeated squaring, the Chinese Remainder Theorem, Montgomery multiplication, and Karatsuba multiplication.

Modular Exponentiation

Suppose we want to compute 6^{20} (mod 29). The obvious approach is to raise 6 to the 20th power, then compute the remainder when this number is divided by 29. For this particular example, we have

$$6^{20} = 3,656,158,440,062,976 = 24 \ (\text{mod } 29).$$

However, this approach is not feasible when the base and exponent are large—as is the case in RSA—since the intermediate result is too large to compute and store. And even if we could somehow deal with such enormous numbers, computing the remainder by long division would be costly.

An improvement would be to do a modular reduction after each multiplication, which would eliminate the problem of large intermediate results. However, there is a better way. A method known as *repeated squaring* allows us to compute a modular exponentiation without having to deal with any extremely large intermediate values and it also dramatically reduces the number of multiplications as compared to the naïve approach. In repeated squaring, we "build up" the exponent one bit at a time, from high-order bit to low-order bit. For example, the exponent 20 is, in binary, 10100, and we have

$$1 = 0 \cdot 2 + 1$$
$$2 = 1 \cdot 2$$
$$5 = 2 \cdot 2 + 1$$
$$10 = 5 \cdot 2$$
$$20 = 10 \cdot 2.$$

Then to find 6^{20} (mod 29) by repeated squaring, we compute

$$6^1 = (6^0)^2 \cdot 6 = 6 \text{ (mod } 29)$$
$$6^2 = (6^1)^2 = 6^2 = 36 = 7 \text{ (mod } 29)$$
$$6^5 = (6^2)^2 \cdot 6 = 7^2 \cdot 6 = 294 = 4 \text{ (mod } 29)$$
$$6^{10} = (6^5)^2 = 4^2 = 16 \text{ (mod } 29)$$
$$6^{20} = (6^{10})^2 = 16^2 = 256 = 24 \text{ (mod } 29).$$

Note that this computation requires five multiplications (as opposed to 20 for the naïve approach) and five modular reductions, and all intermediate values are less than N^2. The repeated squaring algorithm is given in Table 7.4.

Table 7.4: Repeated Squaring

```
// Compute y = x^d (mod N),
// where d = (d_0, d_1, d_2, ..., d_n) in binary, with d_0 = 1
s = x
for i = 1 to n
    s = s^2 (mod N)
    if d_i == 1 then
        s = s · x (mod N)
    end if
next i
return(s)
```

While repeated squaring is clearly preferable to the naïve approach of exponentiation followed by long division, there are many additional refinements that can further improve the efficiency of modular exponentiation. These improvements are necessary for efficient RSA implementations due to the large numbers that arise in RSA. Repeated squaring without further refinements is only used in RSA implementations in extremely resource-constrained environments, such as smartcards.

Another trick that is commonly used to speed up modular exponentiation employs the Chinese Remainder Theorem (CRT). The precise statement of the CRT is given in the Appendix. To see how the CRT applies specifically to RSA, first recall that for an RSA decryption (or signature), we must compute a modular exponentiation of the form C^d (mod N), where $N = pq$ and p and q are large primes. Using the CRT, we can compute the modular exponentiation modulo p and modulo q, then "glue" the two results together to obtain the desired result modulo N. Since p and q are each much smaller than N (each is on the order of $\sqrt{N}$), it is much more efficient to do two modular exponentiations with these relatively small moduli than to do one modular exponentiation with modulus N. The use of CRT provides a speedup of about a factor of four when computing C^d (mod N).

This CRT trick works as follows. Suppose we know C, d, N, p, and q, and we want to compute C^d (mod N). First, we pre-compute

$$d_p = d \ (\mathrm{mod} \ (p-1)) \quad \mathrm{and} \quad d_q = d \ (\mathrm{mod} \ (q-1))$$

and we determine a satisfying

$$a = 1 \ (\mathrm{mod} \ p) \quad \mathrm{and} \quad a = 0 \ (\mathrm{mod} \ q) \tag{7.13}$$

and b satisfying

$$b = 0 \ (\mathrm{mod} \ p) \quad \mathrm{and} \quad b = 1 \ (\mathrm{mod} \ q). \tag{7.14}$$

Then for the given ciphertext C, we compute

$$C_p = C \ (\mathrm{mod} \ p) \quad \mathrm{and} \quad C_q = C \ (\mathrm{mod} \ q)$$

and

$$x_p = C_p^{d_p} \ (\mathrm{mod} \ p) \quad \mathrm{and} \quad x_q = C_q^{d_q} \ (\mathrm{mod} \ q).$$

The desired solution is given by

$$C^d \ (\mathrm{mod} \ N) = (ax_p + bx_q) \ (\mathrm{mod} \ N). \tag{7.15}$$

To see that this actually works, consider the case where $N = 33$, $p = 11$, $q = 3$, $d = 7$ (then $e = 3$, but we do not need the encryption exponent here). Suppose we want to decrypt $C = 5$, that is, we want to determine 5^7 (mod 33). We have

$$d_p = 7 \ (\mathrm{mod} \ 10) = 7 \quad \mathrm{and} \quad d_q = 7 \ (\mathrm{mod} \ 2) = 1$$

and we find that $a = 12$ and $b = 22$ satisfy the required conditions given in (7.13) and (7.14), respectively. Then

$$C_p = 5 \ (\mathrm{mod} \ 11) = 5 \quad \mathrm{and} \quad C_q = 5 \ (\mathrm{mod} \ 3) = 2$$

and, therefore,

$$x_p = C_p^{d_p} = 5^7 = 3 \ (\mathrm{mod} \ 11) \quad \mathrm{and} \quad x_q = C_q^{d_q} = 2^1 = 2 \ (\mathrm{mod} \ 3). \tag{7.16}$$

Finally, we have

$$C^d \ (\mathrm{mod} \ N) = 5^7 = 12 \cdot 3 + 22 \cdot 2 \ (\mathrm{mod} \ 33) = 14,$$

which shows that, at least for this simple example, (7.15) holds.

Another significant speedup in modular exponentiation is provided by Montgomery multiplication [103]. Our discussion here follows the brief but excellent description given in [24].

Suppose we want to compute $ab \pmod{N}$. The most expensive part of this operation is the modular reduction, which, in the naïve approach, requires a division. However, in some cases, modular reduction can be accomplished without division.

One case where the modular reduction is easy occurs when the modulus is of the special form $N = m^k - 1$ for some m and k. Suppose we have a modulus N of this form and we want to determine, say, $ab = c \pmod{N}$. Then there exists c_0 and c_1 such that $c = c_1 m^k + c_0$, with $0 \le c_0 < m^k$. If we can find such c_0 and c_1, then we have

$$
\begin{aligned}
c &= c_1 m^k - c_1 + c_1 + c_0 \\
&= c_1 (m^k - 1) + c_1 + c_0 \\
&= c_1 + c_0 \pmod{(m^k - 1)}.
\end{aligned}
$$

That is, if we can find integers c_0 and c_1 such that $c = c_1 m^k + c_0$, then we have $c \pmod{N} = c_0 + c_1$, provided $N = m^k - 1$. In some cases, it is easy to find the required c_0 and c_1. Consider, for example, $3089 \pmod{99}$. For this example we have

$$
\begin{aligned}
3089 &= 30 \cdot 100 + 89 \\
&= 30 \cdot 100 - 30 + 30 + 89 \\
&= 30(100 - 1) + (30 + 89) \\
&= 30 \cdot 99 + 119 = 119 \pmod{99}.
\end{aligned}
$$

Here, we need one final step where we subtract 99 from 119 to obtain the desired result, namely, $3089 = 20 \pmod{99}$. Provided that $c = ab$ satisfies the condition $c < N^2$ (which will be the case if $a < N$ and $b < N$), the desired result is either $c_0 + c_1$ or, if this sum is greater than N, the desired result is $c_0 + c_1 - N$. In this latter case, we say that an *extra reduction* is required.

The Montgomery multiplication algorithm is somewhat analogous to the process in the previous paragraph, but it works for any modulus N. Again, suppose we want to compute

$$ ab \pmod{N}. \tag{7.17} $$

In the Montgomery algorithm, we choose $R = 2^k$, where k is large enough so that we have $R > N$, and $\gcd(R, N) = 1$. Since R is a power of two, determining any result modulo R is trivial—at least for a computer, where numbers are in binary. Also, since R and N are relatively prime, we can find N' and R' such that

$$ RR' - NN' = 1. $$

Now, instead of dealing directly with a and b we work with the numbers $a' = aR$ (mod N) and $b' = bR$ (mod N). We say that a' and b' are in *Montgomery form*. Converting a and b to Montgomery form appears to be a step backwards, since in (7.17) we only have a single mod N operation, and we now have two such operations (at least). However, dealing with numbers in Montgomery form will actually prove to be highly advantageous when doing modular exponentiation, where repeated multiplication is required. We return to this point below, but for now we simply want to show that we can efficiently multiply two numbers in Montgomery form and obtain a result in Montgomery form.

Observe that

$$a'b' \text{ (mod } N) = abR^2 \text{ (mod } N).$$

We would like this result to be in Montgomery form, that is, we want to have abR (mod N), not abR^2 (mod N). Since $RR' = 1$ (mod N), multiplication by R' yields $abR^2R' = abR$ (mod N), that is, we can obtain the desired result by multiplying by R' and reducing the result modulo N. However, we want to avoid mod N operations, if possible. Therefore, what we chiefly need is an efficient method to convert $a'b'$ to abR (mod N). The Montgomery algorithm provides just such a method.

Let $X = a'b'$ and compute

$$m = (X \text{ (mod } R)) \cdot N' \text{ (mod } R), \qquad (7.18)$$

which is efficient, since all mod R operations are efficient. Next, let

$$x = (X + mN)/R \text{ (mod } R) \qquad (7.19)$$

and return x, unless $x \geq N$, in which case return $x - N$, that is, an extra reduction may be required.

We now want to verify that the algorithm in the previous paragraph gives us abR (mod N). To see that this is the case, first observe that m is the product of N' and the remainder that results when X is divided by R. Also, from the definition of N' we have $NN' = -1$ (mod R). Consequently, $X + mN = X - (X \text{ (mod } R))$, and, therefore, $X + mN$ is divisible by R. Furthermore, since $R = 2^k$, this division is, in binary, simply a shift by k bits and, consequently, the division in (7.19) is trivial to compute. It follows that $xR = X + mN = X$ (mod N) and, therefore, $xRR' = XR'$ (mod N). Finally, from the definition of R' we have $RR' = 1$ (mod N) so that

$$x = xRR' = XR' = abR^2R' = abR \text{ (mod } N),$$

as desired.

An example should clarify the Montgomery algorithm [24]. Suppose that we have $N = 79$ and $a = 61$ and $b = 5$. Since humans prefer powers of 10 to powers of two, and this example is intended for human consumption, we choose $R = 10^2 = 100$. Then

$$a' = 61 \cdot 100 = 17 \ (\text{mod } 79) \ \text{ and } \ b' = 5 \cdot 100 = 26 \ (\text{mod } 79).$$

Via the Euclidean Algorithm, we find

$$64 \cdot 100 - 81 \cdot 79 = 1,$$

which implies $R' = 64$ and $N' = 81$.

In Montgomery form, we have

$$a' = aR \ (\text{mod } N) = 17 \ \text{ and } \ b' = bR \ (\text{mod } N) = 26$$

and we want to determine $abR \ (\text{mod } N)$, which is in Montgomery form. From (7.18) we compute $X = 17 \cdot 26 = 442$, and

$$
\begin{aligned}
m &= (X \ (\text{mod } R)) \cdot N' \ (\text{mod } R) \\
&= (442 \ (\text{mod } 100)) \cdot 81 \ (\text{mod } 100) \\
&= 42 \cdot 81 = 3402 = 2 \ (\text{mod } 100).
\end{aligned}
$$

Then from (7.19) we have

$$
\begin{aligned}
x &= (X + mN)/R \ (\text{mod } R) \\
&= (442 + (2 \cdot 79))/100 \ (\text{mod } 100) \\
&= 600/100 = 6.
\end{aligned}
$$

It is easily verified that this is the correct result, since

$$abR = 61 \cdot 5 \cdot 100 = 30{,}500 = 6 \ (\text{mod } 79).$$

Conversion from Montgomery form into regular (non-Montgomery) form is straightforward, at the cost of one mod N reduction. Given $abR \ (\text{mod } N)$, since $RR' = 1 \ (\text{mod } N)$, we have

$$abRR' \ (\text{mod } N) = ab \ (\text{mod } N).$$

In the example above, $R' = 64$ and we have

$$(abR)R' = 6 \cdot 64 = 384 = 68 \ (\text{mod } 79).$$

We can directly verify that this is the correct answer since

$$ab \ (\text{mod } N) = 61 \cdot 5 = 305 = 68 \ (\text{mod } 79).$$

Montgomery multiplication is certainly more work than it is worth in the simple example considered above. However, suppose that instead of computing $ab \ (\text{mod } N)$, we want to compute $a^d \ (\text{mod } N)$. Then to use the

Montgomery algorithm, we must pay the price of converting a into Montgomery form, but having done so, all of the multiplications required in the computation of $a^d \pmod{N}$ can be computed using (7.18) and (7.19) (and extra reductions, as required), without any expensive division operations. The final result must be converted from Montgomery form back into non-Montgomery form, which requires one additional mod N operation. The bottom line is that only two expensive mod N operations are required, since the multiplications are all computed in Montgomery form which only requires efficient mod R operations. With respect to the timing attacks discussed below, the extra reduction step provides a crucial timing difference that an attacker can exploit in some circumstances.

Other tricks are also used to speed up modular exponentiation. Of these, the sliding window and Karatsuba multiplication are the most significant. A *sliding window* is a straightforward time-memory trade-off applied to the repeated squaring algorithm. That is, instead of processing each bit individually, we process the bits in blocks (say, blocks of five consecutive bits) and use pre-computed tables containing the required factors.

Karatsuba multiplication [76] is the most efficient method to multiply two numbers with the same number of digits—assuming that addition is much cheaper than multiplication. The work factor for Karatsuba multiplication is on the order of $n^{\log_2 3} \approx n^{1.585}$ multiplications, where n is the number of bits in each of the numbers to be multiplied, whereas normal "long multiplication" has a work factor on the order of n^2.

The Karatsuba algorithm is based on a simple observation. The naïve approach to computing the product $(a_0 + a_1 \cdot 10)(b_0 + b_1 \cdot 10)$ is

$$(a_0 + a_1 \cdot 10)(b_0 + b_1 \cdot 10) = a_0 b_0 + (a_0 b_1 + a_1 b_0)10 + a_1 b_1 \cdot 10^2,$$

which requires four multiplications to determine the coefficients of the powers of ten. However, the same can be accomplished with just three multiplications, since

$$\begin{aligned} &(a_0 + a_1 \cdot 10)(b_0 + b_1 \cdot 10) \\ &= a_0 b_0 + [(a_0 + a_1)(b_0 + b_1) - a_0 b_0 - a_1 b_1]10 + a_1 b_1 \cdot 10^2 \end{aligned} \quad (7.20)$$

and this is the essential idea behind Karatsuba multiplication.

The Karatsuba technique can be used for numbers of any magnitude. For example, suppose that we want to find the product

$$(c_0 + c_1 \cdot 10 + c_2 \cdot 10^2 + c_3 \cdot 10^3)(d_0 + d_1 \cdot 10 + d_2 \cdot 10^2 + d_3 \cdot 10^3).$$

We can rewrite the first term as

$$(c_0 + c_1 \cdot 10) + (c_2 + c_3 \cdot 10)10^2 = C_0 + C_1 \cdot 10^2,$$

where $C_0 = c_0 + c_1 \cdot 10$ and $C_1 = c_2 + c_3 \cdot 10$. Similarly, we can rewrite the second term as

$$(d_0 + d_1 \cdot 10) + (d_2 + d_3 \cdot 10)10^2 = D_0 + D_1 \cdot 10^2,$$

where $D_0 = d_0 + d_1 \cdot 10$ and $D_1 = d_2 + d_3 \cdot 10$. In this case, the Karatsuba product is given by

$$(C_0 + C_1 \cdot 10^2)(D_0 + D_1 \cdot 10^2)$$
$$= C_0 D_0 + [(C_0 + C_1)(D_0 + D_1) - C_0 D_0 - C_1 D_1]10^2 + C_1 D_1 \cdot 10^4.$$

Here, the three products involving the C_i and D_j are computed as in (7.20). Consequently, given any product, we can recursively apply the Karatsuba multiplication technique. At each step in the recursion, three multiplications are required, and the numbers are half as big as at the previous step. A straightforward analysis yields the claimed work factor of $n^{1.585}$.

Note that the Karatsuba algorithm holds if the base 10 (or 10^2) is replaced by any other base. Also, the algorithm is most efficient if the two numbers to be multiplied are of about the same magnitude.

At this point, we have more than enough background to discuss the three timing attacks mentioned above. First, we consider Kocher's attack, which only applies to systems that use repeated squaring, but not CRT or Montgomery multiplication. Kocher's attack has been successfully applied to smartcards. Then we discuss Schindler's method, which can be used when CRT and Montgomery multiplication are employed. Finally, we present the justifiably famous Brumley–Boneh attack, which succeeds against RSA as implemented in a version of OpenSSL in a realistic scenario (over a network). The OpenSSL implementation of RSA is highly optimized, using CRT, Montgomery multiplication, sliding windows and Karatsuba's algorithm. As of this writing, the Brumley–Boneh attack stands as the greatest success in the relatively young field of timing attacks. We note in passing that timing attacks have recently been directed at symmetric ciphers [12] but, to date, these have proven far less of a realistic threat than timing attacks on public key cryptosystems.

Kocher's Attack

The basic idea behind Kocher's timing attack [85] is elegant, yet reasonably straightforward. Suppose that the repeated squaring algorithm in Table 7.4 is used for modular exponentiation in RSA. Also, suppose that the time taken by the multiplication operation, $s = s \cdot x \pmod{N}$ in Table 7.4, varies depending on the values of s and x. Furthermore, we assume the attacker is able to determine the timings that will occur, given particular values of s and x.

Given this scenario, Kocher views the problem as a signal detection problem, where the "signal" consists of the timing variations (which are dependent on the unknown private key bits d_i, for $i = 1, 2, \ldots, n$). The signal is corrupted by "noise," which is the result of unknown private key bits, d_i. The objective is to recover the bits d_i one (or a few) at a time, beginning with the first unknown bit, d_1. In practice, it is not necessary to recover all of the bits, since an algorithm due to Coppersmith [31] is feasible once a sufficient number of the high-order bits of d are known.

Suppose we have successfully determined bits $d_0, d_1, \ldots, d_{k-1}$ and we want to determine bit d_k. Then we randomly select several ciphertexts, say, C_j, for $j = 0, 1, 2, \ldots, m - 1$, and for each we obtain the timing $T(C_j)$ for the decryption $C_j^d \pmod{N}$. For each of these ciphertext values, we can precisely emulate the repeated squaring algorithm in Table 7.4 for $i = 1, 2, \ldots, k - 1$, and at the $i = k$ step we can emulate both of the possible bit values, $d_k = 0$ and $d_k = 1$. Then we tabulate the differences between the measured timing and both of the emulated results. Kocher's crucial observation is that the variance of the differences will be smaller for the correct choice of d_k than for the incorrect choice.

For example, suppose we are trying to obtain a private key that is only eight bits in length. Then

$$d = (d_0, d_1, d_2, d_3, d_4, d_5, d_6, d_7) \quad \text{with} \quad d_0 = 1.$$

Furthermore, suppose that we are certain that

$$d_0 d_1 d_2 d_3 \in \{1010, 1001\}.$$

Then we generate some number of random ciphertexts C_j, and for each, we obtain the corresponding timing $T(C_j)$. We can emulate the first four steps of the repeated squaring algorithm for both

$$d_0 d_1 d_2 d_3 = 1010 \quad \text{and} \quad d_0 d_1 d_2 d_3 = 1001$$

for each of these ciphertexts. For a given timing $T(C_j)$, let t_ℓ be the actual time taken in step ℓ for the squaring and multiplying steps of the repeated squaring algorithm. That is, t_ℓ includes the timing of $s = s^2 \pmod{N}$ and, if $d_\ell = 1$, it also includes $s = s \cdot C_j \pmod{N}$ (see the algorithm in Table 7.4). Also, let $\tilde{t}_\ell$ be the time obtained when emulating the square and multiply steps for an assumed private exponent bit ℓ. For $m > \ell$, define the shorthand notation

$$\tilde{t}_{\ell \ldots m} = \tilde{t}_\ell + \tilde{t}_{\ell+1} + \cdots + \tilde{t}_m.$$

Of course, $\tilde{t}_\ell$ depends on the precise bits emulated, but to simplify the notation we do not explicitly state this dependence (it should be clear from context).

Now suppose we select four ciphertexts, C_0, C_1, C_2, C_3, and we obtain the timing results in Table 7.5. In this example we see that for $d_0d_1d_2d_3 = 1010$ we have a mean timing of

$$E(T(C_j) - \tilde{t}_{0...3}) = (7 + 6 + 6 + 5)/4 = 6,$$

while the corresponding variance is

$$\text{var}(T(C_j) - \tilde{t}_{0...3}) = (1^2 + 0^2 + 0^2 + (-1)^2)/4 = 1/2.$$

On the other hand, for $d_0d_1d_2d_3 = 1001$, we have

$$E(T(C_j) - \tilde{t}_{0...3}) = 6,$$

but the variance is

$$\text{var}(T(C_j) - \tilde{t}_{0...3}) = ((-1)^2 + 1^2 + (-1)^2 + 1^2)/4 = 1.$$

Although the mean is the same in both cases, Kocher's attack tells us that the smaller variance indicates that $d_0d_1d_2d_3 = 1010$ is the correct answer. But this begs the question of why we should observe a smaller variance in case of a correct guess for $d_0d_1d_2d_3$.

Table 7.5: Fictitious Timings

		Emulate 1010		Emulate 1001	
j	$T(C_j)$	$\tilde{t}_{0...3}$	$T(C_j) - \tilde{t}_{0...3}$	$\tilde{t}_{0...3}$	$T(C_j) - \tilde{t}_{0...3}$
0	12	5	7	7	5
1	11	5	6	4	7
2	12	6	6	7	5
3	13	8	5	6	7

Consider $T(C_j)$, the timing of a particular computation $C_j^d \pmod{N}$ in Table 7.5. As above, for this $T(C_j)$, let $\tilde{t}_\ell$ be the emulated timing for the square and multiply steps corresponding to the ℓth bit of the private exponent. Also, let t_ℓ be the actual timing of the square and multiply steps corresponding to the ℓth bit of the private exponent. Let u include all timing not accounted for in the t_ℓ. The value u can be viewed as representing the measurement "error". In the example above, we assumed the private exponent d is eight bits, so for this case

$$T(C_j) = t_0 + t_1 + t_2 + \cdots + t_7 + u.$$

Now suppose that the high-order bits of d are $d_0d_1d_2d_3 = 1010$. Then for the timing $T(C_j)$ we have

$$\text{var}(T(C_j) - \tilde{t}_{0...3}) = \text{var}(t_4) + \text{var}(t_5) + \text{var}(t_6) + \text{var}(t_7) + \text{var}(u),$$

since $\tilde{t}_\ell = t_\ell$, for $\ell = 0, 1, 2, 3$ and, consequently, there is no variance due to these emulated timings $\tilde{t}_\ell$. Note that here, we are assuming the t_ℓ are independent and that the measurement error u is independent of the t_ℓ, which appear to be valid assumptions. If we denote the common variance of each t_ℓ by $\mathrm{var}(t)$, we have

$$\mathrm{var}(T(C_j) - \tilde{t}_{0...3}) = 4\,\mathrm{var}(t) + \mathrm{var}(u).$$

However, if $d_0 d_1 d_2 d_3 = 1010$, but we emulate $d_0 d_1 d_2 d_3 = 1001$, then from the point of the first d_j that is in error, our emulation will fail, giving us essentially random timing results. In this case, the first emulation error occurs at d_2 so that we find

$$\begin{aligned}
\mathrm{var}(T - \tilde{t}_{0...3}) &= \mathrm{var}(t_2 - \tilde{t}_2) + \mathrm{var}(t_3 - \tilde{t}_3) + \mathrm{var}(t_4) + \mathrm{var}(t_5) \\
&\quad + \mathrm{var}(t_6) + \mathrm{var}(t_7) + \mathrm{var}(u) \\
&\approx 6\,\mathrm{var}(t) + \mathrm{var}(u),
\end{aligned}$$

since the emulated timings $\tilde{t}_2$ and $\tilde{t}_3$ can vary from the actual timings t_2 and t_3, respectively.

Although conceptually simple, Kocher's technique gives a powerful and practical approach to conducting a timing attack on an RSA implementation that uses repeated squaring (but not CRT or Montgomery multiplication). For the attack to succeed, the variance of the error term u must not vary too greatly between the different cases that are tested. Assuming that a simple repeated squaring algorithm is employed, this would almost certainly be the case since u only includes loop overhead and timing error. For more advanced modular exponentiation techniques, $\mathrm{var}(u)$ could differ greatly for different emulated bits, effectively masking the timing information needed to recover the bits of d.

The amount of data required for Kocher's attack (that is, the number of chosen decryptions that must be timed) depends on the error term u. Note that timings can be reused as bits of d are determined, since, given additional bits of d, only the emulation steps need to change. Therefore, the required number of timings is not nearly as daunting as it might appear at first blush.

The major limitation to Kocher's attack is that repeated squaring, without CRT or Montgomery multiplication, is only used in RSA implementations in highly resource-constrained environments, such as smartcards. In [85], Kocher argues that his timing attack—as discussed in this section—should work for RSA implementations that employ CRT. However, Schindler [129] (among others) disputes this assertion. The next two timing attacks we discuss will succeed against RSA implementations that utilize more highly optimized modular exponentiation techniques.

Schindler's Attack

Schindler [129] gives a timing attack that succeeds against RSA implementations that employ repeated squaring and both CRT and Montgomery multiplication (but not both Karatsuba multiplication and long multiplication). First, we describe the precise modular exponentiation scenario for which Schindler's attack will succeed. Then we discuss Schindler's attack in some detail.

We assume that the Montgomery multiplication algorithm is implemented as given in Table 7.6. The repeated squaring algorithm using Montgomery multiplication is given in Table 7.7.

Table 7.6: Montgomery Multiplication

```
// Find Montgomery product a'b',
// where a' = aR (mod N) and b' = bR (mod N)
// Given RR' − NN' = 1
Montgomery(a', b')
    z = a'b'
    r = (z (mod R))N' (mod R)
    s = (z + rN)/R (mod N)
    if s ≥ N then
        s = s − N // extra reduction
    end if
    return(s)
end Montgomery
```

Table 7.7: Repeated Squaring with Montgomery Multiplication

```
// Find y = x^d (mod N),
// where d = (d_0, d_1, d_2, ..., d_{n-1}) with d_0 = 1
t' = xR (mod N) // Montgomery form
s' = t'
for i = 1 to n − 1
    s' = Montgomery(s', s')
    if d_i == 1 then
        s' = Montgomery(s', t')
    end if
next i
t = s'R' (mod N) // convert to non-Montgomery form
return(t)
```

Suppose that the RSA system we want to attack uses the repeated squaring algorithm in Table 7.7 (which relies on the Montgomery multiplication algorithm in Table 7.6). Also, suppose that the RSA system uses CRT. Then for each mod N reduction, where $N = pq$, we compute a mod p reduction and a mod q reduction, using the algorithm in Table 7.7 for both. We combine these two results to obtain the desired mod N reduction, as discussed above in Section 7.4.1. We assume that the attacker is able to choose ciphertext messages C_j and accurately time the decryption, that is, the computation C_j^d (mod N). Of course, the objective is to determine the private key d.

Schindler's timing attack [129] takes advantage of the extra reduction step in the Montgomery algorithm. Schindler derives precise probabilities that an extra reduction occurs when using the Montgomery algorithm. Suppose that we compute Montgomery(a', B) using the algorithm in Table 7.6, assuming that $a' = aR$ (mod N) and B is randomly-selected in $\{0, 1, 2, \ldots, N-1\}$. Then Schindler shows that for each application of the Montgomery algorithm, the probability of an extra reduction is

$$P(\text{extra reduction in Montgomery}(a', B)) = \frac{a'}{2R}. \qquad (7.21)$$

This gives us a useful probability for an extra reduction in the "multiply" step of the repeated squaring algorithm in Table 7.7. For the "square" step, where the element to be squared, say B, is selected at random in $\{0, 1, 2, \ldots, N-1\}$, Schindler is able to show that

$$P(\text{extra reduction in Montgomery}(B, B)) = \frac{N}{3R}. \qquad (7.22)$$

When computing a modular exponentiation a^d (mod N) using the CRT approach, we first compute a^{d_p} (mod p) using the repeated squaring algorithm in Table (7.7), where $d_p = d$ (mod $(p-1)$). Suppose that when computing a^{d_p} (mod p), we have k_0 multiply steps and k_1 squaring steps. Note that k_0 and k_1 depend only on d_p and, therefore, only on d and p, and not on a. Since the probability (7.21) holds for each multiply, and the probability (7.22) holds for each square, the expected number of extra reductions is

$$k_0 \frac{a' \ (\text{mod} \ p)}{2R} + k_1 \frac{p}{3R}. \qquad (7.23)$$

As a function of a', the expression in (7.23) is piecewise linear—more precisely, it is a linear function with discontinuities at integer multiples of p. Qualitatively, the graph of (7.23) is similar to that in Figure 7.2 (see Problem 2). Note that the total number of extra reductions in the calculation of C^d (mod N) also include extra reductions due to the factor q. Nevertheless, there would still be a discontinuity in the total number of extra reductions at every integer multiple of p (and also q).

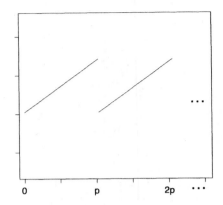

Figure 7.2: Expected number of extra reductions.

The idea behind Schindler's timing attack follows directly from the graph in Figure 7.2. Suppose we select ciphertexts C_0 and C_1, with $C_0 < C_1$. Let $T(C_0)$ and $T(C_1)$ be the timing measurements for the decryption of C_0 and C_1, respectively. Assuming that timing differences are dominated by the number of extra reductions, we would generally expect $T(C_1) - T(C_0)$ to be relatively small, since the number of extra reductions grows slowly (linearly) from C_0 to C_1.

However, suppose that C_0 and C_1 bracket a multiple of p. For example, suppose that we have $C_0 = 2p - k$ and $C_1 = 2p + \ell$, where k and ℓ are reasonably small. Then due to the discontinuity in the number of extra reductions at $2p$, the expected difference $T(C_0) - T(C_1)$ would be relatively large. Therefore, we can select an initial value x and an offset Δ and let

$$C_\ell = x + \ell\Delta, \quad \text{for} \quad \ell = 0, 1, 2, \ldots.$$

Then we compute

$$T(C_\ell) - T(C_{\ell+1}), \quad \text{for} \quad \ell = 0, 1, 2, \ldots,$$

using the chosen ciphertexts C_ℓ. Eventually, we will have $C_\ell < kp < C_{\ell+1}$ for some k and ℓ, and when this occurs we should detect a significant increase in $T(C_\ell) - T(C_{\ell+1})$. Once we have bracketed kp in this manner, we can simply compute $\gcd(n, N)$ for every

$$n \in \{x + \ell\Delta, x + \ell\Delta + 1, x + \ell\Delta + 2, \ldots, x + (\ell + 1)\Delta\}.$$

If kp is actually in the interval, we find it following this approach, since we have $\gcd(kp, N) = p$ while for other values in the interval, $\gcd(n, N) = 1$. Of course, a similar statement holds if we happen to bracket a multiple of q instead of p.

There are several possible refinements to this attack. For example, since the graph in Figure 7.2 represents the expected value (i.e., the average behavior) we would want to test several nearby values before deciding whether we had bracketed a multiple of kp or not. Also, once we have bracketed a multiple of kp, we could use a binary search approach to reduce the size of the interval over which we need to compute the gcds. Determining an optimal size for the increment and good initial starting points are also important issues. These topics are discussed in Schindler's paper [129]. Schindler also gives a detailed analysis of his attack.

It is important to note that in [129], Schindler does not apply his attack to any real-world RSA implementation. Instead, he simulates an RSA decryption routine that uses repeated squaring and Montgomery multiplication as described in this section and he gives empirical results showing that his attack succeeds in every case tested. Also, it is interesting to note that whereas Kocher's timing attack recovers the bits of the private key one (or a few) at a time, Schindler's attack recovers the private key essentially all at once.

Next, we present a timing attack that builds on Schindler's work. This attack, which is due to Brumley and Boneh, succeeds against a sophisticated real-world implementation of RSA.

Brumley–Boneh Attack

Brumley and Boneh [22] consider a timing attack against RSA as implemented in OpenSSL. The attack they develop is practical and sufficiently robust that it can recover a private key over a network that includes several routers and switches between the endpoints, which introduces a significant random timing variation.

The RSA implementation in OpenSSL is highly optimized, using CRT with repeated squaring, Montgomery multiplication and a sliding window (with a window of size of five for a 1024-bit modulus). In addition, the OpenSSL implementation of RSA employs Karatsuba multiplication to compute the product xy whenever x and y consists of the same number of words, and it uses ordinary "long multiplication" when x and y are not of the same word-size. Repeated squaring, CRT, Montgomery multiplication, sliding window and Karatsuba multiplication are all discussed in Section 7.4.1, above.

Kocher's original RSA timing attack [85] does not work when CRT is employed, and Schindler's timing attack [129] does not succeed when Karatsuba multiplication is used (below, it will become clear why Schindler's attack fails in this case). Consequently, Brumley and Boneh had to significantly extend Schindler's approach to successfully attack OpenSSL. Their attack is undoubtedly the most advanced practical timing attack developed to date.

In the OpenSSL implementation of modular exponentiation, there are two algorithmic issues that create significant timing differences. First, there are the extra reductions in the Montgomery algorithm. This is precisely the issue that Schindler exploits in his attack [129]. Second, the use of Karatsuba and normal multiplication creates significant timing differences. However, the timing attack is greatly complicated by the fact that these two timing effects tend to counteract each other.

Suppose we want to decrypt C using the OpenSSL implementation of RSA. When the Montgomery form of C is close to p, but less than p, then the number of extra reductions will be large—as can be seen from Figure 7.2—and therefore the decryption time will increase. On the other hand, if the Montgomery form of C is slightly larger than p, then the number of extra reductions will be relatively small and the decryption time will decrease (again, see Figure 7.2).

When the Montgomery form of C is slightly less than p, then many of the multiplication operations in Table 7.6 will involve numbers that are of about the same magnitude. Consequently, Karatsuba multiplication will predominate in this case, which reduces the time as compared to normal multiplication. On the other hand, when the Montgomery form of C slightly exceeds p, then C is small (due to the mod p reduction) so that more of the multiplication operations in Table 7.6 will involve numbers of significantly differing size. Consequently, the slower normal multiplication routine will predominate.

The Brumley–Boneh attack relies on the fact that these two effects (extra reductions and normal versus Karatsuba multiplication) each dominate during different parts of the attack. This implies that Schindler's attack could not be used to recover those bits where the Karatsuba versus normal multiplication timing effect dominates. Therefore, Schindler's timing attack cannot succeed against the OpenSSL implementation of RSA.

Building on Schindler's work, Brumley and Boneh were able to develop a timing attack against RSA decryption in OpenSSL. Chosen ciphertext messages are decrypted and timing information is obtained. This timing information is used to recover a factor p of the modulus N, where $N = pq$ with $p < q$.

Unlike Schindler's attack (but similar to Kocher's attack), the Brumley–Boneh attack recovers the unknown bits of $p = (p_0, p_1, \ldots, p_n)$, where $p_0 = 1$, one at a time, from the most significant bit to the least significant bit (in our notation, p_1 to p_n). It is not necessary to recover all of the bits of p, since given half of the bits, an algorithm due to Coppersmith [31] can be used to efficiently compute the factorization of N. Of course, the private key d is easily obtained from p, q and the public encryption exponent e.

The Brumley–Boneh attack [22] can be summarized as follows:

1. Suppose that bits $p_1, p_2, \ldots, p_{i-1}$ of p have been determined. Let

$$C_0 = (p_0, p_1, \ldots, p_{i-1}, 0, 0, \ldots, 0),$$

that is, C_0 consists of the known high-order bits of p with the remaining bits all set to 0. Similarly, let

$$C_1 = (p_0, p_1, \ldots, p_{i-1}, 1, 0, \ldots, 0).$$

If the unknown bit p_i is 1, then we have $C_0 < C_1 \leq p$; otherwise, we have $C_0 \leq p < C_1$.

2. For C_0 and C_1, the decryption times $T(C_0)$ and $T(C_1)$, respectively, are measured and we let $\Delta = |T(C_0) - T(C_1)|$. If $C_0 < p < C_1$, then Δ will be "large", indicating that $p_i = 0$. If $C_0 < C_1 < p$, then Δ will be "small," and we infer that $p_i = 1$. Previous values of Δ are used to set thresholds for "large" and "small." Note that this presumes that either the extra reductions or the multiplication (normal versus Karatsuba) predominates at each step. For the 0 bits of p, at those steps where the extra reductions predominate, we have $T(C_0) - T(C_1) > 0$ (as indicated in Figure 7.2), while for those steps where the multiplication effect predominates, we have $T(C_0) - T(C_1) < 0$ (as discussed above).

3. This process is repeated to successively obtain bits $p_{i+1}, p_{i+2}, p_{i+3}, \ldots$ of p, until half of the bits of p have been recovered. Then Coppersmith's algorithm is used to determine p and q, from which d is easily computed.

One complication that arises in this attack is due to the use of sliding windows in OpenSSL, since it greatly reduces the number of multiplications—and thereby the amount of timing information available. In [22], statistical methods are used to compensate for the smaller number of multiplications by C due to sliding windows (in comparison to repeated squaring), as well as for the effects of a networked environment, where timings are inherently less accurate. This compensation is accomplished by performing multiple decryptions for each bit of p. The decryption time is measured for a neighborhood of values, $C, C + 1, \ldots, C + k$, and for each $C + j$ in the neighborhood, the decryption time is measured repeatedly to obtain an average time. While this requires more decryptions, sufficient timing information can be accumulated to exploit small timing differences, in spite of the sliding window and network-induced timing variations.

The neighborhood size and the number of times a decryption is repeated must be large enough to yield a Δ value which strongly indicates the private key bit. Otherwise, the Δ values corresponding to private key bits 1 and 0 will have roughly the same order of magnitude and it will be impossible to discern the bit correctly with a high probability. In Brumley and Boneh's attack [22], private keys corresponding to 1024-bit moduli were recovered, using about 1,433,600 chosen ciphertexts over a realistic network that included several routers and switches. Each attack took about two hours to complete.

It is not too difficult to simulate this timing attack. For example, in [150], the Brumley–Boneh attack was simulated and, using a sample size of seven and a neighborhood size of 3200, many bits of one factor of a 1024-bit modulus were recovered.

Preventing RSA Timing Attacks

A strong defense against timing attacks is provided by *RSA blinding*, which is implemented as follows. To decrypt ciphertext C, we first compute the intermediate value $Y = r^e C \pmod{N}$, where r is a randomly-selected value and e is the RSA encryption exponent. Then Y is decrypted in the usual way, followed by multiplication by $r^{-1} \pmod{N}$. This yields the desired result since

$$r^{-1}Y^d = r^{-1}(r^e C)^d = r^{-1}rC^d = C^d \pmod{N}.$$

Since r is random, Y is random and measuring the decryption time for Y does not reveal any information about the private key d. It is important that a new random r be used for every decryption.

Instead of blinding, an alternative would be to always carry out the extra reduction in the Montgomery algorithm where, if no extra reduction is required, a dummy extra reduction is used. This approach is championed by Schindler [129]. In addition, it is possible to use Karatsuba multiplication in every case. While these modifications would seem to stifle any timing attack, Brumley and Boneh [22] argue against this approach, since, for example, the dummy extra reduction might be optimized into oblivion by an optimizing compiler.

Another approach that has been suggested [18] is to "quantize" RSA decryption, that is, to make all decryptions take some multiple of a specified amount of time (a time "quantum"). Brumley and Boneh [22] note that for this to be completely effective, all decryptions must take the maximum amount of time of any decryption, so the performance penalty might be substantial.

RSA blinding is the preferred method to prevent timing attacks. The drawbacks include a slight performance penalty and the need for a reasonably good source of randomness to generate the blinding factors.

Timing Attacks Conclusion

Timing attacks vividly illustrate that when analyzing the strength of a cryptosystem, all aspects must be considered. In particular, it is not sufficient for a cipher to be mathematically secure, or even secure against "standard" cryptanalytic attacks. Attackers will always look for the weakest link, and they are not obliged to play by any set of presumed rules.

Timing attacks are just one example of a general class of attacks known as side-channel attacks. A side channel is a source of information that—based solely on an analysis of the underlying algorithm—is not supposed to be available to the attacker. Side-channel attacks have been developed which rely on power analysis, fault analysis and electromagnetic fields (EMF). These types of attacks have been very significant recently, particularly in the design of smartcards. Side-channel attacks will undoubtedly continue to play an important role in the design and implementation of systems that use public key cryptography. As mentioned above, timing attacks have recently been developed for symmetric ciphers [12], but, so far at least, these attacks appear to be considerably less practical than timing attacks on public key cryptosystems.

7.4.2 Glitching Attack

In some situations, it is possible to induce a "glitch" or error in an RSA computation. For example, if a smartcard is abused in some way, it might flip a bit or cause some other type of error in the resulting computation. Any system that is in the attacker's possession is potentially subject to such a glitch. An NGSCB "trusted computing" system is one non-smartcard example of such a system [142].

Surprisingly, in some RSA implementations, a single glitch can enable an attacker to factor the modulus, and thereby recover the private key. Specifically, an RSA implementation that employs the CRT (as discussed above) is potentially subject to a glitching attack.

Suppose that an RSA signature is computed for the message M in a system that uses CRT. Then the signature is computed as follows. First,

$$M_p = M \ (\text{mod } p) \ \text{ and } \ M_q = M \ (\text{mod } q),$$

followed by

$$x_p = M_p^{d_p} \ (\text{mod } p) \ \text{ and } \ x_q = M_q^{d_q} \ (\text{mod } q),$$

where $d_p = d \ (\text{mod } (p-1))$ and $d_q = d \ (\text{mod } (q-1))$. The desired signature is given by

$$S = M^d \ (\text{mod } N) = (ax_p + bx_q) \ (\text{mod } N),$$

where the constant a satisfies

$$a = 1 \ (\text{mod } p) \ \text{ and } \ a = 0 \ (\text{mod } q)$$

and b satisfies

$$b = 0 \ (\text{mod } p) \ \text{ and } \ b = 1 \ (\text{mod } q).$$

Now suppose that this system is subject to glitching, and the attacker forces an error in the computation. Suppose that this error occurs so that x_q' is computed instead of x_q, but x_p is correct. That is, the glitch forces an error in the computation $M_q = M \pmod q$ or $x_q = M_q^{d_q} \pmod q$, but the remaining computations are unaffected. Then

$$S' = (ax_p + bx_q') \pmod N$$

is returned instead of S.

The attacker can easily verify that the "signed" value is incorrect, since we have $(S')^e \pmod N \neq M$. But, since $x_p = M_p^{d_p} \pmod p$, by the definitions of a and b,

$$S' \pmod p = x_p = M_p^{d_p} = (M \pmod p))^{d (\bmod \ (p-1))}.$$

It follows (see Problem 15) that

$$(S')^e = M \pmod p.$$

Then the attacker can compute $(S')^e$ and $(S')^e - M$ is a multiple of the factor p. Also, since $x_q' \neq M_q^{d_q} \pmod q$, by the definitions of a and b,

$$(S')^e \neq M \pmod q,$$

which implies that $(S')^e - M$ is not a multiple of q and therefore not a multiple of N. Consequently, the attacker can compute $\gcd(N, (S')^e - M)$ to reveal a nontrivial factor of N.

The bottom line here is that a single glitch can break RSA in certain realistic implementations. Boneh [19] points out that random faults can also be used to attack many RSA implementations that do not employ CRT.

7.4.3   Implementation Attacks Conclusions

RSA has proven to be remarkably robust. Having been carefully scrutinized by many researchers, the underlying algorithm has remained secure since its invention more than three decades ago [19]. Timing attacks and glitching attacks are among the very few known realistic attacks on sound implementations of RSA, and these do not result from any weakness in the underlying algorithms, and, furthermore, there are straightforward defenses against such attacks. Undoubtedly it is for these reasons that RSA is the de facto standard in public key cryptography, and it appears likely to remain so for the foreseeable future.

7.5   Summary

Factoring and discrete log algorithms represent fundamental attacks on the most popular public key systems. Advances in factoring or computing discrete logarithms could significantly change the nature of public key cryptography. At the least, advances in this area would require that larger parameters be used to achieve the same level of security. It is also conceivable that a breakthrough (such as quantum computers) could render entire classes of public key systems vulnerable.

Timing and glitching attacks represent cutting-edge attacks, where cryptography is attacked indirectly. These attacks have proved to be extremely important recently, and there is every indication that this trend will continue. It is important to be aware of the overall system in which cryptography is employed, since seemingly extraneous issues can lead to devastating attacks.

7.6   Problems

1. Construct a simple example (other than the one given in the text) to illustrate the Montgomery multiplication algorithm as discussed in Section 7.4.1.

2. Let $p = 123$ and $R = 128$. For each $x = 0, 1, 2, \ldots, 5p$ let $f(x)$ be the number of extra reductions that occur when using the algorithm in Table 7.7 to compute $x^{31} \pmod{p}$. Plot $f(x)$.

3. Consider the congruence of squares in (7.1).

   a. Show that we cannot be "unlucky" when $x \neq \pm y \pmod{N}$. That is, if $x \neq \pm y \pmod{N}$ then the congruence $x^2 = y^2 \pmod{N}$ must reveal a nontrivial factor of N.

   b. Suppose $x^2 = y^2 \pmod{N}$ but $x = \pm y$. Why can we not factor N?

4. Suppose that in Dixon's Algorithm or the quadratic sieve we are unlucky, that is, $x - y$ and $x + y$ do not reveal a factor of N. Is it necessary to start over and redo all of the work?

5. Empirically estimate the probability that for a given pair x and y that satisfy $x^2 = y^2 \pmod{N}$, we have $x \neq \pm y$.

6. Suppose that the prime p divides $Q(x)$, where $Q(x)$ is defined in (7.6). Show that p divides $Q(x + kp)$ for all integers $k \neq 0$.

7. For Dixon's Algorithm or the quadratic sieve, when determining the factor base, we should exclude any primes p for which

$$\left(\frac{N}{p}\right) \neq 1,$$

where $\left(\frac{N}{p}\right)$ is the Legendre symbol [95]. Why is this the case?

8. Consider the RSA public key cryptosystem. Suppose that the best available attack is to factor the modulus N, and the best available factoring algorithm is the number field sieve. Also assume that the best available attack on a symmetric cipher is an exhaustive key search.

   a. A 1024-bit modulus N provides roughly the same security as a symmetric key of what length?

   b. A 2048-bit modulus N provides roughly the same security as a symmetric key of what length?

   c. What size of modulus N is required to have security roughly comparable to a 256-bit symmetric key?

9. The algorithm described in Section 7.3.2 is actually "giant-step baby-step," since the giant steps are done first. Is there any advantage or disadvantage to doing the baby steps first and the giant steps second?

10. Compute 3^{10i} (mod 101) for $i = 1, 2, \ldots, 10$ and compare your results to the second row in Table 7.3. Explain.

11. Consider the index calculus method of computing the discrete logarithm.

   a. Show that it is possible to find the logarithms, base g, of the elements in the factor base by solving a system of linear equations. Hint: Let $\{p_0, p_1, \ldots, p_{n-1}\}$ be the elements of the factor base. Randomly select $k \in \{0, 1, 2, \ldots, p-2\}$, compute $y = g^k$ (mod p) and try to write y as a product of elements in the factor base, that is,
   $$y = p_0^{c_0} \cdot p_1^{c_1} \cdot p_2^{c_2} \cdots p_{n-1}^{c_{n-1}},$$
   where each $c_i \geq 0$. Take $\log_g$ of both sides.

   b. Let $g = 6$ and $p = 229$ and let the factor base consist of the prime numbers less than 12. Select random values of k as in part a, until you obtain a system of linear equations that can be solved to determine the logarithms, base g, of the elements in the factor base. Solve the system to find the logarithms.

12. Recall the repeated squaring, Montgomery multiplication and CRT methods for efficient modular exponentiation, which are discussed in Section 7.4.1.

   a. Compute 5^{37} (mod 33) by repeated squaring.

    b. Compute 5^{37} (mod 33) using repeated squaring, with Montgomery multiplication and CRT. How many extra reductions occur?

13. Let $a = 31$ and $b = 25$.

    a. Find ab (mod 79) using the Montgomery algorithm.

    b. Find a^b (mod 79) using the Montgomery algorithm.

14. Use two iterations of the Karatsuba algorithm to compute the product $337 \cdot 521$. Clearly show the intermediate steps.

15. Suppose that the RSA signature is computed using CRT as follows. Let M be the message,

$$M_p = M \text{ (mod } p) \text{ and } M_q = M \text{ (mod } q)$$

and

$$x_p = M_p^{d_p} \text{ (mod } p) \text{ and } x_q = M_q^{d_q} \text{ (mod } q),$$

where $d_p = d$ (mod $(p-1)$) and $d_q = d$ (mod $(q-1)$). Then the signature is given by

$$S = M^d \text{ (mod } N) = (ax_p + bx_q) \text{ (mod } N),$$

where the constant a satisfies

$$a = 1 \text{ (mod } p) \text{ and } a = 0 \text{ (mod } q)$$

and b satisfies

$$b = 0 \text{ (mod } p) \text{ and } b = 1 \text{ (mod } q).$$

Suppose that due to a glitch, $x_q' \neq x_q$ is computed but x_p is computed correctly. Let

$$S' = (ax_p + bx_q') \text{ (mod } N).$$

Show that

$$(S')^e = M \text{ (mod } p).$$

16. Write a computer program to implement the following timing attack on RSA [160]. Assume that the repeated squaring algorithm is used (without CRT, Montgomery multiplication or a sliding window), and the decryption exponent is of the form

$$d = (d_0, d_1, \ldots, d_n),$$

where $d_0 = 1$.

    i. Trudy believes she can recover d one bit at a time. To accomplish this, Trudy chooses messages Y_i, where $Y_i^3 < N$ and has Alice decrypt each of them. For each i, let y_i be the time required to decrypt Y_i. Trudy computes y, the average of the times y_i.

    ii. Trudy then chooses messages Z_i, where $Z_i^2 < N < Z_i^3$ and has Alice sign each of them. For each i, let z_i be the time required to sign Z_i. Trudy computes the average z of the times z_i.

    iii. If $d_1 = 1$, then $z_i > y_i$ for each i. On the other hand, if $d_1 = 0$, then $z_i \approx y_i$ for each i. Thus if z is sufficiently larger than y, Trudy deduces that $d_1 = 1$. Otherwise, she concludes that $d_1 = 0$.

    iv. Having recovered d_1, Trudy uses an analogous process to find d_2, where, in this case, the Y_i and Z_i are chosen to satisfy different criteria, depending on the recovered value of d_1. Once, d_2 is known, Trudy proceeds in similar fashion to recover additional bits of d.

Use your program to answer the following questions.

    a. Verify that the attack can be used to recover private key bits d_1 and d_2 for the case where the modulus is $N = 36{,}355{,}783$, the encryption exponent is $e = 3$, and the decryption exponent is given by $d = 24{,}229{,}147$. Also, show that you can recover bits d_1 and d_2 for $N = 13{,}789{,}777$, $e = 3$, and $d = 9{,}188{,}011$.

    b. What percent of the time does this method work? Is it a practical method?

Hint: For part a, instead of trying to actually time the program, you can "cheat", and simply count the number of modular reduction steps that occurs.

17. Suppose Alice's public key is $(N, e) = (667, 3)$.

    a. Find Alice's private key d.

    b. Encrypt $M = 17$.

    c. Decrypt the result of part b using the blinding factor $r = 9$. Show all intermediate steps.

18. Suppose that the work factors for factoring algorithms A through F are given by the following functions, where N is the integer to be factored.

Algorithm	Work Factor
A	$f(N) = N$
B	$f(N) = \sqrt{N}$
C	$f(N) = 2^{\log_2 \log_2 N}$
D	$f(N) = 2^{\log_2 N}$
E	$f(N) = 2^{(\log_2 N)^{1/2}(\log_2 \log_2 N)^{1/2}}$

Which of the algorithms A through E have a polynomial work factor, which have an exponential work factor and which have a subexponential work factor? Recall that the work is determined as a function of the number of bits in N, that is, as a function of $x = \log_2(N)$.

19. Suppose that in Kocher's timing attack, we obtain the timings $T(C_j)$ and the emulated timings $\tilde{t}_{0\ldots2}$ for $d_0 d_1 d_2 \in \{100, 101, 110, 111\}$, as given in the table below.

j	$T(C_j)$	$\tilde{t}_{0\ldots2}$			
		100	101	110	111
0	20	5	7	5	8
1	21	4	7	4	1
2	19	1	6	4	7
3	22	2	8	5	2
4	24	10	6	8	8
5	23	11	5	7	7
6	21	1	1	6	5
7	19	7	1	2	3

a. What is the most likely value of $d_0 d_1 d_2$ and why?

b. Why does this attack not succeed if CRT or Montgomery multiplication is used?

20. Suppose that for Schindler's timing attack, we obtain the the following timing data.

C_j	80	85	90	95	100	105	110	115	120	125	130
$T(C_j)$	50	52	51	56	60	50	52	55	60	56	64

a. Which interval is most likely to contain a factor p of N?

b. Suppose $N = 12{,}827$. For every n in the interval you selected in part a, compute $\gcd(n, N)$. Use this information to factor N.

21. In the Brumley–Boneh attack, the bits are recovered one at a time. Suppose that the following timing information, with a threshold value of $\Delta = 10$, was used to recover bits p_1 through p_9.

	Bit								
Time	1	2	3	4	5	6	7	8	9
$T(C_0)$	98	96	90	85	96	90	80	73	78
$T(C_1)$	91	84	75	88	80	94	95	85	84

    a. What values for the bits p_1 through p_9 were recovered?

    b. For which bits does the extra reduction in the Montgomery algorithm dominate, and for which bits does the normal versus Karatsuba multiplication effect dominate?

22. Suppose Alice's public key is $(N, e) = (33, 3)$. Then Alice's private key is $d = 7$. As discussed in the example on page 337, we can use the Chinese Remainder Theorem (CRT) method of modular exponentiation, with $a = 12$, $b = 22$, $d_p = 7$, and $d_q = 1$. Suppose $M = 5$. Then to sign M, we compute $M_p = 5$ and $M_q = 2$ and, as in (7.16), we compute

$$x_p = M_p^{d_p} = 5^7 = 3 \ (\text{mod} \ 11) \quad \text{and} \quad x_q = M_q^{d_q} = 2^1 = 2 \ (\text{mod} \ 3).$$

Finally, we compute the signature as

$$S = M^d \ (\text{mod} \ N) = 5^7 = (3 \cdot 12 + 22 \cdot 2) \ (\text{mod} \ 33) = 14.$$

Suppose that an attacker forces a glitch error in the computation so that $x'_q = 1$ is computed instead of $x_q = 2$, but all other intermediate quantities are computed correctly.

    a. Find S', the "signature" that is computed using x'_q instead of x_q. How would the attacker know that an error has occurred?

    b. Determine the factors of N from S'.

APPENDIX

A-1 MD5 Tables

The following tables are contained in this appendix. A brief description of each table is provided.

- Table A-1 contains the step constants for the MD5 hash algorithm. The precise values of these constants are not needed to understand the MD5 attack described in the text, but they are necessary to implement the algorithm or the attack.

- Tables A-2 and A-3 give Wang's output differential for the first message block, M_0. The input differential can be deduced from this table and it is also given in (5.47) in Section 5.4. In these tables we use a compact notation for sums of powers. This notation is also used, for example, in Table 5.11 in the text and it is defined on page 239.

- Tables A-4 and A-5 give Wang's output differential for the second message block, M_1. The input differential can be deduced from this table and it is also given in (5.48) in Section 5.4. In these tables we use a compact notation for sums of powers. This notation is also used, for example, in Table 5.11 in the text and it is defined on page 239.

- Table A-6 contains the sufficient conditions for the first message block, M_0, that are satisfied deterministically in Stevens' attack. Note that the conditions on the Q_i, for $i = 0, 1, \ldots, 15$ are satisfied by single-step modifications, while the conditions on the Q_i, for $i = 16, 17, \ldots, 20$ are satisfied by multi-step modifications, as discussed in Section 5.4.5. In this table, a 0 indicates that the particular bit must be a 0, and a 1 indicates the bit is a 1. The character "^" indicates that the bit must equal the bit in the corresponding position of the preceding row, while a "!" indicates that the bit must not equal the bit in the corresponding position of the preceding row and a "." indicates that there is no restriction on the bit.

- Table A-7 contains the sufficient conditions for the first message block, M_0, that are satisfied probabilistically in Stevens' attack. That is, for each putative solution, these conditions are tested. If any of these conditions fail, the putative solution is discarded. In this table, we have the restriction that $I, J, K \in \{0, 1\}$, with $I \neq K$.

- Table A-8 gives information analogous to Table A-6 for M_1, the second message block. See the description of Table A-6, above, for more information on this table.

- Table A-9 gives information analogous to Table A-7 for M_1 the second message block. See the description of Table A-7, above, for more information on this table.

Table A-1: MD5 Step Constants

j	K_j	j	K_j	j	K_j	j	K_j
0	0xd76aa478	16	0xf61e2562	32	0xfffa3942	48	0xf4292244
1	0xe8c7b756	17	0xc040b340	33	0x8771f681	49	0x432aff97
2	0x242070db	18	0x265e5a51	34	0x6d9d6122	50	0xab9423a7
3	0xc1bdceee	19	0xe9b6c7aa	35	0xfde5380c	51	0xfc93a039
4	0xf57c0faf	20	0xd62f105d	36	0xa4beea44	52	0x655b59c3
5	0x4787c62a	21	0x02441453	37	0x4bdecfa9	53	0x8f0ccc92
6	0xa8304613	22	0xd8a1e681	38	0xf6bb4b60	54	0xffeff47d
7	0xfd469501	23	0xe7d3fbc8	39	0xbebfbc70	55	0x85845dd1
8	0x698098d8	24	0x21e1cde6	40	0x289b7ec6	56	0x6fa87e4f
9	0x8b44f7af	25	0xc33707d6	41	0xeaa127fa	57	0xfe2ce6e0
10	0xffff5bb1	26	0xf4d50d87	42	0xd4ef3085	58	0xa3014314
11	0x895cd7be	27	0x455a14ed	43	0x04881d05	59	0x4e0811a1
12	0x6b901122	28	0xa9e3e905	44	0xd9d4d039	60	0xf7537e82
13	0xfd987193	29	0xfcefa3f8	45	0xe6db99e5	61	0xbd3af235
14	0xa679438e	30	0x676f02d9	46	0x1fa27cf8	62	0x2ad7d2bb
15	0x49b40821	31	0x8d2a4c8a	47	0xc4ac5665	63	0xeb86d391

Table A-2: Wang's ΔM_0 Differential (Part 1) [157]

j	Output	W_j	ΔW_j	ΔOutput	∇Output
4	Q_4	X_4	2^{31}	$\overset{-}{6}$	....-++++++ +++++++++ ++......
5	Q_5	X_5	0	$\overset{+}{31}\ \overset{+}{23}\ \overset{-}{6}$	+....... +....... ....-......
6	Q_6	X_6	0	$\overset{-}{27}\ \overset{+}{23}\ \overset{-}{6}\ \overset{-}{0}$	++++++-- -....... ....-+++ ++-+++++
7	Q_7	X_7	0	$\overset{-}{23}\ \overset{-}{17}\ \overset{-}{15}\ \overset{+}{0}$	.... -..-++- +....... ......+
8	Q_8	X_8	0	$\overset{+}{31}\ \overset{-}{6}\ \overset{+}{0}$	-....... ....- ++....+-
9	Q_9	X_9	0	$\overset{+}{31}\ \overset{+}{12}$	+....... ....+-.... ....
10	Q_{10}	X_{10}	0	$\overset{+}{31}\ \overset{+}{30}$	++...... ....
11	Q_{11}	X_{11}	$\overset{+}{15}$	$\overset{+}{31}\ \overset{-}{13}\ \overset{-}{7}$	+....... ....-+++ +++....- +.......
12	Q_{12}	X_{12}	0	$\overset{+}{31}\ \overset{+}{24}$	+.....+- ....
13	Q_{13}	X_{13}	0	$\overset{+}{31}$	+....... ....
14	Q_{14}	X_{14}	$\overset{+}{31}$	$\overset{+}{31}\ \overset{-}{15}\ \overset{+}{3}$	+....... .... -....... ...+...
15	Q_{15}	X_{15}	0	$\overset{+}{31}\ \overset{-}{29}$	+.-..... ....
16	Q_{16}	X_1	0	$\overset{+}{31}$	+....... ....
17	Q_{17}	X_6	0	$\overset{+}{31}$	+....... ....
18	Q_{18}	X_{11}	$\overset{+}{15}$	$\overset{+}{31}\ \overset{+}{17}$	+....... ......+. ....
19	Q_{19}	X_0	0	$\overset{+}{31}$	+....... ....
20	Q_{20}	X_5	0	$\overset{+}{31}$	+....... ....
21	Q_{21}	X_{10}	0	$\overset{+}{31}$	+....... ....
22	Q_{22}	X_{15}	0	0	....
23	Q_{23}	X_4	$\overset{+}{31}$	0	....
24	Q_{24}	X_9	0	0	....
25	Q_{25}	X_{14}	$\overset{+}{31}$	0	....
$\vdots$	$\vdots$	$\vdots$	$\vdots$	$\vdots$	$\vdots$

Table A-3: Wang's ΔM_0 Differential (Part 2) [157]

j	Output	W_j	ΔW_j	ΔOutput	∇Output
$\vdots$	$\vdots$	$\vdots$	$\vdots$	$\vdots$	$\vdots$
34	Q_{34}	X_{11}	$\overset{+}{15}$	$\overset{+}{31}$	$\pm$...... ....
35	Q_{35}	X_{14}	$\overset{+}{31}$	$\overset{+}{31}$	$\pm$...... ....
36	Q_{36}	X_1	0	$\overset{+}{31}$	$\pm$...... ....
37	Q_{37}	X_4	$\overset{+}{31}$	$\overset{+}{31}$	$\pm$...... ....
38	Q_{38}	X_7	0	$\overset{+}{31}$	$\pm$...... ....
$\vdots$	$\vdots$	$\vdots$	$\vdots$	$\vdots$	$\vdots$
44	Q_{44}	X_9	0	$\overset{+}{31}$	$\pm$...... ....
45	Q_{45}	X_{12}	0	$\overset{+}{31}$	$+$...... ....
46	Q_{46}	X_{15}	0	$\overset{+}{31}$	$+$...... ....
47	Q_{47}	X_2	0	$\overset{+}{31}$	$+$...... ....
48	Q_{48}	X_0	0	$\overset{+}{31}$	$+$...... ....
49	Q_{49}	X_7	0	$\overset{+}{31}$	$-$...... ....
50	Q_{50}	X_{14}	$\overset{+}{31}$	$\overset{+}{31}$	$+$...... ....
51	Q_{51}	X_5	0	$\overset{+}{31}$	$-$...... ....
$\vdots$	$\vdots$	$\vdots$	$\vdots$	$\vdots$	$\vdots$
57	Q_{57}	X_{15}	0	$\overset{+}{31}$	$-$...... ....
58	Q_{58}	X_6	0	$\overset{+}{31}$	$+$...... ....
59	Q_{59}	X_{13}	0	$\overset{+}{31}$	$+$...... ....
60	$Q_{60} + A$	X_4	$\overset{+}{31}$	$\overset{+}{31}$	$+$...... ....
61	$Q_{61} + D$	X_{11}	$\overset{+}{15}$	$\overset{+}{31}\ \overset{+}{25}$	$+$.....$+$. ....
62	$Q_{62} + C$	X_2	0	$\overset{+}{31}\ \overset{+}{25}$	$+$....$+-$. ....
63	$Q_{63} + B$	X_9	0	$\overset{+}{31}\ \overset{+}{25}$	$-$.....$+$. ....

Table A-4: Wang's ΔM_1 Differential (Part 1) [157]

j	Output	W_j	ΔW_j	ΔOutput	∇Output
0	Q_0	X_0	0	$\overset{+}{31}\ \overset{+}{25}$	-.....+. ....
1	Q_1	X_1	0	$\overset{+}{31}\ \overset{+}{25}\ \overset{+}{5}$	-.+...+. ....
2	Q_2	X_2	0	$\overset{+}{31}\ \overset{+}{25}\ \overset{+}{16}\ \overset{+}{11}\ \overset{+}{5}$	-+-----. ..+----- ...+-... +--.....
3	Q_3	X_3	0	$\overset{+}{31}\ \overset{+}{25}\ \overset{+}{5}\ \overset{-}{1}$	-....+-. ....+-+++.
4	Q_4	X_4	$\overset{+}{31}$	$\overset{+}{31}\ \overset{+}{9}\ \overset{+}{8}\ \overset{+}{6}\ \overset{+}{0}$	+....... ....+---+ +-.....+
5	Q_5	X_5	0	$\overset{+}{31}\ \overset{-}{20}\ \overset{-}{16}$	+....... ..-+..-+
6	Q_6	X_6	0	$\overset{+}{31}\ \overset{-}{27}\ \overset{-}{6}$	-..-+... ....-+ ++.....
7	Q_7	X_7	0	$31\ \overset{-}{23}\ \overset{-}{17}\ \overset{+}{15}$	-....-++ +.....-+ -.......
8	Q_8	X_8	0	$\overset{+}{31}\ \overset{+}{6}\ \overset{+}{0}$	-....... ....+- --....+-
9	Q_9	X_9	0	$\overset{+}{31}\ \overset{+}{12}$	-....... ....+....
10	Q_{10}	X_{10}	0	$\overset{+}{31}$	-.......
11	Q_{11}	X_{11}	$\overset{-}{15}$	$\overset{+}{31}\ \overset{-}{13}\ \overset{-}{7}$	-....... ....-+++ +++.....
12	Q_{12}	X_{12}	0	$\overset{+}{31}\ \overset{+}{24}$	++------ ....
13	Q_{13}	X_{13}	0	$\overset{+}{31}$	+.......
14	Q_{14}	X_{14}	$\overset{+}{31}$	$\overset{+}{31}\ \overset{+}{15}\ \overset{+}{3}$	+....... .... +....... ....+...
15	Q_{15}	X_{15}	0	$\overset{+}{31}\ \overset{-}{29}$	+.-..... ....
16	Q_{16}	X_1	0	$\overset{+}{31}$	+.......
17	Q_{17}	X_6	0	$\overset{+}{31}$	+.......
18	Q_{18}	X_{11}	$\overset{-}{15}$	$\overset{+}{31}\ \overset{+}{17}$	+....... ......+. ....
19	Q_{19}	X_0	0	$\overset{+}{31}$	+.......
20	Q_{20}	X_5	0	$\overset{+}{31}$	+.......
21	Q_{21}	X_{10}	0	$\overset{+}{31}$	+.......
22	Q_{22}	X_{15}	0	$\overset{+}{31}$	+.......
23	Q_{23}	X_4	$\overset{+}{31}$	$\overset{+}{31}$	+.......
24	Q_{24}	X_9	0	0	....
25	Q_{25}	X_{14}	$\overset{+}{31}$	0	....
$\vdots$	$\vdots$	$\vdots$	$\vdots$	$\vdots$	$\vdots$

Table A-5: Wang's ΔM_1 Differential (Part 2) [157]

j	Output	W_j	ΔW_j	ΔOutput	∇Output
⋮	⋮	⋮	⋮	⋮	⋮
34	Q_{34}	X_{11}	$\overset{-}{15}$	$\overset{+}{31}$	±...... ....
35	Q_{35}	X_{14}	$\overset{+}{31}$	$\overset{+}{31}$	±...... ....
36	Q_{36}	X_1	0	$\overset{+}{31}$	±...... ....
37	Q_{37}	X_4	$\overset{+}{31}$	$\overset{+}{31}$	±...... ....
38	Q_{38}	X_7	0	$\overset{+}{31}$	±...... ....
⋮	⋮	⋮	⋮	⋮	⋮
48	Q_{48}	X_0	0	$\overset{+}{31}$	+...... ....
49	Q_{49}	X_7	0	$\overset{+}{31}$	−...... ....
50	Q_{50}	X_{14}	$\overset{+}{31}$	$\overset{+}{31}$	+...... ....
51	Q_{51}	X_5	0	$\overset{+}{31}$	−...... ....
⋮	⋮	⋮	⋮	⋮	⋮
58	Q_{58}	X_6	0	$\overset{+}{31}$	+...... ....
59	Q_{59}	X_{13}	0	$\overset{+}{31}$	+...... ....
60	$Q_{60} + AA$	X_4	$\overset{+}{31}$	0	....
61	$Q_{61} + DD$	X_{11}	$\overset{-}{15}$	0	....
62	$Q_{62} + CC$	X_2	0	0	....
63	$Q_{63} + BB$	X_9	0	0	....

Table A-6: M_0 Deterministic Sufficient Conditions [144]

	Conditions on M_0				Number
Q_2	....	....0...	....0...	.0......	3
Q_3	1.......	0^^^1^^^	^^^^1^^^	^011....	21
Q_4	1000100.	01..0000	00000000	0010.1.1	27
Q_5	0000001^	01111111	10111100	0100^0^1	32
Q_6	00000011	11111110	11111000	00100000	32
Q_7	00000001	1..10001	0.0.0101	01000000	28
Q_8	11111011	...10000	0.1^1111	00111101	28
Q_9	0111....	0..11111	1101...0	01....00	19
Q_{10}	00100000	1...0001	11000000	11000010	29
Q_{11}	000...00	1000	0001...1	0.......	15
Q_{12}	01....01	1111	111....0	0...1...	14
Q_{13}	0.0...00	1011	111....1	1...1...	14
Q_{14}	0.1...01	0	1.......	....0...	7
Q_{15}	0!1.....	......!.	....	....	4
Q_{16}	0!......	......0.	^.......	....^...	5
Q_{17}	0.^.....	......1.	....	....	3
Q_{18}	0.......	......0.	....	....	2
Q_{19}	0.......	....!..	....	....	2
Q_{20}	0.......	......^.	....	....	2
				Subtotal	287

Table A-7: M_0 Probabilistic Sufficient Conditions [144]

	Conditions on M_0	Number
Q_{21}	0......	1
Q_{22}	0......	1
Q_{23}	1......	1
$Q_{24} - Q_{44}$	....	0
Q_{45}	I......	0
Q_{46}	J......	0
Q_{47}	I......	1
Q_{48}	J......	1
Q_{49}	K......	1
Q_{50}	J......	1
Q_{51}	K......	1
Q_{52}	J......	1
Q_{53}	K......	1
Q_{54}	J......	1
Q_{55}	K......	1
Q_{56}	J......	1
Q_{57}	K......	1
Q_{58}	J......	1
Q_{59}	I......	1
Q_{60}	J......	1
Q_{61}	I......	1
Q_{62}	J......	1
Q_{63}	....	0
	Subtotal	19
	T_j restrictions	2
	IV conditions for M_1	8
	Total conditions	316

Table A-8: M_1 Deterministic Sufficient Conditions [144]

	Conditions from M_0				Number
Q_{-3}	......0.	....	....	....	(1)
Q_{-2}	^....01.	....	....	....	(3)
Q_{-1}	^....00.	....	....	..0.....	(4)
	Conditions on M_1				Subtotal: (8)
Q_0	!...010.	..1....0	....0...	.10.....	9
Q_1	^^^^110.	..0^^^^0	1..^1...	^10..00.	21
Q_2	^011111.	..011111	0..01..1	011^^11.	24
Q_3	^011101.	..000100	...00^^0	0001000^	26
Q_4	!10010..	..101111	...01110	01010000	25
Q_5	^..0010.	1.10..10	11.01100	01010110	25
Q_6	!..1011^	1.00..01	10.11110	00.....1	21
Q_7	^..00100	0.11..10	1.....11	111...^0	19
Q_8	^..11100	0.....01	0..^..01	110...01	18
Q_9	^....111	1...1011	11001.11	11....00	20
Q_{10}	^..00...	1101	11000.11	110...11	19
Q_{11}	^^^00^^^	1000	0001....	1.......	17
Q_{12}	!0111111	0...1111	111.....	0...1...	18
Q_{13}	^1000000	1...1011	111.....	1...1...	18
Q_{14}	01111101	....	00......	....0...	11
Q_{15}	0.10....	......!.	....	....	4
Q_{16}	0!......	......0.	^.......	....^...	5
Q_{17}	0.^.....	......1.	....	....	3
Q_{18}	0.......	......0.	....	....	2
Q_{19}	0.......	.....!..	....	....	2
Q_{20}	0.......	......^.	....	....	2
				Subtotal	309

Table A-9: M_1 Probabilistic Sufficient Conditions [144]

	Conditions on M_1	Number
Q_{21}	O.......	1
Q_{22}	O.......	1
Q_{23}	1.......	1
Q_{24}–Q_{44}	....	0
Q_{45}	I.......	0
Q_{46}	J.......	0
Q_{47}	I.......	1
Q_{48}	J.......	1
Q_{49}	K.......	1
Q_{50}	J.......	1
Q_{51}	K.......	1
Q_{52}	J.......	1
Q_{53}	K.......	1
Q_{54}	J.......	1
Q_{55}	K.......	1
Q_{56}	J.......	1
Q_{57}	K.......	1
Q_{59}	J.......	1
Q_{59}	I.......	1
Q_{60}	J.......	1
Q_{61}	I.......	1
Q_{62}	J.......	1
Q_{63}	....	0
	Subtotal	19
	T_j restrictions	2
	Total conditions	330

A-2 Math

A-2.1 Number Theory

For a positive integer n, the *Euler phi function* (or *totient function*), denoted $\phi(n)$, gives the number of positive integers less than n that are relatively prime to n.

It is not difficult to show that if $n = p_1^{a_1} p_2^{a_2} \cdots p_k^{a_k}$ is the prime factorization of the positive integer n, then

$$\phi(n) = n \left(1 - \frac{1}{p_1}\right) \left(1 - \frac{1}{p_2}\right) \cdots \left(1 - \frac{1}{p_k}\right).$$

Another important fact is that the element $x \in \{0, 1, 2, \ldots, n-1\}$ has a multiplicative inverse modulo n if and only if $\gcd(x, n) = 1$.

Fermat's Little Theorem. If p is a prime number and p does not divide a, then $a^{p-1} = 1 \pmod p$.

Euler's Theorem. If $\gcd(a, n) = 1$, then $a^{\phi(n)} = 1 \pmod n$.

Chinese Remainder Theorem. Let $m_0, m_1, \ldots, m_{k-1}$ be positive integers such that for $i \neq j$, we have $\gcd(m_i, m_j) = 1$. Then given integers $a_0, a_1, \ldots, a_{k-1}$, there is a unique solution $x \pmod{m_0 m_1 \cdots m_{k-1}}$ to the system of simultaneous congruences

$$x = a_0 \pmod{m_0}, \ x = a_1 \pmod{m_1}, \ \ldots, \ x = a_{k-1} \pmod{m_{k-1}}.$$

Example. Find x that satisfies the system of congruences

$$x = 1 \pmod 3, \ x = 2 \pmod 5, \ x = 3 \pmod 7.$$

We first set $M = 3 \cdot 5 \cdot 7 = 105$, $M_0 = 105/3 = 35$, $M_1 = 105/5 = 21$ and $M_2 = 105/7 = 15$. Then we need to solve the congruences

$$35y_0 = 1 \pmod 3$$
$$21y_1 = 1 \pmod 5$$
$$15y_2 = 1 \pmod 7.$$

Easy calculations yield $y_0 = 2 \pmod 3$, $y_1 = 1 \pmod 5$ and $y_2 = 1 \pmod 7$. Then the desired solution to the system of congruences is given by

$$x = 1 \cdot 35 \cdot 2 + 2 \cdot 21 \cdot 1 + 3 \cdot 15 \cdot 1 = 157 = 52 \pmod{105}.$$

Euclidean Algorithm. Let $r_0 = a$ and $r_1 = b$ be non-negative integers with $b \neq 0$. Suppose that the division algorithm is successively applied to obtain $r_j = r_{j+1}q_{j+1} + r_{j+2}$ with $0 < r_{j+2} < r_{j+1}$, for $j = 0, 1, \ldots, n-2$, where $r_n = 0$. Then $\gcd(a, b) = r_{n-1}$, the last non-zero remainder.

Example. Find the greatest common divisor of 27 and 48. Express this gcd as a linear combination of 27 and 48.

From the Euclidean Algorithm, we have

$$48 = 27 \cdot 1 + 21$$
$$27 = 21 \cdot 1 + 6$$
$$21 = 6 \cdot 3 + 3$$
$$6 = 3 \cdot 2 + 0$$

which implies $\gcd(27, 48) = 3$. Using back-substitution, we obtain

$$\begin{aligned}
3 &= 21 - 6 \cdot 3 \\
&= 21 - (27 - 21 \cdot 1) \cdot 3 \\
&= (48 - 27 \cdot 1) - (27 - (48 - 27)) \cdot 3 \\
&= 48 - 27 - (27) \cdot 3 + (48) \cdot 3 - (27) \cdot 3 \\
&= (48) \cdot 4 - (27) \cdot 7.
\end{aligned}$$

A-2.2 Group Theory

A *group* $\langle G, * \rangle$ is a non-empty set G, together with a binary operation $*$ on G, such that the following axioms are satisfied:

- The binary operation $*$ is associative.

- There is an element $e \in G$ such that $e * x = x * e = x$, for all $x \in G$.

- For each $a \in G$, there is an element $a' \in G$ such that $a' * a = a * a' = e$.

A group $\langle G, * \rangle$ is *abelian* (or commutative) if $a * b = b * a$, for all $a, b \in G$.

A-2.3 Ring Theory

A *ring* $\langle R, +, \cdot \rangle$ is a non-empty set R, together with two binary operations $+$ and $\cdot$ (called addition and multiplication, respectively) defined on R such that the following axioms are satisfied:

- $\langle R, +, \cdot \rangle$ is an abelian group.

- Multiplication is associative.

- For all $a, b, c \in R$, we have $a(b + c) = ab + ac$ and $(a + b)c = ac + bc$ hold.

A-2.4 Linear Algebra

Matrix Operations

Addition of matrices is performed elementwise. For example,

$$\begin{bmatrix} 1 & 2 \\ 3 & -1 \end{bmatrix} + \begin{bmatrix} 5 & -1 \\ 2 & 0 \end{bmatrix} = \begin{bmatrix} 6 & 1 \\ 5 & -1 \end{bmatrix}.$$

If the matrices A and B do not have the same dimensions, then $A + B$ is undefined.

Suppose A is an $m \times r$ matrix, denoted $A_{m \times r}$, and B is an $r \times n$ matrix, denoted $B_{r \times n}$. Then the product $C = AB$ is an $m \times n$ matrix, that is, $C_{m \times n} = A_{m \times r} B_{r \times n}$. The entry in row i and column j of C is given by the formula

$$a_{i0}b_{0j} + a_{i1}b_{1j} + a_{i2}b_{2j} + \cdots + a_{i,r-1}b_{r-1,j},$$

where a_{ij} is the element in row i and column j of A, and similarly for b_{ij}. For example,

$$\begin{bmatrix} 1 & 2 \\ 3 & -1 \end{bmatrix} \begin{bmatrix} 5 & -1 \\ 2 & 0 \end{bmatrix} = \begin{bmatrix} 9 & -1 \\ 13 & -3 \end{bmatrix}.$$

A set of vectors $x_0, x_1, \ldots, x_{n-1}$ is *linearly independent* if

$$\sum_{i=0}^{n-1} a_i x_i = 0$$

implies that $a_0 = a_1 = \cdots = a_{n-1} = 0$. If the vectors x_i are not linearly independent, then we say that they are *linearly dependent*.

Example. Consider the set of vectors

$$\left\{ \begin{bmatrix} 2 \\ 1 \end{bmatrix}, \begin{bmatrix} -1 \\ 0 \end{bmatrix}, \begin{bmatrix} 4 \\ 3 \end{bmatrix} \right\}.$$

These are linearly dependent, since

$$3 \begin{bmatrix} 2 \\ 1 \end{bmatrix} + 2 \begin{bmatrix} -1 \\ 0 \end{bmatrix} - 1 \begin{bmatrix} 4 \\ 3 \end{bmatrix} = \begin{bmatrix} 0 \\ 0 \end{bmatrix}.$$

However, the set

$$\left\{ \begin{bmatrix} 2 \\ 1 \end{bmatrix}, \begin{bmatrix} -1 \\ 0 \end{bmatrix} \right\}$$

is linearly independent, since

$$a_0 \begin{bmatrix} 2 \\ 1 \end{bmatrix} + a_1 \begin{bmatrix} -1 \\ 0 \end{bmatrix} = \begin{bmatrix} 0 \\ 0 \end{bmatrix}$$

implies that $a_0 = a_1 = 0$.

Inverse Matrix

Let A be an $n \times n$ matrix and I the $n \times n$ *identity matrix*, that is,

$$I_{n \times n} = \begin{bmatrix} 1 & 0 & 0 & \cdots & 0 \\ 0 & 1 & 0 & \cdots & 0 \\ \vdots & & & \ddots & \\ 0 & 0 & 0 & \cdots & 1 \end{bmatrix}.$$

If there exists an $n \times n$ matrix A^{-1}, such that $AA^{-1} = A^{-1}A = I$, then A is said to be *invertible* and A^{-1} is the *inverse* of A.

Annotated Bibliography

[1] 3GPP home page, at www.3gpp.org/
Cited on page 94

[2] E. Aboufadel, Work by the Poles to break the Enigma codes, at
www.gvsu.edu/math/enigma/polish.htm
Cited on page 34

  • A brief description of the work by the Polish cryptanalysts.

[3] G. Álvarez, D. de la Guía, and F. M. y Alberto Peinado, Akelarre: a
new block cipher algorithm *Proceedings of the SAC'96 Workshop*, 1996,
pp. 1–14
Cited on pages 160, 163, and 169

[4] R. Anderson, 'Trusted computing' frequently asked questions, at
www.cl.cam.ac.uk/~rja14/tcpa-faq.html
Cited on pages 316 and 380

  • An entertaining and enlightening discussion of trusted computing,
    but very one-sided. For a more balanced treatment, see [48].

[5] I. Anshel, M. Anshel, and D. Goldfeld, An algebraic method for public-
key cryptography, *Mathematical Research Letters*, Vol. 6, 1999, pp. 287–
291
Cited on pages 279 and 284

[6] Barbie, at en.wikipedia.org/wiki/Barbie
Cited on page xiii

  • Talking Barbie's infamous "math class is tough" quote, which is
    often misquoted as, "math is hard."

[7] T. Barr, *Invitation to Cryptology*, First edition, Prentice Hall, 2002
Cited on page 1

  • A nice introduction to cryptology for the general reader.

375

[8] F. L. Bauer, *Decrypted Secrets: Methods and Maxims of Cryptology*, third edition, Springer, 2002
     Cited on pages 1 and 5

[9] M. Bellare, S. Goldwasser. and D. Micciancio "Pseudo-random" number generation within cryptographic algorithms: the DDS case, *Advances in Cryptology*, Proceedings of Crypto 1997, LNCS 1294, B. S. Kaliski, Jr., Ed., Springer-Verlag, 1997, pp. 277–291, at theory.lcs.mit.edu/~cis/pubs/shafi/1997-lncs-bgm.pdf
     Cited on page 80

[10] M. Bellare and P. Rogaway, Optimal asymmetric encryption–how to encrypt with RSA, at www.cse.ucsd.edu/users/mihir/papers/oae.pdf
     Cited on page 291

[11] S. M. Bellovin and M. Merritt, Encrypted key exchange: password-based protocols secure against dictionary attacks, at www.windowsecurity.com/uplarticle/4/neke.ps
     Cited on page 278

[12] D. J. Bernstein, Cache-timing attacks on AES, at cr.yp.to/antiforgery/cachetiming-20050414.pdf
     Cited on pages 342 and 353

[13] E. Biham and P. Kocher, A known plaintext attack on the PKZIP stream cipher, *Fast Software Encryption '94*, LNCS 1008, pp. 144–153, B. Preneel, Ed., Springer-Verlag, 1994
     Cited on pages 111, 115, 118, and 378

     • The ideas are undeniably there, but the details are incredibly difficult to pull out of this cryptic paper; see the implementation in [30] for help.

[14] E. Biham and A. Shamir, Differential cryptanalysis of Feal and N-hash, *Advances in Cryptology*, Proceedings of Eurocrypt 1991, LNCS 547, D. W. Davies, Ed., Springer-Verlag, 1991, pp. 1–16
     Cited on pages 170 and 171

[15] J. Birman, K. Ko, and S. Lee, A new approach to the word and conjugacy problems in the braid groups, *Advances in Mathematics*, No. 139, 1998, pp. 322–353
     Cited on page 283

[16] J. Black, M. Cochran, and T. Highland, A study of the MD5 attacks: insights and improvements, at www.cs.colorado.edu/~jrblack/papers/md5e-full.pdf
     Cited on pages 230, 237, and 250

[17] I. Blake, G. Seroussi, and N. Smart, *Elliptic Curves in Cryptography*, London Mathematical Society Lecture Notes 265, Cambridge University Press, 2002
Cited on page 284

[18] M. Blaze, Quantize wrapper library, at
`islab.oregonstate.edu/documents/People/blaze`
Cited on page 352

[19] D. Boneh, Twenty years of attacks on the RSA cryptosystem, *Notices of the AMS*, February 1999, at `www.ams.org/notices/199902/boneh.pdf`
Cited on pages 285, 287, 288, and 354

[20] J. Borst, B. Preneel, and J. Vandewalle, On the time-memory tradeoff between exhaustive key search and table precomputation, at
`www.esat.kuleuven.ac.be/~borst/downloadable/tm.ps.gz`
Cited on page 142

  • An extension of Hellman's original TMTO work. This approach allows for an efficient distributed attack.

[21] D. M. Bressoud, *Factorization and Primality Testing*, Springer-Verlag, New York, 1989
Cited on page 287

[22] D. Brumley and D. Boneh, Remote timing attacks are practical, at
`crypto.stanford.edu/~dabo/papers/ssl-timing.pdf`
Cited on pages 335, 349, 350, 351, and 352

  • A timing attack on the RSA implementation in OpenSSL.

[23] S. Budiansky, *Battle of Wits*, The Free Press, 2000
Cited on pages 26, 37, 38, 48, and 52

[24] D. A. Buell, Montgomery multiplication, at
`www.cse.sc.edu/~buell/csce557/Dlecturenotes/montgomery.pdf`
Cited on pages 338 and 339

[25] D. M. Burton, *Elementary Number Theory*, second edition, Wm. C. Brown Publishers, 1989
Cited on pages 323 and 332

[26] A. Carlson, Simulating the Enigma cypher machine, at
`homepages.tesco.net/~andycarlson/enigma/simulating_enigma.html`
Cited on page 28

  • Describes the double stepping well.

[27] F. Chabaud and A. Joux, Differential collisions in SHA–0, *Advances in Cryptology*, Proceedings of Crypto 1998, LNCS 1462, H. Krawczyk, Ed., Springer-Verlag, 1998
Cited on page 237

[28] W. O. Chan, Sigaba, Master's Thesis, Department of Computer Science, San Jose State University, 2006
Cited on pages 64, 67, and 68

[29] R. Churchhouse, *Codes and Ciphers*, Cambridge University Press, 2002
Cited on page 26

- This contains a nice overview of some classical crypto. In particular, a few chapters are devoted to some of the World War II crypto–machine systems.

[30] P. Conrad, pkcrack, at
`www.unix-ag.uni-kl.de/~conrad/krypto/pkcrack.html`
Cited on pages 111 and 376

- Without this software—which implements Biham and Kocher's PKZIP attack—or something comparable, deciphering Biham and Kocher's paper [13] would be well-nigh impossible. Conrad even includes some valuable comments for the most confusing parts.

[31] D. Coppersmith, Small solutions to polynomial equations, and low exponent RSA vulnerabilities, *Journal of Cryptology*, Vol. 10, 1997, pp. 233–260
Cited on pages 343 and 350

[32] T. H. Cormen, C. E. Leiserson, R. L. Rivest, and C. Stein, *Introduction to Algorithms*, second edition, MIT Press, 2001
Cited on pages 327 and 333

[33] M. Dashu, Xorguinas y Celestinas, excerpt from *Secret History of the Witches*, at
`www.suppressedhistories.net/secret_history/xorguinas.html`
Cited on page 160

[34] M. Daum, Cryptanalysis of hash functions of the MD4-family, Dissertation zur Erlangung des Grades eines Doktor der Naturwissenschaften der Ruhr-Universit at Bochum am Fachbereich Mathematik, at
`www.cits.ruhr-uni-bochum.de/imperia/md/content/magnus/`
`dissmd4.pdf`
Cited on pages 194, 208, 212, 230, 233, 235, 237, 238, 250, and 392

- An excellent source for background information on MD4 and MD5 collision attacks. This dissertation is readable and provides a wealth of relevant information on hash function cryptanalysis. Daum's work was supervised by the late Hans Dobbertin.

[35] M. Daum and S. Lucks, Attacking hash functions by poisoned messages—'the story of Alice and her boss', at
`www.cits.rub.de/MD5Collisions/`
Cited on page 253

[36] H. Delfs and H. Knebl, *Introduction to Cryptography: Principles and Applications*, Springer-Verlag, 2002
Cited on page 291

[37] Y. Desmedt, What happened with knapsack cryptographic schemes?, *Performance Limits in Communication, Theory and Practice*, J. K. Skwirzynski, ed., Kluwer, pp. 113–134, 1988
Cited on page 275

[38] W. Diffie and M. E. Hellman, New directions in cryptography, *IEEE Transactions on Information Theory*, Vol. IT-22, No. 6, 1976, pp. 644–654
Cited on page 276

[39] W. Diffie, P. C. van Oorschot, and M. Wiener, Authentication and authenticated key exchanges, *Designs, Codes and Cryptography*, Vol. 2, 1992, pp. 107–125
Cited on page 278

[40] J. D. Dixon, Asymptotically fast factorization of integers, *Mathematics of Computation*, Vol. 36, 1981, pp. 255–260
Cited on page 317

[41] H. Dobbertin, Cryptanalysis of MD4, *Proceedings of the Third International Workshop on Fast Software Encryption*, LNCS 1039, D. Gollmann, Ed., Springer-Verlag, 1996, pp. 53–69
Cited on page 208

[42] H. Dobbertin, Cryptanalysis of MD4, *Journal of Cryptology*, Vol. 11, No. 4, 1998, pp. 253–271
Cited on pages 199, 208, 210, 216, 219, 224, 225, 231, and 260

- A somewhat difficult attack, but a very well-written article—an exception to the rule in the cryptanalysis literature.

[43] J. R. Durbin, *Modern Algebra: An Introduction*, fifth edition, John Wiley & Sons, Inc., 2004
Cited on page 86

[44] T. ElGamal, A public key cryptosystem and a signature scheme based on discrete logarithms. *Advances in Cryptology*, Proceedings of Crypto 1984, LNCS 196, Springer-Verlag, 1985, pp. 10–18
Cited on page 307

[45] J. H. Ellis, The possibility of secure non-secret digital encryption, CESG Report, January 1970
Cited on page 265

- Ellis was the first to suggest the possibility of public key cryptography.

[46] Enigma, at `www.nsa.gov/public/publi00007.cfm`
Cited on page 27

[47] Enigma Machine, Wikipedia, the free encyclopedia, at `en.wikipedia.org/wiki/Enigma_machine`
Cited on page 26

[48] P. Ericson, TCPA/TCG and NGSCB: benefits and risks for users, School of Humanities and Informatics University of Skövde, Sweden, 2004, at `pericson.com/writings/tcpa-tcg_ngscb/tcpa-tcg_and_ngscb.pdf`
Cited on pages 316 and 375

- A balanced and highly readable discussion of trusted computing (TC). See [4] for the anti-trusted computing viewpoint.

[49] W. Feller, *An Introduction to Probability Theory and Its Applications*, third edition, Wiley, 1968
Cited on pages 185 and 141

- A classic source for information on discrete probability.

[50] N. Ferguson and B. Schneier, Cryptanalysis of Akelarre, *Proceedings of the SAC'97 workshop*, 1997, pp. 201-212
Cited on page 160

[51] S. Fluhrer, I. Mantin, and A. Shamir, Weaknesses in the key scheduling algorithm of RC4, at `www.drizzle.com/~aboba/IEEE/rc4_ksaproc.pdf`
Cited on pages 105, 110, 122, and 385

- Several attacks on RC4 are discussed. Mantin's thesis [96] is much clearer and easier to read.

[52] W. Freeman, G. Sullivan, and F. Weierud, Purple revealed: simulation and computer-aided cryptanalysis of Angooki Taipu B, *Cryptologia*, Vol. XXVII, No. 1, January 2003, pp. 1–43
Cited on pages 39, 46, and 49

- The most detailed source of information on the Purple cipher.

[53] F. Fugate, Frank Rowlett, and David Kahn, at
`cryptome.org/rowlett-kahn.htm`
Cited on page 383

- Fugate, who claims to be Rowlett's nephew, describes an attempt by Kahn to coerce Rowlett into divulging classified information.

[54] E. Fujisaki and T. Okamoto, Secure integration of asymmetric and symmetric encryption schemes, *Advances in Cryptology*, Proceedings of Crypto 1999, LNCS 1666, M. Wiener, Ed., Springer-Verlag, 1999, pp. 537–554
Cited on page 304

[55] M. R. Garey and D. S. Johnson, *Computers and Intractability: A Guide to the Theory of NP-Completeness*, W. H. Freeman & Company, 1979
Cited on page 267

[56] B. Gates, *The Road Ahead*, Penguin, 1995
Cited on page 316

[57] I. Goldberg and D. Wagner, Architectural considerations for cryptanalytic hardware, at
`www.comms.scitech.susx.ac.uk/fft/crypto/paper.pdf`
Cited on page 82

[58] J. Golić, Correlation via linear sequential circuit approximation of combiners with memory, *Advances in Cryptology*, Proceedings of EUROCRYPT '92, LNCS 658, 1993, pp. 113–123
Cited on page 93

[59] S. W. Golomb, *Shift Register Sequences*, Aegean Park Press, 1981 (revised edition)
Cited on page 86

[60] B. Goren, RSA: practical public-key cryptography, at
`www.trumpetpower.com/Papers/Crypto/RSA`
Cited on page 284

[61] M. Goresky and A. M. Klapper, Fibonacci and Galois representations of feedback-with-carry shift registers, *IEEE Transactions on Information*

Theory, Vol. 48, No. 11, November 2002, pp. 2826–2836
Cited on page 83

[62] F. G. Gustavson, Analysis of the Berlekamp-Massey linear feedback
shift-register synthesis algorithm, *IBM Journal of Research and Development*, Vol. 20, May 1976, pp. 204–212
Cited on page 85

[63] D. Hamer, Enigma: actions involved in the 'double-stepping' of the
middle rotor, *Cryptologia*, Vol. 21, No. 1, January 1997, pp. 47–50, at
`www.eclipse.net/~dhamer/downloads/rotorpdf.zip`
Cited on page 28

[64] P. Hawkes, M. Paddon, and G. G. Rose, Musings on the Wang *et al.*
MD5 collision, at `eprint.iacr.org/2004/264.pdf`
Cited on pages 229, 238, 239, 240, 241, 242, 243, 244, 245, 247, and 392

  • A remarkable paper and an absolute necessity for understanding
    the intricate details of Wang's attack.

[65] M. Hellman, A cryptanalytic time-memory tradeoff, *IEEE Transactions
on Information Theory*, vol. 26, pp. 401–406, 1980
Cited on page 133

[66] T. Henderson, ARC shareware license, at
`www.esva.net/~thom/arclicense.html`
Cited on page 110

[67] L. S. Hill, Cryptography in an algebraic alphabet, *American Mathematical Monthly*, No. 36, 1929, pp. 306–312
Cited on page 16

[68] J. Hoffstein, J. Pipher, and J. H. Silverman, NTRU: A ring based public
key cryptosystem, *Algorithmic Number Theory: Third International
Symposium* Proceedings of ANTS-III, LNCS 1423, J. P. Buhler, Ed.,
Springer-Verlag, 1998, pp. 267–288
Cited on pages 293 and 299

[69] J. Hughes and A. Tannenbaum, Length-based attacks for certain group
based encryption rewriting systems, preprint, 2000
Cited on page 283

[70] IBM Research, Horst Feistel, at
`domino.watson.ibm.com/comm/pr.nsf/pages/bio.feistel.html`
Cited on page 131

[71] Investigation of the Pearl Harbor attack, Report of the Joint Committee on the Investigation of the Pearl Harbor Attack, Part I. Diplomatic Background, at `www.ibiblio.org/pha/pha/congress/part_1.html`
Cited on page 39

[72] Japanese "Fourteen Part" message of December 7, 1941, at `www.ibiblio.org/hyperwar/PTO/Dip/Fourteen.html`
Cited on page 38

[73] E. Jaulmes and A. Joux, A chosen-ciphertext attack against NTRU, *Advances in Cryptology*, Proceedings of Crypto 2000, LNCS 1880, M. Blaze, Ed., Springer-Verlag, 2000, pp. 20–35
Cited on pages 302 and 304

[74] D. Kahn, *The Codebreakers: The Story of Secret Writing*, Macmillan, 1967
Cited on pages 1 and 5

- The most complete source for crypto history prior to its original publication date of 1967. But it is important to remember that most of the World War II crypto history was still classified in 1967 and it shows. In particular, Kahn slights Rowlett and, disturbingly, it appears that he knew better at the time [53].

[75] S. A. Kallis, Jr., Codes and cipher, at `www.otr.com/ciphers.shtml`
Cited on page 38

[76] A. Karatsuba and Y. Ofman. Multiplication of many-digital numbers by automatic computers, *Doklady Akad. Nauk SSSR*, Vol. 145, pp. 293-294, 1962 (translation in *Physics-Doklady*, Vol. 7, pp. 595–596, 1963)
Cited on page 341

[77] E. Käsper, Linear cryptanalysis of stream ciphers, at `www.tcs.hut.fi/Studies/T-79.514/slides/S4.Kasper.lc-stream.pdf`
Cited on page 93

- A misleading title since it has nothing to do with linear cryptanalysis. Nevertheless, these notes provide an excellent overview of correlation attacks in general, with some details regarding such attacks on A5/1 (used in GSM) and E_0 (used in Bluetooth).

[78] P. Katz, appnote.txt, at `search.cpan.org/src/NEDKONZ/Archive-Zip-1.14/docs/Appnote.txt`
Cited on page 111

[79] C. Kaufman, R. Perlman, and M. Speciner, *Network Security*, second edition, Prentice Hall, 2002
Cited on page 194

[80] J. Kelsey and T. Kohno, Herding hash functions and the Nostradamus attack, at `eprint.iacr.org/2005/281.pdf`
Cited on pages 203, 204, 206, and 207

[81] V. Klima, Finding MD5 collisions on a notebook PC using multi-message modifications, at `eprint.iacr.org/2005/102.pdf`
Cited on pages 229, 230, 248, and 253

[82] L. R. Knudsen and V. Rijmen, Two rights sometimes make a wrong, *Proceedings of the SAC'97 workshop*, 1997, pp. 213–223
Cited on pages 132, 160, 166, and 169

  • A clever title, but the details are sketchy.

[83] N. Koblitz, *A Course in Number Theory and Cryptography*, second edition, Springer-Verlag, 1994
Cited on page 308

[84] N. Koblitz, A. J. Menezes, Y. H. Wu, and R. J. Zuccherato, *Algebraic Aspects of Cryptography*, Algorithms and Computation in Mathematics, Springer-Verlag, 2004
Cited on page 284

[85] P. Kocher, Timing attacks on implementations of Diffie–Hellman, RSA, DSS, and other systems, at
`www.cryptography.com/resources/whitepapers/TimingAttacks.pdf`
Cited on pages 334, 342, 345, and 349

[86] H. Krawczyk, M. Bellare, and R. Canetti, RFC 2104—HMAC: keyed-hashing for message authentication, at
`www.faqs.org/rfcs/rfc2104.html`
Cited on page 198

[87] D. L. Kreher and D. R. Stinson, *Combinatorial Algorithms: Generation, Enumeration and Search*, CRC Press, 1999
Cited on page 152

  • An excellent approach to an interesting subject. Unfortunately, this otherwise fine book is marred by a large number of typos— which is death for an algorithms (or cryptanalysis) book.

[88] S. Kullback, *General Solution for the Double Transposition Cipher*, Aegean Park Press
Cited on page 8

[89] M. K. Lai, Knapsack cryptosystems: the past and the future, March 2001, at `www.cecs.uci.edu/~mingl/knapsack.html`
Cited on page 275

[90] M. Lee, Cryptanalysis of the SIGABA, Master's Thesis, University of California, Santa Barbara, June 2003, at
`www.cs.ucsb.edu/~kirbysdl/broadcast/thesis/thesis.pdf`
Cited on pages 32 and 59

  • An excellent overview of rotors as cryptographic elements and a nice description of Sigaba. However, the cryptanalysis only covers reduced-rotor versions of the cipher, which are qualitatively different than the full Sigaba.

[91] A. K. Lenstra, H. W. Lenstra, Jr., and L. Lovàsz, Factoring polynomials with rational coefficients, *Mathematische Annalen*, Vol. 261, No. 4, 1982, pp. 515–534
Cited on page 272

[92] K. Lesh, Example of Dixon's squares, at
`www.math.union.edu/~leshk/mth221-06sp/homework/dixon-example.pdf`
Cited on page 319

[93] S. Levy, The open secret, *Wired*, issue 7.04, April 1999, at
`www.wired.com/wired/archive/7.04/crypto_pr.html`
Cited on pages 276 and 284

  • Ellis, Cocks, and Williamson get their due.

[94] J. Liang and X. Lai, Improved collision attack on hash function MD5, at `eprint.iacr.org/2005/425.pdf`
Cited on page 230

[95] Legendre symbol, Wikipedia, the free encyclopedia, at
`en.wikipedia.org/wiki/Legendre_symbol`
Cited on page 356

[96] I. Mantin, Analysis of the stream cipher RC4, at
`www.wisdom.weizmann.ac.il/~itsik/RC4/Papers/Mantin1.zip`
Cited on pages 110 and 380

  • Clearer and more detailed than [51].

[97] M. Matsui, Linear cryptanalysis method for DES cipher, *Advances in Cryptology*, Proceedings of Eurocrypt 1993, LNCS 470, T. Helleseth, Ed., Springer-Verlag, 1994, pp. 386–397
Cited on page 170

[98] M. Matsui and A. Yamagishi. A new method for known plaintext attack on FEAL cipher, *Advances in Cryptology*, Proceedings of Eurocrypt 1992, LNCS 658, R. Rueppel, Ed., Springer-Verlag, 1993, pp. 81–91
Cited on pages 170 and 177

[99] A. Menezes, P. van Oorschot, and S. Vanstone, *Handbook of Applied Cryptography*, CRC Press, 1996
Cited on pages 93, 327, 329, 331, and 333

[100] R. Merkle and M. Hellman, Hiding information and signatures in trapdoor knapsacks, *IEEE Transactions on Information Theory*, Vol. IT-24, No. 5, 1978, pp. 525–530
Cited on pages 267 and 268

[101] T. Meskanen, On the NTRU cryptosystem, TUCS Dissertations No. 63, Turku Centre for Computer Science, June 2005, at
`www.tucs.fi/publications/attachment.php?fname=DISS63.pdf`
Cited on pages 298 and 304

[102] D. Micciancio and S. Goldwasser, *Complexity of Lattice Problems: A Cryptographic Perspective*, Kluwer International Series in Engineering and Computer Science, Vol. 671, Kluwer Academic Publishers, 2002
Cited on page 284

[103] P. Montgomery, Modular multiplication without trial division, *Mathematics of Computation*, Vol. 44, No. 170, 1985, pp. 519–521
Cited on page 338

[104] S. Morris, Cryptology timeline, at
`www.math.cornell.edu/~morris/135/timeline.html`
Cited on page 5

[105] National cryptologic museum, the big machines exhibit, at
`www.nsa.gov/museum/museu00002.cfm`
Cited on pages 49 and 53

[106] M. Nelson, Remembering Phil Katz, at
`www.ddj.com/maillists/compression/do200005cm/do200005cm001.htm`
Cited on page 111

[107] National Institute of Standards and Technology (NIST), Security requirements for cryptographic modules, FIPS PUB 140-2, at
`csrc.nist.gov/publications/fips/fips140-2/fips1402.pdf`
Cited on page 315

[108] NTRU Cryptosystems, at `www.ntru.com`
Cited on pages 294 and 295

[109] A. M. Odlyzko, The rise and fall of knapsack cryptosystems, at
`www.research.att.com/~amo/doc/arch/knapsack.survey.pdf`
Cited on page 275

[110] P. C. van Oorschot and M. J. Wiener, Parallel collision search with application to hash functions and discrete logarithms, at
`www.scs.carleton.ca/~paulv/papers/acmccs94.pdf`
Cited on page 202

[111] Operating instructions for ECM Mark 2 (CSP 888/889) and CCM Mark 1 (CSP 1600), at `www.hnsa.org/doc/crypto/ecm/index.htm`
Cited on page 52

[112] PBS home programs, Creativity and play: fostering creativity, at
`www.pbs.org/wholechild/providers/play.html`
Cited on page 127

[113] R. Pekelney, ECM MARK 2 and CCM MARK 1, at
`www.hnsa.org/doc/crypto/ecm/`
Cited on page 59

[114] PKZIP, Wikipedia, the free encyclopedia, at
`en.wikipedia.org/wiki/Pkzip`
Cited on page 110

[115] C. Pomerance, The quadratic sieve factoring algorithm, *Advances in Cryptology*, Proceedings of Eurocrypt '84, LNCS 209, T. Beth, N. Cot, and I. Ingemarsson, Eds., Springer-Verlag, 1985, pp. 169–182, at
`www.math.dartmouth.edu/~carlp/PDF/paper52.pdf`
Cited on page 327

[116] C. Pomerance, A tale of two sieves, *Notices of the AMS*, December 1996, pp. 1473–1485, at `www.ams.org/notices/199612/pomerance.pdf`
Cited on page 328

[117] Purple cipher switch, at
`www.nsa.gov/public/publi00007.cfm`
Cited on page 38

[118] M. O. Rabin, Digitalized signatures and public key functions as in-
      tractable as factorization. MIT/LCS/TR-212, MIT Laboratory for
      Computer Science, 1979
      Cited on page 289

[119] J. Reeds, Solved: the ciphers in book III of Trithemius's *Steganographia*,
      at www.dtc.umn.edu/~reedsj/trit.pdf
      Cited on page 144

[120] E. Rescorla, RFC 2631—Diffie–Hellman key agreement method, at
      ietf.org/rfc/rfc2631.txt
      Cited on page 276

[121] R. Rivest, RFC 1320—the MD4 message-digest algorithm, April 1992,
      at ftp.rfc-editor.org/in-notes/rfc1320.txt
      Cited on pages 208 and 209

[122] R. Rivest, RFC 1321—the MD5 message-digest algorithm, April 1992,
      at ftp.rfc-editor.org/in-notes/rfc1321.txt
      Cited on pages 225, 226. 227. and 231

[123] R. Rivest, A. Shamir, and L. Adelman, A method for obtaining digital
      signatures and public-key cryptosystems, *Communications of the ACM*,
      Vol. 21, 1978, pp. 120–126
      Cited on page 284

[124] G. Rose, Greg Rose's cryptographic stuff, at
      people.qualcomm.com/ggr/crypto.html
      Cited on page 144

[125] R. Rueppel, *Analysis and Design of Stream Ciphers*, Springer-Verlag,
      1986
      Cited on pages 83, 87, and 95

      • The best book available on the theory of stream ciphers.

[126] L. F. Safford and D. W. Seiler. Control circuits for electric coding ma-
      chines, United States patent number 6,175,625, January 2001
      Cited on page 53

[127] Y. Sasaki, Y. Naito, N. Kunihiro, and K. Ohta, Improved collision
      attack on MD5, at eprint.iacr.org/2005/400.pdf
      Cited on page 230

[128] J. J. G. Savard and R. S. Pekelney, The ECM Mark II: design, history
      and cryptology, *Cryptologia*. Vol. 23, No. 3, July 1999, pp. 211–228
      Cited on page 59

[129] W. Schindler, A timing attack against RSA with the Chinese Remainder Theorem, *CHES 2000*, LNCS 1965, Ç. K. Koç and C. Paar, Eds., Springer-Verlag, 2000, pp. 109–124
Cited on pages 334, 345, 346, 347, 349, 350, and 352

[130] J. Seberry, Hash function tutorial, at
www.uow.edu.au/~jennie/CSCI971/hash1.pdf
Cited on page 193

[131] Shanks-Tonelli algorithm, at
en.wikipedia.org/wiki/Shanks-Tonelli_algorithm
Cited on page 326

[132] A. Shamir, A polynomial-time algorithm for breaking the basic Merkle–Hellman cryptosystem, *IEEE Transactions on Information Theory*, Vol. IT-30, No. 5, September 1984, pp. 699–704
Cited on pages 270 and 272

[133] C. E. Shannon, Communication theory of secrecy systems, *Bell System Technical Journal*, Vol. 28, No. 4, 1949, pp. 656–715, at
www.cs.ucla.edu/~jkong/research/security/shannon1949.pdf
Cited on pages 8, 17, 69, and 182

  • The paper that started it all. This paper remains surprisingly relevant after more than a half-century.

[134] A. Shimizu and S. Miyaguchi, Fast data encryption algorithm FEAL, *Advances in Cryptology*, Proceedings of Eurocrypt '87, LNCS 304, D. Chaum and W. L. Price, Eds., Springer-Verlag, 1987, pp. 267–278
Cited on pages 170 and 171

[135] T. Siegenthaler, Decrypting a class of stream ciphers using ciphertext only, *IEEE Transactions on Computers*, Vol. C–34, No. 1, 1985, pp. 8184
Cited on page 93

[136] J. Silverman, A meet-in-the-middle attack on an NTRU private key, Technical Report 4: Version 1, NTRU Cryptosystems, 1997
Cited on pages 299 and 301

  • Version 2 of this report is available at the NTRU website. However, that version omits many important details and is very unclear.

[137] J. Silverman, Almost inverses and fast NTRU key creation, Technical Report 14, NTRU Cryptosystems, 1999
Cited on page 294

[138] J. Silverman, Estimated breaking times for NTRU lattices, Technical Report 12, NTRU Cryptosystems, 1999
Cited on pages 302, 303, and 304

[139] R. J. Spillman, *Classical and Contemporary Cryptology*, Prentice Hall, 2004
Cited on page 1

[140] Staff Report, U.S. Senate Select Committee on Intelligence, Unclassified summary: involvement of NSA in the development of the Data Encryption Standard, Staff Report, 98th Congress, 2nd Session, April 1978
Cited on page 170

- Unclassified summary of Senate report that cleared the National Security Agency of any wrongdoing in the design of the Data Encryption Standard (DES). This report failed to satisfy the critics, but 30 years of intense cryptanalysis seems to have silenced all but the clinically paranoid.

[141] M. Stamp and C. F. Martin, An algorithm for the k-error linear complexity of binary sequences with period 2^n, *IEEE Transactions on Information Theory*, Vol. IT-39, No. 4, July 1993, pp. 1398–1401
Cited on pages 87, 88, and 121

[142] M. Stamp, *Information Security: Principles and Practice*, Wiley-Interscience, 2005
Cited on pages xv, 28, 93, 94, 103, 129, 130, 131, 133, 196, 199, 258, 270, 305, and 353

[143] M. Stay, ZIP attacks with reduced known plaintext, at
www.woodmann.com/fravia/mike_zipattacks.htm
Cited on page 111

[144] M. Stevens, Fast collision attack on MD5, at
eprint.iacr.org/2006/104.pdf
Cited on pages 230, 235, 242, 248, 252, 367, 368, 369, 370, and 392

- Probably the best implementation of Wang's attack so far—get the source code at win.tue.nl/hashclash/

[145] A. Stubblefield, J. Ioannidis, and A. D. Rubin, Using the Fluhrer, Mantin and Shamir attack to break WEP, at
philby.ucsd.edu/~bsy/ndss/2002/html/2002/papers/stubbl.pdf
Cited on page 106

[146] G. Sullivan, The ECM mark II: some observations on the rotor stepping, *Cryptologia*, Vol. 26, No. 2, pp. 97–100, April 2002
Cited on page 76

[147] Telecommunications Industry Association and Electronic Industry Alliance, TDMA third generation wireless messages subject to encryption, at `ftp.tiaonline.org/UWC136/136-511-A.pdf`
Cited on page 144

[148] W. Trappe and L. C. Washington, *Introduction to Cryptography with Coding Theory*, Prentice Hall, 2002
Cited on page 34

  • The best mathematical introduction to cryptography—bar none.

[149] B. W. Tuchman, *The Zimmermann Telegram*, Ballantine Books, 1985
Cited on page 20

[150] R. Venkataramu, RSA timing attack, at
`cs.sjsu.edu/faculty/stamp/papers/RSATiming.doc`
Cited on page 352

[151] VENONA, at `www.nsa.gov/venona/index.cfm`
Cited on page 19

  • VENONA is an interesting topic, both for its crypto implications and for the historical material. Many of those who vigorously denied they had any role in espionage are implicated by VENONA decrypts. Also, of the hundreds of traitors mentioned (by cover name) in the decrypts, the true identities of more than half remain unknown.

[152] D. Wagner, B. Schneier, and J. Kelsey, Cryptanalysis of the cellular message encryption algorithm, at `www.schneier.com/paper-cmea.pdf`
Cited on pages 144, 151, 156, 157, and 159

[153] D. Wagner, L. Simpson, E. Dawson, J. Kelsey, W. Millan, and B. Schneier, Cryptanalysis of ORYX, at
`www.schneier.com/paper-oryx.pdf`
Cited on pages 94 and 120

[154] J. R. Walker, Unsafe at any key size; an analysis of the WEP encapsulation, at `www.dis.org/wl/pdf/unsafe.pdf`
Cited on page 109

  • A clever title and a good description of some of the many problems with WEP.

[155] X. Wang, X. Lai, D. Feng, H. Chen, and X. Yu, Cryptanalysis of the hash functions MD4 and RIPEMD, at
`www.infosec.sdu.edu.cn/paper/md4-ripemd-attck.pdf`
Cited on pages 229 and 230

[156] X. Wang, D. Feng, X. Lai, and H. Yu, Collisions for hash functions MD4, MD5, HAVAL-128 and RIPEMD, at `eprint.iacr.org/2004/199.pdf`
Cited on pages 229 and 230

- An MD5 collision, but no details on how it was obtained.

[157] X. Wang and H. Yu, How to break MD5 and other hash functions, at
`www.infosec.sdu.edu.cn/paper/md5-attack.pdf`
Cited on pages 229, 230, 231. 237, 363, 364, 365, and 366

- Ironically, this paper is just about the last place you should look for comprehensible information on Wang's MD5 attack. To learn more about the attack, see [34] for the concepts, see [64] for the excruciating details on the derivation of the sufficient conditions and see [144] for a fast implementation (including source code).

[158] D. J. Wheeler and R. M. Needham, TEA, a tiny encryption algorithm, at `www.cix.co.uk/~klockstone/tea.pdf`
Cited on page 132

[159] M. Wiener, Cryptanalysis of short RSA secret exponents, *IEEE Transactions on Information Theory*, Vol. IT-36, No. 3, 1990, pp. 553–558
Cited on page 288

[160] W. Wong, Revealing your secrets through the fourth dimension, *ACM Crossroads*, Spring 2005, pp. 20–24
Cited on page 357

[161] J. Yajima and T. Shimoyama, Wang's sufficient conditions of MD5 are not sufficient, at `eprint.iacr.org/2005/263.pdf`
Cited on page 230

[162] G. Yuval, How to swindle Rabin, *Cryptologia*, Vol. 3, No. 3, 1979, pp. 187–189
Cited on page 202

Index